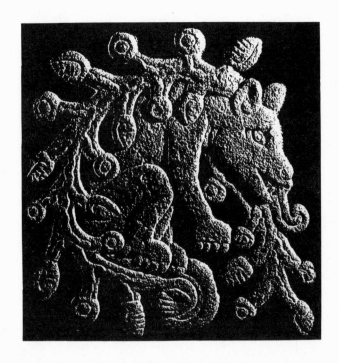

THE EDUCATION OF THE MEXICAN AMERICAN
a selected bibliography

Mario A. Benítez
Texas A&I University

Lupita G. Villarreal
Texas A&I University

Published jointly by

Dissemination and Assessment
Center for Bilingual Education
7703 N. Lamar Boulevard
Austin, Texas 78752
(512) 458-9131

National Clearinghouse
for Bilingual Education
1300 Wilson Boulevard, Suite B2-11
Rosslyn, Virginia 22209
(800) 336-4560/(703) 522-0710

THE EDUCATION OF THE MEXICAN AMERICAN
a selected bibliography

This document is published by InterAmerica Research Associates, Inc., pursuant to contract NIE 400-77-0101 to operate the National Clearinghouse for Bilingual Education. The National Clearinghouse for Bilingual Education is jointly funded by the National Institute of Education and the Office of Bilingual Education and Minority Languages Affairs, U.S. Department of Education. Contractors undertaking such projects under government sponsorship are encouraged to express their judgment freely in professional and technical matters; the views expressed in this publication do not necessarily reflect the views of the sponsoring agencies.

The Evaluation, Dissemination, and Assessment Center for Bilingual Education (EDACBE), formerly known as the Dissemination and Assessment Center for Bilingual Education (DACBE), is a special ESEA bilingual project funded by the Office of Bilingual Education and Minority Languages Affairs, U.S. Department of Education, through the Education Service Center, Region XIII. DACBE selected these materials for dissemination; however, the opinions expressed herein do not necessarily reflect its position or policy nor that of the Education Service Center, Region XIII. Furthermore, DACBE's participation in the publication of this document was performed pursuant to a grant from the U.S. Office of Education, Department of Health, Education, and Welfare. The opinions expressed herein do not necessarily reflect the position or policy of the sponsoring agencies, and no official endorsement by the sponsoring agencies should be inferred.

ISBN: 0-89417-353-7
First printing 1979
Printed in the United States of America

10   9   8   7   6   5   4   3   2

TABLE OF CONTENTS

FOREWORD

One of the important purposes and functions of the National Clearinghouse for Bilingual Education and of the Dissemination and Assessment Center for Bilingual Education is to identify information gaps in our field of interest and concern. Having once identified such gaps, we strive to fill them as promptly and as successfully as possible.

So it is with pride that we present this publication, which indeed fills a glaring gap and fulfills a pressing need. This bibliography was developed at Texas A&I University in Kingsville, edited at the Dissemination and Assessment Center for Bilingual Education in Austin, and printed under the auspices of the National Clearinghouse for Bilingual Education in Rosslyn, Virginia. Many people have combined their efforts and talents to produce it; many people will benefit from its contribution to the field.

Dissemination and Assessment
Center for Bilingual Education

National Clearinghouse
for Bilingual Education

INTRODUCTION

This bibliography is the result of many months of analysis, search, review, and indexing. It represents the first contribution of the Bilingual Education Center at Texas A&I University to the growing body of literature related to the education of the Mexican American. Access to research sources in this topic has been, for the last ten years, a needed dimension in this country. Legislative and judicial landmarks have been made on the basis of research studies which pointed out very clearly the need for improvement of the educational delivery system. The impact of the new legislation and court decisions broke down many social and financial barriers to educational opportunity. Special programs for the Mexican American and other minorities began to proliferate and emphasize a better type of education that became a refreshing aspect of the cultural milieu of the seventies.

It is not necessary to point out the vital role that research has played in the new educational world of the Mexican American. It can safely be said that a substantial number of topics have been investigated, and a new generation of Mexican American researchers have given time and effort to finding solutions to many of the problems they themselves encountered on their way to the top of the academic ladder. Mexican American researchers have not been the only ones interested, by any means. Interest in the Mexican American child has not been bound by color or ethnic background, as this bibliography amply shows.

The research has been done. The availability of the research, as an integrated whole, is a different matter. It is possible to check ERIC or the *Education Index* under the heading "Mexican American" and find articles in education about this minority. However, it is more difficult to find a compilation taxonomically structured that encompasses the most significant educational aspects of the available research on the Mexican American child and his education. This work attempts to do just that for the benefit of scholars both trained and "hopeful." This bibliography offers a meaningful conceptual framework for many studies in many closely related disciplines.

Under normal circumstances no one person can be expected to deal with the literature as it exists today. It is too extensive, too widely distributed among several academic areas, and, at times, it is of doubtful significance or quality. It is hoped that a bibliography such as this one will fill a void that exists at this time in the education of the Mexican American.

The term "Mexican American" is used here to designate an American child of Mexican ancestry. In this sense, the terms "Mexican American" and "Chicano" may be used interchangeably except by those who separate the two terms on the basis of social ideology, political affiliation, or cultural identity.

Purpose

This bibliography has been compiled for the benefit of the inquisitive mind who may ask one or more of the following questions:

(1) What has been written on the education of the Mexican American?
(2) Which authors have done research in this field?
(3) What do the laws and the courts say?

(4) What will a chronological study of the field show?

(5) What topics have been studied more than others?

(6) How can the multitude of the topics (both directly related and tangential) be incorporated into a meaningful conceptual framework?

It is the purpose of this work to help a researcher find answers to these questions. The bibliography has been written with the prospective user in mind, and, hopefully, it offers sufficiently full and accurate bibliographic entries to permit the user the location of any desired item.

Scope

The scope of the bibliography is multiple. It deals with books, monographs, journals, government documents both federal and state, federal laws and federal court decisions, doctoral dissertations and master's theses. It incorporates ERIC entries. It covers significant works from 1896 to 1976. It is centered on the education of the Mexican American child (or adult) as an only topic, but, by necessity, it must cover the demographic, legal, sociocultural, and linguistic determinants of such education. History is incorporated only if it is educational history or if the work is of particular significance and directly related to the education of the Mexican American. The same criterion applies to other sciences and disciplines.

This is a specialized bibliography, including only works directly related to the education of the Mexican American and excluding works on foreign-language methodology or general works on bilingual education. It is arranged into topics of particular significance to the researcher. It includes a substantial number of dissertations and master's theses and significant early-century works seldom cited. It allows for a chronological treatment of themes within topics and subtopics.

Limitations

Due to limitations of time and funds, the following have not been researched and are therefore not a part of this bibliography: (1) book reviews; (2) newspapers; (3) curriculum guides; (4) state laws; (5) state court decisions; (6) testing instruments; (7) publishers' catalogs; (8) textbooks; (9) printed educational materials; and (10) nonprinted educational media such as records, films, filmstrips, slides, tapes, etc. It has been the authors' thought that other bibliographies cover a majority of these items and further coverage is uneconomical. Since the purpose of the bibliography is to collect entries related to the education of the Mexican American, special emphasis has been placed on research studies, while little or no emphasis has been given to materials used in classrooms where Mexican Americans are taught. This is primarily a research bibliography and not a sourcebook for curriculum materials.

Selection of Entries

Five principles have guided the selection process of entries throughout this work.

(1) *Availability*. Only items which were judged to be available to a fairly enterprising researcher were included. Reports and monographs by school districts, university departments, or local agencies not otherwise duplicated or distributed were considered not readily available within the meaning of this principle.

(2) *Relevancy*. Only works directly related to the Mexican American student or, if tangential, possessing a substantial degree of relatedness to the student's education were incorporated. Monographs or books were included only if a substantial or significant portion was directly related. In this sense, a book on bilingual education may or may not be found to be directly related to the Mexican American. Authors of and works on Chicano litera-

ture have been regrettably left out unless the work itself dealt with education. While sociological studies which deal with the Mexican American are not *per se* a part of this bibliography, those studies which bear more significantly upon education are.

(3) *Completeness.* Only entries for which complete bibliographic notation was available were included.

(4) *Length.* Journalistic narratives or one or two pages from journals such as *Time, Newsweek,* or *Reader's Digest* have been left out. The criterion of length was not applied to articles appearing in national or state professional journals.

(5) *Objectivity.* No efforts were made to disregard any point of view no matter how extreme it was.

Examination of Entries

Approximately 90 percent of all entries have been checked for accuracy against original sources by the authors and their staff.

Authorities Consulted

The following authorities were extensively consulted in the design and implementation of this work prior to its release for publication:

> Dr. Julie Bichteler, Graduate School of Library Science, University of Texas at Austin;
>
> Dr. Hensley C. Woodbridge, Department of Foreign Languages, Southern Illinois University;
>
> Mrs. Mary Blanco, Bilingual Center Librarian, Texas A&I University;
>
> Mr. George Boatright, Material Center Library, Texas A&I University;
>
> Mrs. Madeline Peyton, Government Documents Librarian, Texas A&I University;
>
> Mrs. Margarita Calderón, Information Specialist, ERIC/CRESS, New Mexico State University;
>
> Mrs. Ann Graham, Latin American Collection Library, The University of Texas at Austin;
>
> Mr. Nelson Sharpe, Attorney-at-Law, Kingsville, Texas.

Libraries Searched

The following libraries were personally searched by the authors and/or their staff:

> Columbia Teachers College Library
>
> Library of Congress
>
> New York Public Library
>
> North Texas State University Library
>
> Nueces County Law Library
>
> University of Houston Library
>
> University of Texas at Austin Libraries
>> Main Library
>> Collection Deposits Library
>> Communication Library
>> Latin American Collection Library
>> Battle Hall Library

Texas A&I University

Texas Woman's University Library

The following libraries were contacted by phone and/or letter for the purposes of soliciting information on theses and dissertations and checking accuracy of notation for a number of individual entries:

Claremont Graduate School
Pan American University
Southwest Texas State University
Stephen F. Austin State University
University of Arizona
University of New Mexico
Texas A&M University
Texas Technological University

Periodicals Reviewed

Academic Therapy
Adolescence
Adult Leadership
American Academy of Political and Social Sciences
American Anthropologist
American Education
American Educational Research Journal
American Journal of Educational Research
American Journal of Mental Deficiency
American Libraries
American Library
American Scholar
American School and University
American School Board Journal
American Sociological Review
American Speech
American Vocational Journal
Arithmetic Teacher
Arizona English Bulletin
Association of Secondary School Principals
Audiovisual Instruction
Aztlán

Behavioral Science
British Journal of Psychology
Business Education Forum

California Education
California Journal of Educational Research
California Journal of Elementary Education
California Teachers Association Journal
Catholic School Journal
Change
Child Development

Childhood Education
Christian Century
Civil Rights Digest
The Clearing House
College and University Business
College Board Review
Commonweal
Community and Junior College Journal
Community Mental Health Journal
Comparative Education Review
Contemporary Education

Delta Kappa Gamma Bulletin
Developmental Psychology

Education
Educational and Psychological Measurement
Educational Forum
Educational Leadership
Educational Resources and Techniques
Educational Screen
Education Digest
Education for Victory
Elementary Education Series
Elementary English
Elementary School Guidance and Counseling
Elementary School Journal
Encuentro Femenil
English Journal
English Language Teaching Journal
Epoca: The National Concilio for Chicano Studies Journal
ERIC/CRESS Newsletter
Ethnicity
Ethnology
Exceptional Child

Florida Foreign Language Annals
Florida Foreign Language Reporter

Grade Teacher
El Grito

Harvard Educational Review
High Points
High School Journal
Hispania
Houston Law Review
Human Organization

Illinois Education
The Instructor
Integrated Education

Intellect
International American Scene
International Journal of Comparative Sociology
International Migration Review
International Review of Education

Journal of Abnormal and Social Psychology
Journal of Abnormal Psychology
Journal of American Folklore
Journal of Applied Psychology
Journal of Clinical Psychology
Journal of College Student Personnel
Journal of Consulting Psychology
Journal of Counseling Psychology
Journal of Creative Behavior
Journal of Criminal Law, Criminology and Police Science
Journal of Developmental Reading
Journal of Educational Measurement
Journal of Educational Psychology
Journal of Educational Sociology
Journal of Education Research
Journal of Experimental Education
Journal of Genetic Psychology
Journal of Health and Social Behavior
Journal of Home Economics
Journal of Inter-American Studies
Journal of Junior College Personnel
Journal of Learning Disabilities
Journal of Marriage and the Family
Journal of Negro Education
Journal of Personality and Psychology
Journal of Reading
Journal of School Health
Journal of School Psychology
Journal of Social Psychology
Journal of Special Education
Journal of Systems Management
Journal of Vocational Behavior

Language Learning
Liberal Arts
Library Journal
Linguistic Reporter
Linguistics: An International Review

Measurement and Evaluation in Guidance
Media and Methods
Modern Language Journal

Nation

National Education Association Journal
National Elementary Principal
Nations Schools
NCREEO Newsletter
NEA Journal
New Republic

Papers of the Michigan Academy of Sciences, Arts, and Letters
Parents' Magazine
Peabody Journal of Education
Pedagogical Seminary and Journal of Genetic Psychology
Perceptual and Motor Skills
Periodicals of the Modern Language Association
The Personnel and Guidance Journal
Phi Delta Kappan
Phylon
The Progressive
Progressive Education
Psychological Monographs
Psychological Record
Psychological Reports
Psychological Review
Psychology in the Schools
Psychology Today
Public Health Reports

The Quarterly Journal of Speech
Race Relations Reporter
Reading Teacher
Regeneración
Reporter
Review of Educational Research
Review of International Affairs
Rice University Studies
Rural Sociology

Saturday Review
School Counselor
School Life
School Review
Senior Scholastic
Social Education
Social Forces
Social Problems
Social Science Quarterly
Social Service Review
Social Studies
Sociology and Social Research
Sociology of Education

Sociology Quarterly
Sociometry
Southern Education Report
Southern Folklore Society
Southwestern Historical Quarterly
Southwestern Social Science Quarterly
Southwest Review
The Speech Teacher

Teachers College Record
TESOL Quarterly
Theory into Practice
Today's Education
Transcultural Psychiatric Research Review

The University of Texas Bulletin
Urban Education

Western Speech
Wilson Library Bulletin
Wisconsin Journal of Education
World Affairs
Young Children

Bibliographies Searched

Nearly 170 bibliographies on Mexican Americans were searched for materials directly relevant to education. The first bibliographies were published in 1934 and 1935. After these, nine were published in the 40s, five in the 50s, fifty-two in the 60s, and one hundred in the 70s. While some are quite comprehensive in scope (Pino), others (ERIC bibliographies) are merely photocopies of notations on articles and monographs found in the ERIC ED-microfiche collection under the descriptor ''Mexican American.''

Organization

This bibliography is organized under a subject-matter arrangement that, hopefully, will offer readers a meaningful conceptual framework for the literature available. The field is divided into ten basic topics, most of which are broken down into a system of subtopics as shown on the Table of Topical Arrangement. The reader should make every effort to study the topical arrangement and internalize it before attempting to study the bibliographic entries.

The entries under each heading are in chronological rather than alphabetical order but are alphabetized within the same year.

Authenticity

The authors have taken the position that entries should be incorporated exactly as they appear in the sources themselves. Therefore, no diacritical marks (*acentos, diéresis*) have been added unless they are found in the original source. Apparent spelling errors or semantic obscurities have been left untouched for the same reason. It was felt that the purpose of a bibliographer was to record exactly what was found and not to amend it in order to conform to established grammatical principles.

Acknowledgements

Many deserve special mention and expression of gratitude. Ms. Magdalena Benavides Sumpter, Bilingual Curriculum Editor of the National Dissemination and Assessment Center for Bilingual Education, spent many hours carefully editing the complete manuscript and suggesting numerous improvements. The authors are indeed grateful to her untiring dedication to the project. Dr. R. R. Hinojosa-Smith offered comments and suggestions that considerably improved this work. Mrs. Monica Muchetti acted as an administrative assistant and coordinator throughout the typing and editing phases. Her unrelenting drive and passion for accuracy were invaluable to the successful completion of the bibliography. Miss Carolyn Lynch is due special recognition for important contributions to all aspects of this work. Miss Anna Belle Buentello gave generously of her time and effort in the final editing of the manuscript. The authors also wish to express their appreciation to the various university libraries and their staffs who provided much help in tracking down difficult-to-obtain documents and monographs. And last but not least, our most sincere gratitude to Dr. Julie Bichteler, Graduate School of Library Science, University of Texas at Austin, and to Dr. Hensley C. Woodbridge, Department of Foreign Languages, Southern Illinois University, for their professional assistance and guidance.

TABLE OF TOPICAL ARRANGEMENT

1. BIBLIOGRAPHIES

1. *CARTEL: Annotated Bibliography of Bilingual Bicultural Materials.* Austin, Texas: Dissemination and Assessment Center for Bilingual Education, n.d.
2. U.S. Department of Interior. Bureau of Education. *Good References on Language Handicaps of Non-English Speaking Children. Bibliography No. 23.* Washington, D.C.: Government Printing Office, 1934.
3. U.S. Department of Interior. Bureau of Education. *The Education of Native and Minority Groups: A Bibliography, 1923-32. Pamphlet No. 63,* by Katherine M. Cook and Florence E. Reynolds. Washington, D.C.: Government Printing Office, 1935.
4. Nichols, M.W. *A Bibliographical Guide to Materials on American Spanish.* Cambridge, Massachusetts: Harvard University Press, 1941.
5. U.S. Department of Labor. Pan American Union. Division of Labor and Social Information. *Mexicans in the United States, Bibliography.* Washington, D.C.: Government Printing Office, 1942.
6. Saunders, Lyle. *The Education of Spanish-American and Mexican Children: A Selected Bibliography.* Albuquerque: University of New Mexico Press, 1944.
7. Saunders, Lyle. *A Guide to Materials Bearing on Cultural Relations in New Mexico.* Albuquerque: University of New Mexico Press, 1944.
8. Saunders, Lyle. *Spanish Speaking Americans and Mexican Americans in the United States: A Selected Bibliography.* New York: Bureau for Intercultural Education, 1944.
9. Kelley, Victor H. "Selected Bibliography: The Teaching of the Spanish-Speaking Child." Photostat. Tucson: University of Arizona, 1946.
10. Riemer, Ruth. *An Annotated Bibliography of Material on Ethnic Problems in Southern California.* Los Angeles: University of California at Los Angeles, The Haynes Foundation, 1947.
11. Whittenburg, Clarice T., and Sánchez, George I., eds. *Materials Relating to the Education of Spanish-Speaking People: A Bibliography.* Inter-American Occasional Papers, no. 2. Austin: University of Texas Press, 1948.
12. "Mexican-Americans. Bibliographic Series, No. 7, 1949." Mimeographed. Chicago, Illinois: American Council on Race Relations, 1949.
13. U.S. Department of Agriculture. *Migratory Agricultural Labor in the United States. Annotated Bibliography of Selected References,* by Joseph C. Folson. Washington, D.C.: Government Printing Office, 1953.
14. "Selected Bibliography and Notes on Intensive Training for Teachers in Field of Teaching English to the Foreign Born." Mimeographed. New York: National Council on Naturalization and Citizenship, Committee on Education, 1955.
15. Haugen, Einar. *Bilingualism in the Americas: A Bibliography and Research Guide.* Tuscaloosa: University of Alabama Press, 1956. Also in: *American Dialect Society Publications,* no. 26 (November 1956): 125-56.

16. U.S. Department of Labor. Labor Standard Bureau. *Selected References on Migratory Workers and Their Families, Problems and Programs, 1950-56.* Washington, D.C.: Government Printing Office, 1956.

17. *Mexican-Americans.* California: Los Angeles City School District, Division of Instructional Planning and Services, Professional Library, 1958.

18. "Education of Children of Agricultural Migrants." 1962. ERIC ED 020 838.

19. U.S. Department of Health, Education, and Welfare. Office of Education. *Selected References on Migrant Education,* by George E. Haney. Washington, D.C.: Government Printing Office, 1963.

20. Potts, Alfred M., ed. "Knowing and Educating the Disadvantaged: An Annotated Bibliography." Alamosa, Colorado: Adams State College, 1965. ERIC ED 012 189.

21. *Selected References on Migrant Children's Education.* New York: National Committee on the Education of Migrant Children, 1965. ERIC ED 020 809.

22. *Bibliography: Mexican American Study Project. Advance Report No. 3.* Los Angeles: University of California at Los Angeles, Graduate School of Business Administration, Mexican American Study Project, 1966.

23. Ohannessian, S., and Wineberg, R. *Teaching English as a Second Language in Adult Education Programs. An Annotated Bibliography.* Washington, D.C.: Center for Applied Linguistics, 1966.

24. U.S. Department of Agriculture. *Research Data on Minority Groups: An Annotated Bibliography of Economic Research Service Reports, 1955-1965,* by Vera J. Banks, Elsie S. Manny, and Nelson L. LeRoy. Washington, D.C.: Government Printing Office, 1966.

25. U.S. Department of Health, Education, and Welfare. Office of Education. *Education of Disadvantaged Children. Bibliography,* by Lois B. Watt. Washington, D.C.: Government Printing Office, 1966.

26. U.S. Department of Health, Education, and Welfare. Office of Education. *Education of Disadvantaged Children in the Elementary School: An Annotated Bibliography,* by Gertrude M. Lewis and Esther Murrow. Washington, D.C.: Government Printing Office, 1966.

27. Charles, Edgar B., comp. "Youth in Rurality; A Bibliography." University Park: New Mexico State University, 1967. ERIC ED 025 337.

28. Colorado. State Department of Education. *Materiales tocante los Latinos (A Bibliography of Materials on the Spanish-American),* by Joan Harrigan. Denver: Colorado State Department of Education, 1967. ERIC ED 018 292.

29. Forbes, Jack D. *Mexican-Americans: A Handbook for Educators.* Berkeley, California: Far West Laboratory for Educational Research and Development, 1967. ERIC ED 013 164.

30. *An Index to Multi-Ethnic Teaching Materials and Teacher Resources.* Washington, D.C.: National Education Association, PR&R Committee on Civil and Human Rights of Educators, 1967.

31. Keating, Charlotte Matthews. *Building Bridges of Understanding.* Tucson, Arizona: Palo Verde Publishing Co., Inc., 1967.

32. Lewis, F. *Bibliography of Bilingualism.* Hamburg: UNESCO Institute for Education, 1967.

33. Messinger, Milton Albert. "The Forgotten Child; A Bibliography with Special Emphasis on Materials Relating to the Education of 'Spanish-Speaking' People in the United States." Austin: University of Texas at Austin, 1967.

34. *Mexican Heritage: A Selected Book List for all Ages.* Colorado: Denver Public Library, 1967.

35. U.S. Department of Labor. *Mexican-Americans, Selected References.* Washington, D.C.: Government Printing Office, 1967.

36. Rugh, Patricia A., and Scardamalia, Marlene L. *Learning Problems of the Migrant Child: An Annotated Bibliography.* Lewisburg, Pennsylvania: Bucknell University, 1967.

37. *Bibliography on the Problems of Southwestern Minority Groups and for Teachers of Adult Students from Different Cultural Backgrounds.* Denver: Colorado Migrant Council Press, 1968.

38. *Black Brown Bibliography.* Northridge, California: San Fernando State College, 1968.

39. Caskey, O.L., and Hodges, J. "A Resource and Reference Bibliography on Teaching and Counseling the Bilingual Student." Lubbock: Texas Technological College, 1968. ERIC ED 032 966.

40. Charles, Edgar B., ed. *Mexican American Education, A Bibliography.* University Park: New Mexico State University, 1968. ERIC ED 016 562.

41. Fifield, Ruth, comp. "English as a Second Language Bibliography." El Centro, California: Imperial County Education Center, 1968. ERIC ED 024 513.

42. Martínez, Gilbert T. *Bibliography on Mexican-Americans.* California: Sacramento City Unified School District, 1968.

43. Strange, Susan, and Priest, Rhea P. "Bibliography: The Mexican-American in the Migrant Labor Setting." East Lansing: Michigan State University, Department of Sociology, Rural Manpower Center, 1968. ERIC ED 032 188.

44. "An Annotated Bibliography of Migrant Related Materials." Boca Raton: Florida Atlanta University, 1969. ERIC ED 030 523.

45. Barnes, Regina. "A Selected ERIC Bibliography on Teaching Ethnic Minority Group Children in the United States of America." New York: Columbia University, 1969. ERIC ED 027 360.

46. *Bibliography of Studies Concerning the Spanish Speaking Population of the American Southwest.* Greeley: Colorado State College, Museum of Anthropology, 1969.

47. Ching, D.C. "Reading, Language Development and the Bilingual Child: An Annotated Bibliography." *Elementary English* 46, no. 5 (May 1969): 622-28.

48. Colorado. State Department of Education. *More Materials Tocante Los Latinos. A Bibliography of Materials on the Spanish-American,* by Joan Harrigan, comp. Denver: Colorado State Department of Education, 1969. ERIC ED 031 344.

49. Cortez, Ruben, and Navarro, Joseph. *Mexican-American History; A Critical Selective Bibliography.* Santa Barbara, California: Mexican-American Historical Society, 1969.

50. Florida. State Department of Education. *An Annotated Bibliography of Migrant Related Materials.* Boca Raton: Florida State Department of Education, 1969. ERIC ED 030 523.

51. García, George J., comp. "Selected Reading Materials on the Mexican and Spanish American." Denver, Colorado: Denver Committee on Community Relations, 1969. ERIC ED 039 047.

52. Garza, Ben. *Chicano Bibliography. Education . . . the Last Hope of the Poor Chicano. (Educación . . . la última esperanza del pobre chicano.)* Davis, California: Movimiento Estudiantil Chicano de Aztlán, 1969. ERIC ED 034 642.

53. Heathman, James E., comp. "Migrant Education: A Selected Bibliography." University Park: New Mexico State University, 1969. ERIC ED 028 011.

54. Heathman, James E., and Martínez, Cecilia J., comps. "Mexican American Education; A Selected Bibliography." University Park: New Mexico State University, 1969. ERIC ED 031 352.

55. Hillyer, Mildred. "Bibliography of Spanish and Southwestern Indian Cultures Library Books." 1969. ERIC ED 047 846.

56. "Hispanic Heritage. An Annotated Bibliography." Denver, Colorado: University of Denver, School of Education, 1969. ERIC ED 048 079.

57. Holland, Nora. "A Selected ERIC Bibliography on the Education of Urban American Indian and Mexican American Children. ERIC-IRCD Urban Disadvantaged Series, No. 5." New York: Columbia University, 1969. ERIC ED 029 935.

58. Ibarra, Herb. "Bibliography of ESL/Bilingual Teaching Materials." San Diego, California: San Diego Public Schools, 1969. ERIC ED 028 002.

59. Karr, Ken. "A Selected Bibliography Concerning the Education of Mexican-American Migrant Children." Las Vegas, Nevada: American Personnel and Guidance Association, 1969. ERIC ED 028 014.

60. "The Mexican American: A Selected and Annotated Bibliography." Palo Alto, California: Stanford University, Center for Latin American Studies, 1969.

61. *Mexican Americans: A Selective Guide to Materials in the UCSB Library.* Santa Barbara: University of California at Santa Barbara, 1969. ERIC ED 032 150.

62. Mickey, Barbara A. *A Bibliography of Studies Concerning the Spanish-Speaking Population of the American Southwest. Museum of Anthropology Miscellaneous Series, No. 4.* Greeley: Colorado State College, Museum of Anthropology, 1969. ERIC ED 042 548.

63. Navarro, Eliseo G. "Annotated Bibliography of Materials on the Mexican American." Austin: University of Texas at Austin, Graduate School of Social Work, 1969. ERIC ED 034 633.

64. Saldaña, Nancy. "Mexican-Americans in the Midwest: An Annotated Bibliography. Rural Manpower Center Special Paper No. 10." East Lansing: Michigan State University, Department of Sociology, Rural Manpower Center, Mexican-American Research Project, 1969.

65. Tuttle, Lester E., Jr., and Hooker, Dennis A., eds. *An Annotated Bibliography of Migrant Related Materials.* 3rd ed. Boca Raton: Florida Atlanta University, 1969. ERIC ED 032 171.

66. U.S. Department of Health, Education, and Welfare. Office of Education. *Chicano! A Selected Bibliography of Materials by and about Mexico and Mexican-Americans,* by Keith Revelle. Washington, D.C.: Government Printing Office, 1969. ERIC ED 039 381.

67. U.S. Department of Health, Education, and Welfare. Office of Education. Inter-Agency Committee on Mexican American Affairs. *A Guide to Materials Relating to Persons of Mexican Heritage in the United States. The Mexican American, A New Focus on Opportunity.* Washington, D.C.: Government Printing Office, 1969. ERIC ED 034 644.

68. U.S. Department of Health, Education, and Welfare. Office of Education. Mexican American Affairs Unit. *Language, Culture, Education, Articles, Books, Unpublished Materials, 1962-68.* Washington, D.C.: Government Printing Office, 1969.

69. Wurster, Stanley R., and Heathman, James E. "Rural Education and Small Schools: A Selected Bibliography." University Park: New Mexico State University, 1969. ERIC ED 033 257.

70. Altus, David M., comp. "Bilingual Education; A Selected Bibliography." Las Cruces, New Mexico: Educational Resource Information Center, 1970. ERIC ED 047 853.

71. Anderson, Bernard F., et al. "Urban-Rural Cross Cultural Adjustment Problems of Indians and Mexican Americans. A Survey of Literature." Flagstaff: Northern Arizona University, 1970. ERIC ED 119 893.

72. Caseli, Ron; Anderson, Edward; and Arreguin, José, comps. "The Minority Experience—A Basic Bibliography of American Ethnic Studies." Santa Rosa, California: Sonoma County Superintendent of Schools, 1970. ERIC ED 038 221.

73. Clark y Moreno, Joseph A. "A Bibliography of Bibliographies Relating to Mexican American Studies." El Grito 3, no. 4 (summer 1970): 25-31.

74. Heathman, James E., comp. "Migrant Education, A Selected Bibliography. Supplement No. 1." University Park: New Mexico State University, 1970. ERIC ED 040 002.

75. Hedman, Kenneth, and McNeil, Patsy, comps. Mexican American Bibliography; A Guide to the Resources of the Library at the University of Texas at El Paso. El Paso: University of Texas at El Paso Library, 1970.

76. "Mexican American History: A Critical Selective Bibliography." Journal of Mexican American History 1 (fall 1970): 68-86.

77. Pennsylvania. State Department of Education. American Diversity: A Bibliography of Resources on Racial and Ethnic Minorities for Pennsylvania Schools, by Elizabeth S. Haller, comp. Harrisburg: Pennsylvania State Department of Education, 1970. ERIC ED 054 031.

78. Poliakoff, Lorraine, comp. "Ethnic Groups: Negroes, Spanish-Speaking, American Indians, and Eskimos, Part 4 of a Bibliographic Series on Meeting Special Educational Needs." Washington, D.C.: ERIC Clearinghouse on Teacher Education, 1970. ERIC ED 044 384.

79. Poliakoff, Lorraine, comp. "Some Selected Topics, Part 5 of a Bibliographic Series on Meeting Special Educational Needs." Washington, D.C.: ERIC Clearinghouse on Teacher Education, 1970. ERIC ED 044 385.

80. "Portraits: The Literature of Minorities: An Annotated Bibliography of Literature by and about Four Ethnic Groups in the United States for Grades 7-12." California: Los Angeles County Superintendent of Schools, 1970. ERIC ED 042 771.

81. Quezada, María. "Chicano Resource Materials." Paper presented at the Chicano Studies Institutes in Aztlán [sic], Washington, D.C., summer 1970. Available from: University of Texas at Austin, Benson Latin American Collection Library.

82. Schramko, Linda Fowler, comp. Chicano Bibliography: Selected Materials on Americans of Mexican Descent. Bibliographic Series No. 1. California: Sacramento State College Library, 1970. ERIC ED 047 829.

83. Segreto, Joan, comp. "Bibliographía: A Bibliography on the Mexican-American." Houston, Texas: Houston Independent School District, 1970. ERIC ED 046 616.

84. U.S. Department of Health, Education, and Welfare. Office of Education. Bibliography of Mexican-American Studies on Various Subjects, by Jesús J. Gonzales, comp. Washington, D.C.: Government Printing Office, 1970. ERIC ED 050 839.

85. U.S. Department of Housing and Urban Development. The Mexican Americans: A Bibliography. Washington, D.C.: Government Printing Office, 1970.

86. Weinberg, Meyer, comp. The Education of the Minority Child: A Comprehensive Bibliography of 10,000 Selected Entries. Chicago, Illinios: Integrated Education Associates, 1970.

87. Winnie, William W., Jr.; Stegner, John F.; and Kopachevsky, Joseph P. *Persons of Mexican Descent in the United States: A Selected Bibliography*. Fort Collins: Colorado State University, Center for Latin American Studies, 1970.

88. Albright, Cora; Bernath, Kathleen, et al. *Chicano: A Selected Bibliography*. San Bernardino, California: The Inland Library System, 1971.

89. Altus, David M., comp. "Mexican American Education; A Selected Bibliography. Supplement No. 1." University Park: New Mexico State University, 1971. ERIC ED 048 961.

90. Altus, David M., comp. "Migrant Education; A Selected Bibliography. Supplement No. 2." University Park: New Mexico State University, 1971. ERIC ED 055 706.

91. Barrios, Ernie, ed. *Bibliografía de Aztlán: An Annotated Chicano Bibliography*. San Diego, California: Centro de Estudios Chicanos Publications, San Diego State College, 1971.

92. Birdwell, Gladys B., and Little, Perry G. *Chicanos; A Selected Bibliography*. Houston, Texas: University of Houston Libraries, 1971. ERIC ED 048 987.

93. Bridgford, Clay. *Teaching about Minorities: An Annotated Bibliography on Blacks, Chicanos, and Indians*. Boulder, Colorado: Social Science Education Consortium, Inc., 1971. ERIC ED 049 970.

94. Castañeda, Alfredo, et al., eds. "Mexican Americans and Educational Change. Symposium (University of California, Riverside, May 21-22, 1971)." Riverside: University of California at Riverside, Mexican American Studies Program, May 1971. ERIC ED 063 988.

95. Cotera, Martha P., comp. and ed. *Educator's Guide to Chicano Resources*. Crystal City, Texas: Crystal City Memorial Library, 1971.

96. Feeney, Joan V., comp. "Chicano Special Reading Selections. Bibliography." 1971. ERIC ED 065 255.

97. Mackey, William F. *International Bibliography on Bilingualism*. Quebec: Les Presses de l' Université Laval, 1971.

98. Nogales, Luis G., ed. "The Mexican American: A Selected and Annotated Bibliography." Palo Alto, California: Stanford University, 1971. ERIC ED 050 865.

99. Rosen, Pamela, and Horne, Eleanor V. *Tests for Spanish-Speaking Children: An Annotated Bibliography*. Princeton, New Jersey: Educational Testing Service, 1971. ERIC ED 056 084.

100. Sánchez, George I., and Putnam, Howard. *Materials Relating to the Education of Spanish-Speaking People in the United States: An Annotated Bibliography*. Westport, Connecticut: Greenwood Press, 1971.

101. Sprague, Juliene C. "United States Government Publications on Mexican Americans." *Texas Libraries* 33 (spring 1971): 47-58.

102. U.S. Cabinet. Committee on Opportunity for Spanish Speaking People. *The Spanish Speaking in the United States: A Guide to Materials*. Washington, D.C.: Government Printing Office, 1971.

103. U.S. Department of Health, Education, and Welfare. Office of Education. *Listing of Resource Material Concerned with the Spanish Speaking*, by Manuel H. Guerra, Arturo Y. Cabrera, and Susan S. Benson. Washington, D.C.: Government Printing Office, 1971. ERIC ED 059 930.

104. U.S. Department of Health, Education, and Welfare. Office of Education. Committee to Recruit Mexican American Librarians. *Chicanismo*. Washington, D.C.: Government Printing Office, 1971. ERIC ED 068 268.

105. "We Talk, You Listen: A Selected Bibliography." *Personnel and Guidance Journal* 50, no. 2 (October 1971): 145-46.

106. Clark y Moreno, Joseph A., comp. "A Bibliography of Bibliographies Relating to Studies of Mexican Americans." *El Grito* 5, no. 2 (winter 1971-72): 47-79.

107. Link, Albert D., comp. "Mexican American Education; A Selected Bibliography. ERIC/CRESS Supplement No. 2." May 1972. ERIC ED 065 217.

108. Loventhal, Milton; Lauritzen, Robert L.; and Simpson, Christine. "Bibliografía de materiales tocante al Chicano: A Bibliography of Materials Relating to the Chicano in the Library, California State University." 1972. ERIC ED 088 630.

109. Meier, Matt S., and Rivera, Feliciano. *A Bibliography for Chicano History.* San Francisco: R and E Research Associates, 1972.

110. Onouye, Wendy. "A Guide to Materials for Ethnic Studies." 1972. ERIC ED 090 111.

111. Ortego, Philip D. *Selective Mexican American Bibliography.* El Paso, Texas: Border Regional Library Association, 1972.

112. Osborne, Zelda L., et al., comps. *Mexican Americans: A Selected Bibliography.* Texas: University of Houston Libraries, Office of the Assistant Director for Collection Development, 1972.

113. Suarez, Cecilia C.-R., and Cabello-Argandoña, Roberto. *Early Childhood Education: A Selected Bibliography.* Los Angeles: University of California at Los Angeles, Chicano Research Library of the Chicano Studies Center, 1972.

114. U.S. Department of Defense. Naval Personnel Bureau. *Indians and Mexican Americans, Selective Annotated Bibliography.* Washington, D.C.: Government Printing Office, 1972.

115. *CARTEL: Annotated Bibliography of Bilingual Bicultural Materials No. 12 Cumulative Issue—1973.* Austin, Texas: Dissemination and Assessment Center for Bilingual Education, 1973. ERIC ED 806 429.

116. *Chicano Bibliography.* 2 vols. Salt Lake City: University of Utah Marriott Library, 1973.

117. Conley, Howard K. "An Annotated Bibliography of Dissertations on American Indian, Mexican American, Migrant and Rural Education." March 1973. ERIC ED 080 251.

118. Cordova, Marcella, and Roybal, Rose Marie. *Bibliografía de la Chicana—Bibliography on the Chicana.* Lakewood, Colorado: M. Cordova, 1973.

119. Gómez-Quiñones, Juan. *Selective Bibliography on Chicano Labor Materials.* Austin: University of Texas at Austin, Center for Mexican-American Studies, 1973.

120. Gómez-Quiñones, Juan. *Selected Materials for Chicano Studies.* Austin: University of Texas at Austin, Center for Mexican-American Studies, 1973.

121. Jablonsky, Adelaide, comp. "Mexican Americans. An Annotated Bibliography of Doctoral Dissertations. ERIC-IRCD Doctoral Research Series, No. 1." 1973. ERIC ED 076 714.

122. Jordan, Lois B. *Mexican Americans: Resources to Build Cultural Understanding.* Littleton, Colorado: Libraries Unlimited, Inc., 1973.

123. Maryland. State Department of Education. *Bibliography of the Sources for the Evaluation and Selection of Instructional Materials Which Will Insure Proper Recognition of Ethnic and Cultural Minorities.* Baltimore: Maryland State Department of Education, 1973. ERIC ED 095 885.

124. "Mexican American Education. A Selected Bibliography. ERIC/CRESS Supplement No. 3." 1973. ERIC ED 082 881.

125. "Migrant Education. A Selected Bibliography (with ERIC Abstracts). ERIC/CRESS Supplement No. 3." University Park: New Mexico State University, 1973. ERIC ED 075 162.

126. Romano, Octavio I.V., and Rios, Herminio C., eds. "Toward a Chicano/Raza Bibliography: Drama, Prose, Poetry." *El Grito* 7, no. 2 (December 1973): 1-85.

127. *A Selected Annotated Bibliography of Material Relating to Racism, Blacks, Chicanos, Native Americans and Multi-Ethnicity.* Vol. 2. East Lansing: Michigan Education Association, Division of Minority Affairs, 1973. ERIC ED 117 230.

128. "Selected Bibliography Pertaining to La Raza in the Midwest and Great Lake States (1924-1973)." Revised edition. Notre Dame, Indiana: University of Notre Dame, June 1973. ERIC ED 091 141.

129. Talbot, Jane Mitchell, and Cruz, Gilbert R. *A Comprehensive Chicano Bibliography 1960-1972.* Austin, Texas: Jenkins Publishing Co., 1973.

130. Tash, Steven, and Nupoll, Karin. *La Raza; A Selective Bibliography of Library Resources.* Northridge: University of California at Northridge, 1973.

131. "Bilingual Bicultural Materials; A Listing for Library Resource Centers." EL Paso, Texas: El Paso Public Schools, Model Bilingual/Bicultural Learning Resource Center, 1974.

132. Bills, Garland D., ed. *Southwest Areal Linguistics.* San Diego, California: San Diego State University, School of Education, 1974.

133. Bodnar, John E. *Ethnic History in Pennsylvania: A Selected Bibliography.* Harrisburg: Pennsylvania Historical Commission, 1974. ERIC ED 098 111.

134. Cotera, Martha P. *Selected Sources for Bilingual/Bicultural Material for the Migrant Child.* Austin, Texas: Juarez-Lincoln Center, 1974.

135. Gómez-Quiñones, Juan, and Camarillo, Alberto. *Selected Bibliography for Chicano Studies.* Los Angeles: Aztlán Publications, University of California at Los Angeles, Chicano Studies Center, 1974.

136. *A Guide to Publications on Latinos at Indiana University Library.* Pueblo Latino Volume 1: The Chicanos. Bloomington: Indiana University, 1974.

137. Guzmán, Ralph. *Mexican American Study Project. Advanced Report No. 3, Revised Bibliography.* Los Angeles: University of California at Los Angeles, 1974. ERIC ED 015 078.

138. Hyland, Anne, comp. "A Mexican American Bibliography: A Collection of Print and Non-Print Materials." Toledo, Ohio: Toledo Public Schools, 1974. ERIC ED 103 331.

139. Leyba, Charles. "A Brief Bibliography on Teacher Education and Chicanos." 1974. ERIC ED 090 147.

140. "Mexican American Education. A Selected Bibliography. ERIC/CRESS Supplement No. 4." 1974. ERIC ED 097 187.

141. "Migrant Education. A Selected Bibliography (with ERIC Abstracts). ERIC/CRESS Supplement No. 4." University Park: New Mexico State University, 1974. ERIC ED 087 599.

142. Ney, James W., and Eberle, Donella K. *A Selected Bibliography of Bilingual/Bicultural Education. CAL. ERIC/CLL Series on Languages and Linguistics, No. 2.* Arlington, Virginia: Center for Applied Linguistics, 1974. ERIC ED 098 813.

143. Pino, Frank. *Mexican Americans: A Research Bibliography.* 2 vols. East Lansing: Michigan State University, 1974.

144. Sandoval, R., and Nilsen, A.P. "Mexican-American Experience." *English Journal* 63 (January 1974): 61-63.

145. *A Selected Annotated Bibliography of Material Relating to Racism, Blacks, Chicanos, Native Americans and Multi-Ethnicity.* Vol. 3. East Lansing: Michigan Education Association, Division of Minority Affairs, 1974. ERIC ED 117 231.

146. "Selected Collections of the Chicano Studies Library." *Chicano Studies Library* No. 1- (February 1974-)Berkeley: University of California at Berkeley.

147. Spencer, Mimi, comp. "Bilingual Education for Spanish-Speaking Children: An Abstract Bibliography." 1974. ERIC ED 091 075.

148. Teschner, Richard V., comp. *Spanish-Surnamed Populations in the United States: A Catalog of Dissertations.* Ann Arbor, Michigan: Xerox University Microfilms, 1974.

149. U.S. Department of Health, Education, and Welfare. National Institute of Mental Health, Alcohol, Drug Abuse, and Mental Health Administration. *Latino Mental Health: Bibliography and Abstracts,* by Amado M. Padilla and Paul Aranda. Washington, D.C.: Government Printing Office, 1974.

150. Wilson, James A. *Tejanos, Chicanos and Mexicanos: A Partially Annotated, Historical Bibliography for Texas Public School Teachers.* San Marcos: Southwest Texas State University, 1974.

151. Zúñiga, Alfredo H. *Mexico and the Southwest Collection: A Bibliography and Directory of Materials, Services and Agencies Relating to the Chicano.* Fullerton: University of California at Fullerton Library, 1974.

152. Cahir, Stephen; Jeffries, Brad; and Montes, Rosa, eds. "A Selected Bibliography on Mexican American and Native American Bilingual Education in the Southwest. CAL ERIC/CLL Series on Languages and Linguistics, No. 6." 1975. ERIC ED 103 148.

153. Cohen, David, comp. *Multiethnic Media: Selected Bibliographies.* Chicago, Illinois: American Library Association, Office for Library Service to the Disadvantaged, 1975.

154. *Evaluation Instruments for Bilingual Education: An Annotated Bibliography.* Austin, Texas: The Dissemination Center for Bilingual Bicultural Education, 1975.

155. *Higher Education for Mexican Americans, A Selected Bibliography.* Las Cruces, New Mexico: ERIC/CRESS, 1975. ERIC ED 108 818.

156. Márquez, Benjamin, ed. *Chicano Studies Bibliography: A Guide to the Resources of the Library at the University of Texas at El Paso.* 4th ed. El Paso: University of Texas at El Paso, 1975. ERIC ED 119 923.

157. "Migrant Education. A Selected Bibliography (with ERIC Abstracts). ERIC/CRESS Supplement No. 5." University Park: New Mexico State University, 1975. ERIC ED 101 909.

158. Oller, John W., Jr. *Research with Cloze Procedure in Measuring the Proficiency of Non-Native Speakers of English: An Annotated Bibliography.* Arlington, Virginia: ERIC Clearinghouse on Languages and Linguistics, no. 13, 1975. ERIC ED 104 154.

159. Scott, Frank, et al., comps. *M.A. Theses on the Mexican-American in the University Archives of the University of Texas at El Paso Library.* El Paso: University of Texas at El Paso, 1975. ERIC ED 116 830.

160. Teschner, Richard V.; Bills, Garland D.; and Craddock, Jerry R., eds. *Spanish and English of United States Hispanos: A Critical, Annotated, Linguistic Bibliography.* Arlington, Virginia: Center for Applied Linguistics, 1975.

161. Trejo, Arnulfo D. *Bibliografía Chicana: A Guide to Information Sources.* Detroit, Michigan: Gale Research Co., 1975.

162. *Words Like Freedom: A Multi-Cultural Bibliography*. Burlingame: California Association of School Librarians, Human Relations Committee, 1975.

163. Cabello-Argandoña, Roberto, et al. *The Chicana: A Comprehensive Bibliographical Study*. Los Angeles: University of California at Los Angeles, Chicano Studies Center, 1976.

164. Cashman, Marc, and Klein, Barry, eds. *Bibliography of American Ethnology*. Rye, New York: Todd Publications, 1976.

165. "Migrant Education. A Selected Bibliography (with ERIC Abstracts). ERIC/CRESS Supplement No. 6." University Park: New Mexico State University, 1976. ERIC ED 118 292.

166. Miller, Wayne C., and Vowell, Faye N. *A Comprehensive Bibliography for the Study of American Minorities*. 2 vols. New York: New York University Press, 1976.

167. Tatum, Charles M. *A Selected and Annotated Bibliography of Chicano Studies*. n.p.: Society of Spanish and Spanish-American Studies, 1976.

168. Woods, Richard D. *Reference Materials on Mexican Americans: An Annotated Bibliography*. Metuchen, New Jersey: The Scarecrow Press, Inc., 1976.

2. GENERAL

2.1 The Mexican American

169. Bogardus, Emory S. *The Mexican in the United States*. New York: Arno Press, 1970; reprint from: Los Angeles: University of California Press, 1934.
170. Falits, Joseph. "Understanding Our Students of Mexican Extraction." *California Teachers Association Journal* 47, no. 2 (February 1951): 11.
171. McWilliams, Carey. "America's Disadvantaged Minorities: Mexican-Americans." *Journal of Negro Education* 20, no. 3 (Summer 1951): 301-9.
172. U.S. Federal Security Agency. Office of Education. *Young Spanish-Speaking Children in Our Schools*. Elementary Education Series, No. 30. Washington, D.C.: Government Printing Office, 1951.
173. Talbert, Robert H. *Spanish-Name People in the Southwest and West. Socio-Economic Characteristics of White Persons of Spanish Surname in Texas, Arizona, California, Colorado, and New Mexico*. Fort Worth: Potishman Foundation, Texas Christian University, 1955.
174. Landes, Ruth. *Latin Americans of the Southwest*. New York: Webster Division, McGraw-Hill Book Co., 1965.
175. Moore, Joan W. "Mexican-Americans: Problems and Prospects." Madison: University of Wisconsin, Institute for Research on Poverty, 1966. ERIC ED 028 856.
176. Sánchez, George I. *Forgotten People: A Study of New Mexicans*. Albuquerque, New Mexico: Calvin Horn, Publisher, Inc., 1967.
177. Nava, Julian. *Mexican-Americans: Past, Present and Future*. New York: American Book Co., 1969.
178. Burma, John H., ed. *Mexican Americans in the United States: A Reader*. Cambridge, Massachusetts: Schenkman Publishing Company, Inc., 1970.
179. Barragán, Miguel Francisco. *¡Adelante!* Phoenix, Arizona: Bronze Artists, 1970.
180. Galarza, Ernesto; Gallegos, Herman; and Samora, Julian. *Mexican-Americans in the Southwest*. 2nd ed. Santa Barbara, California: McNally & Loftin, Publishers, 1970.
181. Grebler, Leo; Moore, Joan; Guzmán, Ralph C., et al. *The Mexican American People: The Nation's Second Largest Minority*. New York: The Free Press, 1970.
182. Haddox, John Herbert. "Los Chicanos: An Awakening People." El Paso: University of Texas at El Paso, Southwestern Studies, monograph no. 28, 1970. 44 pp.
183. Lamb, Ruth S. *Mexican Americans: Sons of the Southwest*. Claremont, California: Ocelot Press, 1970.
184. Vásquez, Richard. *Chicano*. New York: Doubleday, 1970.
185. Villarreal, José Antonio. *Pocho*. Garden City, New York: Doubleday, 1970.
186. Acuña, Rudy. "Problems Confronting the Mexican American in Education." In *A Mexican American Chronicle*, pp. 141-44. New York: American Book Company, 1971.

187. Cabrera, Y. Arturo. *Emerging Faces: The Mexican-Americans.* Dubuque, Iowa: William C. Brown Company, 1971. ERIC ED 047 868.
188. Carranza, Eliu. *Pensamientos On los Chicanos.* 2nd ed. Berkeley, California: California Book Company, Ltd., 1971.
189. Wagner, Nathaniel L., and Haug, Marsha J., eds. *Chicanos: Social and Psychological Perspectives.* Saint Louis: The C.V. Mosby Company, 1971.
190. Davis, Charlotte D., and Stickney, Edith P., eds. *The Emerging Minorities in America: A Resource Guide for Teachers.* Santa Barbara, California: CLIO Press, 1972. ERIC ED 091 458.
191. de Leon, Nephtali. *Chicanos: Our Background and Our Pride.* Lubbock, Texas: Trucha Publications, 1972.
192. Kuenster, John. *The Mexicans in America.* Chicago, Illinois: Claretina Publications, 1972.
193. Cardenas, Blandina, and Cardenas, Jose A. "Chicano—Bright-Eyed Bilingual, Brown, and Beautiful." *Today's Education* 62 (February 1973): 49-51.
194. de la Garza, Rudolph O.; Kruszewski, Z. Anthony; and Arciniega, Tomás A., eds. *Chicanos and Native Americans: The Territorial Minorities.* Englewood Cliffs, New Jersey: Prentice-Hall, Inc., 1973.
195. Gómez, David F. *Somos Chicanos. Strangers in Our Own Land.* Boston: Beacon Press, 1973.
196. Cortés, Carlos E., ed. *The Mexican American.* New York: Arno Press, 1974.
197. Rodríguez, Richard. "Going Home Again: The New American Scholarship Boy." *American Scholar* 44 (winter 1974): 15-28.
198. Fadala, Sam. "Eddie: A Living Letter." *Integrated Education* 13, no. 2 (March 1975): 16-18.

2.2 Demographic Studies

2.2.1 General

199. Howard, Donald Stephenson. "A Study of the Mexican, Mexican-American and Spanish-American Population in Pueblo, Colorado, 1929-1930." Master's thesis, University of Denver, 1932.
200. Manuel, Herschel T. "The Mexican Population of Texas." *Southwestern Social Science Quarterly* 15, no. 1 (June 1934): 29-51.
201. Hunt, William Andrew, Jr. "Migration and Population Changes and Their Educational Implications." Master's thesis, University of Texas at Austin, 1941.
202. Longmore, T. Wilson, and Hitt, Homer L. "A Demographic Analysis of First and Second Generation Mexican Population of the United States." *Southwestern Social Science Quarterly* 24, no. 2 (September 1943): 138-49.
203. U.S. Department of Commerce. Bureau of the Census. *Internal Migration 1935-40, Economic Characteristics of Migrants,* by Joel Williams and Robert J. Milliken. Washington, D.C.: Government Printing Office, 1946.
204. U.S. Department of Commerce. Bureau of the Census. *Internal Migration, 1935-40, Social Characteristics of Migrants,* by Leon E. Truesdell. Washington, D.C.: Government Printing Office, 1946.
205. Crain, Forest Burr. "The Occupational Distribution of Spanish-Name People in Austin, Texas." Master's thesis, University of Texas at Austin, 1948.

206. Massey, Ellis Leonard. "Migration of the Spanish-Speaking People of Hidalgo County." Master's thesis, University of Texas at Austin, 1953.

207. Beegle, J. Allan; Goldsmith, Harold F,; and Loomis, Charles P. "Demographic Characteristics of the United States-Mexican Border." *Rural Sociology* 25, no. 1 (March 1960): 107-62.

208. Gómez, Raymond L. "The Latin American Population in 1950: The Interrelations of Factors of Social and Economic Development." Master's thesis, University of Chicago, 1962.

209. Browning, Harley L., and McLemore, Dale S. *A Statistical Profile of the Spanish-Surname Population of Texas.* Austin: University of Texas at Austin, Bureau of Business Research, 1964.

210. California. State Department of Industrial Relations. *Californians of Spanish Surname, Population, Employment, Income, Education.* San Francisco: California State Department of Industrial Relations, 1964. ERIC ED 021 680.

211. Gel, Walter Local Emerald. *Education and Income of Mexican Americans in the Southwest.* Los Angeles: University of California at Los Angeles, Graduate School of Business Administration, Division of Research, 1965.

212. Alvarez, José Hernández. "A Demographic Profile of the Mexican Immigration to the United States, 1910-1950." *Journal of Inter-American Studies and World Affairs* 8, no. 3 (July 1966): 471-96.

213. Moore, Joan W., and Mittelbach, Frank G. *Residential Segregation in the Urban Southwest: A Comparative Study. Advance Report No. 4.* Los Angeles: University of California, Graduate School of Business Administration, Mexican American Study Project, 1966.

214. Upham, W. Kennedy, and Lever, Michael F. *Differentials in the Incidence of Poverty in Texas.* Departmental Information Report 66-9. Prepared by Texas A&M University, College Station, Texas, 1966. ERIC ED 035 481.

215. Fogel, W. *Education and Income of Mexican Americans in the Southwest. Advance Report No. 1 by the Mexican American Study Project.* Los Angeles: University of California, Graduate School of Business Administration, 1967.

216. Grebler, Leo. *Mexican Immigration to the United States: The Record and Its Implications. Advance Report No. 2 by the Mexican American Study Project.* Los Angeles: University of California, Graduate School of Business Administration, 1967.

217. U.S. Department of Commerce. Bureau of the Census. *Population Characteristics of Selected Ethnic Groups in Five Southwestern States,* by Charles E. Johnson and Tobia Bressler. Washington, D.C.: Government Printing Office, 1968.

218. Goodman, Mary Ellen; Beman, Alma; des Jarlais, Don, et al. "The Mexican-American Population of Houston: A Survey in the Field, 1965-1970. Monograph in Cultural Anthropology." *Rice University Studies* 57, no. 3 (summer 1971): 1-125.

219. U.S. Department of Commerce. Bureau of the Census. *Ethnic Origin and Educational Attainment: November 1969. Population Characteristics, Current Population Reports,* by Charles E. Johnson, Jr. Washington, D.C.: Government Printing Office, 1971. ERIC ED 051 931.

220. U.S. Department of Commerce. Bureau of the Census. *Persons of Spanish Origin in the United States: November 1969. Population Characteristics, Current Population Reports,* by Tobia Bressler. Washington, D.C.: Government Printing Office, 1971.

221. U.S. Department of Commerce. Bureau of the Census. *Selected Characteristics of Persons and Families of Mexican, Puerto Rican, and Other Spanish Origin: March 1971. Population Characteristics: Current Population Reports*, by Larry E. Suter. Washington, D.C.: Government Printing Office, 1971. ERIC ED 065 224.

222. "Data on the Spanish-Speaking Population of Suburban Cook County, Illinois." Mimeographed. Cook County, Illinois: Cook County Office of Economic Opportunity, The Task Force on Spanish Speaking Affairs, 1972.

223. U.S. Department of Commerce. Bureau of the Census. *Selected Characteristics of Persons and Families of Mexican, Puerto Rican, and Other Spanish Origin: March 1972, Current Population Reports: Series P-20, Population Characteristics*. Washington, D.C.: Government Printing Office, July 1972. ERIC ED 070 546.

224. Fernández, Edward W., and Cresce, Arthur. "Persons of Spanish Origin in the United States: March 1973. Current Population Reports, Population Characteristics." ERIC ED 091 119.

225. U.S. Department of Commerce. Bureau of the Census. *Persons of Spanish Ancestry. 1970 Census of Population, Supplementary Report PC(S1)-30.* Washington, D.C.: Government Printing Office, 1973.

226. Shepherd, George. "Population Profiles, Vol. 5: Demographic and Socioeconomic Profiles of the American Indian, Black, Chinese, Filipino, Japanese, Spanish Heritage, and White Populations of Washington State in 1970." July 1974. ERIC ED 097 184.

227. Mindiola, Tatcho. "A Demographic Profile of Texas and Selected Cities: Some Recent Trends, 1950-1970." 1974. ERIC ED 097 147.

228. U.S. Commission on Civil Rights. *Counting the Forgotten: The 1970 Census Count of Spanish Speaking Background in the United States*, by Jaime Taronji, Jr. Washington, D.C.: Government Printing Office, 1974. ERIC ED 089 929.

2.2.2 School

229. New Mexico. State Department of Education. *The Age-Grade Status of the Rural Child in New Mexico, 1931-1932*, by George I. Sánchez. Santa Fe: New Mexico State Department of Education, 1932.

230. Wood, Herbert Sidney. "A Pupil Survey of James A. Garfield High School, Los Angeles." Master's thesis, University of Southern California, 1937.

231. Grout, Paul Asbury. "Trends in Scholastics, Enrollment, Average Daily Attendance, and Age-Grade Distribution, of Spanish-American Pupils in Lyford, Texas Public Schools, 1933-1938." Master's thesis, Texas A&I University, at Kingsville, 1938.

232. Martínez, Arnulfo Simeon. "A Study of the Scholastic Census of the Spanish Speaking Children in Texas." Master's thesis, University of Texas at Austin, 1944.

233. Texas. Education Agency. *State-Wide Survey of Enumeration, Enrollment, Attendance and Progress of Latin American Children in Texas Public Schools, 1943-1944.* Austin: Texas Education Agency, 1944.

234. Whitaker, J.M. "Survey of Socioeconomic Status of the Pupils of Franklin D. Roosevelt Elementary School." Master's thesis, University of Texas at El Paso, 1948.

235. Johnson, Vally L. "Survey of Spanish-Speaking Scholastics in Brewster County, Texas." Doctoral dissertation, Colorado State College, 1950.

236. Hnatek, Margaret. "A Survey of Population Factors Relating to the Education of Migrant Children in Victoria County, Texas." Master's thesis, University of Texas at Austin, 1952.

237. Texas. Education Agency. *Report of Pupils in Texas Public Schools Having Spanish Surnames, 1955-56.* Austin: Texas Education Agency, Division of Research, 1957.
238. Record, Wilson. "Racial Diversity of California Public Schools." *Journal of Negro Education* 27, no. 1 (winter 1959): 15-25.
239. Texas. Education Agency. *Estimated Number of Potential School Dropouts for Children and Average Daily Attendance in Public Schools in 1960 and of Current Dropouts of 1960 for School Age Children with Percent of Population Who Are Latin-American and Non-White Population.* Austin: Texas Education Agency, [1960?]
240. California. State Department of Education. Bureau of Intergroup Relations. *Distribution of Racial and Ethnic Groups in California Public Schools.* Sacramento: California State Department of Education, 1968.
241. California. State Department of Education. *Racial and Ethnic Survey of California Public Schools.* Sacramento: California State Department of Education, 1969.
242. New York. State Department of Education. *Racial/Ethnic Distribution of Public School Students and Staff in New York, 1972-73.* Albany: New York State Department of Education, 1973. ERIC ED 089 901.
243. Shepherd, George. *Population Profiles, Vol. 2: 1970 Demographic and Socioeconomic Profiles of the Populations of Washington State School Districts with Over 400 Students.* 1973. ERIC ED 097 181.
244. Shepherd, George. *Population Profiles, Vol. 3: 1970 Demographic and Socioeconomic Profiles of the Population of Washington State School Districts with Less Than 400 Students.* 1973. ERIC ED 097 182.
245. Jiménez, Luis A., and Upham, W. Kennedy. "Rural Youth in Five Southwestern States: The Population under Age 25 in Arizona, California, Colorado, New Mexico, and Texas. Information Report No. 73-2." 1974. ERIC ED 096 090.
246. Suter, Larry E., et al. "Social and Economic Characteristics of Students: October 1972. Current Population Reports, Series P-20, NC." 1974. ERIC ED 093 728.

2.3 Education

247. Stanley, Grace C. "Special Schools for Mexicans." *Survey* 44 (15 September 1920).
248. Davis, E.E. "A Report on Illiteracy in Texas." *University of Texas at Austin Bulletin No. 2328,* 22 July 1923.
249. Works, George A. *The Non-English Speaking Children and the Public School.* Austin, Texas: Texas Education Survey Commission, 1925.
250. Emerson, Ralph Waddell. "Education for the Mexican in Texas." Master's thesis, Southern Methodist University, 1929.
251. Manuel, Herschel T. *The Education of Mexican and Spanish-Speaking Children in Texas.* Austin: The University of Texas Press, 1930.
252. Sisk, William O. "Mexican in Texas Schools." *Texas Outlook* 14, no. 12 (December 1930): 10-12.
253. Cortés, Carlos E., advisory ed. *Education and the Mexican American.* New York: Arno Press, Inc., 1974; reprint from: articles by various authors published in 1930, 1933, 1944, and 1951.
254. Armour, Basil T. "Problems in the Education of the Mexican Child." *Texas Outlook* 16, no. 12 (December 1932): 29-31.
255. U.S. Department of Interior. Bureau of Education. *The Education of Spanish-Speaking Children in Five Southwestern States. Bulletin No. 11,* by Annie Reynolds. Washington, D.C.: Government Printing Office, 1933.

256. Sánchez, George I. "The Education of Bilinguals in a State School System." Doctoral dissertation, University of California, 1934.

257. Taylor, J.T., Mrs. "Americanization of Harlingen's Mexican School Population." *Texas Outlook* 18, no. 9 (September 1934): 37-38.

258. Taylor, Paul Schuster. *An American-Mexican Frontier, Nueces County, Texas*. Chapel Hill: University of North Carolina Press, 1934.

259. Enciso, F.B. "Rights and Duties of a Mexican Child." *Progressive Education* 13, no. 2 (February 1936): 123.

260. Hamill, Mary H. "Teaching the Foreign Beginner." *Texas Outlook* 21, no. 6 (June 1937): 38-39.

261. Andrus, Ethel Percy. "Social Living Classes for the Underprivileged." *California Journal of Secondary Education* 14, no. 7 (November 1939): 414-17.

262. Arizona. State Department of Public Instruction. *Instruction of Bilingual Children*. Phoenix: Arizona State Department of Public Instruction, 1939.

263. Murphy, Laura F. "Experiment in Americanization." *Texas Outlook* 23, no. 11 (November 1939): 23-24.

264. Davis, Allison, and Dollard, John. *Children of Bondage*. Washington, D.C.: American Council of Education, 1940.

265. Kaderli, Albert Turner. "The Educational Problem in Americanization of the Spanish Speaking Pupils of Sugarland, Texas." Master's thesis, University of Texas at Austin, 1940.

266. "Problems of Spanish-Speaking Pupils in Our Public Schools." Los Angeles, California: Los Angeles County Board of Education, 1940.

267. Wooten, Kate. "The Anglo-Latin-American Spanish Class." *Texas Outlook* 25, no. 10 (October 1941): 14-16.

268. Hughes, Marie M., and Palm, Reuben R. "Workshop in Education of Mexican and Spanish-Speaking Pupils." Los Angeles, California: Los Angeles County Superintendent of Schools, 1942.

269. Hutton, E.R. "We Mexicans—Meeting the Language and Social Needs of Mexican Children." In *Foreign Languages and Cultures in American Education*, pp. 29-41. Edited by W.V. Kaulfers et al. New York: McGraw-Hill, 1942.

270. "In the Interest of Understanding: Some Recent Studies Concerned with Education of Minority Groups." *Education for Victory* 1, no. 13 (September 1942): 18-20.

271. Andrus, Ethel Percy. "Workshop Studies—Education of Mexican-Americans." *California Journal of Secondary Education* 18, no. 6 (October 1943): 328-30.

272. McGorray, W.E. "Needs of a Mexican Community." *California Journal of Secondary Education* 18, no. 6 (October 1943): 349-50.

273. Russell, Daniel. "Problems of Mexican Children in the Southwest." *Journal of Educational Sociology* 17, no. 4 (December 1943): 216-22.

274. Trillingham, C.C., and Hughes, Marie M. "Good-Neighbor Policy for Los Angeles County." *California Journal of Secondary Education* 18, no. 6 (October 1943): 342-46.

275. Brown, F.F., and Roucek, J.S. *Our Racial and National Minorities*. New York: Prentice-Hall, 1945.

276. Davis, Harold E. "Education Program for Spanish-Speaking Americans." *World Affairs* 108 (March 1945): 43-48.

277. Borrego, Eva R. "American Child with a Two Language Heritage." *National Elementary Principal* 25, no. 6 (June 1946): 32-35.

278. McWilliams, Carey. "Chapter III. The Forgotten Mexican." In *Brothers Under the Skin*, pp. 114-46. Boston: Little, Brown and Company, 1948.

279. Rouse, Lura. "A Study of the Education of Spanish Speaking Children in Dimmit County, Texas." Master's thesis, University of Texas at Austin, 1948.

280. Tireman, Lloyd Spencer. *Teaching Spanish-Speaking Children*. Albuquerque: University of New Mexico Press, 1948.

281. Connor, Ruth P. "Some Community, Home, and School Problems of Latin-American Children in Austin, Texas." Master's thesis, University of Texas at Austin, 1949.

282. Roberts, Kathryn. "The Contribution of the Southern Presbyterian Church to the General Education of Latin-American Youth through Its Texas Mission Schools." Master's thesis, Southwest Texas State University, 1950.

283. Castañeda, Carlos D. "Some of Our Earliest Americans Await the Magic Touch." *Texas Outlook* 37, no. 1 (January 1953): 22-23 +.

284. DuPrey, Virginia. *Techniques of Minority Bilingual Groups*. New York: MacMillan Co., 1955.

285. Calderón, Carlos I. "Fewest Words to Open the Widest Doors." *Texas Outlook* 40, no. 7 (July 1956): 14-16.

286. "Teaching the Spanish-Speaking Child: Report of the Second Annual Workshop." Alpine, Texas: Sul Ross State College, 1956.

287. Beals, Ralph, and Humphrey, Norman. *No Frontier to Learning: The Mexican American Student in the United States*. Minneapolis: University of Minnesota Press. 1957.

288. Chávez, Simon J., and Erickson, Twila L. "Teaching American Children from Spanish-Speaking Homes." *Elementary School Journal* 57, no. 4 (January 1957): 198-203.

289. U.S. Department of Health, Education, and Welfare. Office of Education. *The Educational Problem of the Mexican-American*. Washington, D.C.: Government Printing Office, [1960?]

290. Burma, John H. "Spanish-Speaking Children." In *The Nation's Children*. Vol. 3: *Problems and Prospects*, pp. 78-102. Edited by Eli Ginzberg. New York: Columbia University Press, 1960.

291. U.S. President. White House Conference on Children and Youth. *Needs of Mexican American Children and Youth Today*, by George I. Sánchez. Washington, D.C.: Government Printing Office, 1961.

292. Woolsey, A. Wallace. "What Are We Doing for the Spanish-Speaking Student?" *Hispania* 44, no. 1 (March 1961): 119-23.

293. Bullock, Paul, and Singleton, Robert. "The Minority Child and the Schools." *The Progressive* 26 (November 1962): 33-36.

294. Roucek, Joseph S. "Some Educational Problems of Children from Immigrant, Refugee and Migrant Families in U.S.A." *International Review of Education* 8, no. 2 (1962): 225-35.

295. U.S. Department of Health, Education, and Welfare. Office of Education. Educational Policies Commission. *Education and the Disadvantaged American*. Washington, D.C.: Government Printing Office, 1962.

296. Samora, Julian. "The Educational Status of a Minority." *Theory into Practice* 2 (June 1963): 144-50.

297. Singleton, Robert, and Bullock, Paul. "Some Problems in Minority-Group Education in the Los Angeles Public Schools." *Journal of Negro Education* 32, no. 2 (spring 1963): 137-45.

298. Howsden, Arley L. "Where's the Camp, Mister?" [Summer School for Migrant Children at the Gridley Farm Labor Camp in Butte County.] *California Teachers Association Journal* 60, no. 3 (May 1964): 14-16.

299. Maglietto, Lois B. "Where Are They? How Are They Educated? Teaching the Non-English Speaking Children in Our Public Schools." 1964. ERIC ED 002 508.

300. Potts, Alfred M. *Providing Opportunities for Disadvantaged Children.* Denver: Colorado State Department of Education, 1964.

301. Rice, Joseph P., Jr. "Education of Subcultural Groups." *School and Society* 92 (28 November 1964): 360-62.

302. U.S. Department of Health, Education, and Welfare. Office of Education. *Problems and Difficulties in Planning and Development in Areas with Large Minority Groups,* by Clark S. Knowlton. Washington, D.C.: Government Printing Office, 1964. ERIC ED 013 129.

303. Berman, Mark L. *Some Considerations in the Education of Indigenous Groups in the Southwest.* Santa Monica, California: System Development Corp., 1965. ERIC ED 016 387.

304. Christian, Chester C., Jr., and Lado, R., eds. *Our Bilinguals: Social and Psychological Barriers; Linguistic and Pedagogical Barriers. Reports.* El Paso, Texas: Southwest Council of Foreign Language Teachers, 1965.

305. Landes, Ruth. *Culture in American Education: Anthropological Approaches to Minority and Dominant Groups in the Schools.* New York: John Wiley and Sons, 1965.

306. McKenney, J. Wilson. "The Dilemma of the Spanish Surname People of California." *California Teachers Association Journal* 61, no. 2 (March 1965): 17, 38, 40.

307. Manuel, Herschel T. *Spanish Speaking Children of the Southwest, Their Education and the Public Welfare.* Austin: University of Texas at Austin Press, 1965.

308. "Mexican-American Study Project. Revised Prospectus and Interim Report." Los Angeles: University of California at Los Angeles, 25 February 1965. ERIC ED 011 530.

309. Mulvaney, Iris. "Teaching Students from Bilingual or Non-English Speaking Homes." *Audiovisual Instruction* 10, no. 1 (January 1965): 34-35.

310. U.S. Department of Health, Education, and Welfare. Office of Education. *Discussion of Planning and Implementation of Government and Private Agency Programs in Northern New Mexico,* by Clark S. Knowlton. Washington, D.C.: Government Printing Office, 1965. ERIC ED 013 154.

311. Berlin, Irving N. "Special Learning Problems of Deprived Children." *National Education Association Journal* 55, no. 3 (March 1966): 23-24.

312. Fielding, Byron. "Federal Funds to Meet Local Needs." *National Education Association Journal* 55, no. 6 (September 1966): 23-26.

313. U. S. Department of Health, Education, and Welfare. Office of Education. *Dignity of Their Own. Helping the Disadvantaged Become First-Class Citizens,* by William H. Koch. Washington, D.C.: Government Printing Office, 1966. ERIC ED 012 195.

314. U.S. Department of Health, Education, and Welfare. Office of Education. *Educational Programs for Mexican-Americans Administered by the U.S. Office of Education.* Washington, D.C.: Government Printing Office, [1966?]

315. Wilson, Alan B. *The Education of Disadvantaged Children in California.* Berkeley: University of California, Survey Research Center, 1966.

316. California. State Department of Education. *Pattern Transmission in a Bicultural Community.* Sacramento: California State Department of Education, 1967. ERIC ED 014 366.

317. Colorado. State Legislature. General Assembly. *Report of the Colorado General Assembly: The Status of Spanish-Surnamed Citizens of Colorado.* Denver: Colorado Commission on Spanish Surnamed Citizens, 1967.

318. Cordasco, Frank M. "Knocking Down the Language Walls: [Proposed Amendment to Elementary and Secondary Education Act to Establish Education Programs]." *Commonweal* 87 (6 October 1967): 6-8.

319. Gómez, Severo. "The Meaning and Implications of Bilingualism for Texas Schools." In *Improving Educational Opportunities of the Mexican-American. Proceedings of the First Texas Conference for the Mexican-American, San Antonio, Texas, April 13-15, 1967*, pp. 42-63. Edited by Dwain M. Estes and David W. Darling. Austin: Southwest Educational Development Laboratory, 1967.

320. Gonzales, H.B. "The Hope and the Promise." In *Improving Educational Opportunities of the Mexican-American. Proceedings of the First Texas Conference for the Mexican-American, San Antonio, Texas, April 13-15, 1967*, pp. 112-22. Edited by Dwain M. Estes and David W. Darling. Austin: Southwest Educational Development Laboratory, 1967.

321. Grebler, Leo. "The Schooling Gap: Signs of Progress (Advance Report 7.)" Los Angeles: University of California at Los Angeles, Division of Research, Mexican-American Study Project, 1967.

322. Lamanna, Richard A., and Samora, Julian. "Recent Trends in Educational Status of Mexican-Americans in Texas." In *Improving Educational Opportunities of the Mexican-American. Proceedings of the First Texas Conference for the Mexican-American, San Antonio, Texas, April 13-15, 1967*, pp. 20-41. Edited by Dwain M. Estes and David W. Darling. Austin: Southwest Educational Development Laboratory, 1967.

323. Lloyd, Clay. "Remembering Forgotten Americans." *National Education Association Journal* 56, no. 9 (December 1967): 58-59.

324. Moreno, Edward. "View from the Margin." *Claremont College Reading Conference Yearbook* 31 (1967): 88-100.

325. Parker, Ann. "Mess, You Goin' To Be Real Teacher Now, Don'cha?" *American Education* 3, no. 5 (May 1967): 14-16.

326. Rivera, Carlos. "The Meaning and Implication of Bilingualism for Texas Schools." In *Improving Educational Opportunities of the Mexican-American. Proceedings of the First Texas Conference for the Mexican-American, San Antonio, Texas, April 13-15, 1967*, pp. 67-69. Edited by Dwain M. Estes and David W. Darling. Austin: Southwest Educational Development Laboratory, 1967.

327. Samora, Julian, and Lamanna, Richard A. *Mexican-American Study Project. Advance Report 8, Mexican-Americans in a Midwest Metropolis—A Study of East Chicago.* Los Angeles: University of California at Los Angeles, 1967. ERIC ED 015 079.

328. Stocker, Joseph. "Help for Spanish-Speaking Youngsters." *American Education* 3, no. 5 (May 1967): 17-18, 24.

329. U.S. Department of Health, Education, and Welfare. Office of Education. *Federal Programs to Improve Mexican American Education,* by Clayton Brace et al. Washington, D.C.: Government Printing Office, 1967. ERIC ED 014 338.

330. Bonilla, Joe. "Back to the Neighborhood." *Grade Teacher* 86, no. 4 (December 1968): 47-48.

331. Cordasco, Frank M. "The Challenge of the Non-English-Speaking Child in American Schools." *School and Society* 96 (30 March 1968): 198-201.

332. Elliott, W. Floyd, and Cox, Robert L., comps. "Educational Communication for the Deprived Child: Report and Suggestions. Texas A&I University, Kingsville, Texas, Teacher Corps Project Report. First Cycle Program 1966-1968." Kingsville: Texas A&I University at Kingsville, 1968. ERIC ED 071 786.

333. Howe, Harold, II. "Cowboys, Indians and American Education." Paper presented at the National Conference on Educational Opportunities for Mexican Americans, Austin, Texas, 25 April 1968. ERIC ED 020 810.

334. Palomares, Uvaldo H. "Special Needs of Mexican-Americans: PROJECT DESIGN. Educational Needs, Fresno, 1968, Number 27." Fresno, California: Fresno City Unified School District, 1968. ERIC ED 038 765.

335. Rodríguez, Armando M. "Mexican-American Education: An Overview." Speech presented at the Workshop to Develop Human Resources among Mexican-American Teachers in the Denver Metropolitan Area, Denver, Colorado, 6 June 1968. ERIC ED 030 509.

336. Rodríguez, Armando M. "Mexican-American Education, Special Report." Paper presented at the Ford Foundation Leadership Seminar, Albuquerque, New Mexico, 23 August 1968. ERIC ED 030 510.

337. Rosenau, Fred S. "New Hope for the Culturally Different." *California Teachers Association Journal* 64, no. 3 (May 1968): 9-11.

338. *Search Lights on Education on the Mexican American Youth.* Austin, Texas: Southwest Educational Development Laboratory, 1968.

339. Ulibarri, Horacio. "Educational Needs of the Mexican-American." University Park: New Mexico State University, 1968. ERIC ED 016 538.

340. U.S. Department of Health, Education, and Welfare. Office of Education. *Viva la Raza, Mexican-American Education, A Search for Identity.* Washington, D.C.: Government Printing Office, 1968.

341. U.S. Department of Health, Education, and Welfare. Office of Education. Mexican-American Affairs Unit. *Mexican-American Education. Special Report.* Washington, D.C.: Government Printing Office, 1968. ERIC ED 023 510.

342. *Afro- and Mexican-Americans. Mexico-Americana.* California: Fresno State College Library, 1969.

343. Arizona. State Department of Public Instruction. *Mexican American Educational Needs: A Report for the State Superintendent of Public Instruction.* Phoenix: Arizona Department of Public Instruction, 1969. ERIC ED 041 691.

344. Cabrera, Y. Arturo. "The Chicano Voice is Being Heard." *California Teachers Association Journal* 65, no. 4 (October 1969): 26-27.

345. California. State Department of Education. *Report of Recommendations Concerning Educational Programs for the Non-English Speaking Adult Population.* Sacramento: California State Department of Education, 1969. ERIC ED 036 719.

346. *First Annual Report: February, 1968-1969.* Phoenix, Arizona: Southwest Council of La Raza, 1969.

347. Forbes, Jack D. "La Raza Brings Much to the School." *California Teachers Association Journal* 65, no. 4 (October 1969): 15-17.

348. "Mexican American Education Research Program: Solutions in Communication. Report to the California State Department of Education." San Jose, California: Santa Clara County Office of Education, 1969. ERIC ED 033 806.

349. Post, Don. "Mexican-Americans and 'La Raza.' " *Christian Century* 86 (5 March 1969): 325-26 + .

350. Rodríguez, Armando M. "The Mexican-American—Disadvantaged? Ya Basta!" *Florida FL Reporter: A Language Education Journal (Special Anthology Issue: Linguistic-Cultural Differences and American Education)* 7, no. 1 (spring/summer 1969): 35-36, 160.

351. Bahr, Jerome. "Federally Funded Education Projects Help Spanish-Speaking Americans Join National Mainstream." *Adult Leadership* 18, no. 8 (February 1970): 239-40.

352. California. State Department of Education. *Mexican-American Education Research Project. Fourth Annual Nuevas Vistas Conference of the California State Department of Education.* Sacramento: California State Department of Education, 1970.

353. California. State Legislature. Assembly. *Report on the Education of Children in the Ghetto School: A Legislative Program for Reform.* Sacramento: California Legislature, Assembly, 1970.

354. California. State Legislature. Senate. Committee on Education. *Hearings, 1970. The Education of Mexican-American Pupils. Proceedings of Hearings, Stockton, California.* Sacramento: California State Legislature, 1970.

355. Carter, Thomas P. "Mexican Americans: How the Schools Have Failed Them." *College Board Review* 75 (spring 1970): 5-11.

356. Carter, Thomas P.; Samora, Julian; and Sánchez, George I. "Interviews." *The National Elementary Principal* 50, no. 2 (November 1970): 93-104.

357. Casso, Henry J. "Ya Basta, The Siesta Is Over." In *Educating the Mexican American,* pp. 93-99. Edited by Henry Sioux Johnson and William J. Hernández-M. Valley Forge, Pennsylvania: Judson Press, 1970.

358. "Education for the Spanish Speaking." *National Elementary Principal* 50, no. 2 (November 1970): 15-122.

359. Hernández, Deluvina. *Mexican American Challenge to a Sacred Cow.* Los Angeles: University of California at Los Angeles, Mexican American Cultural Center, 1970.

360. Jensen, Arthur R. "Do Schools Cheat Minority Children?" Berkeley: University of California at Berkeley, Institute of Human Learning, 1970. ERIC ED 046 976.

361. Johnson, Henry Sioux, and Hernández-M., William J., comps. *Educating the Mexican American.* Valley Forge, Pennsylvania: Judson Press, 1970.

362. *Mexicans in California: Report of Governor C.C. Young's Mexican Fact-Finding Committee.* San Francisco: R and E Research Associates, 1970.

363. Moore, John W., and Cuéllar, Alfredo. *Mexican-Americans.* Englewood Cliffs, New Jersey: Prentice-Hall, Inc.,1970.

364. Palomares, Uvaldo H. "Communication Begins with Attitude." *The National Elementary Principal* 50, no. 2 (November 1970): 47-49.

365. Peterson, Lorraine D. *Teacher's Guide for Cultures in Conflict, Problems of the Mexican Americans.* New York: Charter School Books, Inc., 1970.

366. Rivera, Feliciano. *A Mexican American Source Book.* Menlo Park, California: Educational Consulting Association, 1970.

367. Rodríguez, Armando M. "The Challenge for Educators." *The National Elementary Principal* 50, no. 2 (November 1970): 18-19.

368. U.S. Cabinet. Committee on Opportunity for Spanish Speaking People. *New Era, Spanish Speaking People of the United States,* by Carlos Conde. Washington, D.C.: Government Printing Office, 1970.

369. Valencia, Atilano A. *Research and Development Needs and Priorities for the Education of the Spanish-Speaking People.* Albuquerque, New Mexico: Southwestern Cooperative Educational Lab., 1970. ERIC ED 041 521.

370. Aragón, John A., and Ulibarri, Sabine R. "Learn, Amigo, Learn." *Personnel and Guidance Journal* 50, no. 2 (October 1971): 87-89.

371. California. State Department of Education. Bureau of Intergroup Relations. *Intergroup Relations and the Education of Mexican American Children. An Advisory Report to the Board of Education, Norwalk-La Mirada Unified School District.* Sacramento: California State Department of Education, 1971. ERIC ED 052 854.

372. Coles, Robert. "Uprooted Children." *National Elementary Principal* 50, no. 3 (January 1971): 6-14.

373. García, Ernest J. "A Synthesis of Current Research in Mexican American Education." Master's thesis, University of California at Los Angeles, 1971.

374. González, Simon. *Education for Minorities: The Mexican Americans.* New York: John Wiley and Sons, 1971.

375. Henderson, George, ed. *America's Other Children; Public Schools Outside Suburbia.* Norman: University of Oklahoma Press, 1971.

376. Ludwig, Ed, and Santibañez, James. *The Education of Mexican Americans.* Baltimore, Maryland: Penguin Books, Inc., 1971.

377. *National Education Task Force De La Raza. Annual Report, 1971.* Los Angeles, California: National Education Task Force, 1971. ERIC ED 075 145.

378. Pacheco, Manuel T. "Approaches to Bilingualism: Recognition of a Multilingual Society." In *Britannica Review of Foreign Language Education.* Vol. 3, pp. 97-124. Chicago: Encyclopaedia Britannica, Inc., 1971.

379. Pranzo, Mary Louise. "Studies in Production Relationships in Secondary Education for Minority Groups in the United States." Doctoral dissertation, University of Pittsburgh, 1971.

380. Valencia, Atilano A. *Research and Development Needs and Priorities for the Education of the Spanish-Speaking People.* Albuquerque, New Mexico: Southwestern Cooperative Educational Lab., 1971. ERIC ED 052 886.

381. "Aid to Mexican-American Education: Grant to the National Education Task Force de la Raza." *Intellect* 101 (December 1972): 143-44.

382. Ballesteros, David. "Meeting Instructional Needs of Chicano Students." *NCREEO Newsletter* 3, no. 3 (February 1972). ERIC ED 072 164.

383. Cabrera, Y. Arturo. "Chicano Educational Priorities: Mindongo, Hash, or Potpourri." Paper presented at the workshop on Southwest Ethnic Groups: Sociopolitical Environment and Education, El Paso, Texas, 1972. ERIC ED 071 814.

384. "Educación, basta." *Edcentric* (October-November issue, 1972.) [Washington, D.C.: U.S. National Student Association, Center for Educational Reform.]

385. García, Nelda C. "Teaching the Spanish-American." *Business Education Forum* 26, no. 5 (February 1972): 19-20.

386. Guerra, Manuel H. "Educating Chicano Children and Youths." *Phi Delta Kappan* 53, no. 5 (January 1972): 313-14.

387. Health, G. Louis. *Red, Brown, and Black Demands for Better Education*. Philadelphia, Pennsylvania: Westminster Press, 1972.

388. Kuvlesky, William P. "Children Who Are Short-Changed: Rural Blacks and Chicanos." College Station: Texas A&M University and Texas Agricultural Experiment Station, 1972. ERIC ED 067 203.

389. Marland, S.P., Jr. "Completing the Revolution." Speech presented at the inauguration of Dr. Frank Angel as president of New Mexico Highlands University, Las Vegas, New Mexico, 1972. ERIC ED 066 288.

390. Minnesota. Governor's Interracial Commission. *The Mexican in Minnesota: A Report to Governor C. Elmer Anderson of Minnesota by the Governor's Interracial Commission*. San Francisco: R and E Research Associates, 1972.

391. Nelsen, Jerald. "Open-Minded, Thought-Filled Education." Ellensburg, Washington: Central Washington State College, 1972. ERIC ED 068 166.

392. Ornstein, Jacob. "Report on a Project to Apply Sociolinguistic Research Findings to Educational Needs of Mexican American Bilingual/Biculturals." Paper presented at the sixth annual meeting of the American Council on the Teaching of Foreign Languages, Atlanta, Georgia, 25 November 1972. ERIC ED 077 296.

393. Wahab, Abdul Zaher. "The Mexican American Child and the Public School." Doctoral dissertation, Stanford University, 1972. ERIC ED 096 034.

394. Zimmerman, Barry J., and Ghozeil, Sue. "Feedback: Educational Strategies." Tucson: University of Arizona, Arizona Center for Early Childhood Education, October 1972. ERIC ED 094 860.

395. Almaraz, Felix D., Jr. "Current Issues in Mexican American Education." In *Proceedings of the 2nd Annual Mexican American Conference on Education, May 3-4, 1973*. Lincoln: University of Nebraska, Institute for Ethnic Studies, TTT Project, 1973.

396. Drake, Diana. "Culture and Education: Mexican American and Anglo American." *Elementary School Journal* 74, no. 2 (November 1973): 97-105.

397. Hall, William S., et al. "Policy, Programs and Research in Child Development: A Review and Assessment from a Minority Perspective. Final Report." 1973. ERIC ED 091 982.

398. Hamilton, Andrew. "Education and La Raza; With Editorial Comment." *American Education* 9, no. 6 (July 1973): inside cover, 4-8.

399. Litsinger, Dolores Escobar. *The Challenge of Teaching Mexican-American Students*. New York: American Book Co., 1973.

400. Reyes, Donald J. "Helping the Chicano Pupil." *Clearing House* 48, no. 2 (October 1973): 110-12.

401. Ruiz, Julliette, ed. *Chicano Task Force Report*. New York: Chicano Task Force, Council on Social Work Education, 1973.

402. U.S. Department of Health, Education, and Welfare. National Institute of Education. *The Elementary Education of Black and Chicano Children: An Iatrogenic Dilemma. Final Report*, by Lee Conway. Washington, D.C.: Government Printing Office, 1973. ERIC ED 078 034.

403. Walsh, Donald D. "Spanish-Speaking Children in American Schools: The Story of an Educational Crime." Paper presented at the annual (63rd) meeting of the National Council of Teachers of English, Philadelphia, 22-24 November 1973. ERIC ED 088 103.

404. Castañeda, Alfredo, et al. *The Educational Needs of Minority Groups*. Lincoln, Nebraska: Cliffs Notes, Inc., 1974. ERIC ED 118 515.

405. Michigan. State Board of Education. *Quality Educational Services to Michigan's Spanish Speaking Community. [Report by the La Raza Citizens Advisory Committee to the Michigan State Board of Education]*, by Carlos Falcón et al. Lansing: Michigan State Board of Education, January 1974. ERIC ED 097 177.

406. Quintana, Francis, comp. "The Brown Paper: Education and Chicanos in New Mexico, 1973-74." Las Vegas: New Mexico Highlands University, 1974. ERIC ED 113 120.

407. Wilson, Herbert B. "Quality Education in a Multicultural Classroom." *Childhood Education* 50, no. 3 (January 1974): 153-56.

408. Bane, Mary E. "Education Futurism and the Mexican-American Student." 1975. ERIC ED 119 925.

409. Gonzales, Tobias, and Gonzales, Sandra, eds. "Perspectives on Chicano Education." Palo Alto, California: Stanford University, Office of Chicano Affairs, 1975.

410. *La Raza: Ford Foundation Assistance to Mexican Americans.* New York: Ford Foundation, 1975.

411. Nava, Julian. "Educational Challenges in Elementary and Secondary Schools." In *Mexican-Americans Tomorrow: Educational and Economic Perspectives*, pp. 107-36. Edited by Gus Tyler. Albuquerque: University of New Mexico Press, 1975.

412. Palomares, Uvaldo H. "El Gringo no es pendejo, mijo." *Education Digest* 40, no. 8 (April 1975): 24-27.

413. San Miguel, Guadalupe, Jr. "No One Single Solution." In *Perspectives on Chicano Education.* Edited by Tobias Gonzales and Sandra Gonzales. California: Stanford University, Office of Chicano Affairs, 1975.

414. Tyler, Gus, ed. *Mexican-Americans Tomorrow: Educational and Economic Perspectives.* Albuquerque: University of New Mexico Press, 1975.

2.4 Educational History

415. Jones, Anita Edgar. "Conditions Surrounding Mexicans in Chicago." Master's thesis, University of Chicago, 1928.

416. Bowers, Gladine. "Mexican Education in East Donna." *Texas Outlook* 15, no. 3 (March 1931): 29-30.

417. Johnson, Roberta Muriel. "History of the Education of Spanish Speaking Children in Texas." Master's thesis, University of Texas at Austin, 1932.

418. Leis, Ward William. "The Status of Education for Mexican Children in Four Border States." Master's thesis, University of Southern California, 1932.

419. Treff, S.L. "The Education of Mexican Children in Orange County." Master's thesis, University of Southern California, 1934.

420. Kaderli, James Nicholas. "A Study of Mexican Education at Atascosa County with Specific Reference to Pleasanton Elementary School." Master's thesis, University of Texas at Austin, 1938.

421. Bennett, Cathrine. "The History of Education in Laredo, Texas." Master's thesis, University of Texas at Austin, 1939.

422. Little, Wilson. *Spanish-Speaking Children in Texas.* Austin: University of Texas Press, 1944.

423. Kibbe, Pauline R. *Latin Americans in Texas.* Albuquerque: The University of New Mexico Press, 1946.

424. Berger, Max. "Education in Texas during the Spanish and Mexican Periods." *South western Historical Quarterly* 51, no. 1 (July 1947): 41-53.

425. Cromack, Isabel C. "Latin-Americans: A Minority Group in the Austin Public Schools." Master's thesis, University of Texas at Austin, 1949.

426. Richey, Herman G. "Educational Status of Important Population Groups between the First and Second World Wars." *School Review* 57, no. 1 and no. 2 (January and February 1949) 16-27, 89-100.

427. Ginzberg, Eli, and Bray, Douglas W. *The Uneducated.* New York: Columbia University Press, 1953.

428. McDonagh, Edward C. *Ethnic Relations in the United States.* New York: Appleton-Century-Crofts, Inc., 1953.

429. Ramírez, Sara Leonil. "The Educational Status and Socioeconomic Backgrounds of Latin American Children in Waco, Texas." Master's thesis, University of Texas at Austin, 1957.

430. Meador, Bruce Staffel. "Minority Groups and Their Education in Hay County, Texas." Doctoral dissertation, University of Texas at Austin, 1959.

431. McClendon, Juliette Jane Canfield. "Spanish-Speaking Children of Big Spring: An Educational Challenge." Doctoral dissertation, University of Texas at Austin 1964.

432. U.S. Department of Health, Education, and Welfare. Office of Education. *Spanish-American Schools in the 1960's.* Washington, D.C.: Government Printing Office, 1966. ERIC ED 012 194.

433. California. State Advisory Committee. *Education and the Mexican American Community in Los Angeles County. Report of the California State Advisory Committee to the U.S. Commission on Civil Rights.* Sacramento: California State Advisory Committee, 1968. ERIC ED 025 355.

434. Cuéllar, Robert A. *A Social and Political History of the Mexican-American Population of Texas, 1929-1963.* San Francisco: R and E Research Associates, 1974; master's thesis, North Texas State University, 1969.

435. Carter, Thomas P. *Mexican Americans in School: A History of Educational Neglect.* Princeton, New Jersey: College Entrance Examination Board, 1970.

436. Feeley, Dorothy Louise Young. "Mexican Americans in Texas: A View of Their History and Education in the Texas Public Schools." Master's thesis, University of Texas at Austin, 1970.

437. Hamilton, James. "Mexican American Problems and Trends in Corpus Christi, Texas." Master's thesis, St. Mary's University, 1970.

438. Lozano, Diana. "Historical Perspective." *National Elementary Principal* 50, no. 2 (November 1970): 20-23.

439. Keller, Robert Andrew. "The Educational Aspirations and Achievements of Mexican-Americans in a Northern Community—A Historical-Descriptive Study." Doctoral dissertation, Wayne State University, 1971.

440. Gamboa, Erasmo. "Chicanos in the Northwest: An Historical Perspective." *El Grito* 6, no. 4 (summer 1973): 57-70.

441. Evans, Charles L. *Mexican American Education Study. Report 1: Employment, Enrollment, and School Success of Mexican Americans.* Fort Worth, Texas: Fort Worth Independent School District, Department of Research and Evaluation, 1974. ERIC ED 100 548.

2.5 Equal Opportunity

2.5.1 General

442. Bogardus, Emory S. "The Mexican Immigrant and Segregation." *American Journal of Sociology* 36, no. 1 (July 1930): 74-80.

443. Carpenter, C.C. "Mexicans in California—A Case Study of Segregation versus Non-Segregation of Mexican Children." Master's thesis, University of Southern California, 1934.

444. Bynum, H.E. "Inequality of Educational Opportunity in New Mexico." Master's thesis, University of Southern California, 1936.

445. Gilbert, Ennis Hall. "Some Legal Aspects of the Education of Spanish-Speaking Children in Texas." Master's thesis, University of Texas at Austin, 1947.

446. Cooke, Henry W. "The Segregation of Mexican-American School Children in Southern California." *School and Society* 67 (5 June 1948): 417-21.

447. Peters, Mary M. "The Segregation of Mexican-American Children in the Elementary Schools of California: Its Legal and Administrative Aspects." Master's thesis, University of California at Los Angeles, 1948.

448. Strickland, Virgil E., and Sánchez, George I. "Spanish Name Spells Discrimination." *Nation's Schools* 41, no. 1 (January 1948): 22-24.

449. Texas. Education Agency. *Instructions and Regulations to All School Officers of County, City, Town and School Districts: Concerning Segregation of Pupils of Mexican or Other Latin American Descent.* Austin: Texas Education Agency, 1948.

450. Arizona. Council for Civic Unity. *Close the Breach: A Study of School Segregation in Arizona.* Phoenix: Arizona Council for Civic Unity, 1949.

451. Ashton, Price Richard. "The Fourteenth Amendment and the Education of Latin American Children in Texas." Master's thesis, University of Texas at Austin, 1949.

452. Broyles, Harvey Lloyd. "Some Phases of Spanish-Culture Segregation in South Texas." Master's thesis, Texas A&I University at Kingsville, 1949.

453. Huszar, George B., ed., comp. *Equality in America: The Issue of Minority Rights.* New York: The H.W. Wilson Company, 1949.

454. Phillips, Lester H. "Segregation in Education; A California Case Study." *Phylon* 10, no. 4 (winter 1949): 407-13.

455. Texas. Education Agency. *Statement, Discussion and Decision on the Segregation in the Del Rio Public Schools,* by the Texas State Superintendent of Public Instruction. Austin: Texas Education Agency, 1949.

456. Sánchez, George I. "Concerning Segregation of Spanish-Speaking Children in the Public Schools." In *Inter-American Education, Occasional Papers,* no. 9, pp. 1-75. Austin: University of Texas Press, 1951.

457. Edwards, N. "Segregation of Spanish-Speaking Children in Public Schools." *Elementary School Journal* 52, no. 6 (February 1952): 318.

458. Dawson, Howard A. "Disadvantaged: Education and Other Social Opportunities." *National Education Association Journal* 42, no. 1 (January 1953): 29-30.

459. Simpson, George Eaton, and Yinger, J. Milton. *Racial and Cultural Minorities: An Analysis of Prejudice and Discrimination.* New York: Harper & Brothers, 1953.

460. Clinchy, Everett. "Equality of Opportunity for Latin Americans in Texas." Doctoral dissertation, Columbia University, 1954.

461. Teel, Dwight. "Preventing Prejudice against Spanish-Speaking Children." *Educational Leadership* 12, no. 2 (November 1954): 94-98.

462. Brookshire, Marjorie S. "Some Notes on the Integration of Mexican-Americans since 1929, Nueces County, Texas." *Industrial Relations Research Association Annual Proceedings* 8 (December 1955): 356-61.

463. *Minority Groups; Segregation and Integration.* Edited by National Conference of Social Work. New York: Columbia University Press, 1955.

464. Cohn, Jack. "Integration of Spanish Speaking Newcomers in a 'Fringe Area' School." *National Elementary Principal* 39, no. 6 (May 1960): 29-33.

465. Winnie, William W., Jr. "The Spanish Surname Criteria for Identifying Hispanos in the Southwestern United States: A Preliminary Evaluation." *Social Forces* 38, no. 4 (May 1960): 363-66.

466. Sexton, Patricia Cayo. *Education and Income: Inequalities of Opportunity in Our Public Schools.* New York: The Viking Press, 1961.

467. Pinkney, Alfonso. "Prejudice toward Mexican and Negro Americans: A Comparison." *Phylon* 24, no. 4 (winter 1963): 353-59.

468. Grimes, Alan Pendleton. *Equality in America: Religion, Race, and the Urban Majority.* New York: Oxford University Press, 1964.

469. "New Voices of the Southwest; Symposium: The Spanish-Speaking Child in the Schools of the Southwest." Proceedings of the Third Professional Rights and Responsibilities Conference on Civil and Human Rights in Education sponsored by the National Education Association, Tucson, Arizona, 30-31 October 1966.

470. U.S. Congress. House. *The Hope and the Promise—Poverty in the Southwest. Proceedings and Debates of the 89th Congress, 2nd Session, May 12, 1966.* Washington, D.C.: Government Printing Office, 1966.

471. Anderson, James G., and Safar, Dwight. "The Influence of Differential Community Perceptions on the Provision of Equal Educational Opportunities." In *Chicanos: Social and Psychological Perspectives,* pp. 244-52. Edited by Nathaniel L. Wagner and Marsha J. Haug. Saint Louis: The C.V. Mosby Company, 1971; reprint from: *Sociology of Education,* 40, no. 3 (1967): 219-320.

472. California. State Department of Education. *Mexican-American Education Research Project. Prospectus for Equitable Educational Opportunities for Spanish-Speaking Children.* Sacramento: California State Department of Education, 1967.

473. California. State Department of Education. Bureau of Intergroup Relations. *Recruiting Minority Teachers; An Equal Opportunity Guide.* Sacramento: California State Department of Education, 1967.

474. U.S. Commission on Civil Rights. *Racial Isolation in the Public Schools; A Report.* Washington, D.C.: Government Printing Office, 1967. [Commonly known both as the Hannah report and as the Taylor report.]

475. Bailey, Stephen D., and Mosher, Edith K. *ESEA: The Office of Education Administers a Law.* New York: Syracuse University Press, 1968.

476. Kerby, Phil. "Minorities Oppose Los Angeles School System; Persistent Segregation." *Christian Century* 85 (4 September 1968): 1119-22.

477. Leiva, Richard. "Special Education Classes, Barrier to Mexican Americans." *Civil Rights Digest* 1, no. 3 (fall 1968): 36-39.

478. Mack, Raymond W., ed. *Our Children's Burden; Studies of Desegregation in Nine American Communities.* New York: Random House, 1968.

479. "The Mexican American: Quest for Equality." Washington, D.C.: National Advisory Committee on Mexican American Education, 1968. ERIC ED 049 841.

480. Rodríguez, Armando M. "Speak up, Chicano: Fight for Educational Equality." *American Education* 4, no. 5 (May 1968): 25-27.

481. U.S. Commission on Civil Rights. *The Mexican-American Paper,* by Helen Rowan. Washington, D.C.: Government Printing Office, 1968. ERIC ED 035 509.

482. U.S. Commission on Civil Rights. *Stranger in One's Own Land. Report. Hearings by the U.S. Commission on Civil Rights in San Antonio, Texas, December 1968,* by Rubén Salazar. Washington, D.C.: Government Printing Office, 1968. ERIC ED 054 908.

483. U.S. Commission on Civil Rights. *A Study of Equality of Educational Opportunity for Mexican Americans in Nine School Districts of the San Antonio Area. Staff Report.* Washington, D.C.: Government Printing Office, 1968. ERIC ED 047 828.

484. U.S. Department of Health, Education, and Welfare. Office of Civil Rights. "Policies on Elementary and Secondary School Compliance with Title VI of the Civil Rights Act of 1964." *Federal Register* 33, no. 58 (23 March 1968): 4955-56.

485. U.S. President (Johnson, Lyndon Baines). *A New Focus on Opportunity for the Spanish Speaking American; Statement of the President.* Washington, D.C.: Government Printing Office. 1968. ERIC ED 023 523.

486. California. State Department of Education. Bureau of Intergroup Relations. *Procedures to Correct Racial and Ethnic Imbalance in School Districts.* Sacramento: California State Department of Education, 1969.

487. California. State Legislature. Joint Committee on Higher Education. *Increasing Opportunities for Disadvantaged Students; A Preliminary Outline.* Sacramento: California State Legislature, 1969.

488. Radojkovic, Milos. "The Protection of Minorities under International Law, I." *Review of International Affairs* 20, no. 453 (20 February 1969): 25-27.

489. Radojkovic, Milos. "The Protection of Minorities under International Law, II." *Review of International Affairs* 20, no. 454 (5 March 1969): 14, 19-20.

490. U.S. Commission on Civil Rights. *Hearing before the United States Commission on Civil Rights, San Antonio, Texas, December 9-14, 1968.* Washington, D.C.: Government Printing Office, 1969. ERIC ED 042 839.

491. U.S. Congress. House. *Cabinet Committee on Opportunities for Spanish Speaking People. Report from Committee on Government Operations.* Washington, D.C.: Government Printing Office, 1969.

492. California. State Department of Education. *Placement of Underachieving Minority Group Children in Special Classes for the Educable Mentally Retarded.* Sacramento: California State Department of Education, 1970.

493. Mercado, Edward. "What Price Inglés." *Civil Rights Digest* 3, no. 3 (summer 1970): 32-35.

494. Ramírez, Henry. "Report from the U.S. Commission on Civil Rights." *National Elementary Principal* 50, no. 2 (November 1970): 78-79.

495. Steinfield, Melvin. *Cracks in the Melting Pot: Racism and Discrimination in American History.* Beverly Hills: Glencoe Press, 1970.

496. Turner, H.C. "Team Teaching, Employing a Variety of Methods for Spanish/Anglo-American Integration. Title IV, 1969-70. Final Report." Las Vegas, New Mexico: Las Vegas City Schools, 1970. ERIC ED 056 130.

497. U.S. Commission on Civil Rights. *Equal Educational Opportunities for the Spanish Speaking Child: Bilingual and Bicultural Educational Programs.* Washington, D.C.: Government Printing Office, 1970. ERIC ED 073 866.

498. U.S. Congress. Senate. *Select Committee on Equal Educational Opportunity, United States Senate, Ninety-First Congress, Second Session, September 1970. Interim Report. Report No. 91-743.* Washington, D.C.: Government Printing Office, 1970. ERIC ED 053 846.

499. U.S. Department of Health, Education, and Welfare. Office of Civil Rights. "Identification of Discrimination and Denial of Services on the Basis of National Origin." *Federal Register* 35, no. 139 (18 July 1970): 11549-608.

500. Cardenas, José A. "Deprivation of Poverty; Excerpts from Hearings before the Senate Select Committee on Equal Educational Opportunity." *Integrated Education* 9, no. 3 (May 1971): 45-49.

501. Carter, Thomas P. "School Discrimination: The Mexican American Case." University Park: New Mexico State University, 1971. ERIC ED 048 969.

502. Floca, Kathryn Priscilla Haines. "The Legality of Chicano Education." Master's thesis, University of Texas at Austin, 1971.

503. McMurrin, Sterling M., ed. "The Conditions for Educational Equality. CED Supplementary Paper, Number 34." New York: Committee for Economic Development, 1971. ERIC ED 057 118.

504. Salinas, Guadalupe, ed. "Mexican-Americans and the Desegregation of Schools in the Southwest." *Houston Law Review* 8 (1971): 929-51.

505. U.S. Commission on Civil Rights. *Mexican American Educational Series, Report 2: The Unfinished Education; Outcomes for Minorities in the Five Southwestern States.* Washington, D.C.: Government Printing Office, October 1971.

506. U.S. Commission on Civil Rights. *Mexican American Education Study, Report 1: Ethnic Isolation of Mexican Americans in the Public Schools of the Southwest.* Washington, D.C.: Government Printing Office, April 1971. ERIC ED 052 849.

507. U.S. Congress. *Equal Educational Opportunity Hearings. Ninety-First Congress, 2nd Session.* Washington, D.C.: Government Printing Office, 1971. ERIC ED 054 273.

508. U.S. Congress. Senate. *Equal Educational Opportunity: Hearings before the Select Committee on Equal Educational Opportunity of the United States Senate, Ninety-First Congress, Second Session on Equal Educational Opportunity, Part 4—Mexican American Education.* Washington, D.C.: Government Printing Office, 1971. ERIC ED 052 877.

509. Blair, Philip M. *Job Discrimination and Education: An Investment Analysis, A Case Study of the Mexican American in Santa Clara County, California.* New York: Praeger, 1972.

510. Brischetto, Robert, and Arciniega, Tomás A. "The Concept of Equal Educational Opportunity and the Chicano: Methodological Footnotes on a Study of School Systems in the Southwest." Paper presented at the annual meeting of the Rocky Mountain Educational Research Association, Las Cruces, New Mexico, 17 November 1972. ERIC ED 071 788.

511. Cooke, Henry W. *The Segregation of Mexican American School Children in Southern California.* New York: Macmillan Company, 1972.

512. Floyd, Harold William. "A Study of Student Rights and School Authority with Regard to Long-Term Suspensions." Master's thesis, New Mexico State University, 1972. ERIC ED 067 179.

513. González, Simón. "Implications of the Serrano and Rodríguez Cases on the Education of Mexican Americans." Paper presented at the Leadership Institute for Chicano Educators, El Paso, Texas, 17-18 November 1972. ERIC ED 077 602.

514. "La Raza: The Race for Equality." *Senior Scholastic* 99, no. 13 (10 January 1972): 4-9.

515. Mangold, Margaret M., ed. *La Causa Chicana: The Movement for Justice.* New York: Family Service Association of America, 1972.

516. Sánchez, David J., Jr. "Equal Opportunity for the Spanish-Speaking American." *Educational Forum* 36, no. 3 (March 1972): 383-87.

517. U.S. Commission on Civil Rights. *Methodological Appendix of Research Methods Employed in the Mexican American Education Study.* Washington, D.C.: Government Printing Office, 1972. ERIC ED 064 025.

518. U.S. Commission on Civil Rights. *Mexican American Education Study, Report 3: The Excluded Student; Educational Practices Affecting Mexican Americans in the Southwest.* Washington, D.C.: Government Printing Office, May 1972. ERIC ED 062 069.

519. U.S. Commission on Civil Rights. *Mexican American Education Study, Report 4: Mexican American Education in Texas: A Function of Wealth.* Washington, D.C.: Government Printing Office, August 1972.

520. U.S. Commission on Civil Rights. *The Study of Mexican American Education in the Southwest: Implications of Research by the Civil Rights Commission,* by Susan Navarro. Washington, D.C.: Government Printing Office, July 1972.

521. U.S. Congress. House. *Education of the Spanish Speaking Hearings before the Civil Rights Oversight Subcommittee (Subcommittee No. 4) of the Committee on the Judiciary, House of Representatives, Ninety-Second Congress, Second Session on Reports of the U.S. Commission on Civil Rights. Serial No. 35.* Washington, D.C.: Government Printing Office, June 1972. ERIC ED 071 803.

522. Brischetto, Robert, and Arciniega, Tomás. "Inequalities in Educational Opportunity and the Chicano. A Study of School Systems in the Southwest. Final Report." El Paso: University of Texas at El Paso, 1973. ERIC ED 082 935.

523. California. State Advisory Committee. *Negligencia en la educación de estudiantes México-Americanos en el distrito escolar unificado Lucía Mar, Pismo Beach, California. (Educational Neglect of Mexican-American Students in Lucia Mar Unified School District, Pismo Beach, California.)* Sacramento: California State Advisory Committee, 1973. ERIC ED 091 099.

524. California. State Advisory Committee. *The Schools of Guadalupe. . . . A Legacy of Educational Oppression.* Sacramento: California State Advisory Committee, 1973. ERIC ED 087 584.

525. Casso, Henry Joseph. "A Descriptive Study of Three Legal Challenges for Placing Mexican American and Other Linguistically and Culturally Different Children into Educably Mentally Retarded Classes." Doctoral dissertation, University of Massachusetts, 1973.

526. Jackson, Gregg, and Cosca, Cecilia. "The Equality of Educational Opportunity within Ethnically Mixed Classrooms." Paper presented at the American Educational Research Association meetings, New Orleans, Louisiana, 1 March 1973. ERIC ED 073 862.

527. "Mexican Americans as a Legal Minority: U.S. Court of Appeals Decision." *Integrated Education* 11 (March 1973): 68-74.

528. U.S. Commission on Civil Rights. *Hearing before the United States Commission on Civil Rights, New York, New York, February 14-15, 1972.* Washington, D.C.: Government Printing Office, 1973.

529. U.S. Commission on Civil Rights. *To Know or Not to Know, Collection and Use of Racial and Ethnic Data in Federal Assistance Programs. A Report of the U.S. Commission on Civil Rights,* by Cynthia Norris et al. Washington, D.C.: Government Printing Office, February 1973. ERIC ED 091 110.

530. U.S. Commission on Civil Rights. *Mexican American Education Study, Report 5: Teachers and Students; Differences in Teacher Interaction with Mexican American and Anglo Students.* Washington, D.C.: Government Printing Office, March 1973.

531. U.S. Commission on Civil Rights. *Mexican American Education Study, Report 6: The Final Report.* Washington, D.C.: Government Printing Office, 1973.

532. Baca, Leonard Marcus. "A Survey of the Testing, Labeling and Placement Procedures Utilized to Assign Mexican-American Students into Classes for Educable Mentally Retarded in the Southwest." Doctoral dissertation, University of Northern Colorado, 1974.

533. Brischetto, Robert, and Arciniega, Tomás A. "Inequalities in Educational Resources: Their Impact on Minorities and the Poor in Texas and California. Final Report." San Antonio, Texas: Our Lady of the Lake College, 1974. ERIC ED 108 322.

534. Cardenas, Blandina. "Defining Equal Access to Educational Opportunity for Mexican-American Children: A Study of Three Civil Rights Actions Affecting Mexican-American Students and the Development of a Conceptual Framework for Effecting Institutional Responsiveness to the Educational Needs of Mexican-American Children." Doctoral dissertation, University of Massachusetts, 1974.

535. Carroll, John M. "Internal Colonialism as an Explanation for the Political and Social Marginality of Mexican-Americans." Master's thesis, University of Texas at El Paso, 1974.

536. Jackson, Gregg, and Cosca, Cecilia. "Inequality of Educational Opportunity in the Southwest: An Observational Study of Ethnically Mixed Classrooms." *American Educational Research Journal* 11, no. 3 (summer 1974): 219-29.

537. Nieto, Consuelo. "Chicanas and the Woman's Rights Movement: A Perspective." *Civil Rights Digest* 6, no. 3 (spring 1974): 36-42.

538. U.S. Commission on Civil Rights. *The Mexican American Education Study. Reports 1-6.* Washington, D.C.: Government Printing Office, April 1971-February 1974. [Note: Report 2 has title: *Mexican American Educational Series.*]

539. U.S. Commission on Civil Rights. *Para los niños—For the Children: Improving Education for Mexican Americans,* by Frank Sotomayor. Washington, D.C.: Government Printing Office, October 1974.

540. U.S. Commission on Civil Rights. *Toward Quality Education for Mexican Americans. Mexican American Education Study,* by Cecilia Preciado de Burciaga et al. Washington, D.C.: Government Printing Office, 1974. ERIC ED 086 407.

541. U.S. Department of Health, Education, and Welfare. Office of Civil Rights. *Task Force Findings Specifying Remedies Available for Eliminating Past Educational Practices Ruled Unlawful under Lau v. Nichols.* Washington, D.C.: Government Printing Office, summer 1975.

542. U.S. Department of Health, Education, and Welfare. Office of Education. "Bilingual Education: Proposed Regulation." *Federal Register* 41, no. 69 (8 April 1976): 14986-96.

2.5.2   Court Decisions

Note: These listings are arranged in alphabetical, not in chronological, order.

543. *Arvizu* v. *Waco Independent School District*, 373 F. Supp. 1264 (1973).

544. *Arvizu* v. *Waco Independent School District*, 495 F. 2d 499, C. A. 5 (1974).

545. *Aspira of New York, Inc.*, v. *Board of Education of City of New York*, 394 F. Supp. 1161 (1975).

546. *Bradley* v. *Milliken*, C.A. no. 35, 257, E.D. Michigan, (1975).

547. *Bradley* v. *Milliken*, 402 F. Supp. 1096, 1144 (1975).

548. *Brown* v. *Board of Education*, 347 U.S. 483 (1954).

549. *Cisneros* v. *Corpus Christi Independent School District*, 350 F. Supp. 1241 (1971).

550. *Cisneros* v. *Corpus Christi Independent School District*, 467 F. 2d 142, C.A. 5 (1972).

551. *Cisneros* v. *Corpus Christi Independent School District*, 413 U.S. 920 (1973).

552. *Delgado* v. *Bastrop Independent School District*, Civil Action No. 388, United States District Court, 1948. (Unreported.)

553. *Evans* v. *Buchanan*, C.A. Nos. 1816-1822, D. Delaware, (1975).

554. *Gonzales* v. *Sheeley*, 96 F. Supp. 1004 (D.Ariz. 1951).

555. *Hernández* v. *Driscoll Consolidated Independent School District*, 2 Race Rel. L. Rep. 329 (S.D. Tex. 1957).

556. *Hernández* v. *Texas*, 347 U.S. 475 (1954).

557. *Independent School District* v. *Salvatierra*, 33 S.W. 2d 790 (1930).

558. *Keyes* v. *School District No. 1*, Denver, Colorado, 303 F. Supp. 279 (1969).

559. *Keyes* v. *School District No. 1*, Denver, Colorado, 303 F. Supp. 289 (1969).

560. *Keyes* v. *School District No. 1*, Denver, Colorado, 313 F. Supp. 61 (1970).

561. *Keyes* v. *School District No. 1*, Denver, Colorado, 313 F. Supp. 90 (1970).

562. *Keyes* v. *School District No. 1*, Denver, Colorado, 445 F. 2d 990, C.A. 10 (1971).

563. *Keyes* v. *School District No. 1*, Denver, Colorado, 368 F. Supp. 207 (1973).

564. *Keyes* v. *School District No. 1*, Denver, Colorado, 413 U.S. 189 (1973).

565. *Keyes* v. *School District No. 1*, Denver, Colorado, 380 F. Supp. 673 (1974).

566. *Keyes* v. *School District No. 1*, Denver, Colorado, 521 F. 2d 465, C.A. 10 (1975).

567. *Lau* v. *Nichols*, 483 F. 2d 791 C.A. No. 9 (1973).

568. *Lau* v. *Nichols*, 414 U.S. 563 (1974).

569. *Méndez* v. *Westminister School District*, 64 F. Supp. 544 (1946).

570. *Morales* v. *Shannon*, 366 F. Supp. 813 (1974).

571. *Morales* v. *Shannon*, 516 F. 2d 411, C.A. 5 (1975).

572. *Morgan* v. *Kerrigan*, 401 F. Supp. 216, 242 (1975).

573. *Otero* v. *Mesa County Valley School District No. 51*, C.A. No. 74-W-279, D. Colorado, (1975).

574. *Pérez* v. *Sonora Independent School District*, Civil Action No. 6-224 (N.D. Tex., Nov. 5, 1970).

575. *Romero* v. *Weakley*, 131 F. Supp. 818, 820 (S.D. Cal.), rev'd, 226 F. 2d 399, (9th Cir. 1955).

576. *Ross* v. *Eckels*, 434 F. 2d 1140 (5th Cir. 1970).

577. *San Antonio Independent School District* v. *Rodríguez*, 337 F. Supp. 280 (1971).

578. *San Antonio Independent School District* v. *Rodríguez*, 411 U.S. 1 (1973).

579. *Serna* v. *Portales Municipal Schools*, 351 F. Supp. 1279 (1973).

580. *Serna* v. *Portales Municipal Schools*, 499, F. 2d 1147, C.A. 10 (1974).

581. *United States* v. *Texas Education Agency,* 467 F. 2d 848, C.A. 5 (1972).
582. *United States* v. *Texas Education Agency,* 470 F. 2d 1001, C.A. 5 (1973).
583. *United States* v. *Texas* (San Felipe Del Rio School District), 321 F. Supp. 1043 (1971).
584. *United States* v. *Texas* (San Felipe Del Rio School District), 342 F. Supp. 24 (1971).
585. *United States* v. *Texas* (San Felipe School District), 466 F. 2d 518, C.A. 5 (1972).

2.6 Conferences

586. "Conference on Educational Problems in the Southwest." Typewritten. Committee reports of the Conference on Educational Problems in the Southwest with special reference to the educational problems in Spanish-speaking communities, under the auspices of the University of New Mexico, New Mexico Highlands University, and the Coordinator of Inter-American Affairs, held at Santa Fe, New Mexico, 19-24 August 1943.

587. "Workshop in the Education of Mexican and Spanish-Speaking Pupils." Los Angeles, California: Los Angeles City and County Schools, July 1943.

588. Sánchez, George I. "First Regional Conference on the Education of Spanish Speaking People in the Southwest; A Report." In *Inter-American Education, Occasional Papers, No. 1,* pp. 1-22. Austin: University of Texas Press, March 1946.

589. *Southwest Council on the Education of Spanish-Speaking People. Proceedings of the Fifth Annual Conference, George Pepperdine College.* Los Angeles, California: Southwest Council on the Education of Spanish-Speaking People, 1951.

590. "Summary of Proceedings of Conference on Educational Problems of Students of Mexican Descent." Los Angeles: University of California at Los Angeles, Department of Education, 26 March 1955.

591. *First Annual Report on Mexican American Education Conference Proceedings.* Los Angeles, California: Council of Mexican-American Affairs, 1956.

592. Eide, Carla, and Nance, Afton Dill. "Conference on the Education of Spanish-Speaking Children and Youth." Union City, California: Decoto Elementary School District, April 1963. ERIC ED 002 513.

593. California. State Department of Education. *Report of the Conference on Understanding and Teaching Mexican-American Youth.* Concord, California (16-17 October 1964). Sacramento: California State Department of Education, 1964.

594. *Our Bilinguals—Social and Psychological Barriers, Linguistic and Pedagogical Barriers (2nd Annual Conference of the Southwest Council of Foreign Language Teachers, El Paso, November 13, 1965).* El Paso, Texas: Southwest Council of Foreign Language Teachers, 13 November 1965. ERIC ED 019 899.

595. New Mexico. State Department of Education. *New Mexico State Conference on Education of the Disadvantaged, 1966. Report of the Proceedings.* Santa Fe: New Mexico State Department of Education, January 1966.

596. U.S. Department of Health, Education, and Welfare. Office of Education. *National Conference on Education of the Disadvantaged. July 18-20, 1966.* Washington, D.C.: Government Printing Office, 1966.

597. Estes, Dwain M., and Darling, David W., eds. *Improving Educational Opportunities of the Mexican-American: Proceedings of the First Texas Conference for the Mexican-American, April 13-15, 1967, San Antonio, Texas.* Austin: Southwest Educational Development Laboratory, 1967.

598. Manuel, Herschel T. "The Spanish-Speaking Child in Texas Schools." In *Improving Educational Opportunities of the Mexican-American: Proceedings of the First Texas Conference for the Mexican-American, April 13-15, 1967, San Antonio, Texas,* pp. 72-86. Edited by Dwain M. Estes and David W. Darling. Austin: Southwest Educational Development Laboratory, 1967.

599. California. State Department of Education. *Nuevas Vistas: A Report of the First Annual Conference of the California State Department of Education.* Sacramento: California State Department of Education, 1968.

600. Helm, June, ed. *Spanish-Speaking People in the United States. Proceedings of the 1968 Annual Spring Meeting of the American Ethnological Society.* Seattle: University of Washington Press, 1968.

601. Méndez, Aida, and Lee, Caroline, eds. "Trends Conference on Education of the Mexican-American in San Diego County (San Diego University, May 13, 1967)." California: San Diego City Schools, January 1968. ERIC ED 022 821.

602. *Proceedings. National Conference on Educational Opportunities for Mexican-Americans, April 25-26, 1968, Austin, Texas.* Austin: Southwest Educational Development Laboratory, 1968.

603. California. State Department of Education. *The Education of the Mexican-American. A Summary of the Proceedings of the Lake Arrowhead and Anaheim Conferences.* Sacramento: California State Department of Education, 1969. ERIC ED 050 844.

604. California. State Department of Education. *Nuevas Vistas: A Report of the Second Annual Conference of the California State Department of Education.* Sacramento: California State Department of Education, 1969.

605. *The Melting Pot, The Mold and Resultant Rejects. National Conference on Equal Educational Opportunity.* Washington, D.C.: National Education Association, Publications-Sales Section, 1969. ERIC ED 035 708.

606. U.S. Congress. House. Government Operations Committee. *Establishing Cabinet Committee on Opportunities for Spanish Speaking People. Hearings before Subcommittee, 91st Congress, 1st Session.* Washington, D.C.: Government Printing Office, 1969.

607. U.S. Department of Health, Education, and Welfare. Office of Education. *Report of Conferences on Improving Education of Disadvantaged Children, November 25-December 3, 1968, Silver Spring, Maryland; December 11-12, 1968, Denver, Colorado.* Washington, D.C.: Government Printing Office, 1969.

608. California. State Department of Education. *Nuevas Vistas: A Report of the Third Annual Conference of the California State Department of Education.* Sacramento: California State Department of Education, 1970.

609. Castañeda, Alfredo, et al., eds. "Mexican Americans and Educational Change. Symposium (University of California, Riverside, May 21-22, 1971)." Riverside: University of California at Riverside, Mexican American Studies Program, May 1971. ERIC ED 063 988.

610. Texas. Education Agency. *Proceedings: National Conference on Bilingual Education (Austin, Texas, April 14-15, 1972).* Austin: Texas Education Agency, 1972. ERIC ED 080 282.

611. U.S. Department of Health, Education, and Welfare. Office of Education. *Chicano Education and the National Institute of Education. Report of a Planning Conference for the NIE Planning Unit,* by Juan Aragón et al. Washington, D.C.: Government Printing Office, July 1972. ERIC ED 110 260.

612. Esquibel, Antonio, and Casso, Henry J. *A Report on the National Institute of Education/National Education Task Force de la Raza Symposium (Albuquerque, New Mexico, July 25-26, 1974)*. Albuquerque: National Education Task Force de la Raza, July 1974. ERIC ED 110 261.

3. MEXICAN AMERICAN STUDENTS

3.1 Physical Traits

613. Paschal, Franklin C. *Racial Influences in the Mental and Physical Development of Mexican Children.* Baltimore: The Williams & Wilkins Company, 1925.

614. Lamb, Emily O. "Racial Differences in Bi-Manual Dexterity of Latin and American Children." *Child Development* 1, no. 3 (September 1930): 204-31.

615. Manuel, Herschel T. "Physical Measurements of Mexican Children in American Schools." *Child Development* 5, no. 3 (September 1934): 237-52.

616. Rollins, E.L. "A Snellen Chart Technique Study of Visual Acuity of the Spanish Culture Pupils in the Stephen F. Austin Public Elementary School, Kingsville, Texas." Master's thesis, Texas A&I University at Kingsville, 1937.

617. Kramme, Clyde Ira. "A Comparison of Anglo-Culture with Spanish-Culture Elementary Students in Physical Development as Determined by Height, Weight, and Vital Capacity Measurements." Master's thesis, Texas A&I University at Kingsville, 1939.

618. Habermacher, Andrew Lee. "Physical Development of Anglo and Spanish-Culture School Boys and Girls, Ages 13-18 Inclusive." Master's thesis, Texas A&I University at Kingsville, 1940.

619. Jones, Hubert Ledyard. "A Comparison of Physical Skill and Intelligence of Negro and Spanish-American Boys of Junior High School Age." Master's thesis, University of Denver, 1940.

620. Keen, Marvin Spruce. "A Comparative Study of the Motor Ability of Latin American and Anglo American Boys." Master's thesis, University of Texas at Austin, 1941.

621. Nicoll, James Stewart. "A Comparison of the Physical Development, Motor Capacity and Strength of Anglo American and Spanish American Boys." Master's thesis, University of Southern California, 1943.

622. Goldstein, Marcus S. "Infants of Mexican Descent. I. Physical Status of Neonates." *Child Development* 18, nos. 1-2 (March-June 1947): 3-10.

623. Bell, Myrtle Lee. "A Comparative Study of Anglo-Culture and Latin-Culture School Girls in General Motor Capacity, Ability, and Achievement." Master's thesis, Texas A&I University at Kingsville, 1951.

624. Raven, Lillian Margaret. "Comparative Study of Sociometric Status and Athletic Ability of Anglo-American and Latin-American Sixth Grade Boys." Master's thesis, University of Texas at Austin, 1951.

625. Shaw, Bruce Walsh. "Sociometric Status and Athletic Ability of Anglo-American and Latin-American Boys in a San Antonio Junior High School." Master's thesis, University of Texas at Austin, 1951.

626. Cobb, Albert F. "Comparative Study of the Athletic Ability of Latin-American and Anglo-American Boys on a Junior High School Level." Master's thesis, University of Texas at Austin, 1952.

627. Lowry, Sarah J. "A Comparison of Certain Physical Abilities of Anglo and Latin American Fifth and Sixth Grade Girls." Master's thesis, University of Texas at Austin, 1952.

628. Meredith, Howard V., and Goldstein, Marcus S. "Studies on the Body Size of North American Children of Mexican Ancestry." *Child Development* 23, no. 2 (June 1952): 91-110.

629. Jayagopal, Rajabather. "Problem Solving Abilities and Psychomotor Skills of Navajo Indians, Spanish Americans and Anglos in Junior High School." Doctoral dissertation, University of New Mexico, 1970.

630. Sasser, Connie. "Motor Development of the Kindergarten Spanish-Speaking Disadvantaged Child." Master's thesis, Texas Woman's University, 1970. ERIC ED 067 186.

631. Brogdon, Gayle Lyndon. "A Comparison of Physical Fitness and Anthropometric Measures of Pre-Adolescent Mexican-American and Anglo-American Males." Doctoral dissertation, North Texas State University, 1972.

3.2 Health

3.2.1 Mental

632. Garth, Thomas R.; Holcomb, Walter M.; and Gesche, Irma. "Mental Fatigue of Mexican School Children." *Journal of Applied Psychology* 16, no. 6 (1932): 675-80.

633. Allinsmith, Wesley, and Goethals, George W. "Cultural Factors in Mental Health: An Anthropological Perspective." *Review of Educational Research* 26, no. 5 (December 1956): 429-50.

634. Jaco, E. Gartly. "Social Factors in Mental Disorders in Texas." *Social Problems* 4, no. 4 (April 1957): 322-28.

635. Jaco, E. Gartly. "Mental Health of the Spanish-American in Texas." In *Culture and Mental Health: Cross-Cultural Studies*, pp. 467-85. Edited by Marvin K. Opler. New York: The Macmillan Company, 1959.

636. Texas. State Department of Health. *The Forgotten Egg; A Study of the Mental Health Problems of Mexican American Residents in the Neighborhood of the Good Samaritan Center, San Antonio, Texas*, by Fred R. Crawford. Austin: Texas State Department of Health, 1961. ERIC ED 048 956.

637. Karno, Marvin; Ross, Robert N.; and Caper, Robert S. "Mental Health Roles of Physicians in a Mexican American Community." *Community Mental Health Journal* 5, no. 1 (February 1969): 62-69.

638. Fabrega, Horacio, Jr. "Mexican Americans of Texas: Some Social Psychiatric Features." In *Behavior in New Environments: Adaptation of Migrant Populations*, pp. 249-73. Edited by Eugene G. Brody. Beverly Hills: Sage Publications, 1970.

639. Morales, Armando. "Mental and Public Health Issues: The Case of the Mexican Americans in Los Angeles." *El Grito* 3, no. 2 (winter 1970): 3-11.

640. Opler, Marvin K.; Stoker, David H.; Zurcher, Louis A., et al. "Women in Psychotherapy: A Cross-Cultural Comparison." *Transcultural Psychiatric Research Review* 7 (October 1970): 203-5.

641. Karno, Marvin, and Morales, Armando. "A Community Mental Health Service for Mexican-Americans in a Metropolis." In *Chicanos: Social and Psychological Perspectives,* pp. 281-85. Edited by Nathaniel L. Wagner and Marsha J. Haug. Saint Louis: The C.V. Mosby Company, 1971.

642. Morales, Armando. "The Impact of Class Discrimination and White Racism on the Mental Health of Mexican-Americans." In *Chicanos: Social and Psychological Perspectives,* pp. 257-62. Edited by Nathaniel L. Wagner and Marsha J. Haug. Saint Louis: The C.V. Mosby Company, 1971.

643. U.S. Department of Health, Education, and Welfare. National Institute of Mental Health, Alcohol, Drug Abuse, and Mental Health Administration. *East Los Angeles and Comprehensive Mental Health Planning Perspectives. Report to National Institute of Mental Health,* by Ray Valle. Washington, D.C.: Government Printing Office, 1971.

644. Atencio, Tomás. "Mental Health and the Spanish Speaking." In *Mental Health Planning Conference for the Spanish Speaking,* pp. 19-32. Baltimore, Maryland: National Institute of Mental Health, 1972.

645. Martínez, Cervando. "Community Mental Health and the Chicano Movement." *American Journal of Orthopsychiatry* 43, no. 4 (July 1973): 595-601.

646. Aguilar, Ignacio, and Wood, Virginia N. "Aspects of Death, Grief and Mourning in the Treatment of Spanish-Speaking Mental Patients." Paper presented at the annual meeting of the American Anthropology Association, 73rd, Mexico City, Mexico, 19-24 November 1974. ERIC ED 101 887.

647. U.S. Department of Health, Education, and Welfare. National Institute of Mental Health, Alcohol, Drug Abuse, and Mental Health Administration. *Latino Mental Health: A Review of the Literature,* by Amado M. Padilla and René A. Ruiz. Washington, D.C.: Government Printing Office, 1974.

648. Durán, Rubén, et al., eds. "Salubridad Chicana: su preservación y mantenimiento—The Chicano Plan for Mental Health." Boulder, Colorado: Western Interstate Commission for Higher Education, Mental Health Manpower Office, 15 March 1975. ERIC ED 121 526.

3.2.2 Physical

649. Smith, Helen P. "Health and Nutrition of Mexican Infants and Pre-School Children." Master's thesis, University of Texas, 1930.

650. Barfell, Lawrence Otto. "A Study of the Health Program among Mexican Children with Special Reference to the Prevalence of Tuberculosis and Its Causes." Master's thesis, University of Southern California, 1937.

651. Goribund, Antonio. "Food Patterns and Nutrition of Two Spanish-American Communities." Master's thesis, University of Chicago, 1943.

652. Heller, Christine A. "Regional Patterns of Dietary Deficiency: The Spanish-Americans of New Mexico and Arizona." *American Academy of Political and Social Science* 225 (January 1943): 49-51.

653. Pijoan, Michel. *Nutrition and Certain Related Factors of Spanish-Americans in Northern Colorado.* Denver: Rocky Mountain Council on Inter-American Affairs, 1943.

654. Humphrey, Norman D. "Some Dietary and Health Practices of Detroit Mexicans." *Journal of American Folklore* 58 (July-September 1945): 255-58.

655. Shapiro, Harold A. "Health Conditions in San Antonio, Texas, 1900-1947." *Southwestern Social Science Quarterly* 34, no. 3 (December 1953): 60-76.

656. Harrison, Inez Anne. "Health Needs and Interests of Spanish-Speaking Children of Intermediate Grades." Master's thesis, University of California at Los Angeles, 1957.

657. Clark, Margaret. *Health in the Mexican-American Culture; A Community Study.* 2nd ed. San Francisco, California: El Dorado Distributors, 1970; 1st ed. Berkeley: University of California Press, 1959.

658. Madsen, William. *Society and Health in the Lower Rio Grande Valley.* Austin, Texas: Hogg Foundation for Mental Health, 1961. ERIC ED 043 401.

659. Mann, Virginia R. "Food Practices of the Mexican-American in Los Angeles County." San Jose, California: Santa Clara County Health Department, 1963.

660. Nall, Frank C., II, and Speilberg, Joseph. "Social and Cultural Factors in the Responses of Mexican-Americans to Medical Treatment." *Journal of Health and Social Behavior* 8 (December 1967): 299-308.

661. Bowden, Shirley. "Nutritional Beliefs and Food Practices of Mexican-American Mothers." Master's thesis, Fresno State College, 1968. ERIC ED 050 837.

662. Rosenthal, Ted L.; Henderson, Ronald W.; Hobson, Arline, et al. "Social Strata and Perception of Magical and Folk-Medical Child-Care Practices." *Journal of Social Psychology* 77, no. 1 (February 1969): 3-13.

663. Stanley, Grace C. "The Selection and Condition of Clothing of Low-Income Mexican American Pre-School Children." Master's thesis, University of Arizona, 1969.

664. Aranda, Robert G., et al. "A Preliminary Study of Nutritional Status in Mexican American Pre-School Children. I. Experimental Design, Selection of Subjects, Data Collection and Description of Families." San Diego: University of California at San Diego, 1970. ERIC ED 054 897.

665. Weaver, Thomas. "Use of Hypothetical Situations in a Study of Spanish American Illness Referral Systems." *Human Organization* 29, no. 2 (summer 1970): 140-54.

666. Lewis, Jane S., et al. "Nutritional Status of Mexican American Preschool Children in East Los Angeles and San Diego." Paper presented at the American Institute of Nutrition annual meeting, Chicago, Illinois, 16 April 1971. ERIC ED 054 898.

667. Thornberry, Spencer Lee. "Dental Health Care of Elementary School Students at Canutillo, Texas, Four Years after Their Participation in Head Start Dental Program." Master's thesis, University of Texas at El Paso, 1971.

668. U.S. Department of Health, Education, and Welfare. National Institute of Mental Health, Alcohol, Drug Abuse, and Mental Health Administration. *Chicano Comprehensive Health Planning: Final Report,* by Esmeralda J. Vallejo. Washington, D.C.: Government Printing Office, 1971.

669. Lewis, Jane S., et al. "Food Buying Practices of Mexican Americans in East Los Angeles." Paper presented at the American Home Economics Association meeting, Detroit, Michigan, 27 June 1972. ERIC ED 067 192.

670. Lewis, Jane S., et al. "A Pilot Survey of Food Frequencies, Meal Frequencies and Meal Patterns of Preschool Children in East Los Angeles." Paper presented at the American Home Economics Association meeting, Detroit, Michigan, 27 June 1972. ERIC ED 067 193.

671. Lurie, Hugh J., and Lawrence, George L. "Communication Problems between Rural Mexican-American Patients and Their Physicians: Description of a Solution." *American Journal of Orthopsychiatry* 42, no. 5 (October 1972): 777-83.

672. Lindstrom, Carol Jane. "Health and Illness of Mexican-American Children in an Upper Midwest Urban Setting." Doctoral dissertation, Michigan State University, 1974.

673. U.S. Congress. Senate. Select Committee on Nutrition and Human Needs. *National Nutrition Policy: Prepared for the Senate Select Committee on Nutrition and Human Needs, 93rd Congress, 2nd Session,* by Freeman H. Quimby and Cynthia. B. Chapman. Washington, D.C.: Government Printing Office, 1974. ERIC ED 094 041.

674. Woteki, Catherine O'Connor. "Some Nutritional Considerations of Lactose Malabsorption in Mexican American Children." Doctoral dissertation, Virginia Polytechnic Institute and State University, 1974.

675. Solís, Enrique, Jr. "Factors Discriminant of Dental Health Care Behavior Orientation in Southwest Cultures." Doctoral dissertation, New Mexico State University, 1975.

3.3 Cultural Traits

3.3.1 General

676. Parr, Eunice Elvira. *A Comparative Study of Mexican and American Children in the Schools of San Antonio, Texas.* San Francisco: R and E Research Associates, 1971; master's thesis, University of Chicago, 1926.

677. Bogardus, Emory S. "Second Generation Mexicans." *Sociology and Social Research* 13 (January-February 1929): 276-83.

678. Dodd, Elmer Cecil. "A Comparison of Spanish-Speaking and English-Speaking Children in Brownsville, Texas." Master's thesis, University of Texas at Austin, 1930.

679. Ream, Glen O. "A Study of Spanish Speaking Pupils in Albuquerque High School." Master's thesis, Yale University, 1930.

680. Knight, James. "A Laboratory Study of the Reading Habits of Spanish Speaking Children." Doctoral dissertation, University of Texas at Austin, 1931.

681. Schneider, Virginia. "Abilities of Mexican and White." Master's thesis, University of Southern California, 1931.

682. Manuel, H.T. "The Mexican Child in Texas." *Southwest Review* 17, no. 3 (spring 1932): 290-302.

683. Sánchez, George I. "Group Differences and Spanish-Speaking Children: A Critical Review." *Journal of Applied Psychology* 16 (October 1932): 549-58.

684. Brown, Willie Leonzo. "Knowledge of Social Standards among Mexican and Non-Mexican Children." Master's thesis, University of Texas at Austin, 1934.

685. Taylor, Harry Franklin. "The Musical Abilities of Spanish-American Children." Master's thesis, University of Denver, 1934.

686. Gunn, Ewing Leyton. "An Eye Movement Study of the Reading Habits of Spanish Speaking Children." Master's thesis, University of Texas at Austin, 1935.

687. Pintner, Rudolf, et al. "The Measurement of Pupil Adjustment." *Journal of Educational Research* 28 (January 1935): 334-46.

688. Porter, Charles Jesse. "Recreational Interests and Activities of High School Boys of the Lower Rio Grande Valley of Texas." Master's thesis, University of Texas, 1940.

689. Beard, E. Alice. "A Study of the Mexican Pupils in Fremont Junior High School." Master's thesis, University of Southern California, 1941.

690. Milor, John H. "Problems of a Junior High for Mexicans." *California Journal of Secondary Education* 16, no. 8 (December 1941): 482-84.
691. Sprinkle, Eunice Caroline. "A Comparative Study of the Reading Interests of Mexican and White Children." Master's thesis, University of Southern California, 1941.
692. Tramel, Mrs. Lucile. "Play Interests of Preschool Mexican Children." Master's thesis, Southwest Texas State University, 1941.
693. Withers, Charles Dinnijes. *Problems of Mexican Boys.* San Francisco: R and E Research Associates, 1974; master's thesis, University of Southern California, 1942.
694. Knopf, Arthur Carlyle. "Some Mexican Characteristics and Their Educational Significance." Master's thesis, University of Southern California, 1943.
695. Jones, Robert C. "Mexican Youth in the United States." *Texas Outlook* 29, no. 8 (August 1945): 11-13.
696. Fraser, William McKinley. "A Study of the Abilities of Spanish-Speaking and English-Speaking Children of Kinney County, Texas." Master's thesis, University of Texas at Austin, 1946.
697. Riggins, Rachael T. "Factors in Social Background Which Influence the Mexican Child." Master's thesis, University of Arizona, 1946.
698. Anderson, Amelia B. "The Number Abilities and Concepts of Spanish Speaking Children." Master's thesis, University of Texas at El Paso, 1948.
699. Jones, Robert C. "Mexican American Youth." *Sociology and Social Research* 32, no. 4 (March-April 1948): 793-97.
700. Altus, William D. "The American Mexican: The Survival of a Culture." *Journal of Social Psychology* 29, no. 2 (May 1949): 211-20.
701. Hill, Myles Eugene. "An Attitude Test toward Mexican Americans." Master's thesis, Arizona State University, 1950.
702. Anderson, Mary. "A Comparative Study of the English-Speaking Beginners in the Public Schools." Master's thesis, University of Texas at Austin, 1951.
703. de la Vega, Marguerite. *Some Factors Affecting Leadership of Mexican-Americans in a High School.* San Francisco: R and E Research Associates, 1974; master's thesis, University of Southern California, 1951.
704. Kluckhohn, Florence Rockwood. "Cultural Factors in Social Work Practice and Education [Mexican Culture as an Example of Diversity in Cultural Orientations]." *Social Service Review* 25, no. 1 (March 1951): 38-45.
705. Ramírez, Alfonso René. "A Study of the Reactions of Latin American Pupils to English and Spanish Film Commentaries." Master's thesis, University of Texas at Austin, 1951.
706. Ramírez, Emilia S. " 'Wetback' Children in South Texas." Master's thesis, University of Texas at Austin, 1951.
707. California. State Department of Education. "Spanish-Speaking Children." *California State Department of Education Bulletin* 21, no. 14 (1952).
708. Saunders, Maxine. "An Analysis of Some Educational Problems of the Spanish Speaking Children at the Intermediate Grade Level." Master's thesis, University of Texas at Austin, 1952.
709. Booth, Leroy L.J. "A Normative Comparison of the Responses of Latin-American and Anglo-American Children to the Children's Apperception Test." Doctoral dissertation, Texas Technological College, 1953.
710. California. State Department of Education. *Some Solutions to Problems of Students of Mexican Descent in Secondary Schools,* by Helen Heffernan. Sacramento: California State Department of Education, 1953.

711. Garnett, Hattie Mae. "Boy-Girl Relationships of Latin American Children as Shown in Anecdotal Records by Teachers." Master's thesis, University of Texas at Austin, 1953.

712. McCrary, Mallie Muncy. "These Minorities in Our Midst with Emphasis on Latin Americans in Texas." Master's thesis, University of Texas at Austin, 1953.

713. Shaftel, George. "The Needs and Anxieties of Spanish Speaking Students." *California Journal of Secondary Education* 28, no. 3 (March 1953): 168-70.

714. Houle, Bettie Eckhardt. "Some Significant Characteristics Associated with Popularity in American and Mexican Elementary School Children." Doctoral dissertation, University of Chicago, 1954.

715. Rivera, Orland Arthur. "A Descriptive Study of Students of Spanish-Speaking Descent at West High School." Doctoral dissertation, University of Utah, 1954.

716. Sánchez, Luisa Guerrero G. "The 'Latin-American' of the Southwest; Backgrounds and Curricular Implications." Doctoral dissertation, University of Texas at Austin, 1954.

717. Saunders, Lyle. *Cultural Difference and Medical Care: The Case of the Spanish-Speaking People of the Southwest.* New York: Russell Sage Foundation, 1954.

718. Corona, Bert Charles. "Study of Adjustment and Interpersonal Relations of Adolescents of Mexican Descent." Doctoral dissertation, University of California at Berkeley, 1955.

719. Wilson, D. "Concomitants of Peer Acceptance in Two 7th Grade Classes." Master's thesis, University of Texas at Austin, 1956.

720. Jensen, James Maurice. "The Mexican American in an Orange County Community." Master's thesis, Claremont Graduate School, 1957.

721. Ulibarri, Horacio. "The Effect of Cultural Difference in the Education of Spanish-Americans." Albuquerque: University of New Mexico, September 1958. ERIC ED 019 156.

722. Rubel, Arthur J. "Concepts of Disease in Mexican-American Culture." *American Anthropologist* 62, no. 5 (October 1960): 795-814.

723. Festersen, John C. "A Study of the Bilingual Student at Roseville Union High School." Master's thesis, Sacramento State College, 1961.

724. Jensen, Arthur R. "Learning Abilities in Mexican-American and Anglo-American Children." *California Journal of Educational Research* 12, no. 4 (September 1961): 147-59.

725. Mullins, Martha Mersman. "The Personality Differences between Unilingual and Bilingual Ninth Grade Students in a Depressed Area." Master's thesis, University of New Mexico, 1961.

726. Simmons, Ozzie G. "The Mutual Images and Expectations of Anglo-Americans and Mexican-Americans." *Daedalus* 90, no. 2 (spring 1961): 286-99.

727. Nall, Frank C., II. "Role Expectations: A Cross Cultural Study." *Rural Sociology* 27, no. 1 (March 1962): 28-41.

728. Peck, Robert F., and Galliani, Cono. "Intelligence, Ethnicity, and Social Roles in Adolescent Society." *Sociometry* 25, no. 1 (March 1962): 64-72.

729. Villarreal, Eduardo. "A Study of Group Processes in Two Small Natural Groups of Latin-American Adolescents." Master's thesis, University of Texas at Austin, 1962.

730. Wolman, Marianne. "Cultural Factors and Creativity." *Journal of Secondary Education* 37, no. 8 (December 1962): 454-60.

731. Barrett, Donald N., and Samora, Julian. *The Movement of Spanish Youth from Rural to Urban Settings.* Washington, D.C.: National Committee for Children and Youth, September 1963.

732. Cabrera, Ysidro Arturo. *A Study of American and Mexican-American Culture Values and Their Significance in Education.* San Francisco: R and E Research Associates, 1972; doctoral dissertation, University of Colorado, 1963.

733. Lin, Paul Ming-Chang. "Voluntary Kinship and Voluntary Association in a Mexican-American Community." Master's thesis, University of Kansas, 1963.

734. Brooks, Richard Martin. "The Psychological and Cultural Bases of Magical Disease Beliefs." Doctoral dissertation, University of Arizona, 1964.

735. California. State Department of Social Welfare. *Implications of Cultural Values to Education.* Sacramento: California Department of Social Welfare, 1964.

736. Tullis, David Sherman. "A Comparative Study of Negro, Latin, and Anglo Children in a West Texas Community." Doctoral dissertation, Texas Technological College, 1964.

737. Guerra, Manuel H. "The Mexican-American Child: Problems or Talents?" Paper presented at the Second Annual Conference on the Education of Spanish-Speaking Children and Youth, South San Gabriel, California, 20 November 1965. ERIC ED 045 243.

738. Jackson, Gail Craghead. "Implications for Teachers from a Study of the Culture of Mexican Americans." Master's thesis, University of Texas at Austin, 1965.

739. Romano-V., Octavio Ignacio. "Charismatic Medicine, Folk-Healing, and Folk-Sainthood." *American Anthropologist* 67, no. 5 (1965): 1151-73.

740. Andersen, Martha D. "Latin American Teenagers and the News in Ten Rio Grande Valley Districts." Master's thesis, University of Texas at Austin, 1966.

741. Belliaeff, Alexander. "Understanding the Mexican-American in Today's Culture, San Diego Project—Elementary and Secondary Education Act." California: San Diego City Schools, 1966. ERIC ED 014 365.

742. Currier, Richard L. "The Hot-Cold Syndrome and Symbolic Balance in Mexican and Spanish-American Folk Medicine." *Ethnology* 5, no. 3 (1966): 251-63.

743. Doan, William Franklin. "The Effect of Response Meaningfulness on Verbal Paired-Associated Learning in Anglo-American and Mexican-American Fifth-Grade Children." Doctoral dissertation, University of Texas at Austin, 1966.

744. Heller, Celia S. *Mexican American Youth: Forgotten Youth at the Crossroads.* New York: Random House, 1966.

745. Parmee, Leila Khazanchand. "Perception of Personal-Social Problems by Students of Different Ethnic Backgrounds." Doctoral dissertation, University of Arizona, 1966.

746. Cohen, Rosalie A. "Conceptual Styles, Culture Conflict, and Nonverbal Tests of Intelligence." *American Anthropologist* 71, no. 5 (October 1967): 828-56.

747. Demak, Leonard Sidney. "A Study of the Meanings of Selected Educational Concepts to Culturally Diverse Groups, Using the Semantic Differential." Doctoral disseration, Wayne State University, 1967.

748. Goldstein, Lillian Faidar. "A Comparison of the Auditory Discrimination Ability of Lower Class Negro and Mexican American Children in Kindergarten and First Grade." Master's thesis, University of California at Los Angeles, 1967.

749. Hernández, Luis F. "The Culturally Disadvantaged Mexican American Student: Part I." *Journal of Secondary Education* 42, no. 2 (February 1967): 59-65.

750. Hernández, Luis F. "The Culturally Disadvantaged Mexican American Student. Part II." *Journal of Secondary Education* 42, no. 3 (March 1967): 123-28.

751. Ihrig, Maxwell J. "A Study of the Motivation of Students Who Completed the Junior Year of High School, and Who Are Members of Socially, Economically and Culturally Deprived Areas." Doctoral dissertation, University of New Mexico, 1967.

752. Leppke, Ronald Dean. "Perceptual Approaches for Disadvantaged Anglo- and Mexican-American Students." Doctoral dissertation, University of the Pacific, 1967.

753. Mason, Evelyn P. "Comparison of Personality Characteristics of Junior High Students from American Indian, Mexican, and Caucasian Ethnic Backgrounds." *Journal of Social Psychology* 73 (December 1967): 145-55.

754. Mittelbach, F.G., and Marshall, G. *The Burden of Poverty. Advance Report No. 5.* Los Angeles: University of California, Graduate School of Business Administration, Mexican American Study Project, 1967. ERIC ED 015 800.

755. Orr, R.G. "The Relationship of Social Character and Dogmatism among Spanish American Young Adults in Three Selected Institutions in New Mexico." Doctoral dissertation, University of New Mexico, 1967.

756. Penalosa, Fernando. "Changing Mexican-American in Southern California." *Sociology and Social Research* 51 (July 1967): 405-17.

757. Plott, Curtis Ellsworth. "An Analysis of the Characteristics of Mexican-American and Anglo-American Participants in Co-Curricular Activities." Doctoral dissertation, University of Southern California, 1967.

758. Wilstach, Ilah Muller. "Vocational Maturity of Mexican American Youth." Doctoral dissertation, University of Southern California, 1967.

759. Brody, Eugene B., ed. *Minority Group Adolescents in the United States.* Baltimore: The Williams & Wilkins Company, 1968.

760. Cairncross, Elba Bains. "Concept Development for the Spanish-Speaking Child in The Southwest." Doctoral dissertation, Texas Technological College, 1968.

761. *Classroom Strategies: Culture and Learning Styles.* Albuquerque, New Mexico: Southwestern Cooperative Educational Laboratory, 1968.

762. Cohen, Rosalie A. "The Relation between Socio-Conceptual Styles and Orientation to School Requirements." *Sociology of Education* 41, no. 2 (spring 1968): 201-20.

763. Durrett, Mary E., and Huffman, Wanda. "Playfulness and Divergent Thinking among Mexican American Children." *Journal of Home Economics* 60, no. 5 (May 1968): 355-58.

764. Fabrega, Horacio, Jr., and Wallace, Carole A. "Value Identification and Psychiatric Disability: An Analysis Involving Americans of Mexican Descent." *Behavioral Science* 13, no. 5 (September 1968): 362-71.

765. Garber, Malcolm. "Ethnicity and Measures of Educability: Differences among Navajo, Pueblo and Rural Spanish American First Graders on Measures of Learning Style, Hearing Vocabulary, Entry Skills, Motivation and Home Environment Processes." Doctoral dissertation, University of Southern California, 1968.

766. Haddox, J.H. "Hispanic Culture in the Southwest." In *Bilingual Education in Three Cultures,* pp. 30-32. El Paso, Texas: Southwest Council for Bilingual Education. November 1968.

767. Hardt, Annanelle. "Bi-cultural Heritage of Texas." Doctoral dissertation, University of Texas at Austin, 1968.

768. Littlefield, Robert P. "An Analysis of the Self-Disclosure Patterns on Ninth-Grade Public School Students in Three Selected Sub-Cultural Groups." Doctoral dissertation, Florida State University, 1968.

769. Mason, Evelyn P. "Sex Difference in Personality Characteristics of Deprived Adolescents." *Perceptual and Motor Skills* 27, no. 3, part 1 (1968): 934.

770. Neill, Richard Glenn. "A Study of Behavior in Spanish-Speaking Children in Special Education and the Regular Grades." Master's thesis, University of Utah, 1968.

771. Penalosa, Fernando, and McDonagh, Edward C. "Education, Economic Status and Social-Class Awareness of Mexican-Americans." *Phylon* 29 (summer 1968): 119-26.

772. Phillips, Beeman N., and McNeil, K. *Differences between Anglo and Non-Anglo Children on Factorial Dimensions of School Anxiety and Copying Style.* Washington, D.C.: American Educational Research Association, 1968.

773. Quijano, Teresa. "A Cross-Culture Study of Sex Differences among First-Graders on a Verbal Test." Master's thesis, Texas Woman's University, 1968. ERIC ED 026 191.

774. Reynolds, Carl Akard. "Characteristic Differences in Creativity among Mexican-American, Mexican, and Anglo-American Children." Master's thesis, Texas A&I University, 1968.

775. Rodríguez, Minerva D. "Reinforcement Expectations and Effectiveness among Mexican-American Migrant and Non-Migrant Children." Denton, Texas: Texas Woman's University Library, August 1968. ERIC ED 028 001.

776. Romano-V., Octavio Ignacio. "The Anthropology and Sociology of the Mexican-Americans: A Distortion of Mexican-American History." *El Grito* 2, no. 1 (fall 1968): 13-26.

777. Vigil, Joaquin Thomas. "A Comparison of Selected Perceptions of Spanish Speaking Students and Non-Spanish Speaking Students." Doctoral dissertation, Colorado State College, 1968.

778. Anderson, James G., et al. "Mexican-American Students in a Metropolitan Context: Factors Affecting the Social-Emotional Climate of the Classroom." University Park: New Mexico State University, July 1969. ERIC ED 030 521.

779. Blue, Arthur W. "Prediction of Learning Ability across Culture." Doctoral dissertation, Iowa State University, 1969.

780. Casavantes, Edward J. *A New Look at the Attributes of the Mexican American.* Albuquerque: Southwestern Cooperative Educational Laboratory, March 1969. ERIC ED 028 010.

781. Fujitani, Shigeaki. "Subcultural Differences in Instrumental Preference for Reinforcers." Doctoral dissertation, University of Utah, 1969.

782. Grimmett, Sadie A. "Problem Solving on the Same Twenty Questions by Males of Four Ethnocultural Groups at Two Grade Levels." Doctoral dissertation, George Peabody College for Teachers, 1969.

783. Mason, Evelyn P. "Cross-Validation Study of Personality Characteristics of Junior High Students from American Indian, Mexican, and Caucasian Ethnic Backgrounds." In *Chicanos: Social and Psychological Perspectives,* pp. 150-55. Edited by Nathaniel L. Wagner and Marsha J. Haug. Saint Louis: The C.V. Mosby Company, 1971; reprint from: *Journal of Social Psychology* 77, no. 1 (February 1969): 15-24.

784. "Mexican American Cultural Differences. A Brief Survey to Enhance Teacher Pupil Understanding." Moses Lake, Washington: Moses Lake Intermediate School District 104, Migrant Education Center, 1969. ERIC ED 041 665.

785. Nelson, Bill Jacob. "Case Studies of Selected Spanish-American Junior and Senior High School Students from Lark, Utah." Master's thesis, University of Utah, 1969.

786. Penalosa, Fernando. "Education-Income Discrepancies between Second and Later-Generation Mexican-Americans in the Southwest." *Sociology and Social Research* 53, no. 4 (July 1969): 448-54.

787. Scullen, Kathleen Walozak. "Mexican American Secondary School Students' Perceptions of Their Teachers." Master's thesis, University of California at Los Angeles, 1969.

788. Silberstein, Ruth Leibowitz. "Risk-Taking Behavior in Preschool Children from Three Ethnic Backgrounds." Master's thesis, University of California at Los Angeles, 1969.

789. Wasserman, Susan Arnesty. "Expressed Humanitarian and Success Values of Four-Year-Old Mexican-American, Negro, and Anglo Blue-Collar and White-Collar Children." Doctoral dissertation, University of California at Los Angeles, 1969.

790. Arndt, Richard Werner. "La Fortalecita: A Study of Low-Income (Urban) Mexican Americans and the Implications for Education." Doctoral dissertation, University of New Mexico, 1970.

791. Baxter, James C. "Interpersonal Spacing in Natural Settings." *Sociometry* 33, no . 4 (December 1970): 444-56.

792. Bryson, Juanita Eastman. "Comparison of Bilingual Vs. Single Language Instruction in Concept Learning in Mexican-American Four-Year-Olds." Master's thesis, University of California at Los Angeles, 1970. ERIC ED 062 043.

793. Burruel, José Mariá. "A Study of Mexican-American Tenth-Grade Students Showing the Relationship between Parental Attitudes and Socio-Economic Level." Doctoral dissertation, Arizona State University, 1970.

794. Dunigan, Joseph L., Jr. "The Religious Socialization of Mexican-Americans: A Functional Analysis of Catholic Education." Master's thesis, University of Texas at El Paso, 1970.

795. Mallory, Sadie Grimmett. "Effect of Stimulus Presentation on Free Recall of Reflective and Impulsive Mexican-American Children." *Journal of Psychology* 76, no. 2 (November 1970): 193-98.

796. Powell, Isola Russ. "Identification of Cultural Styles of the Spanish Speaking People for Use in Prescribing Educational Experiences for the Spanish Speaking Child." Master's thesis, University of Texas at Austin, 1970.

797. Sánchez, Luisa Guerrero G. "Spanish-Speaking Minority Holds Historical Past as Common Bond." *Delta Kappa Gamma Bulletin* 36, no. 3 (spring 1970): 23-28.

798. Shane, James Felton. "Time Perception: A Comparative Study of Mexican-American and Anglo-American Subjects Involving Temporal Sense and Perspective." Doctoral dissertation, Oklahoma State University, 1970.

799. "Talk with a Young Mexican American: Interview." *Social Education* 34, no. 6 (October 1970): 643-47.

800. Weaver, Charles N. "Accidents as a Measure of the Cultural Adjustment of Mexican-Americans." *Sociology Quarterly* 11, no. 1 (winter 1970): 119-25.

801. Aiello, John R., and Jones, Stanley E. "Field Study of the Proxemic Behavior of Young School Children in Three Subcultural Groups." *Journal of Personality and Social Psychology* 19, no. 3 (September 1971): 351-56.

802. Arciniega, T.A. "Adaptive Mechanisms Employed by Bicultural Students in Urban Secondary Schools." *Urban Education* 6, nos. 2-3 (July/October 1971): 233-41.

803. Arciniega, T.A. "The Urban Mexican American: A Sociocultural Profile." University Park: New Mexico State University, July 1971. ERIC ED 050 887.

804. Bernal, Ernest M. "Comparative Concept Learning among Anglo, Black, and Mexican-American Children under Standard and Facilitation Conditions of Task Administration." Paper presented at the Symposium of the Effects of Cultural Variables on the Mexican-American at the meetings of the American Psychological Association, Washington, D.C., 1971.

805. Bernal, Ernest M. "Concept Learning among Anglo, Black, and Mexican-American Children Using Facilitation Strategies and Bilingual Techniques." Doctoral dissertation, University of Texas at Austin, 1971.

806. Blauner, R. "Chicano Sensibility." *Transaction* 8, no. 4 (1971): 51-56.

807. Bongers, Lael Shannon. "A Developmental Study of Time Perception and Time Perspective in Three Cultural Groups: Anglo American, Indian American, and Mexican American." Doctoral dissertation, University of California at Los Angeles, 1971.

808. Byrne, David Ronald. "Mexican-American Secondary Students: Salt Lake City School District." Doctoral dissertation, University of Utah, 1971.

809. Engle, Patricia Lee. "Free Recall of Categorizable Objects by Mexican American and Anglo American Children after Training." Doctoral dissertation, Stanford University, 1971.

810. Goodman, Mary Ellen, and Beman, Alma. "Child's-Eye-Views of Life in an Urban Barrio." In *Chicanos: Social and Psychological Perspectives,* pp. 109-22. Edited by Nathaniel L. Wagner and Marsha J. Haug. Saint Louis: The C.V. Mosby Company, 1971.

811. Gottlieb, David, and Heinsohn, Annie L., eds. *America's Other Youth: Growing Up Poor.* Englewood Cliffs, New Jersey: Prentice-Hall, Inc., 1971.

812. Hudelson, Sarah Jane. "Male-Female Role Patterns of Mexican American Children in a South Texas School." Master's thesis, University of Texas at Austin, 1971.

813. Kagan, Spencer, and Madsen, Millard C. "Cooperation and Competition of Mexican, Mexican-American, and Anglo-American Children of Two Ages under Four Instructional Sets." *Developmental Psychology* 5, no. 1 (July 1971): 32-39.

814. Kuvlesky, William P.; Wright, David; and Juárez, Rumaldo Z. "Status Projections and Ethnicity: A Comparison of Mexican American, Negro, and Anglo Youth." *Journal of Vocational Behavior* 1, no. 2 (April 1971): 137-51.

815. Logan, Donald Moody. "Need Affiliation of Mexican-Americans and Anglo-Americans of South Texas." Doctoral dissertation, Texas Tech University, 1971.

816. McAnany, Emile G. "Cross-Cultural Cognitive Development: Two Experiments in Stimulus Mode Presentation." Doctoral dissertation, Stanford University, 1971.

817. Morales, Armando. "Distinguishing Psychodynamic Factors from Cultural Factors in the Treatment of the Spanish-Speaking Patient." In *Chicanos: Social and Psychological Perspectives,* pp. 279-80. Edited by Nathaniel L. Wagner and Marsha J. Haug. Saint Louis: The C.V. Mosby Company, 1971.

818. Naylor, Gordon Hardy. "Learning Styles at Six Years in Two Ethnic Groups in a Disadvantaged Area." Doctoral dissertation, University of Southern California, 1971.

819. Padilla, Amado M. "Psychology and the Mexican American: An Awareness of Cultural and Social Factors." Paper presented at the Symposium on the Effects of Cultural Variables on the Mexican American at the annual meeting of the American Psychological Association, Washington, D.C., 1971.

820. Padilla, Eligio R. "The Relationship between Psychology and Chicanos: Failures and Possibilities." In *Chicanos: Social and Psychological Perspectives*, pp. 286-94. Edited by Nathaniel L. Wagner and Marsha J. Haug. Saint Louis: The C.V. Mosby Company, 1971.

821. Palomares, Uvaldo H., ed. "Culture as a Reason for Being: Special Issue." *The Personnel and Guidance Journal* 50, no. 2 (October 1971): 82-147.

822. Pike, Earl Oswald. "Observationally-Induced Question-Asking Behavior in Disadvantaged Mexican-American Children." Doctoral dissertation, University of Oregon, 1971.

823. Ramírez, Manuel, III; Taylor, Clark, Jr.; and Petersen, Barbara. "Mexican-American Cultural Membership and Adjustment to School." In *Chicanos: Social and Psychological Perspectives*, pp. 221-28. Edited by Nathaniel L. Wagner and Marsha J. Haug. Saint Louis: The C.V. Mosby Company, 1971; reprint from: *Developmental Psychology* 4, no. 2 (1971): 141-48.

824. Roberts, Alan H., and Greene, Joel E. "Cross-Cultural Study of Relationships among Four Dimensions of Time Perspective." *Perceptual and Motor Skills* 33, no. 1 (August 1971): 163-73.

825. Schmidt, Linda, and Gallessich, June. "Adjustment of Anglo-American and Mexican-American Pupils in Self-Contained and Team-Teaching Classrooms." *Journal of Educational Psychology* 52, no. 2 (August 1971): 328-32.

826. Streiff, Virginia. "Question Generation by First Graders: A Heuristic Model." Paper presented at the Conference on Child Language, Chicago, Illinois, 22-24 November 1971. ERIC ED 061 807.

827. Swize, Myron Theodore. "Prediction of Piagetian Conservation for Second Grade Mexican-American and Anglo-American Children." Doctoral dissertation, University of Northern Colorado, 1971.

828. TenHouten, Warren D.; Lei, Tzuen; Kendall, Francoise, et al. "School Ethnic Composition, Social Contexts, and Educational Plans of Mexican-American and Anglo High School Students." *American Journal of Sociology* 77, no. 1 (July 1971): 89-107.

829. Thomas, Elizabeth C., and Yamamoto, Kaoru. "Minority Children and Their School-Related Perceptions." *Journal of Experimental Education* 40, no. 1 (fall 1971): 89-96.

830. Aramoni, Aniceto. "Machismo." *Psychology Today* 5, no. 8 (January 1972): 69-72.

831. Belding, Nancye, et al. *A Survey of the Literature Relevant to Spanish-Surname Rural Youth in the Southwestern States. Final Report of Phase 1.* Minneapolis, Minnesota: North Star Research and Development Institution, 10 May 1972.

832. Burger, Henry G. " 'Ethno-Lematics': Evoking 'Shy' Spanish-American Pupils by Cross-Cultural Mediation." *Adolescence* 7, no. 25 (spring 1972): 61-76.

833. Castañeda, Alfredo; Ramírez, Manuel, III; and Herold, Leslie. "Culturally Democratic Learning Environments: A Cognitive Styles Approach." Riverside: University of California at Riverside, Multi-Lingual Assessment Project, Riverside Component, 1972.

834. Flores, Juan Modesto. "A Study of Mexican American Cultural Characteristics as Perceived by Members of 100 Impoverished Mexican American Families and Its Educational Implications." Doctoral dissertation, University of Houston, 1972.

835. Kershner, John R. "Ethnic Group Differences in Children's Ability to Reproduce Direction and Orientation." *Journal of Social Psychology* 88, no. 1 (October 1972): 3-13.

836. Kuzma, Kay J., and Stern, Carolyn. "Effects of Three Preschool Intervention Programs on the Development of Autonomy in Mexican-American and Negro Children." *Journal of Special Education* 6, no. 3 (fall 1972): 197-205.

837. López, Thomas R., Jr. "Prospects for the Spanish American Culture of New Mexico: An Educational View." Doctoral dissertation, University of New Mexico, 1972.

838. Meeker, Frederick B., and Kleinke, Chris L. "Knowledge of Names for In- and Out-Group Members of Different Sex and Ethnic Groups." *Psychological Reports* 31, no. 3 (December 1972): 832-34.

839. Muñoz, Leo. "Attributed Meanings of Selected Cultural Concepts by Mexican-American and Anglo-American Secondary School Male Students." Doctoral dissertation, University of Arizona, 1972.

840. Palomares, Uvaldo. "The Psychology of the Mexican-American." In *Adelante: An Emerging Design for Mexican-American Education.* Edited by Manuel Reyes Mazon. Austin: University of Texas at Austin, Center for Communication Research, 1972.

841. Zimmerman, Barry J., and Pike, Earl O. "Effects of Modeling and Reinforcement on the Acquisition and Generalization of Question-Asking Behavior." *Child Development* 43, no. 3 (September 1972): 892-907.

842. Zimmerman, Barry J., and Rosenthal, Ted L. "Observation, Repetition, and Ethnic Background in Concept Attainment and Generalization." *Child Development* 43, no. 2 (June 1972): 605-13.

843. Bonura, James Victor. "Effects of Success and Failure on a Direct Measure of Personal Space in Anglo-American and Mexican-American Children." Doctoral dissertation, California School of Professional Psychology at Los Angeles, 1973.

844. Brekke, Alice M. "Evaluational Reactions of Adolescent and Preadolescent Mexican-American and Anglo-American Students to Selected Samples of Spoken English." Doctoral dissertation, University of Minnesota, 1973.

845. Escotet, Miguel A. "A Comparison between Mexican-American and South American Students: A Cross-Cultural Study." Paper presented at the Comparative and International Education Society, 1973 National Convention, San Antonio, Texas, 25-27 March 1973. ERIC ED 079 010.

846. Justin, Neal E. "Mexican-American Reading Habits and Their Cultural Basis." *Journal of Reading* 16, no. 6 (March 1973): 467-73.

847. Kagan, Spencer Monte. "Adaptation Mode and Behavior of Urban Anglo American and Rural Mexican Children." Doctoral dissertation, University of California at Los Angeles, 1973.

848. Ramírez, Manuel, III. "Cognitive Styles and Cultural Democracy in Education." *Social Science Quarterly* 53, no. 4 (March 1973): 895-904.

849. Suarez, Cecilia C.-R. "Sexual Stereotypes—Psychological and Cultural Survival." *Regeneración* 2, no. 3 (1973): 17-21.

850. Achor, Shirley Coolidge. "Of Thorns and Roses: Variations in Cultural Adaptations among Mexican-Americans in an Urban Texas Barrio." Doctoral dissertation, Southern Methodist University, 1974.

851. Adams, Georgia B. "A Case Study of Specific Life-Space Experiences of Academically Successful and Non-Successful Intermediate Grade Level Mexican-American Migrant Boys in Dade County, Florida." Doctoral dissertation, University of Miami, 1974.

852. Baird, Frank L. "An Anglo View of Mexican Americans." *Public Service* 1, no. 2 (February 1974): 1-5, ERIC ED 101 897.

853. Broncato, Jacob S., Jr. "Effects of the Aggression of Spanish Speaking Preschool Children by Deliberately Contrived Television Models of Violence." Doctoral dissertation, Northern Illinios University, 1974.

854. Gonzales, Sylvia Alicia. "A Process for Examining Cultural Relevancy for Educational Compatability of the Mexican-American in the United States." Doctoral dissertation, University of Massachusetts, 1974.

855. Gruen, Gerald E.; Korte, John R.; and Baum, John F. "Group Measure of Locus of Control." *Developmental Psychology* 10, no. 5 (September 1974): 683-86.

856. Henry, William F., and Miles, Guy H. *Perspectives of Adjustment: Rural Chicano Youth.* Vol. 1. Minneapolis, Minnesota: North Star Research and Development Institute, April 1974. ERIC ED 100 538.

857. Hernández, Nellie M. "Sex-Role Development of Preschool Middle- and Lower-Class Mexican-American and Anglo-American Males." Master's thesis, University of Texas at El Paso, 1974.

858. Lindberg, Dormalee H. "Creativity and the Culturally Different." 1974. ERIC ED 090 154.

859. Littlefield, Robert P. "Self-Disclosure among Some Negro, White, and Mexican American Adolescents." *Journal of Counseling Psychology* 21, no. 2 (March 1974): 133-36.

860. McClintock, Charles G. "The Development of Social Motives in Anglo-American and Mexican-American Children." *Journal of Personality and Social Psychology* 29, no. 3 (March 1974): 348-54.

861. Price-Williams, D.R., and Ramírez, M., III. "Ethnic Differences in Delay of Gratification." *Journal of Social Psychology* 93, no. 1 (July 1974): 23-30.

862. Stewart, Ida S. "Cultural Differences in the Attributions and Intentions of Anglos and Chicanos in an Elementary School." Paper presented at the 1974 AERA meeting, Chicago, Illinios, April 1974. ERIC ED 088 627.

863. Sultemeier, Barbara. "Assessing Sex Role Development of Kindergarten Mexican-American Boys." Master's thesis, Texas A&I University at Kingsville, 1974.

864. Acevedo, Homero E. "A Sociological Analysis of Differences in Student Motivation: A Case Study of Two School Districts in Texas." Doctoral dissertation, Walden University, 1975. ERIC ED 108 828.

865. Cushing, James Francis. "A Comparison of Mexican-American and Anglo-American Tenth-Grade Students in the West Valley Complex of the Granite School District." Doctoral dissertation, University of Utah, 1975.

866. Deakins, Myrtle Lynn. "Machismo: An Empirical Investigation of Aggression in Mexican-American and Anglo-American Children in a School Setting." Master's thesis, University of California at Long Beach, 1975.

867. Gilmore, George; Chandy, Jean; and Anderson, Thomas. "Bender Gestalt and the Mexican American Student: A Report." *Psychology in the Schools* 12, no. 2 (April 1975): 172-75.

868. Pérez, Antonio. "An Investigation of the Effect of the Follow Through Program on Selected Behavior and Personality Constructs of Mexican-American Pupils." Doctoral dissertation, University of Houston, 1975.

869. Venegas, Moises, and Kuvlesky, William. "Do Metropolitan and Nonmetropolitan Chicano Youth Differ: A Study of South Texas Teen-Agers—1973." Paper presented at the annual meeting of the Rural Sociological Society, San Francisco, California, 21-24 August 1975. ERIC ED 121 514.

870. Wisener, Robert Henry. "Factors Affecting Piagetian Classification and Seriation Skills in a Sample of Mexican-American and Anglo-American Children." Doctoral dissertation, University of Northern Colorado, 1975.

871. McBurnette, Patrick E., and Kunetka, James W. "Mexican American Perceptions of Isolation in Desegregated School Settings." Paper presented at the annual meeting of the American Educational Research Association, San Francisco, California, April 1976. ERIC ED 121 555.

872. Monk, Phillip M., and Medina, Dennis. "Residence Projections of Mexican-American Youth from the Border Area of South Texas: A Study of Changes over Time." Paper presented at the annual meeting of the Southwestern Sociological Association, Dallas, Texas, 9 April 1976. ERIC ED 121 508.

873. Salinas, Medardo. "A Comparison of the Levels of Personal and Social Adjustment between Anglo-American and Mexican-American Adolescents in Six AAAA Schools of the Rio Grande Valley of Texas." Master's thesis, Pan American University, 1976.

874. Stewart, Ida S. "Cultural Differences between Anglos and Chicanos." *Educational Digest* 41, no. 7 (March 1976): 29-31.

3.3.2 Attitudes and Values

875. Peek, R.B. "The Religious and Social Attitudes of the Mexican Girls of the Constituency of the All Nations Foundation in Los Angeles." Master's thesis, University of Southern California, 1929.

876. Chávez, Simon J. "An Experimental Study to Determine the Effects of a Group of Short Stories Translated from Spanish-American Literature on the Attitudes of a Group of Sixth Grade Children toward Spanish Americans." Doctoral dissertation, University of Colorado at Boulder, 1933.

877. Coole, Mrs. Ruth. "A Comparison of Anglo-American and Latin-American Girls in Grades V-XI with Reference to Their Vocational, Academic, and Recreational Preferences, and Aversions." Master's thesis, University of Texas at Austin, 1937.

878. Smith, Mrs. Avis Dowis. "A Comparative Study of Some Attitudes and Interests of Latin American and Anglo American Boys." Master's thesis, University of Texas at Austin, 1940.

879. Cruz, María Angelita. "Spanish-Speaking Children's Expressed Attitudes toward Money Values." Master's thesis, University of Texas at Austin, 1942.

880. Johnson, Granville B. "The Origin and Development of the Spanish Attitude toward the Spanish." *Journal of Educational Psychology* 41, no. 7 (1950): 428-39.

881. Johnson, Granville B. "Relationship Existing between Bilingualism and Racial Attitude." *Journal of Educational Psychology* 42, no. 5 (May 1951): 357-65.

882. Roca, P. "The Construction of an Interest Inventory for Students of Different Linguistic and Cultural Backgrounds." Doctoral dissertation, University of Texas at Austin, 1952.

883. Cooper, Elizabeth K. "Attitude of Children and Teachers toward Mexican, Negro and Jewish Minorities." Master's thesis, University of California at Los Angeles, 1955.

884. Woods, Sister Frances Jerome. *Cultural Values of American Ethnic Groups.* New York: Harper & Brothers, Publishers, 1956.

885. Demos, George D. "Attitudes of Mexican-American and Anglo-American Groups toward Education." *Journal of Social Psychology* 57, no. 2 (August 1962): 249-56.

886. Verdi, Lida Frances. "Needs and Values of Mexican American and Anglo American High School Students." Master's thesis, University of Arizona, 1965.

887. Romero, Fred Emilio. "A Study of Anglo and Spanish-American Culture Value Concepts and Their Significance in Secondary Education." Doctoral dissertation, University of Denver, 1966.

888. Ramírez, Manuel, III, and Taylor, Clark L. "Sex Role Determinants in Attitudes toward Education among Mexican-American Adolescents. Final Report." Sacramento, California: Sacramento State College, November 1967. ERIC ED 039 957.

889. Shasteen, Amos Eugene. "Value Orientations of Anglo and Spanish American High School Sophomores." Doctoral dissertation, University of New Mexico, 1967.

890. Derbyshire, Robert L. "Children's Perceptions of the Police: A Comparative Study of Attitudes and Attitude Change." In *Chicanos: Social and Psychological Perspectives*, 175-83. Edited by Nathaniel L. Wagner and Marsha J. Haug. Saint Louis: The C.V. Mosby Company, 1971; reprint from: *Journal of Criminal Law, Criminology and Police Science* 59, no. 2 (June 1968): 183-90.

891. Bradish, Damaris. "Achievement Attitudes of Hispanos." Doctoral dissertation, Colorado State University at Fort Collins, 1969.

892. Fink, Harold Otto. "The World of Work as Perceived by Anglo Americans and Mexican American Secondary School Students in a Border Community." Doctoral dissertation, University of Arizona, 1969.

893. Botha, Elize. "The Effect of Language on Values Expressed by Bilinguals." *The Journal of Social Psychology* 80, no. 2 (April 1970): 143-45.

894. Rivera-Ortega, Manuel Geoffrey. "Interpersonal Values of California Mexican-American and Non-Mexican American High School Students." Master's thesis, University of Utah, 1970.

895. Stokes, Vernon Dee. "Selected Value Concepts of Seventh-Grade Mexican-American Students." Doctoral dissertation, Texas Tech University, 1970.

896. Barnes, Bernice Marie. "Attitudes of Minority and Non-Minority Students toward Nonskill Aspects of Office Work." Doctoral dissertation, Arizona State University, 1971.

897. Bockman, John F., and Videen, Darleen A. "A Study to Determine the Relationship between Spanish Listening Comprehension Proficiency and Cultural Attitudes of Various Groups of Native and Non-Native Students of the Spanish Language in Three High Schools: Cholla, Pueblo, and Tucson." Tucson, Arizona: Tucson Public Schools, May 1971. ERIC ED 057 674.

898. Caskey, Owen L., and Webb, Doris J. "Keys to the Elementary School Environment (with Subgroup Reference Norms): How Children Perceive Their School Environment." Lubbock: Texas Technological College, School of Education, 1971. ERIC ED 059 822.

899. Church, Virginia Klewer. "A Comparative Study of the Attitudes and Aspirations of Bilingual Mexican American Students with Monolingual Mexican American Students." Master's thesis, University of Toledo, 1971. ERIC ED 085 136.

900. Farias, Hector, Jr. "Mexican-American Values and Attitudes toward Education." *Phi Delta Kappan* 52, no. 10 (June 1971): 602-4.

901. Wasserman, Susan A. "Values of Mexican-American, Negro, and Anglo Blue-Collar and White-Collar Children." *Child Development* 42, no. 5 (November 1971): 1624-28.

902. Zurich, M. "Perceptions of Indian, Mexican, Negro, and White Children Concerning the Development of Responsibility." *Perceptual and Motor Skills* 32, no. 3 (June 1971): 796-98.

903. Solomon, Daniel; Ali, Faizunisa A.; Kfir, Drora, et al. "The Development of Democratic Values and Behavior among Mexican-American Children." *Child Development* 43, no. 2 (June 1972): 625-38.

904. Howell, Maryon. "A Study of the Effects of Reading upon the Attitudes of Fifth-Graders toward Mexican-Americans." Doctoral dissertation, Southern Illinois University, 1973.

905. Jackson, Stephan L., and McCallon, Earl. "The Cross-Cultural Attitude Inventory: A Report on Item Analysis and Stability." Paper presented at the American Educational Research Association meeting, New Orleans, Louisiana, 1973. ERIC ED 073 885.

906. Montenegro, Raquel. "Educational Implications of Cultural Values and Attitudes of Mexican-American Women." Doctoral dissertation, Claremont Graduate School, 1973.

907. Politzer, Robert L., and Ramírez, Arnulfo. "Judging Personality from Speech: A Pilot Study of the Effects of Bilingual Education on Attitudes toward Ethnic Groups. Research and Development Memorandum No. 106." Palo Alto, California: Stanford University, Stanford Center for Research and Development in Teaching, February 1973. ERIC ED 076 278.

908. Politzer, Robert L., and Ramírez, Arnulfo. "Judging Personality from Speech: A Pilot Study of the Attitudes toward Ethnic Groups of Students in Monolingual Schools. Research and Development Memorandum No. 107." Palo Alto, California: Stanford University, Stanford Center for Research and Development in Teaching, June 1973. ERIC ED 078 992.

909. Flores, Nancy de la Zerda, and Whitehead, Jack. "Mexican American Self-Referents and Linguistic Attitudes." Paper presented at the annual meeting of the International Communication Association, New Orleans, Louisiana, 17-20 April 1974. ERIC ED 098 641.

910. MacIntosh, Roderick, and Ornstein, Jacob. "Brief Sampling of West Texas Teacher Attitudes toward Southwest Spanish and English Language Varieties." *Hispania* 57, no. 4 (December 1974): 920-26.

911. Quintanar, Rosalinda. "A Comparative Study of Students' Attitudes toward Education." Master's thesis, New Mexico State University, 1974. ERIC ED 093 521.

912. Ryan, Ellen Bouchard, and Carranza, Miguel A. "A Methodological Approach to Study of Evaluative Reactions of Adolescents toward Speakers of Different Language Varieties." Paper presented at the annual meeting of the Southwestern Sociological Association, Dallas, Texas, March 1974. ERIC ED 088 619.

913. Calhoun, Emory Everett. "Value Orientations of Mexican American and Anglo American Ninth Grade Students." Doctoral dissertation, New Mexico State University, 1975.

914. Castro, John Gonzales. "A Guttman Facet Designed Multidimensional Attitude-Behavior Scale Analysis of Internal-External Locus of Control of Mexican Americans and Mexican Nationals." Doctoral dissertation, Michigan State University, 1975.

915. Hernández, Mike Angel. "A Comparative Study of Attitudes toward Athletics as Expressed by Mexican American and Non-Mexican American High School Boys." Doctoral dissertation, University of Utah, 1975.

916. Stans, Patricia A. Hanusik. "Attitudes of Eleventh Grade Students in Selected Southern New Mexico Public High Schools Concerning Some Aspects of School Life." Doctoral dissertation, New Mexico State University, 1975.

917. Whatley, George Alfred. "A Study of Basic Values Systems among Mexican-Americans of the First, Second, Third, and Fourth Generations in Whittier, California, in 1975." Doctoral dissertation, Brigham Young University, 1976.

3.3.3 Self-Concept

918. Nicoll, John. "A Study of the Self and Social Adjustment Patterns of Equated Mexican American Groups Entering Excelsior High School, Norwalk, California from Both Mixed and Segregated Elementary Schools." Master's thesis, Claremont Graduate School, 1949.

919. Zeligs, Rose. "Children's Concepts and Stereotypes of Dutch, French, Italian, Mexican, Russian, and Negro." *Journal of Educational Research* 43 (1950): 367-75.

920. Wilkinson, D.H. "Self-Realization and Group Living through Language Development." *Elementary English* 31 (April 1954): 210-13.

921. Najmi, Mohamed Abdul Khalique. "Comparison of Greeley's Spanish-American and Anglo-White Elementary School Children's Response to Instruments Designed to Measure Self-Concepts and Some Related Variables." Doctoral dissertation, Colorado State College, 1962.

922. Farris, Buford, and Brymer, Richard A. "Differential Socialization of Latin and Anglo-American Youth: An Exploratory Study of the Self-Concept." Paper presented at the meetings of the Texas Academy of Science, Dallas, 1965.

923. Firme, Thereza P. "Effects of Social Reinforcement on Self-Esteem of Mexican-American Children. Long Abstract." 1967. ERIC ED 033 767.

924. Carter, T.P. "Negative Self-Concept of Mexican-American Students." *School and Society* 96 (30 March 1968): 217-19.

925. Firme, Thereza P. "Effects of Social Reinforcement on Self-Esteem of Mexican-American Children." Doctoral dissertation, Stanford University, 1969.

926. Gallegos, Katherine Powers, ed. "Indio and Hispano Child: Improving His Self Image." New Mexico: Los Lunas Consolidated Schools, 19 May 1969. ERIC ED 044 206.

927. Healey, Gary W. *Self-Concept: A Comparison of Negro-, Anglo-, and Spanish-American Students across Ethnic, Sex, and Socioeconomic Variables.* San Francisco: R and E Research Associates, 1974; doctoral dissertation, New Mexico State University, 1969.

928. Hishiki, Patricia C. "Self-Concepts of Sixth Grade Girls of Mexican-American Descent." *California Journal of Educational Research* 20, no. 2 (March 1969): 56-62.

929. DeBlassie, Richard. "Self Concept: A Comparison of Spanish American, Negro, and Anglo Adolescents across Ethnic, Sex and Socioeconomic Variables." Las Cruces, New Mexico, 1970. ERIC ED 037 287.

930. Giltner, Mary Annette. "An Experimental Study of Self-Concept in Selected Second Grade Children." Master's thesis, University of Arizona, 1970.

931. Heller, Celia S. "Chicano is Beautiful: The New Militancy and Mexican-American Identity." *Commonweal* 91 (23 January 1970): 454-58.

932. Hepner, Ethel Marion. "Self-Concepts, Values, and Needs of Mexican-American Underachievers." Doctoral dissertation, University of Southern California, 1970.

933. Hepner, Ethel Marion. "Self-Concepts, Values, and Needs of Mexican-American Underachievers or (Must the Mexican-American Child adopt a Self-Concept That Fits the American School?)." Paper presented at the American Psychological Association National Convention, Miami, Florida, 3 September 1970. ERIC ED 048 954.

934. Hodges, Jimmy Ross. "Goal-Setting Behavior and Self Concepts of Elementary Mexican-American Children." Doctoral dissertation, Texas Tech University, 1970.

935. Palomares, Geraldine Dunn. *The Effects of Stereotyping on the Self-Concept of Mexican-Americans.* Albuquerque, New Mexico: Southwestern Cooperative Educational Lab., 1970. ERIC ED 056 806.

936. Penalosa, Fernando. "Recent Changes among the Chicanos." *Sociology and Social Research* 55, no. 1 (October 1970): 47-52.

937. Cooper, James G. "Perception of Self and Others as a Function of Ethnic Group Membership." Albuquerque: University of New Mexico, September 1971. ERIC ED 057 965.

938. Dworkin, Anthony Gary. "National Origin and Ghetto Experience as Variables in Mexican American Stereotypy." In *Chicanos: Social and Psychological Perspectives,* pp. 80-84. Edited by Nathaniel L. Wagner and Marsha J. Haug. Saint Louis: The C.V. Mosby Company, 1971.

939. Dworkin, Anthony Gary. "Stereotypes and Self-Images Held by Native-Born and Foreign-Born Mexican Americans." In *Chicanos: Social and Psychological Perspectives,* pp. 72-79. Edited by Nathaniel L. Wagner and Marsha J. Haug. Saint Louis: The C.V. Mosby Company, 1971.

940. Gustafson, Richard A., and Owens, Thomas. "Children's Perceptions of Themselves and Their Teacher's Feelings toward Them Related to Actual Teacher Perceptions and School Achievement." Paper presented at the 51st annual meeting of the Western Psychological Association, San Francisco, California, April 1971. ERIC ED 053 848.

941. Gustafson, Richard A., and Owens, Thomas R. "The Self-Concept of Mexican-American Youngsters and Related Environmental Characteristics." Paper presented at the annual meeting of the California Educational Research Association, San Diego, 30 April 1971. ERIC ED 053 195.

942. Aguirre, Ree Walker. "The Effects of a Parental Involvement Program on Self Concepts and School Attitudes of Mexican-American First Grade Children." Doctoral dissertation, University of Houston, 1972.

943. López, Meliton. "Bilingual-Bicultural Education and Self-Concept of Mexican-American Children." Doctoral dissertation, Wayne State University, 1972.

944. Maldonado, Bonnie Buckley. "The Impact of Skin Color by Sex on Self Concept of Low Socioeconomic Level Mexican-American High School Students." Doctoral dissertation, New Mexico State University, 1972. ERIC ED 066 284.

945. Renas, Warner Allen. "The Mexican American Image as Perceived by Selected Anglo-American and Mexican-American Students." Doctoral dissertation, United States International University, 1972.

946. Rodríguez, Valerio Sierra. "Mexican American Pupil's Self-Concept in Public Elementary Schools." Doctoral dissertation, United States International University, 1972.

947. Beckley, Cynthia J. "Self-Concept; a Function of Achievement, Socioeconomic Status, and Minority Ethnic Group Membership." Master's thesis, University of Texas at El Paso, 1973.

948. Christensen, Jack Dean. "The Effects of Teacher and Curricular Variables on the Self-Concept and School Related Behavior of Mexican-American Children." Doctoral dissertation, Stanford University, 1973.

949. Felice, Lawrence G. "Mexican American Self-Concept and Educational Achievement: The Effects of Ethnic Isolation and Socioeconomic Deprivation." *Social Science Quarterly* 53, no. 4 (March 1973): 716-26.

950. Gecas, Viktor. "Self-Conceptions of Migrant and Settled Mexican Americans." *Social Science Quarterly* 54, no. 3 (December 1973): 579-95.

951. Greene, John F., and Zirkel, Perry A. "The Influence of Language and Ethnicity on the Measurement of Self-Concept of Spanish-Speaking Migrant Pupils." Paper presented at the annual meeting of the National Council of Measurement in Education, New Orleans, February 1973. ERIC ED 071 816.

952. Leonetti, Robert. "A Primary Self-Concept Scale for Spanish-Surnamed Children, Grades K-4." Doctoral dissertation, New Mexico State University, 1973. ERIC ED 071 813.

953. Teske, Raymond, Jr., and Nelson, Bardin H. "Two Scales for the Measurement of Mexican-American Identity." Paper presented at the Southwestern Sociological Society meeting, Dallas, Texas, March 1973. ERIC ED 075 152.

954. Albright, Vitia Harrison. "A Comparison between the Self Concept of Mexican American Pupils Taught in a Bilingual Program and Those Taught in a Monolingual Program." Doctoral dissertation, George Washington University, 1974.

955. Healey, Gary W., and DeBlassie, Richard R. "A Comparison of Negro, Anglo, and Spanish-American Adolescents' Self Concepts." *Adolescence* 9, no. 33 (spring 1974): 15-24.

956. Medeiros, Francine, and Reck, John D. "Self-Esteem and Academic Performance: Using a Self-Image Improvement Package with Emphasis on the Chicano Student." Walnut, California: Mt. San Antonio College, June 1974. ERIC ED 093 522.

957. Nielsen, Mildred D. "Self Concept Variables as Related to Level of Achievement and Anxiety." Master's thesis, Texas A&I University at Kingsville, 1974.

958. Reeves, Robert. "A Study of Self-Concept of Title I Third Grade Mexican-American Students." Doctoral dissertation. University of Nebraska, 1974.

959. Koeller, Shirley Ann Lipian. "The Effect of Listening to Excerpts from Children's Stories about Mexican-Americans on the Self-Concepts and Attitudes of Sixth-Grade Children." Doctoral dissertation, University of Colorado, 1975.

960. Nasseri, Gholamreza. "Self-Esteem, Test Anxiety and General Anxiety among Students of Three Ethnic Groups in Grades Nine through Twelve." Doctoral dissertation, Northern Illinois University, 1975.

3.3.4 Acculturation

961. Borrego, Eva R. "Some Educational Aspects Affecting Acculturation of the Spanish-Culture Background Student in the San Luis Valley." Master's thesis, Adams State College, 1946.

962. Senter, Donovan, and Hawley, Florence. "The Grammar School as the Basic Acculturating Influence for Native New Mexicans." *Social Forces* 24, no. 4 (May 1946): 398-407.

963. Allen, Joseph E. "A Sociological Study of Mexican Assimilation in Salt Lake City." Master's thesis, University of Utah, 1947.

964. Landman, Ruth Hallo. "Some Aspects of the Acculturation of Mexican Immigrants and Their Descendants to American Culture." Doctoral dissertation, Yale University, 1953.

965. Reyes, Ignacio. *Americanization of the Mexican American.* San Francisco: R and E Research Associates, 1972; master's thesis, University of Southern California, 1957.

966. Jones, Benton McLain. "A Study of the Acculturation and Social Aspirations of Sixty Junior High School Students from the Mexican Ethnic Group." Master's thesis, University of Texas at Austin, 1962.

967. Goldkind, Victor. "Factors in the Differential Acculturation of Mexicans in a Michigan City." Doctoral dissertation, Michigan State University, 1963.

968. Christian, Chester C., Jr. "The Acculturation of the Bilingual Child." *Modern Language Journal* 49, no. 3 (March 1965): 160-65.

969. Crampton, H.M. "Acculturation of the Mexican-American in Salt Lake County, Utah." Master's thesis, University of Utah, 1967.

970. Graves, Theodore D. "Acculturation, Access, and Alcohol in a Tri-Ethnic Community." *American Anthropologist* 69, nos. 3-4 (June-August 1967): 306-21.

971. Cordova, Ignacio Ruben. "The Relationship of Acculturation, Achievement, and Alienation and Spanish American Sixth Grade Students." Doctoral dissertation, University of New Mexico, 1968.

972. Newton, Harry Gene. "An Analysis of the Relationship between Certain Selected Aspects of Acculturation and the School Adjustment of Mexican-American Students in the Seventh Grade." Doctoral dissertation, Texas Tech University, 1969.

973. Ulibarri, Horacio. *The Spanish-American: A Study of Acculturation.* Albuquerque: University of New Mexico, College of Education, 1969.

974. Cardenas, Rene. "Three Critical Factors That Inhibit Acculturation of Mexican Americans." Doctoral dissertation, University of California, Berkeley, 1970.

975. del Campo, Philip E. "An Analysis of Selected Factors in the Acculturation Process of the Mexican-American Elementary School Child." Doctoral dissertation, United States International University, 1970.

976. Derbyshire, Robert L. "Adaptation of Adolescent Mexican Americans to United States Society." In *Behavior in New Environments: Adaptation of Migrant Populations,* pp. 275-90. Edited by Eugene B. Brody. Beverly Hills: Sage Publications, 1970.

977. López, Richard E. *Anxiety, Acculturation and the Urban Chicano; The Relationship between Stages of Acculturation and Anxiety Levels of EOP Students.* Berkeley: California Book Co., 1970.

978. Ramírez, Manuel, III. *Effects of Cultural Marginality on Education and Personality.* Albuquerque, New Mexico: Southwestern Cooperative Educational Lab., 1970. ERIC ED 056 805.

979. Aranda, Robert G., and Acosta, Phyllis B. "Migration, Culture and Health of Mexican Americans in an Acculturation Gradient." San Diego: University of California at San Diego, 1971. ERIC ED 055 722.

980. Lampe, Philip E. "Comparative Study of the Assimilations of Mexican-Americans: Parochial Schools vs. Public Schools." Doctoral dissertation, Louisiana State University and Agricultural and Mechanical College, 1973.

981. Jensen, Jannette J. "Assimilation among Mexican-Americans: Differences in the Father-Eldest Son Authority Role Relationship as a Function of Social Class, Generation, and Assimilation: The Case of Selected Lower-Class and Middle-Class Urbanized Mexican-American Families in the San Diego Standard Metropolitan Statistical Area." Doctoral dissertation, Fordham University, 1974.

982. Shannon, Lyle W., et al. "A Longitudinal Study of the Economic Absorption and Cultural Integration of Mexican-American and Negro Immigrants to Racine, Wisconsin." 1974. ERIC ED 099 449.

983. Lampe, Philip E. "Comparative Study of the Assimilation of Mexican Americans: Parochial Schools Versus Public Schools." Paper presented at the annual meeting of the Southwestern Sociological Association, San Antonio, Texas, 26-29 March 1975. ERIC ED 104 619.

984. Martin, William Lee. "Cognitive Performance and Exposure to Acculturation among Children of Transient and Settled-Out Mexican-American Migrants in Vermilion County, Illinois." Doctoral dissertation, University of Illinois at Urbana-Champaign, 1975.

985. Nay, Daniel Lyman. "A Comparison of the Rate of Acculturation of the Urban Mexican-American in the United States to That of Selected Urban Immigrant Groups Which Entered the United States between 1880 and 1914." Doctoral dissertation, University of Southern California, 1976.

3.3.5 Cultural Identity

986. Patterson, William Rex Albert. "Group Formation in Middle Childhood." Doctoral dissertation, University of Texas at Austin, 1954.

987. Sommers, Vita S. "The Impact of Dual Cultural Membership on Identity." *Psychiatry* 27, no. 4 (November 1964): 332-44.

988. Parsons, Theodore William, Jr. "Ethnic Cleavage in a California School." Doctoral dissertation, Stanford University, 1965.

989. Juárez, Rumaldo Z., and Kuvlesky, William P. "Ethnic Group Identity and Orientations toward Education Attainment; A Comparison of Mexican-American and Anglo Boys." Paper presented at the annual meeting of the Southwestern Sociological Association, Dallas, Texas, April 1968. ERIC ED 023 497.

990. Durrett, Mary E., and Davy, Achsah J. "Racial Awareness in Young Mexican-American, Negro and Anglo Children." *Young Children* 26, no. 1 (October 1970): 16-24.

991. Patella, Victoria Morrow. "A Study of the Validity of Language Usage as an Indicator of Ethnic Identification." Master's thesis, Texas A&M University, 1971. ERIC ED 051 943.

992. Suarez, Cecilia Cota-Robles De. "Skin Color as a Factor of Racial Identification and Preference of Young Chicano Children." *Aztlán* 2, no. 1 (spring 1971): 107-50.

993. Miller, James. "Patterns of Racial Preference and Racial Self-Identification among Young Black and Mexican American Children: A Preliminary Comparison." Doctoral dissertation, Wayne State University, 1972.

994. Salazar, John H. "Self-Designation Patterns of a Traditional Ethnic Minority in a Modern Society—Conflict, Consensus, and Confusion in the Identity Crisis." Paper presented at the Third World Congress for Rural Sociology, Baton Rouge, Louisiana, 22-27 August 1972. ERIC ED 066 256.

995. Leyba, Charles F. "Cultural Identity: Problems and Dilemmas." *Journal of Teacher Education* 24, no. 4 (winter 1973): 272-76.

996. Miller, Michael V. " 'Chicanos' and 'Anti-Chicanos': Selected Status Indicators of Ethnic Identity Polarization." Paper presented at the annual meeting of the Southwestern Sociological Association, Dallas, Texas, April 1976. ERIC ED 121 501.

3.3.6 Cultural Conflict

997. Rice, Theodore D. "Some Contributing Factors in Determining the Social Adjustment of the Spanish-Speaking People in Denver and Vicinity." Master's thesis, University of Denver, 1927.

998. Mason, Florence Gordon. "A Case Study of Thirty Adolescent Mexican Girls and Their Social Conflicts and Adjustment within the School." Master's thesis, University of Southern California, 1928.

999. Van Velzer, Francis. "Race Relation Problems of 50 Normal Adolescent Mexican-American Boys in Los Angeles." Master's thesis, University of Southern California, 1936.

1000. Jerden, Cecil M. "A Study in Racial Differences in the El Paso Public Schools." Master's thesis, Southern Methodist University, 1939.

1001. Humphrey, Norman Daymond. "The Stereotype and the Social Types of Mexican-American Youths." *Journal of Social Psychology* 22, no. 1 (August 1945): 69-78.

1002. Rice, Roy C. "Intergroup Relations in Arizona." *Journal of Educational Sociology* 21, no. 4 (1947): 243-49.

1003. Taylor, Travis H. "Intergroup Relations at Cosmopolitan Junior High." *Journal of Educational Sociology* 21, no. 4 (December 1947): 220-25.

1004. Batista y Calderón, Judith. "A Study of Counter-Prejudice in a Mexican Spanish Community in the Surroundings of Des Moines, Iowa." Master's thesis, Drake University, 1948.

1005. Adams, Ruth Loraine. "Inter-Group Relations in a Class in the Carrizo Springs Public Schools." Master's thesis, University of Texas at Austin, 1949.

1006. Loomis, Nellie Holmes. "Spanish-Anglo Ethnic Cleavage in a New Mexican High School." Doctoral dissertation, Michigan State University, 1955.

1007. Pierce-Jones, John; Reid, Jackson B.; and King, F.J. "Adolescent Racial and Ethnic Group Differences in Social Attitudes and Adjustment." *Psychological Reports* 5, no. 3 (September 1959): 549-52.

1008. Witherspoon, Paul. "A Comparison of the Problem of Certain Anglo and Latin American Junior High School Students." *Journal of Educational Research* 53, no. 8 (April 1960): 295-99.

1009. Madsen, William. "Value Conflicts and Folk Psychotherapy in South Texas." In *Magic, Faith and Healing*, pp. 420-40. Edited by Ari Kiev. New York: Free Press of Glencoe, 1964.

1010. Zurcher, Louis A., Jr.; Meadow, Arnold; and Zurcher, Susan Lee. "Value Orientation, Role Conflict, and Alienation from Work: A Cross-Cultural Study." *American Sociological Review* 30, no. 4 (August 1965): 539-48.

1011. Bauer, Evelyn Cohen. "Conflicting Cultural Values between the Lower-Class Mexican Americans and Their Effect on the Mexican American Child's Adjustment to the School." Master's thesis, University of California at Los Angeles, 1967.

1012. Cabrera, Y. Arturo. "Schizophrenia in the Southwest, Mexican-Americans in Anglo-Land." *Claremont Reading Conference Yearbook, 31st Yearbook* (1967): 101-6.

1013. Henderson, George. "Opportunity and Alienation in Public Schools." *The Record* 69, no. 2 (November 1967): 151-57.

1014. Peck, Robert F., and Diaz-Guerrero, Rogelio. "Two Core-Culture Patterns and the Diffusion of Values across Their Border." *International Journal of Psychology* 2, no. 4 (1967): 275-82.

1015. Ericksen, Charles A. "Uprising in the Barrios: Concerning East Los Angeles High School Walkouts." *American Education* 4, no. 10 (November 1968): 29-31.

1016. Ramírez, Manuel, III. "Value Conflicts Experienced by Mexican-American Students." Riverside: University of California at Riverside, 1968. ERIC ED 059 829.

1017. Werner, Norma E., and Evans, Idella M. "Perception of Prejudice in Mexican American Preschool Children." *Perceptual and Motor Skills* 27, no. 3, pt. 2 (1968): 1039-46.

1018. Lombrozo, Muriel P. "Ethnic, Racial and Social Class Differences as Measured by Free-Association Cognitive Responses to Verbal and Pictorial Stimuli." Doctoral dissertation, University of Southern California, 1969.

1019. Donnelly, Jerry D., and Anaya, Carlos. "Alienation in the Barrio: Eastern New Mexico." Boulder: University of Colorado, Mexican-American Studies Department, 1970. ERIC ED 081 535.

1020. González, Nancie L. "Positive and Negative Effects of Chicano Militancy on the Education of the Mexican American." Albuquerque, New Mexico: Southwestern Cooperative Educational Lab., 1970.

1021. Karr, Kathleen. "Protest: Mexican-American Style; Three Films." *Media and Methods* 6, no. 8 (April 1970): 54-56.

1022. Kelso, James A. *Mexican Americans in a Middle Class Anglo American Society; A Study of Intergroup Value Conflict.* Berkeley: California Book Co., 1970.

1023. Espinoza, Marta. "Cultural Conflict in the Classroom." Paper presented at the Fifth Annual TESOL Convention, New Orleans, Louisiana, 4 March 1971. ERIC ED 054 669.

1024. Heusenstamm, F.K. "Student Strikes in the East Los Angeles High Schools." *School and Society* 100 (March 1972): 182-85.

1025. Meza, Ruth Ann. "Ethnic Stereotypes: A Semantic Differential Analysis of Mexican-American and Anglo-American Names." Master's thesis, University of Texas at El Paso, 1972.

1026. Frisbie, Parker. "Militancy among Mexican American High School Students." *Social Science Quarterly* 53, no. 4 (March 1973): 865-83.

1027. Justin, Neal. "Mexican-Americans Exhibit Culture Conflict." *Education Forum* 37, no. 2 (January 1973): 229-30.

1028. Calloway, Aubrey. "The West Coast: More Gang Violence Hits LA Schools." *Race Relations Reporter* 5, no. 5 (March 1974): 5-6.

1029. Garwood, S. Gray, and McDavid, John W. "Ethnic Factors in Stereotypes of Given Names." Paper presented at the annual meeting of the American Psychological Association (82nd), New Orleans, Louisiana, 30 August-3 September 1974. ERIC ED 097 994.

1030. Gutiérrez, Armando George. "The Socialization of Militancy: Chicanos in a South Texas Town." Doctoral dissertation, University of Texas at Austin, 1974.

1031. Shockley, John Staples. *Chicano Revolt in a Texas Town.* Notre Dame, Indiana: University of Notre Dame Press, 1974.

3.3.7 Social Mobility

1032. Pratt, P.S. "A Comparison of the Social Achievement and Socio-Economic Background of Mexican and White Children in a Delta, Colorado Elementary School." Master's thesis, University of Southern California, 1938.

1033. Howard, Raymond G. "Acculturation and Social Mobility among Latin-Americans in Rasaca City." Master's thesis, University of Texas at Austin, 1952.

1034. Nall, Frank. "Levels of Aspiration of Mexican Americans in El Paso Schools." Doctoral dissertation, Michigan State University, 1959.

1035. de Hoyos, Arturo. *Occupational and Educational Levels of Aspiration of Mexican-American Youth.* San Francisco: R and E Research Associates, 1971; doctoral dissertation, Michigan State University, 1961.

1036. Waddell, Jack. "Value Orientations of Young Mexican-American Males as Reflected in Their Work Patterns and Employment Preferences." Master's thesis, University of Texas at Austin, 1962.

1037. Atonna, Peter. "A Comparison of Travel Patterns of a Mexican American Neighborhood with Those of an Anglo American Neighborhood in Tucson, Arizona." Master's thesis, University of Arizona, 1964.

1038. Heller, Celia Stopnicka. "Ambitions of Mexican-American Youth: Goals and Means of Mobility of High School Seniors." Doctoral dissertation, Columbia University, 1964.

1039. Robles, Ernest A. "An Analytic Description of Peer Group Pressures on Mobility-Oriented Mexican American Junior High Students." Master's thesis, University of Redlands, 1964.

1040. Heller, Celia Stopnicka. "Class as an Explanation of Ethnic Differences in Mobility Aspirations. The Case of the Mexican Americans." *International Migration Review* 2, no. 1 (fall 1967): 31-39.

1041. Palomares, Uvaldo Hill. "A Study of the Role of Mobility in the Acculturation Process of Rural Migrant and Non-Migrant Disadvantaged Mexican-Americans in the Coachella Valley." Doctoral dissertation, University of Southern California, 1967.

1042. Egelund, Larry Dwayne. "A Comparative Analysis of the Educational and Occupational Aspirations of High School Students: The Case of Selected Latin and Anglo-American Students in Laramie, Wyoming." Master's thesis, University of Wyoming, 1968.

1043. Juárez, Rumaldo Z. "Educational Status Orientations of Mexican American and Anglo American Youth in Selected Low-Income Counties of Texas." Master's thesis, Texas A&M University, 1968. ERIC ED 023 511.

1044. Wright, David E., Jr. "Occupational Orientations of Mexican American Youth in Selected Texas Counties." Master's thesis, Texas A&M University, 1968. ERIC ED 023 512.

1045. Marcus, Betty Elliot. "Replication Study of Ethnic Group Achievement Aspirations for the Young." Master's thesis, University of California at Riverside, 1969.

1046. Hindelang, Michael J. "Educational and Occupational Aspirations among Working Class Negro, Mexican-American and White Elementary School Children." *Journal of Negro Education* 39, no. 4 (fall 1970): 351-53.

1047. Kuvlesky, William P., and Patella, Victoria M. "Strength of Ethnic Identification and Intergenerational Mobility Aspirations among Mexican American Youth." Paper presented at the Southwestern Sociological Association meetings, Dallas, Texas, 26-28 March 1970. ERIC ED 040 777.

1048. Burstein, Alvin G., and Kobos, Joseph. "Psychological Testing as a Device to Foster Social Mobility." *American Psychologist* 26, no. 11 (November 1971): 1041-42.

1049. Heller, Celia Stopnicka. *New Converts to the American Dream? Mobility Aspirations of Young Mexican Americans.* New Haven, Connecticut: College & University Press, 1971.

1050. Kleibrink, Michael Charles. "Value Orientations of Retrained-Relocated Mexican-Americans." Master's thesis, Texas A&M University, 1971. ERIC ED 078 981.

1051. Kuvlesky, William P., and Patella, Victoria M. "Degree of Ethnicity and Aspirations for Upward Social Mobility among Mexican American Youth." *Journal of Vocational Behavior* 1, no. 3 (July 1971): 231-44.

1052. Penalosa, Fernando, and McDonagh, Edward C. "Social Mobility in a Mexican-American Community." In *Chicanos: Social and Psychological Perspectives,* pp. 85-92. Edited by Nathaniel L. Wagner and Marsha J. Haug. Saint Louis: The C.V. Mosby Company, 1971.

1053. Versteeg, Arlen, and Hall, Robert. "Level of Aspiration, Achievement, and Sociocultural Differences in Preschool Children." *Journal of Genetic Psychology* 119, no. 1 (September 1971): 137-42.

1054. Merkin, Donald H. "Ethnic Differences in Mobility Attitudes: A Comparison of Mexican American and Anglo Female High School Students." Master's thesis, Colorado State University, 1972. ERIC ED 078 977.

1055. Stilwell, William E., and Thoresen, Carl E. "Social Modeling and Vocational Behaviors of Mexican-American and Non-Mexican-American Adolescents." *Vocational Guidance Quarterly* 20, no. 4 (June 1972): 279-86.

1056. Wright, David E., Jr., et al. "Ambitions and Opportunities for Social Mobility and Their Consequences for Mexican Americans as Compared with Other Youth." Paper presented at the Workshop on Southwest Ethnic Groups: Sociopolitical Environment and Education, El Paso, Texas, July 1972. ERIC ED 066 285.

1057. Kuvlesky, William P. "Use of Spanish and Aspirations for Social Mobility among Chicanos: A Synthesis and Evaluation of Texas and Colorado Findings." College Station: Texas A&M University, 1973. ERIC ED 075 128.

1058. Orta, Simon L. "Occupational Aspirations of Mexican-American and Anglo-American Senior High School Students." Doctoral dissertation, University of Nebraska, 1973.

1059. Venegas, Moises. "Educational and Occupational Aspirations and Expectations of El Paso High School Students." Doctoral dissertation, New Mexico State University, 1973.

1060. Kuvlesky, William P., and Venegas, Moises. "Aspirations of Chicano Youth from the Texas Border Region: A Metropolitan-Non-Metropolitan Comparison." Paper presented at the 1974 annual meetings of the Rocky Mountain Social Science Association, El Paso, Texas, April 1974. ERIC ED 091 093.

1061. Moerk, Ernst L. "Age and Epogenic [sic] Influences of Aspirations of Minority and Majority Group Children." *Journal of Counseling Psychology* 21, no. 4 (July 1974): 294-98.

1062. Crawford, Harold B. "Educational and Occupational Aspirations and Expectations of Galveston High School Students." Doctoral dissertation, New Mexico State University, 1975.

1063. Kuvlesky, William P., and Monk, Philip M. "Historical Change in Status Aspirations and Expectations of Mexican American Youth from the Border Area of Texas: 1967-1973." Paper presented at the annual meeting of the Southwestern Sociological Association, San Antonio, Texas. 27 March 1975. ERIC ED 104 591.

3.3.8 Politics

1064. McAlister, Robert Theron. "Relationship of Education and Income to Partisan Vote: The Case of El Paso." Master's thesis, University of Texas at El Paso, 1967.

1065. López y Rivas, Gilbert. "Chicano: o, la explotación de la raza." Master's thesis, Escuela Nacional de Antropología e Historia, 1969.

1066. Love, Joseph L. "La Raza: Mexican-Americans in Rebellion." *Transaction* 6 (February 1969): 35-41.

1067. Cornbleth, Catherine Rae. "Political Socialization and the Schools: The Mexican American Student." Master's thesis, University of Texas at Austin, 1970.

1068. García, Richard A. "Political Ideology: A Comparative Study of the Chicano Youth Organizations." Master's thesis, University of Texas at El Paso, 1970.

1069. Messick, Rosemary G. "Political Awareness among Mexican-American High School Students." *High School Journal* 54, no. 2 (November 1970): 108-18.

1070. Peregrino, Santiago. "The Political Ideology of the Mexican American in a Southwestern City: El Paso." Master's thesis, University of Texas at El Paso, 1970.

1071. Button, Christine Bennett. "The Development of Experimental Curriculum to Effect the Political Socialization of Anglo, Black, and Mexican-American Adolescents." Doctoral dissertation, University of Texas at Austin, 1972.

1072. Button, Christine Bennett. "The Effects of Experimental Government Units on Students' Feelings of Political Efficacy, Political Cynicism and Political Knowledge: A Tri-Ethnic Study." Paper presented at the annual meeting of the American Educational Research Association, Chicago, Illinios, 5 April 1972. ERIC ED 088 769.

1073. Cárdenas, José A. "Politics and Education." In *Adelante: An Emerging Design for Mexican-American Education.* Edited by Manuel Reyes Mazón. Austin: University of Texas, Center for Communication Research, 1972.

1074. Rodríguez, Roy C. "A Measurement of Political Attitudes in Mexican American Civic Organizations." Master's thesis, University of Texas at El Paso, 1972.

1075. Sica, Morris G. "An Analysis of the Political Orientations of Mexican-American and Anglo-American Children. Final Report." Fullerton: University of California at Fullerton, 1972. ERIC ED 066 418.

1076. García, F. Chris. "Orientations of Mexican American and Anglo Children toward the U.S. Political Community." *Social Science Quarterly* 53, no. 4 (March 1973): 814-29.

1077. García, F. Chris. *Political Socialization of Chicano Children. A Comparative Study with Anglos in California Schools.* New York: Praeger Publishers, 1973.

1078. García, F. Chris. "The Political World of the Chicano Child." Paper presented at the annual meeting of the American Political Science Association, New Orleans, Louisiana, September 1973. ERIC ED 101 905.

1079. Loyola, José Gabriel. "Political Socialization in a Comparative of Different Ethnic School Children in Newark and El Paso." Master's thesis, University of Texas at El Paso, 1973.

1080. Mathis, William Jefferson. "Political Socialization in a Mexican American High School." Doctoral dissertation, University of Texas at Austin, 1973.

1081. Paris, Philip Lee. "The Mexican American Informal Polity and the Political Socialization of Brown Students: A Case Study in Ventura County, California." Doctoral dissertation, University of Southern California, 1973.

1082. Presnall, Barbara Ann. "The Political Socialization of Mexican American and Anglo Children: A Comparison." Doctoral dissertation, American University, 1973.

1083. García, F. Chris, ed. *La Causa Política. A Chicano Politics Reader.* Notre Dame, Indiana: University of Notre Dame Press, 1974.

1084. García, Neftali Gerardo, et al. "Ethnic Identification and Political Attitudes among Mejicano Youth in San Antonio, Texas." Paper presented at the annual meeting of the Rocky Mountain Social Science Association, El Paso, Texas, April 1974. ERIC ED 101 885.

1085. Post, Donald Eugene. "Ethnic Competition for Control of Schools in Two South Texas Towns." Doctoral dissertation, University of Texas at Austin, 1974. ERIC ED 101 867.

1086. Rosen, Gerald. "The Chicano Movement and the Politicization of Culture." *Ethnicity* 1, no. 3 (October 1974): 279-93.

1087. García, Neftali Gerardo. "Mexican-American Youth: Orientations toward Political Authority." Doctoral dissertation, North Texas State University, 1975.

3.3.9 Family

1088. Culp, Alice Bessie. "A Case Study of the Living Conditions of Thirty-Five Mexican Families of Los Angeles with Special Reference to Mexican Children." Master's thesis, University of Southern California, 1921.

1089. Jordan, R. Harding. "Retention of Foreign Language in the Home." *Journal of Educational Research* 3 (1921): 35-42.

1090. Bishop, Hazel Peck Campbell. "A Case Study of the Improvements of Mexican Homes through Instruction in Homemaking." Master's thesis, University of Southern California, 1937.

1091. Underwood, Marion L. "A Study of the Homes of One Hundred Latin American Girls in Corpus Christi to be Used as a Basis for a Homemaking Education Program in the Elementary Schools." Master's thesis, University of Texas at Austin, 1937.

1092. Wilson, William Nathan. "Analysis of the Academic and Home Problems of the Pupils in a Mexican Junior High School." Master's thesis, University of Southern California, 1938.

1093. Garza, George J. "Social and Economic Status of Mexicans of San Marcos and Its Bearing upon the Education of Mexican Children." Master's thesis, Southwest Texas State University, 1940.

1094. Nami, Julia. "A Study of the Family Life, In Its Relation to Education of Pupils in the Second Grade of the Anthony Margil School, San Antonio, Texas." Master's thesis, University of Texas at Austin, 1940.

1095. Humphrey, Norman Daymond. "The Changing Structure of the Detroit Mexican Family." *American Sociological Review* 9, no. 6 (December 1944): 622-26.

1096. Saenz, Nora A. "Position in the Family as Related to School Programs and Success." Master's thesis, University of Texas at Austin, 1952.

1097. Solien de González, Nancie L. "Family Organization in Five Types of Migratory Wage Labor." *American Anthropologist* 63, no. 6 (December 1961): 1264-80.

1098. Ramírez, Manuel. "Identification with Mexican Family Values and Authoritarianism in Mexican-Americans." *Journal of Social Psychology* 73 (October 1967): 3-11.

1099. Anderson, James G., and Johnson, William H. "Social and Cultural Characteristics of Mexican-American Families in South El Paso, Texas. Interim Report of the Mathematics Education Program." Las Cruces: New Mexico State University, 27 December 1968. ERIC ED 026 175.

1100. Penalosa, Fernando. "Mexican Family Roles." *Journal of Marriage and the Family* 30, no. 4 (November 1968): 680-89.

1101. Tharp, Roland G.; Meadow, Arnold; Lennhoff, Susan G., et al. "Changes in Marriage Roles Accompanying the Acculturation of the Mexican-American Wife." *Journal of Marriage and the Family* 30, no. 3 (August 1968): 404-12.

1102. "Cultural Stability and Change Among Mexican-American Families in an Urban Setting: A Comparison of Generations in El Paso, Texas." Paper presented at the American Educational Research Association Convention, Minneapolis, Minnesota, 2-6 March 1970. ERIC ED 039 552.

1103. Kearns, Bessie J. "Childrearing Practices among Selected Culturally Deprived Minorities." *Journal of Genetic Psychology* 116, no. 2 (June 1970): 149-55.

1104. Montiel, Miguel. "The Social Science Myth of the Mexican American Family." *El Grito* 3, no. 4 (summer 1970): 56-63.

1105. Murillo, Nathan. "The Mexican American Family." In *Chicanos: Social and Psychological Perspectives,* pp. 97-108. Edited by Nathaniel L. Wagner and Marsha J. Haug. Saint Louis: The C.V. Mosby Company, 1971.

1106. Staples, Robert. "The Mexican-American Family: Its Modifications over Time and Space." *Phylon* 32, no. 2 (summer 1971): 179-92.

1107. Stedman, James M., and McKenzie, Richard E. "Family Factors Related to Competence in Young Disadvantaged Mexican-American Children." *Child Development* 42, no. 5 (November 1971): 1602-7.

1108. Uhlenberg, Peter. "Marital Instability among Mexican Americans: Following the Patterns of Blacks?" *Social Problems* 20, no. 1 (summer 1972): 49-56.

1109. Cooksey, Robbie Choate. "Parental Role-Perception by the Young Mexican-American Child." Doctoral dissertation, University of Texas at Austin, 1974.

1110. Johnson, Aileen Seacat. "An Assessment of Mexican-American Parent Childrearing Feelings and Behavior." Doctoral dissertation, University of Arizona, 1975.

1111. Miller, Michael V. "Variations in Mexican-American Family Life: A Review Synthesis." College Station: Texas A&M University, 1975. ERIC ED 111 536.

1112. Moller, Darlene A. Townsend. "Family Interaction in the Development of Gender Identity in Mexican-American and Anglo Adolescents." Doctoral dissertation, Washington State University, 1975.

3.4 Language

3.4.1 General

1113. Manuel, Herschel T., and Wright, Carrie E. "Language Difficulty of Mexican Children." *Journal of Genetic Psychology* 36, no. 3 (September 1929): 458-68.

1114. Haught, B.F. "The Language Difficulty of Spanish American Children." *Journal of Applied Psychology* 15 (1931): 92-95.

1115. Blackman, Robert D. "The Language Handicap of Spanish American Children." Master's thesis, University of Arizona, 1940.

1116. Bain, Winifred E. "Mother Tongue or Other Tongue." *Parents' Magazine and Better Homemaking* 17, no. 3 (March 1942): 26-27, 40.

1117. Nelson, Lowry. "Speaking of Tongues." *American Journal of Sociology* 54, no . 3 (November 1948): 202-10.

1118. Holland, William R. "Language Barrier as an Educational Problem of Spanish-Speaking Children." In *The Disadvantaged Learner: Knowing, Understanding, Educating*, pp. 338-49. Edited by S.W. Webster. San Francisco: Chandler Publishing Co., 1966; reprint from : *Exceptional Children* 27, no. 1 (1960): 42-50.

1119. Carrell, Theresa, and Stevens, Traxel. "Leaping the Language Barrier." *Texas Outlook* 45, no. 9 (September 1961): 19-20.

1120. Dawson, Clarence W. "Spanish by Accident." *Texas Outlook* 46, no. 1 (January 1962): 22-24.

1121. Calderón, Carlos I. "Four Keys to a Better Speech." *Texas Outlook* 47, no. 4 (April 1963): 32-33.

1122. Galbraith, Clare Kearney. "Spanish-Speaking Children Communicate." *Childhood Education* 42, no. 2 (October 1965): 70-74.

1123. Macaulay, R.K.S. "Vocabulary Problems for Spanish Learners." *English Language Teaching* 20, no. 2 (January 1966): 130-36.

1124. Schaer, Bertha A. "A New Language for José." *Texas Outlook* 50, no. 12 (December 1966): 32-33.

1125. Soriano, Jesse M., and McClafferty, James. "Spanish Speakers of the Midwest: They Are Americans Too." *Foreign Language Annals* 2, no. 3 (March 1969): 316-24.

1126. U.S. Department of Health, Education, and Welfare. Office of Education. *The Mexican-American and His Language*, by Armando Rodríguez. Washington, D.C.: Government Printing Office, 1969. ERIC ED 030 508.

1127. Spector, Sima. "Patterns of Difficulty in English in Bilingual Mexican-American Children." Master's thesis, Sacramento State College, 1972. ERIC ED 066 083.

1128. Zimmerman, Ira Lee; Steiner, Violette; and Pond, Roberta L. "Language Status of Preschool Mexican American Children—Is There a Case against Early Bilingual Education?" *Perceptual and Motor Skills* 38, no. 1 (February 1974): 227-30.

3.4.2 Descriptive Studies

1129. Bourke, J.G. "Notes on the Language and Folk-Usage of the Rio Grande Valley." *Journal of American Folklore* 9, (April-June 1896): 81-116.

1130. Espinosa, Aurelio M. *The Spanish Language in New Mexico and Southern Colorado.* Santa Fe, New Mexico: Historical Society of New Mexico, 1911.

1131. Espinosa, Aurelio M. "Speech Mixture in New Mexico: The Influence of the English Language on the New Mexican Spanish." In *The Pacific Ocean in History*, pp. 408-28. Edited by Stephens H. Morse and Herbert E. Bolton. New York: The Macmillan Co., 1917.

1132. Turney, Douglas. "The Mexican Accent." *American Speech* 4, no. 6 (August 1929): 434-39.

1133. Brown, Carroll Edgar. "Foreign-Language Errors of Chicago Children." *English Journal* 20 (June 1931): 469-74.

1134. Bentley, Harold W. *A Dictionary of Spanish Terms in English with Special Reference to the American Southwest.* New York: Columbia University Press, 1932.

1135. Baugh, Lila. "A Study of the Preschool Vocabulary of Spanish Speaking Children." Master's thesis, University of Texas at Austin, 1933.

1136. Schupp, Ona E. "Oral and Written Language Errors of Sixth Grade Pupils." Master's thesis, University of New Mexico, 1933.

1137. McSpadden, George E. *Some Semantic and Philological Facts of the Spanish Spoken in Chilili, New Mexico.* Albuquerque: University of New Mexico Press, 1934.

1138. Kelly, R. *Mexican Spanish Language along the Border.* Waco, Texas: Baylor University Press, 1937.

1139. Jackson, Mrs. Lucile Prim. "An Analysis of the Language Difficulties of the Spanish Speaking Children of the Bowie High School, El Paso, Texas." Master's thesis, University of Texas at Austin, 1938.

1140. Johnson, Loaz W. "A Comparison of the Vocabularies of Anglo-American and Spanish-American High-School Pupils." *Journal of Educational Psychology* 29, no. 2 (February 1938): 135-44.

1141. Lynn, Klonda. "A Phonetic Analysis of the English Spoken by Mexican Children in the Elementary Schools of Arizona." Doctoral dissertation, Louisiana State University, 1940.

1142. Moran, Mrs. Mattie Belle. "A Study of the Oral and Reading Vocabularies of Beginning Spanish Speaking Children." Master's thesis, University of Texas at Austin, 1940.

1143. Rogers, Marjorie Katherine. "A Study of the Pronounciation Difficulties of Spanish-Culture Beginners." Master's thesis, Texas A&I University at Kingsville, 1940.

1144. Mitchell, Frederic Francis. "Shortcomings in the Written English of Spanish American Ninth Grade Pupils at the Schools of Tucson, Arizona." Master's thesis, University of Arizona, 1942.

1145. Ochoa, Hermelinda. "Linguistic Errors Made by Spanish-Speaking Children in Written English." Master's thesis, University of Texas at Austin, 1942.

1146. Reynolds, Selma Fay. "Some Aspects of Spanish as Spoken and Written by Spanish Speaking Students of a Junior High School in Texas." Master's thesis, Texas State College for Women, 1945.

1147. Tireman, Lloyd S. "A Study of Fourth-Grade Reading Vocabulary of Native Spanish-Speaking Children." *Elementary School Journal* 46, no. 4 (December 1945): 223-27.

1148. Tireman, Lloyd S. *Spanish Vocabulary of Four Native Spanish-Speaking Pre-First-Grade Children.* Albuquerque: University of New Mexico Press, 1948.

1149. Diaz-Risa, Ignacio. "A Speech Survey of Eighty Spanish-Speaking Children in Four Elementary Schools of Austin, Texas." Master's thesis, University of Texas at Austin, 1952.

1150. Cerda, Gilberto; Cabaza, Berta; and Farias, Julieta. *Vocabulario Español de Texas.* Austin: University of Texas Press, 1953.

1151. Keele, Jewel Aden. "A Study of the Variations and Misspellings of Anglo American and Spanish American Children." Master's thesis, University of Texas at Austin, 1953.

1152. Galvan, Robert Arispe. "El dialecto español de San Antonio, Texas." Doctoral dissertation, Tulane University, 1954.

1153. Massey, Gloria Mae Walker. "Spanish in Texas Junior High Schools." Master's thesis, University of Texas at Austin, 1954.

1154. Naunheim, Elizabeth. "Spanish in Corpus Christi." *Hispania* 37, no. 1 (March 1954): 77-78.

1155. Servey, Richard E. "An Analysis of Written Language Structure of English Speaking and Spanish Speaking Children in Grades 4, 5, and 6." Master's thesis, University of California at Los Angeles, 1955.

1156. Sawyer, Janet Beck Moseley. "A Dialect Study of San Antonio, Texas: A Bilingual Community." Doctoral dissertation, University of Texas at Austin, 1958.

1157. Page, Gwen Allison. "A Comparative Study of Spelling Errors for Third Grade Children of Anglo and Bilingual Backgrounds." Master's thesis, University of Texas at El Paso, 1959.

1158. Braddy, Haldeen. "Pachucos and Their Argot." *Southern Folklore Quarterly* 24, no. 4 (December 1960): 255-71.

1159. Contreras, Hales W. "The Phonological System of a Bilingual Child." Doctoral dissertation, Indiana University, 1961.

1160. Garrison, Pearl Runnels. "A Study of Vocabulary in Fourth Grade Bilingual Children." Master's thesis, Texas A&I University at Kingsville, 1961.

1161. Starkey, Roberta Johnston. "A Synthesis and Interpretation of Research Findings Which Pertained to Teaching Spanish-Speaking Children." Doctoral dissertation, Texas Technological College, 1961.

1162. Klinger, Herbert. "Imitated English Cleft Palate Speech in a Normal Spanish-Speaking Child." *Journal of Speech and Hearing Disorders* 27, no. 4 (November 1962): 379-81.

1163. Lorenzini, August Peter. "A Study of the Pattern of Communication Used by Fifty Negro and Fifty Spanish-Named Residents of Phoenix, Arizona." Doctoral dissertation, University of Denver, 1962.

1164. Montemayor, Elsa Diana. "A Study of the Spanish Spoken by Certain Bilingual Students of Laredo, Texas." Master's thesis, Texas Woman's University, 1966.

1165. Olpin, Bonnie Le Blanc. "Some Linguistic Differences between Bilingual Mexican American Children and Monolingual Anglo American Children on the Second Grade Level." Master's thesis, University of California at Santa Barbara, 1966.

1166. Mahoney, Mary Katherine. "Spanish and English Language Usage by Rural and Urban Spanish American Families in Two South Texas Counties." Master's thesis, Texas A&M University, 1967.

1167. Peña, Albar Antonio. "A Comparative Study of Selected Syntactical Structures of the Oral Language Status in Spanish and English Disadvantaged First-Grade Spanish-Speaking Children." Doctoral dissertation, University of Texas at Austin, 1967.

1168. Amsden, Constance E. "A Study of the Syntax of the Oral English Used by Thirty Selected Mexican-American Children Three to Five Years Old in a Preschool Setting." Doctoral dissertation, Claremont Graduate School and University Center, 1968.

1169. González, Gustavo. "A Linguistic Profile on the Spanish Speaking First Grades in Corpus Christi (Texas)." Master's thesis, University of Texas at Austin, 1968.

1170. Wakefield, Mary W. "A Comparative Study of Language Patterns in Low Socioeconomic First Graders." Doctoral dissertation, Arizona State University, 1968.

1171. Fishman, Joshua A., and Herasimchuk, Eleanor. "The Multiple Predication of Phonological Variables in a Bilingual Speech Community." *American Anthropologist* 7, no. 4 (August 1969): 648-57.

1172. García, Anita H. "Identification and Classification of Types of Common Deviations from Standard Spanish Made by Representative Native Speakers in South Texas." Master's thesis, Texas A&I University at Kingsville, 1969.

1173. González, Gustavo. *The Phonology of Corpus Christi Spanish. Final Report.* Austin, Texas: Southwest Educational Development Laboratory, Program Research and Evaluation Division, 1969.

1174. Lawson, Jack. "Bobby and John: A Study of the Spanish of Two American Boys of Mexican Descent." Master's thesis, Fresno State University, 1969.

1175. Natalicio, Eleanor Diana Siedhoff. "Formation of the Plural in English: A Study of Native Speakers of English and Native Speakers of Spanish." Doctoral dissertation, University of Texas at Austin, 1969.

1176. Ornstein, Jacob. "Language Varieties along the U.S.-Mexican Border." Paper presented at the Sociolinguistics Section of the 2nd International Congress of Applied Linguistics, Cambridge, England, 8-12 September 1969. ERIC ED 032 520.

1177. Smith, G.M. "Some Comments on the English of Eight Bilinguals." In *A Brief Study of Spanish-English Bilingualism: Final Report.* College Station: Texas A&M University, Research Project ORR-Liberal Arts-15504, 1969. (Unpublished document.)

1178. Wakefield, Mary W., and Silvaroli, N.J. "A Study of Oral Language Patterns of Low Socioeconomic Groups." *Reading Teacher* 22, no. 7 (1969): 622-24, 663.

1179. Allred, Forrest Rich. "Errors in Oral English Usage of Mexican-American Pupils with a Spanish Background in Grade III in the State of Colorado." Doctoral dissertation, University of Northern Colorado, 1970.

1180. Benitez, Carrahlee. "A Study of Some Non-Standard English Features in the Speech of Seventh-Grade Mexican-Americans Enrolled in a Remedial Reading Program in an Urban Community of South Texas." Master's thesis, Texas A&I University at Kingsville, 1970.

1181. Doggett, Elizabeth Belk. "A Linguistic and Cultural Profile of First Grade Mexican American Children in Austin, Texas." Master's thesis, University of Texas at Austin, 1970.

1182. Elías-Olivares, Lucia Ernestina. "Study of the Oral Spanish Vocabulary of Ten High School Mexican American Students in Austin (Texas)." Master's thesis, University of Texas at Austin, 1970.

1183. Hicks, Jerral Robert. "Errors in Oral English Usage of Mexican-American Pupils with a Spanish Language Background in Grade II in the State of Colorado." Doctoral dissertation, University of Northern Colorado, 1970.

1184. Mazeika, Edward John. "A Descriptive Analysis of the Language of a Bilingual Child." Doctoral dissertation, University of Rochester, 1970.

1185. Pauls, Leo Wayne. "Errors in Oral English Usage of Mexican American Pupils with a Spanish Language Background in Grade V in the State of Colorado." Doctoral dissertation, University of Northern Colorado, 1970.

1186. Roberts, Neil Alden. "Errors in Oral English Usage of Mexican-American Pupils with a Spanish Language Background in Grade IV in the State of Colorado." Doctoral dissertation, University of Northern Colorado, 1970.

1187. Said, Sally Eugenia Sneed. "A Descriptive Model of Austin Spanish Syntax." Master's thesis, University of Texas at Austin, 1970.

1188. Spears, Mary Ann. "A Partial Linguistic Profile of the Mexican American First Grader in Austin, Texas." Master's thesis, University of Texas at Austin, 1970.

1189. Broussard, Neonetta Cabrera. "The Spelling Errors of Mexican-American High School Students Tested at UCLA." Master's thesis, University of California at Los Angeles, 1971.

1190. Bussey, Jo Ann Keslar. "A Comparative Study of Phonological Variation among First, Second and Third Grade Linguistically Different Children in Five San Antonio (Texas) Schools: 1970." Doctoral dissertation, University of Texas at Austin, 1971.

1191. January, William Spence. "The Chicano Dialect of the Mexican American Communities of Dallas and Fort Worth." Master's thesis, Texas Christian University, 1971.

1192. Serrano, Rodolfo G. "The Language of the Four Year Old Chicano." Paper presented at the Rocky Mountain Educational Research Association meeting, Boulder, Colorado, 28-29 October 1971. ERIC ED 071 791.

1193. Valls, Dolores, L. "Linguistic Description of Samples of Oral Spanish Spoken by California High School Students of Mexican Background." Master's thesis, Sacramento State University, 1971.

1194. Brisk, María Estela. "The Spanish Syntax of the Pre-School Spanish American: The Case of New Mexican Five-Year-Old Children." Doctoral dissertation, University of New Mexico, 1972.

1195. Castro-Gingras, Rosario. *An Analysis of the Linguistic Characteristics of the English Found in a Set of Mexican-American Child Data.* Los Alamitos, California: Southwest Regional Lab for Educational Research and Development, 1972. ERIC ED 111 002.

1196. Frydendall, Dennis Joe. "Errors in Oral English Usage of Mexican-American Pupils with a Spanish Language Background in Grade VI in the State of Colorado." Doctoral dissertation, University of Northern Colorado, 1972.

1197. Mace, Betty J. "A Linguistic Profile of Children Entering Seattle Public School Kindergartens in September, 1971, and Implications for Instruction." Master's thesis, University of Texas at Austin, 1972.

1198. Ornstein, Jacob. "Toward a Classification of Southwest Spanish Nonstandard Variants." *Linguistics: An International Review* 93 (1972): 70-87.

1199. Robinson, Virginia Hope. "Comparison of Standard English Patterns Produced by Head Start Participants and Comparable Children with No Head Start Experience." Doctoral dissertation, Arizona State University, 1972.

1200. Van Metre, Patricia Downer. "Syntactical Characteristics of Selected Bilingual Children." Doctoral dissertation, University of Arizona, 1972.

1201. Cervantes, Alfonso. "A Selected Vocabulary of Anglicisms Used by the Spanish-Speaking First Grade Students of the Elementary Schools of Del Rio, Texas." Master's thesis, Southwest Texas State University, 1973.

1202. García, Ricardo L. "Identification and Comparison of Oral English Syntactic Patterns of Spanish-English Speaking Adolescent Hispanos." Doctoral dissertation, University of Denver, 1973.

1203. Hensey, Fritz G. "Grammatical Variables in Southwestern American Spanish." *Linguistics: An International Review* 108 (July 1973): 5-26.

1204. Natalicio, Luiz F.S., and Natalicio, Diana S. "An Investigation into Linguistic Cues Involved in English Noun Pluralization of Six-Year-Old Mexican-American Children. Final Report." El Paso: University of Texas at El Paso, August 1973. ERIC ED 108 521.

1205. Pastrana, Sonia. "Características sociolingüísticas de dos grupos de alumnos de secundaria recién llegados de México." Master's thesis, University of Texas at El Paso, 1973.

1206. Politzer, Robert L., and Ramírez, Arnulfo G. "An Error Analysis of the Spoken English of Mexican-American Pupils in a Bilingual School and a Monolingual School. Research and Development Memorandum No. 103." Palo Alto, California: Stanford University, Stanford Center for Research and Development in Teaching, February 1973. ERIC ED 073 879.

1207. Poulter, Virgil Leroy. "A Phonological Study of the Speech of Mexican-American College Students Native to Fort Worth-Dallas." Doctoral dissertation, Louisiana State University and Agricultural and Mechanical College, 1973.

1208. Axelrod, Jerome. "Some Pronunciation and Linguistic Problems of Spanish-Speaking Children in American Classrooms." *Elementary English* 51, no. 2 (February 1974): 203-6.

1209. Brisk, María Estela. "New Mexican Spanish Syntax of the Five-Year-Old." In *Southwest Areal Linguistics*, pp. 225-39. Edited by Garland D. Bills. San Diego, California: San Diego State University, Institute for Cultural Pluralism, 1974.

1210. Ramírez, Arnulfo G. "The Spoken English of Spanish-Speaking Pupils in a Bilingual and Monolingual School Setting: An Analysis of Syntactic Development. Technical Report No. 40." Palo Alto, California: Stanford University, Stanford Center for Research and Development in Teaching, June 1974. ERIC ED 094 569.

1211. Rodríguez, Raymond J. "A Comparison of the Written and Oral English Syntax of Mexican-American Bilingual and Anglo-American Monolingual Fourth-Grade and Ninth-Grade Students." Doctoral dissertation, University of New Mexico, 1974.

1212. Hartford, Beverly Ann Slattery. "The English of Mexican-American Adolescents in Gary, Indiana: A Sociolinguistic Description." Doctoral dissertation, University of Texas at Austin, 1975.

1213. Hernández-Chávez, Eduardo; Cohen, Andrew D.; and Beltramo, Anthony F., eds. *El lenguaje de los Chicanos: Regional and Social Characteristics Used by Mexican Americans.* Arlington, Virginia: Center for Applied Linguistics, 1975.

1214. Jacobson, Rodolfo. "Semantic Compounding in the Speech of Mexican-American Bilinguals: A Reexamination of the Compound-Coordinate Distinction." Paper presented at the meeting of the Rocky Mountain Modern Language Association, Denver, Colorado, 1975. ERIC ED 115 112.

3.4.3 Sociolinguistics

1215. Ajubita, María Luisa. "Language in Social Relations with Special Reference to the Mexican-American Problem." Master's thesis, Tulane University, 1943.

1216. Barker, George C. *Pachuco: An American-Spanish Argot and Its Function in Tucson, Arizona.* Tucson, Arizona: University of Arizona Press, 1950.

1217. Tsuzaki, Stanley Mamoru. "English Influences in the Phonology and Morphology of the Spanish Spoken in the Mexican Colony in Detroit, Michigan." Doctoral dissertation, University of Michigan, 1963.

1218. Fishman, Joshua A., and Nahirny, Vladimir C. "The Ethnic Group School and Mother Tongue Maintenance in the United States." *Sociology of Education* 37, no. 4 (summer 1964): 306-17.

1219. Linn, George Byron. *A Study of Several Linguistic Functions of Mexican-American Children in a Two-Language Environment.* San Francisco: R and E Research Associates 1971; doctoral dissertation, University of Southern California, 1965.

1220. Protheroe, Donald Wesley. "The Language Used by Children of Contrasting Socio-Economic Groups in Tasks Related to Concept Formation." Doctoral dissertation, Wayne State University, 1967.

1221. Ramos, M., et al. *The Determination and Implementation of Language Policy.* Quezon City: Alemar-Phoenix, 1967.

1222. Hensey, Frederick G. "Linguistic Consequences of Culture Contact in a Border Community." Doctoral dissertation, University of Texas at Austin, 1968.

1223. Sechrest, Lee; Flores, L.; and Arellano, Lourdes. "Language and Social Interaction in a Bilingual Culture." *Journal of Social Psychology* 76, no. 2 (December 1968): 155-61.

1224. Scott, Carmen Casillas. "Spanish Language Maintenance and Loyalty in El Paso-Juárez: A Sociolinguistic Study of the Contact Situations in a Highly Bilingual Area." Master's thesis, University of Texas at El Paso, 1969.

1225. Smith, Dennis R. "The Effect of Selected Communication Patterns on Level of Abstraction, Length, and Complexity of Sentence in Speech of Children. Final Report." Buffalo: State University of New York, Research Foundation, January 1969. ERIC ED 028 004.

1226. Christian, Chester C., Jr. "The Analysis of Linguistic and Cultural Differences: A Proposed Model." In *Bilingualism and Language Contact: Anthropological, Linguistic, Psychological Aspects,* pp. 149-62. Edited by J.E. Alatis. George Town Monograph Series on Language and Linguistics, No. 23. Washington, D.C.: Georgetown University Press, 1970.

1227. Cohen, Andrew David. "A Sociolinguistic Approach to Bilingual Education: The Measurement of Language Use and Attitudes toward Language in School and Community, with Special Reference to the Mexican American Community of Redwood City, California." Master's thesis, Stanford University, 1970. ERIC ED 043 007.

1228. Ornstein, Jacob. *Sociolinguistics and New Perspectives in the Study of Southwest Spanish.* El Paso: Texas Western Press, 1970.

1229. Sharp, John M. "The Origin of Some Non-Standard Lexical Items in the Spanish of El Paso." In *Studies in Language and Linguistics, 1969-70,* pp. 207-32. Edited by Ralph W. Ewton, Jr., and Jacob Ornstein. El Paso: Texas Western Press, 1970.

1230. Skrabanek, R.L. "Language Maintenance among Mexican-Americans." *International Journal of Comparative Sociology* 11, no. 4 (December 1970): 272-82.

1231. García, Nelda Carola. "Language Factors in the Employment of Bilingual Mexican-Americans: A Case Study Analysis." Doctoral dissertation, Michigan State University, 1971.

1232. Mallory, Gloria Griffin. "Sociolinguistic Considerations for Bilingual Education in an Albuquerque Community Undergoing Language Shift." Doctoral dissertation, University of New Mexico, 1971.

1233. Ornstein, Jacob. "Sociolinguistic Research on Language Diversity in the American Southwest and Its Educational Implications." *The Modern Language Journal* 55, no. 4 (April 1971): 223-29.

1234. Teel, Tommy Lou. "A Sociolinguistic Study of Spanish Linguistic Interference and Nonstandard Grammatical Phenomena in the Written English of Selected Mexican American Bilinguals." Master's thesis, University of Texas at El Paso, 1971.

1235. Thompson, Roger M. "Language Loyalty in Austin, Texas: A Study of a Bilingual Neighborhood." Doctoral dissertation, University of Texas at Austin, 1971.

1236. Barker, George C. *Social Functions of Language in a Mexican-American Community. Anthropological Papers of the University of Arizona Number 22.* Tucson, Arizona: University of Arizona Press, 1972.

1237. Beltramo, Anthony Fred. "Lexical and Morphological Aspects of Linguistic Acculturation by Mexican Americans in San Jose, California." Doctoral dissertation, Stanford University, 1972.

1238. Christian, Chester C., Jr. "Criteria for Cultural-Linguistic Subdivision in the Southwest." In *Bilingualism in the Southwest,* pp. 39-49. Edited by Paul Turner. Tucson, Arizona: University of Arizona Press, 1972.

1239. Donofrio, Rosalie S. Maggio. "Situations and Language: A Sociolinguistic Investigation." Doctoral dissertation, University of New Mexico, 1972.

1240. Serrano, Rodolfo Gaitan. "Sociocultural Influence on the Development of Mexican American Language Styles." Doctoral dissertation, University of Arizona, 1972.

1241. García, Rodolfo. "Language Interference and Socioeconomic Status as Factors in the Acquisition of Standard Oral English of Mexican American and Anglo Migrant Children." Doctoral dissertation, Ohio State University, 1973.

1242. Patella, Victoria, and Kuvlesky, William P. "Situational Variation in Language Patterns of Mexican American Boys and Girls." *Social Science Quarterly* 53, no. 4 (March 1973): 855-64.

1243. Domínguez, Domingo. "A Theoretical Model for Classifying Dialectal Variations of Oral New Mexican Spanish." Doctoral dissertation, University of New Mexico, 1974.

1244. Grieshop, James I., and Harris, Mary B. "Effects of Mode of Modeling, Model Age, and Ethnicity on Rule-Governed Language Behaviors." *Journal of Educational Psychology* 66, no. 6 (December 1974): 974-80.

1245. Ortego, Philip D. "Sociolinguistics and Language Attitudinal Change." Mimeographed. In *Sociolinguistics in the Southwest,* pp. 75-80. Edited by Bates Hoffer and Jacob Ornstein. San Antonio, Texas: Trinity University, Department of English, 1974.

1246. Thompson, Roger M . "The 1970 U.S. Census and Mexican American Language Loyalty: A Case Study." In *Southwest Areal Linguistics,* pp. 65-78. Edited by Garland D. Bills. San Diego: Institute for Cultural Pluralism, San Diego State University, 1974.

1247. García, Ricardo L. "Mexican American Bilingualism and English Language Ethnocentrism in Public Education." Paper presented at the annual meeting of the Conference of College Composition and Communication, 26th, Saint Louis, Missouri, 13-15 March 1975. ERIC ED 105 494.

1248. Patella, Victoria M ., and Kuvlesky, William P. "Bilingual Patterns of Nonmetropolitan Mexican American Youth: Variations by Social Context, Language Use, and Historical Change." College Station: Texas A&M University, 21 August 1975. ERIC ED 113 108.

1249. Fantini, Alvino E. *Language Acquisition of a Bilingual Child: A Sociolinguistic Perspective.* Brattleboro, Vermont: Experiment Press, 1976.

1250. Rodríguez del Pino, Salvador, et al., eds. *Proceedings of the National Exploratory Conference on Chicano Sociolinguistics (Las Cruces, New Mexico, November 6-8, 1974).* University Park, New Mexico: National Council for Chicano Sociolinguistic Research, February 1976. ERIC ED 118 330.

3.4.4 Development

1251. Callicutt, Laurie Timmons. "Word Difficulties of Mexican and Non-Mexican Children." Master's thesis, University of Texas at Austin, 1934.

1252. Tireman, Lloyd S.; Dixon, N.; and Cornelius, V. "Vocabulary Acquisition of Spanish-Speaking Children." *Elementary English* 12, no. 5 (May 1935): 118-19, 144.

1253. Rodríguez-Bou, Ismael. "A Study of the Parallelism of English and Spanish Vocabularies." Doctoral dissertation, University of Texas at Austin, 1944.

1254. Saylor, Thelma I. "A Study of the Language Development of Spanish-Speaking Children." Master's thesis, Arizona State College, 1946.

1255. Hughes, Maria. "The English Language Facility of Mexican American Children Living and Attending School in a Segregated Community." Doctoral dissertation, Stanford University, 1952.

1256. Carrow, Sister Mary Arthur. "A Comparative Study of the Linguistic Function of Bilingual Spanish-American Children and Monolingual Anglo-American Children at the Third Grade Level." Doctoral dissertation, Northwestern University, 1955.

1257. Tireman, Lloyd S. "The Bilingual Child and His Reading Vocabulary." *Elementary English* 32 (January 1955): 33-35.

1258. Carrow, Sister Mary Arthur. "Linguistic Functioning of Bilingual and Monolingual Children." *Journal of Speech and Hearing* 22, no. 3 (September 1957): 371-80.

1259. Beberfall, Lester. "Some Linguistic Problems of Spanish-Speaking People of Texas." *Modern Language Journal* 42, no. 2 (February 1958): 87-90.

1260. Hess, Stephen Grant. "A Comparative Study of the Understanding of the Multiple Meanings of English Words." Master's thesis, University of New Mexico, 1963.

1261. García, Ernest Felix. "Interference by Textual Stimuli on Selected Elements of Spanish Pronunciation." Doctoral dissertation, University of California at Los Angeles, 1966.

1262. Heiler, Barbara. "An Investigation of the Causes of Primary Stress Mislocation in the English Speech of Bilingual Mexican-American Students." Master's thesis, University of Texas at El Paso, 1966.

1263. Kernan, Keith, T., and Blount, B.G. "The Acquisition of Spanish Grammar by Mexican Children." *Anthropological Linguistics* 8, no. 9 (December 1966): 1-14.

1264. Harrison, Helene W. "A Methodological Study in Eliciting Linguistic Data from Mexican-American Bilinguals." Doctoral dissertation, University of Texas at Austin, 1967.

1265. Hendrix, Leland Jacob. "Auditory Discrimination Differences between Culturally Deprived and Non-Deprived Preschool Children." Doctoral dissertation, Brigham Young University, 1967.

1266. Linn, George B. "Linguistic Functions of Bilingual Mexican-American Children." *Journal of Genetic Psychology* 3, no. 2 (December 1967): 183-93.

1267. Hilton, Darla Chris. "An Investigation of the Internalization of Phonological Rules in Monolingual and Bilingual Children." Master's thesis, University of Texas at Austin, 1969.

1268. Taylor, Thomasine Hughes. "A Comparative Study of the Effects of Oral-Aural Language Training on Gains in English Language for Fourth and Fifth Grade Disadvantaged Mexican-American Children." Doctoral dissertation, University of Texas at Austin, 1969. ERIC ED 041 252.

1269. Thornhill, D.E. "A Quantitative Analysis of the Development of Syntactical Fluency of Four Young Adult Spanish Speakers Learning English." Doctoral dissertation, Florida State University, 1969.

1270. Annicchiarico, James Robert. "Syntactically Mediated Paired-Associate Learning of Normal and Educationally Retarded Anglo- and Mexican-American Children." Doctoral dissertation, University of Texas at Austin, 1970.

1271. Arnold, Richard D., and Wist, Anne H. "Auditory Discrimination Abilities of Disadvantaged Anglo- and Mexican-American Children." *Elementary School Journal* 70, no. 6 (March 1970): 295-99.

1272. González, Gustavo. "The Acquisition of Spanish Grammar by Native Spanish Speakers." Doctoral dissertation, University of Texas at Austin, 1970.

1273. Munsell, Paul E. "The Relationship between Aural Discrimination and Oral Production." Doctoral dissertation, University of Michigan, 1970.

1274. Politzer, Robert L. "Auditory Discrimination Performance of Pupils from English and Spanish-Speaking Homes." Palo Alto, California: Stanford University, Stanford Center for Research and Development in Teaching, July 1970. ERIC ED 050 853.

1275. Jorstad, Dorothy. "Psycholinguistic Learning Disabilities in 20 Mexican American Students." *Journal of Learning Disabilities* 4, no. 3 (March 1971): 143-49.

1276. Monette, Elizabeth M. "Educational Problems Relating to the Spanish-Speaking Children with Emphasis on Language Development." Master's thesis, University of Texas at Austin, 1971.

1277. Young, Rodney W. "Semantics as a Determiner of Linguistic Comprehension across Language and Cultural Boundaries." Doctoral dissertation, University of New Mexico, 1971.

1278. Carrow, Elizabeth [Sister Mary Arthur]. "Auditory Comprehension of English by Monolingual and Bilingual Preschool Children." *Journal of Speech and Hearing Research* 15, no. 2 (June 1972): 407-12.

1279. Cordova, Joe E. "English Proficiency and Behavioral Change in Spanish-Speaking Children." Pueblo, Colorado: Southern Colorado State College, 23 August 1972. ERIC ED 066 996.

1280. Dillon, David Andrew. "An Analysis of the Written Syntactic Maturity in English of Mexican-American Migrant Students." Master's thesis, Southwest Texas State University, 1972.

1281. Gonzales, James Lee. "Effects of Maternal Stimulation on Early Language Development of Mexican American Children." Doctoral dissertation, University of New Mexico, 1972.

1282. Kirk, Samuel A. "Ethnic Differences in Psycholinguistic Abilities." *Exceptional Child* 39, no. 2 (October 1972): 112-18.

1283. Alvarez, Salvador. "The Influence of Phonological Characteristics upon Orthography in Mexican-American Second-Graders." Doctoral dissertation, University of Texas at Austin, 1973.

1284. Grieshop, James Ivo. "Modeling and Cognitive Behavior: The Effects of Modeling. Modes of Modeling and Selected Model Attributes on Rule-Governed Language Behavior." Doctoral dissertation, University of New Mexico, 1973. ERIC ED 085 135.

1285. Murthy, Marilyn. "The Effects of Modeling and Repetition upon the Acquisition of Three Standard English Patterns by Spanish-Speaking First-Grade Children." Doctoral dissertation, University of New Mexico, 1973.

1286. Pialorsi, Frank Paul. "The Production and Recognition of Grammatical and Ungrammatical English Word Sequences by Bilingual Children." Doctoral dissertation, University of Arizona, 1973.

1287. Chesnut, Norman Jennings. "Linguistic Development among Mexican-American and Anglo Primary Students in the Public Schools." Doctoral dissertation, University of Arizona, 1974.

1288. Dulay, Heidi C., and Burt, Marina K. "Natural Sequences in Child Second Language Acquisition." *Language Learning* 24, no. 1 (June 1974): 37-53.

1289. Evans, Joyce S. "Word-Pair Discrimination and Imitation Abilities of Preschool Spanish-Speaking Children." *Journal of Learning Disabilities* 7, no. 9 (November 1974): 573-80.

1290. González, Gustavo. "The Acquisition of Questions in Texas Spanish." In *Southwest Areal Linguistics,* pp. 251-66. Edited by Garland D. Bills. California: San Diego State University, Institute for Cultural Pluralism, 1974.

1291. Stewart, Adela Artola. "The Relative Oral Spanish Proficiency (Lexical) of Second Generation Mexican-American Kindergarten Children in Tucson, Arizona." Doctoral dissertation, University of Arizona, 1974.

1292. McClure, Erica, and Wentz, James. "Code-Switching in Children's Narratives." Paper presented at the Mid-American Linguistics Conference, University of Kansas, 1975. ERIC ED 119 524.

1293. Trepper, Terry Steven. "A Comparison of English and Spanish Verbal Facility of Mexican-American Children." 1975. ERIC ED 121 547.

3.4.5 Language and Education

1294. Shields, Virginia. "Oral Expression, Remedial Speech and English for the Migrant Child, Grades One-Twelve." Naples, Florida: Collier County Board of Public Instruction, n.d. ERIC ED 010 745.

1295. Finckinger, Paul Lawrence. "A Study of Certain Phases of the Language Problem of Spanish-American Children." Master's thesis, University of New Mexico, 1930.

1296. Vetters, Mrs. Anna Hill. "Speech Correction among Spanish-Speaking Children in an Elementary School." Master's thesis, University of Texas at Austin, 1942.

1297. Humphrey, Norman D. "The Education and Language of Detroit Mexicans." *Journal of Educational Sociology* 17, no. 9 (May 1944): 534-42.

1298. Condit, Eleanor Daly. "An Appraisal of Certain Methods of Treating Bi-Lingualism in the Claremont Elementary School." Master's thesis, University of Southern California, 1946.

1299. Rohr, Thurman G. "A Study of the Correction of English Pronunciation of Latin American Pupils." Master's thesis, University of Texas at Austin, 1948.

1300. Brown, Wrinkle Mary H. "Pitch Improvement in Anglo and Latin American Children." Master's thesis, University of Texas at Austin, 1950.

1301. Torres, J.A. "Spanish-Speaking Students Correct Defective English." *Texas Outlook* 41, no. 3 (March 1957): 22 + .

1302. Calderón, Carlos I. "Put the Accent on Speech Errors " Texas Outlook 43, no. 2 (February 1959): 26-28.

1303. Paulos, William T. "They Learn Basic English before School Starts." Texas Outlook 43, no. 8 (August 1959): 15-16.

1304. Riley, Frances Lucile. "A Longitudinal Evaluation of the Pre-First Grade Language Experiences in the McAllen Public Schools." Master's thesis, Texas A&I University at Kingsville, 1961.

1305. Powell, D.R. "Initial Clusters and the Spanish-Speaking Learner." English Language Teaching 16, no. 2 (1962): 95-101.

1306. Rohn, Ramona. "Improvement of Oral English in the First Grade in the Santo Domingo School." Master's thesis, University of New Mexico, 1963.

1307. Powell, D.R. "Final Cluster and the Spanish-Speaking Learner." English Language Teaching 20, no. 1 (October 1965): 17-22.

1308. Dillard, J.L. "The English Teacher and the Language of the Newly Integrated Student." The Record-Teachers College 69, no. 2 (November 1967): 115-20.

1309. Gallagher, Betty. "The Effect of Teacher Attitudes on Children's Response to Defective Articulation." Journal of Educational Research 60, no. 10 (1967): 456-58.

1310. Collier, Maggie S. "A Study of the Effects of Customary Language Usage upon the Learning of Concepts by a Group of Second Grade Children." Doctoral dissertation, Texas Technological College, 1968.

1311. Lastra, Yolanda. "El habla y la educación de los niños de origen Mexicano en Los Angeles." Paper presented at the V Simposio del Programa Interamericano de Lingüística y Enseñanza de Idiomas, São Paulo, Brazil, 9-14 January 1969. ERIC ED 018 286.

1312. Taylor, Thomasine Hughes. "English Language Proficiency for Fourth and Fifth Grade Spanish-Speaking Children." San Antonio, Texas: San Antonio Independent School District, March 1970. ERIC ED 040 391.

1313. Venesky, Richard L. "Nonstandard Language and Reading." Elementary English 47, no. 3 (March 1970): 334-35.

1314. Wasserman, Susan. "Raising the English Language Proficiency of Mexican American Children in the Primary Grades." California English Journal 6, no. 2 (April 1970): 22-27.

1315. Saville, M.R. "Interference Phenomena in Language Teaching." Elementary English 48, no. 3 (March 1971): 396-405.

1316. Spence, Allyn G.; Mishra, Shitala P.; and Ghozeil, Susan. "Home Language and Performance on Standardized Tests." Elementary School Journal 71, no. 6 (March 1971): 309-13.

1317. Williams, Frederick, and Van Wart, Geraldine. "On the Relationship of Language Dominance and the Effects of Viewing CARRASCOLENDAS." Austin: University of Texas at Austin, Center for Communication Research, September 1972. ERIC ED 066 058.

1318. Hernández-Chávez, Eduardo. "Home Language of Chicanos as a Medium of Instruction." Claremont Reading Conference, Yearbook 37 (1973): 28-36.

1319. Sutton, Arlene Vigil. "The Effects of the Bilingual Spanish/English Television Series 'Carrascolendas' on the Oral Language Skills of Selected Primary Children." Doctoral dissertation, University of Colorado, 1973.

1320. Lindsey, Peggy Jane. "A Study of the Effect of an Oral-Aural Language Program upon the Vocabulary Development of Bilingual and Bicultural Fourth-Grade Children." Master's thesis, University of Texas at El Paso, 1974.

1321. López, Sarah Jane Hudelson. "The Use of Context by Native Spanish Speaking Mexican-American Children When They Read Spanish." Doctoral dissertation, University of Texas, 1975.

3.4.6 Bilingualism

1322. Smith, Frank. "Bilingualism and Mental Development." *British Journal of Psychology* 13 (1921-1923): 271-82.
1323. Predmore, R.L. "Bilingualism and the First Year of School." Master's thesis, Rutgers University, 1931.
1324. Sánchez, George I. "Bilingualism and Mental Measures; A Word of Caution." In *Chicanos: Social and Psychological Perspectives,* pp. 232-36. Edited by Nathaniel L. Wagner and Marsha J. Haug. Saint Louis: The C.V. Mosby Company, 1971; reprint from: *Journal of Applied Psychology* 18, no. 6 (1934): 765-72.
1325. Pintner, Rudolf, and Arsenian, Seth. "The Relation of Bilingualism to Verbal Intelligence and School Adjustment." *Journal of Educational Research* 31, no. 4 (December 1937): 255-63.
1326. Seidl, Julius Carl Pfrorer. "The Effect of Bilingualism on Intelligence." Doctoral dissertation, Fordham University, 1937.
1327. Hoffman, Howardine G. "Bi-Lingualism and Oral and Written Expression of Fifth Grade Children." Master's thesis, University of Southern California, 1938.
1328. Marshall, M.V., and Phillips, R.H. "The Effect of Bilingualism upon College Grades." *Journal of Educational Research* 36 (October 1942): 131-32.
1329. Darcy, Natalie T. "The Effect of Bilingualism upon the Measurement of the Intelligence of Children of Preschool Age." Doctoral dissertation, Fordham University, 1945.
1330. Lynn, Klonda. "Bilingualism in the Southwest." *The Quarterly Journal of Speech* 31, no. 2 (April 1945): 175-80.
1331. Langley, Willard. "A Study of Bilingualism for the Purpose of Doing a Better Job in Understanding and Teaching Eighth Grade Spanish Speaking Children in Arizona." Master's thesis, Arizona State University, 1951.
1332. Darcy, Natalie T. "A Review of the Literature on the Effects of Bilingualism upon Measurement of Intelligence." *Journal of Genetic Psychology* 82 (March 1953): 21-57.
1333. Johnson, Granville B. "Bilingualism as Measured by a Reaction-Time Technique and the Relationship between a Language and Non-Language Intelligence Quotient." *Journal of Genetic Psychology* 82, no. 1 (March 1953): 3-9.
1334. Marx, Meyer. "The Problem of Bi-Lingualism among Spanish-Speaking Groups in the United States—A Review of the Literature. Project Report." Los Angeles: University of Southern California, August 1953.
1335. Wallace, Almina. "Bilingualism and Retardation." *Elementary English* 33 (May 1956): 303-4.
1336. Lambert, W.E.; Havelka, J.; and Crosby, C. "The Influence of Language-Acquisition Contexts on Bilingualism." *The Journal of Abnormal and Social Psychology* 56, no. 2 (March 1958): 239-44.
1337. Kittel, Jack E. "Bilingualism and Language and Non-Language Intelligence Scores of Third Grade Children." *Journal of Educational Research* 52 (1959): 263-68.
1338. Dudding, Christine. "An Investigation into the Bilingual Child's Comprehension of Antonyms." Master's thesis, University of New Mexico, 1960.

1339. Mercer, Veta Walker. "The Efficiency of the Bilingual Child in Understanding Analogies in the English Language." Master's thesis, University of New Mexico, 1960.

1340. Norman, Ralph D., and Mead, Donald F. "Spanish-American Bilingualism and the Ammons Full-Range Picture Vocabulary Test." *Journal of Social Psychology* 51, no. 2 (May 1960): 319-30.

1341. Schneider, A.A. *An Investigation of Bilingualism and Achievement in Reading in the Fourth Grade of the Parochial School System in the Archdiocese of Santa Fe, 1957-58.* Albuquerque: University of New Mexico Press, 1961.

1342. Jensen, J. Vernon. "Effects of Childhood Bilingualism." *Elementary English* 39, nos. 2, 4 (February, April 1962): 132- 43, 358-66.

1343. Johnson, Bruce Edward. "Ability, Achievement and Bilingualism: A Comparative Study Involving Spanish-Speaking and English-Speaking Children at the Sixth Grade Level." Doctoral dissertation, University of Maryland, 1962.

1344. Darcy, Natalie T. "Bilingualism and the Measurement of Intelligence: Review of a Decade of Research." *Journal of Genetic Psychology* 103, no. 2 (December 1963): 259-82.

1345. Sawyer, Janet Beck. *Social Aspects of Bilingualism in San Antonio, Texas.* University, Alabama: University of Alabama Press, 1964.

1346. Dimitrijevic, N.R. "Bilingual Child." *English Language Teaching* 20, no. 1 (October 1965): 23-28.

1347. Diebold, A.R., Jr. "The Consequences of Early Bilingualism in Cognitive Development and Personality Formation." Palo Alto, California: Stanford University, 1966.

1348. Gaarder, A. Bruce, et al. "Bilingualism: From the Viewpoint of the Administrator and Counselor." Paper presented at the annual conference of the Southwest Council of Foreign Language Teachers, El Paso, Texas, 4-5 November 1966. ERIC ED 018 286.

1349. Jacobs, John F., and Pierce, Marnell L. "Bilingualism and Creativity." *Elementary English* 43, no. 5 (May 1966): 499-503.

1350. Stubing, C., ed. *Bilingualism, Annual Conference of the Southwest Council of Foreign Language Teachers. Reports.* El Paso: Southwest Council of Foreign Language Teachers, 1966.

1351. Cervenka, Edward J. "The Measurement of Bilingualism and Biculturalism Socialization of the Child in the School Setting—The Development of Instruments. Section VI, Final Report on Head Start Evaluation and Research, 1966-1967, to the Institute for Educational Development." Austin: University of Texas at Austin, Child Development Evaluation and Research Center, 1967.

1352. Galvan, Robert R. "Bilingualism as It Relates to Intelligence Test Scores and School Achievement among Culturally Deprived Spanish-American Children." Doctoral dissertation, East Texas State University, 1967.

1353. Texas. Education Agency. *Addresses and Reports Presented at the Conference on Development of Bilingualism in Children in Varying Linguistic and Cultural Heritages,* by W.R. Goodson, ed. Austin: Texas Education Agency, 1967.

1354. Boyd, Dorothy L. "Bilingualism as an Educational Objective." *The Educational Forum* 32, no. 3 (March 1968): 309-13.

1355. Harding, Dee Anne. "A Comparative Analysis of the Relation of Bilingualism and Cultural Deprivation to Psycholinguistic Abilities in First, Second, and Third Grade Children." Master's thesis, University of California at Santa Barbara, 1968.

1356. Smith, Marguerite. "English as a Second Language for Mexican Americans." Paper presented at the National Conference on Educational Opportunities for Mexican Americans, Las Cruces, New Mexico, 1968. ERIC ED 016 560.

1357. U.S. Department of Health, Education, and Welfare. Office of Education. *The Influence of Bilingualism on Tested Verbal Ability in Spanish and English. Final Report,* by John E. Riley, Washington, D.C.: Government Printing Office, 7 June 1968. ERIC ED 026 935.

1358. Gaarder, A. Bruce. "Bilingualism." In *A Handbook for Teachers of Spanish and Portuguese,* pp. 149-72. Edited by Donald D. Walsh. Lexington, Massachusetts: D.C. Heath, 1969.

1359. Hittinger, Marsha S. "Bilingualism and Self-Identity." *Educational Leadership* 27, no. 3 (December 1969): 247-49.

1360. Lance, Donald M. "A Brief Study of Spanish-English Bilingualism: Final Report, Research Project ORR-Liberal Arts-15504." College Station, Texas: Texas A&M University, College of Liberal Arts, 25 August 1969. ERIC ED 032 529.

1361. Krear, Serafina E. "The Role of the Mother Tongue at Home and at School in the Development of Bilingualism." In *Chicanos: Social and Psychological Perspectives,* pp. 229-31. Edited by Nathaniel L. Wagner and Marsha J. Haug. Saint Louis: The C.V. Mosby Company, 1971; reprint from: *English Language Teaching* 24, no. 1 (October 1969): 2- 4.

1362. California. State Department of Education. *An Overview of Research on Bilingualism,* by Marie E. Taylor. Sacramento: California State Department of Education, 1970. ERIC ED 049 876.

1363. Gilbert, Glenn G., ed. *Texas Studies in Bilingualism: Spanish, French, German, Czech, Polish, Serbian, and Norwegian in the Southwest, With a Concluding Chapter on Code-Switching and Modes of Speaking in American Swedish.* Berlin: De Gruyter, 1970.

1364. Lance, Donald M. "The Code of the Spanish-English Bilingual." *TESOL* 4, no. 4 (December 1970): 343-51.

1365. Lugo, James Oscar. "A Comparison of Degrees of Bilingualism and Measure of School Achievement among Mexican-American Pupils." Doctoral dissertation, University of Southern California, 1970.

1366. Rouchdy, Aleya Aly. "A Case of Bilingualism: An Investigation in the Area of Lexical and Syntactic Interference in the Performance of the Bilingual Child." Doctoral dissertation, University of Texas at Austin, 1970.

1367. Carrow, Elizabeth. "Comprehension of English and Spanish by Preschool Mexican American Children." *Modern Language Journal* 55, no. 5 (May 1971): 299-306.

1368. Gingras, Rosario C. "A Critical Review of Standard Procedures for Studying Spanish-English Bilingualism." Los Alamitos, California: Southwest Regional Laboratory for Educational Research and Development, 5 April 1971. ERIC ED 110 206.

1369. Palmer, Michael B. "The Effects of Categorization, Degree of Bilingualism, and Language upon the Recall of Select Monolinguals and Bilinguals." Doctoral dissertation, Arizona State University, 1971.

1370. Rodríguez, Darío E. "Some Physiological and Educational Aspects of Bilingualism." *Aztlán* 2, no. 1 (spring 1971): 79-106.

1371. Timmins, Kathleen M. "An Investigation of the Relative Bilingualism of Spanish Surnamed Children in an Elementary School in Albuquerque." Doctoral dissertation, University of New Mexico, 1971.

1372. Carringer, Dennis Clyde. "The Relationship of Bilingualism to the Creative Thinking Abilities of Mexican Youth." Doctoral dissertation, University of Georgia, 1972.

1373. Hickey, Tom. "Bilingualism and the Measurement of Intelligence and Verbal Learning Ability." *Exceptional Child* 39, no. 1 (September 1972): 24-28.

1374. Penalosa, Fernando. "Chicano Multilingualism and Multiglossia." *Aztlán* 3, no. 2 (fall 1972): 215-22.

1375. Steiner, Violette G., and Zimmerman, Ira Lee. "Assessing Bilingual Language Ability in the Mexican-American Preschool Child." Paper presented at the annual convention of the Western Psychological Association, Portland, Oregon, 26-29 April, 1972. ERIC ED 073 831.

1376. Ulibarri, Horacio. "Bilingualism." In *ACTFL Review of Foreign Language Education*. Vol. 1: *Foreign Language Education: An Overview*, pp. 229-58. Edited by Emma M. Birkmaier. Skokie, Illinios: National Textbook Company, 1972.

1377. Van Duyne, John H., and Gutiérrez, George. "The Regulatory Function of Language in Bilingual Children." *Journal of Educational Research* 66, no. 3 (1972): 122-24.

1378. García, Ricardo L. "Bilingualism and Language Development: The Effect of the Mexican American's Bilingualism on His English Language Development." Manhattan, Kansas: Kansas State University, Institute on Cultural Understanding, 1973. ERIC ED 086 031.

1379. Hollomon, John Wesley. "Problems of Assessing Bilingualism in Children Entering School." Doctoral dissertation, University of New Mexico, 1973.

1380. Johnson, Nancy Ainsworth. "A Psycholinguistic Study of Bilingual Language Acquisition." Doctoral dissertation, University of Texas at Austin, 1973.

1381. Reyes, Donald J. "Another Look at Bilingualism." *Integrated Education* 11, no. 6 (November-December 1973): 27-28.

1382. Turner, Paul R., ed. *Bilingualism in the Southwest*. Tucson: University of Arizona Press, 1973. ERIC ED 104 133.

1383. García, Ricardo L. "Mexican American Bilingualism and English Language Development." *Journal of Reading* 17, no. 6 (March 1974): 467-73.

1384. Hoffer, Bates. "Bilingual Language Development and Bilingual Education." Mimeographed. In *Sociolinguistics in the Southwest*, pp. 81-90. Edited by Bates Hoffer and Jacob Ornstein. San Antonio, Texas: Trinity University, Department of English, 1974.

1385. Johnson, Nancy A. "Zombies and Other Problems: Theory and Method in Research on Bilingualism." *Language Learning* 24, no. 1 (June 1974): 105-33.

1386. Nelson, Charles Robert. "Effects of Bilingual Language Proficiency on Learning Achievement." Master's thesis, Texas A&I University at Kingsville, 1974.

1387. Trueba, Henry T. " 'Bilingualism in the Southwest': Review." *Research in the Teaching of English* 8, no. 1 (spring 1974): 69-74.

1388. García, Ricardo L. *Learning in Two Languages*. Bloomington, Indiana: Phi Delta Kappa Educational Foundation, 1976.

3.4.7 Testing

1389. Roca, Pablo. "A Study of a Test of Word-Relations for Spanish-Speaking Children." Master's thesis, University of Texas at Austin, 1948.

1390. Rose, Anna Augusta. "Testing the Vocabulary of the Pre-Primer Spanish-Speaking Child." Master's thesis, Southwest Texas State University, 1950.

1391. Chenault, Vivian Margaret. "A Study of the Cooperative Inter-American Tests of General Ability and Reading at the Primary Level." Master's thesis, University of Texas at Austin, 1951.

1392. Lado, R. "Measurement in English as a Foreign Language with Special Reference to Spanish-Speaking Adults." Doctoral dissertation, University of Michigan, 1951.

1393. Nichols, Paul Edward. "A Study of the Cooperative Inter-American Tests of Language Usage at the Junior High School Level." Master's thesis, University of Texas at Austin, 1952.

1394. Rea, George Harold. "A Study of Four Cooperative Inter-American Tests." Master's thesis, University of Texas at Austin, 1954.

1395. Manuel, Herschel T. *The Preparation of and Evaluation of Inter-Language Testing Materials.* Austin: University of Texas Press, 1963.

1396. Jameson, Gloria Ruth. "The Development of a Phonemic Analysis for an Oral English Proficiency Test for Spanish-Speaking School Beginners." Doctoral dissertation, University of Texas at Austin, 1967.

1397. U.S. Department of Health, Education, and Welfare. Office of Education. Division of Higher Education Research. Language Research Section. *The Measurement and Description of Language Dominance in Bilinguals. Third Progress Report,* by Joshua A. Fishman. Washington, D.C.: Government Printing Office, 1967.

1398. Arnold, Richard D. "Reliability Coefficients of Certain Tests Used in the San Antonio Language Research Project." Directed by Thomas D. Horn. Austin: University of Texas at Austin; San Antonio: San Antonio Language Research Project, February 1968.

1399. Fowler, Elaine D. "An Evaluation of the Brengelman-Manning Linguistic Capacity Index as a Predictor of Reading Achievement of Spanish-Speaking First-Grade Children." Doctoral dissertation, University of Texas at Austin, 1968.

1400. Mycue, Elena Inez de Los Santos. "Testing in Spanish and the Subsequent Measurement of English Fluency." Master's thesis, Texas Woman's University, 1968. ERIC ED 026 193.

1401. U.S. Department of Health, Education, and Welfare. Office of Education. *Predicting Pronunciation and Listening Skills of Native Speakers of Spanish. Speaking Exploratory Study,* by J. Donald Ragsdale. Washington, D.C.: Government Printing Office, March 1968. ERIC ED 020 516.

1402. Card, Judy A . "A Study of Some Oral Language Test Instrument Variables Concerning Mexican American Bilingual Children." Master's thesis, University of Texas at Austin, 1970.

1403. Natalicio, Diana S., and Williams, Frederick. "What Characteristics Can 'Experts' Reliably Evaluate in the Speech of Black and Mexican-American Children?" *TESOL Quarterly* 6, no. 2 (June 1972): 121-27.

1404. Toronto, Allen Sharp. "A Developmental Spanish Language Analysis Procedure for Spanish-Speaking Children." Doctoral dissertation, Northwestern University, 1972.

1405. Zirkel, Perry A. "A Method for Determining and Depicting Language Dominance." *TESOL Quarterly* 8, no. 1 (March 1974): 7-16.

1406. Randle, Janice Ann Whitehead. "A Bilingual Oral Language Test for Mexican-American Children." Doctoral dissertation, University of Texas at Austin, 1975.

1407. Silverman, Robert J., et al. *Oral Language Tests for Bilingual Students: An Evaluation of Language Dominance and Proficiency Instruments.* Portland, Oregon: Northwest Regional Educational Laboratory, 1976.

1408. Yeh, Mary C.L. "The Issues in the Measurement of Bilingual Language Dominance." Paper presented at the annual meeting of the American Educational Research Association, 60th, San Francisco, California, 19-23 April 1976. ERIC ED 121 853.

3.5 Intelligence

1409. Brown, G.L. "Intelligence as Related to Nationality." *Journal of Educational Research* 5 (1921): 324-27.

1410. Coxe, Warren W. "School Variation in General Intelligence." *Journal of Educational Research* 4, no. 3 (October 1921): 187-94.

1411. Berry, Charles S. "The Classification by Tests of Intelligence of Ten Thousand First Grade Pupils." *Journal of Educational Research* 6 (October 1922): 185-203.

1412. Pintner, Rudolf, and Keller, Ruth. "Intelligence Tests of Foreign Children." *Journal of Educational Psychology* 13, no. 4 (April 1922): 214-22.

1413. Texas. Education Agency. Educational Survey Commission. *A Comparative Study of the Performance of White, Mexican, and Negro School Children in Certain Standard Intelligence Tests,* by Helen L. Koch and Rietta Simmons. Austin: Texas Education Agency, 1925.

1414. Koch, Helen L., and Simmons, Rietta. "A Study of the Test Performance of American, Mexican, and Negro Children." *Psychological Monographs* 35, no. 5 (1926): 1-166.

1415. Coon, Mary W. "The Language Difficulty in Measuring the Intelligence of Spanish American Students." Master's thesis, University of New Mexico, 1927.

1416. Flores, Zella K. Jordan. "The Relation of Language Difficulty to Intelligence and School Retardation in a Group of Spanish-Speaking Children." Master's thesis, University of Chicago, 1927.

1417. Delmet, Don T. "A Study of the Mental and Scholastic Abilities of Mexican Children in the Elementary Schools." Master's thesis, University of Southern California, 1928.

1418. Garth, Thomas R. "The Intelligence of Mexican School Children." *School and Society* 27 (30 June 1928): 791-94.

1419. Hughes, Lois S. "A Comparative Study of the Intelligence of Mexican and Non-Mexican Children." Master's thesis, University of Texas at Austin, 1928.

1420. Randals, Edwyna Henrietta. "A Comparison of the Intelligence Test Results of Mexican and Negro Children in Two Elementary Schools." Master's thesis, University of Southern California, 1929.

1421. Sirkin, M. "The Relation between Intelligence, Age, and Home Environment of Elementary School Pupils." *School and Society* 30 (31 August 1929): 304-8.

1422. Brigham, Carl C. "Intelligence Tests of Immigrant Groups." *Psychological Review* 37 (March 1930): 158-65.

1423. Hanson, Edith Josephine. "A Study of Intelligence Test Results for Mexican Children Based on English and Mexican Test Forms." Master's thesis, University of Southern California, 1931.

1424. Page, Dorothy. "Performance of Spanish American Children on Verbal and Non-Verbal Intelligence Tests." Master's thesis, University of New Mexico, 1931.

1425. Davenport, E. Lee. "Intelligence Quotients of Mexican and Non-Mexican Siblings." *School and Society* 36 (3 September 1932): 304-6.

1426. González, Aurora Marjorie. "A Study of the Intelligence of Mexican Children in Relation to Their Socio-Economic Status." Master's thesis, University of Texas at Austin, 1932.

1427. Jones, H.E., et al. *Environmental Handicap in Mental Test Performance.* Berkeley: University of California Press, 1932.

1428. Manuel, Herschel T., and Hughes, Lois S. "The Intelligence and Drawing Ability of Young Mexican Children." *Journal of Applied Psychology* 16, no. 4 (1932): 382-87.

1429. Garth, Thomas R., and Johnson, Harper D. "The Intelligence and Achievement of Mexican Children in the United States." *Journal of Abnormal and Social Psychology* 29, no. 2 (1934): 222-29.

1430. Sánchez, George I. "The Implications of a Basal Vocabulary to the Measurement of the Abilities of Bilingual Children." *Journal of Social Psychology* 5, no. 3 (1934): 395-402.

1431. Senour, A.C. "Necessity for Use of a Non-Language Mental Test in Group Intelligence Testing." *Journal of Educational Research* 27 (February 1934): 435-41.

1432. Manuel, Herschel T. "Spanish and English Editions of the Stanford-Binet in Relation to the Abilities of Mexican Children." *The University of Texas Bulletin,* no. 3532 (22 August 1935).

1433. Garth, Thomas R.; Elson, Thomas H.; and Marton, Margaret M. "The Administration of Non-Language Intelligence Tests to Mexicans." *Journal of Abnormal and Social Psychology* 31 (1936/1937): 53-58.

1434. Hill, Harry Segner. "Resemblance of Bilingual Siblings in Verbal Intelligence." *School and Society* 43 (22 February 1936): 271-72.

1435. Merryweather, Rose. "A Study of the Comparative Ability of the Mexican and American Children in the Upper Elementary Grades." Master's thesis, University of Southern California, 1937.

1436. Mitchell, A.J. "The Effect of Bilingualism in the Measurement of Intelligence." *Elementary School Journal* 28, no. 1 (September 1937): 29-37.

1437. Cox, L.M. "Analysis of the Intelligence of Sub-Normal Negro, Mexican and White Children." Master's thesis, University of Southern California, 1938.

1438. Chauncey, Marlin R. "The Relation of the Home Factor to Achievement and Intelligence Test Scores." *Journal of Educational Research* 20 (September 1939): 88-90.

1439. Mahakian, Charles. "Measuring Intelligence and Reading Capacity of Spanish-Speaking Children." *Elementary School Journal* 39, no. 10 (June 1939): 760-68.

1440. Bayley, Nancy. *Factors Influencing the Growth of Intelligence in Young Children. Its Nature and Nurture, Part 2, Original Studies and Experiments.* Bloomington, Illinois: Public School Publishing Company, 1940.

1441. Cattell, Raymond B. "A Culture-Free Intelligence Test I." *Journal of Educational Psychology* 31, no. 3 (March 1940): 161-79.

1442. Fussell, William D. "Comparable Norms for Anglo and Latin American Pupils on a Scholastic Aptitude Test." Master's thesis, University of Texas at Austin, 1940.

1443. Holder, Helen Lee. "Family Resemblances in the Intelligence Quotients of Mexican Children and Their Socio-Economic Status." Master's thesis, Southwest Texas State University, 1940.

1444. Michea, Claude Angus. "The Intelligence of Nine and Ten Year Old Mexican Children as Measured by the Leiter International Performance Scale." Master's thesis, University of California, 1941.

1445. Carlson, Hilding B., and Henderson, Norman. "The Intelligence of American Children of Mexican Parentage." *Journal of Abnormal and Social Psychology* 45, no. 3 (July 1945): 544-51.

1446. Wilhauk, Ralph Clyde. "A Study of Inter-American Tests in Relation to the Stanford-Binet Tests." Master's thesis, University of Texas at Austin, 1946.

1447. Henderson, Norman B. "A Study of Intelligence of Children of Mexican and Non-Mexican Parentage." Doctoral dissertation, Occidental College, 1948.

1448. Altus, William D., and Clark, Jerry H. "The Effect of Adjustment Patterns upon the Intercorrelation of Intelligence Subtest Variables." *Journal of Social Psychology* 30, no. 1 (August 1949): 39-48.

1449. Goulard, Lowell Jack. "A Study of the Intelligence of Eleven and Twelve Year Old Mexicans by Means of the Leiter Inter-National Performance Scale." Master's thesis, University of Southern California, 1949.

1450. Munson, John. "Intelligence Rating for Ninety-Seven Mexican Children in St. Paul, Minnesota." Doctoral dissertation, University of Minnesota, 1950.

1451. Cook, John M., and Arthur, Grace. "Intelligence Rating of 97 Mexican-American Children in St. Paul, Minnesota." *Journal of Exceptional Children* 18, no. 1 (1951): 14-15 +.

1452. Jiménez, Carmina A. "Performances on English and Spanish Editions of the Stanford-Binet by Spanish-American Children." Master's thesis, University of New Mexico, 1951.

1453. Pasamanick, Benjamin. "The Intelligence of American Children of Mexican Parentage: A Discussion of Uncontrolled Variables." *Journal of Abnormal and Social Psychology* 46, no. 4 (October 1951): 598-602.

1454. Altus, Grace T. "WISC Patterns of a Selective Sample of Bilingual School Children." *Journal of Genetic Psychology* 83, no. 4 (December 1953): 241-48.

1455. Keston, Morton J., and Jiménez, Carmina A. "A Study of the Performance on English and Spanish Editions of the Stanford-Binet Intelligence Test by Spanish-American Children." *Journal of Genetic Psychology* 85, no. 4 (December 1954): 263-69.

1456. Nathan, Jerome M. "The Relationship of English Language Deficiency to Intelligence Test Scores of Mentally Retarded Mexican American Children." Master's thesis, University of California at Los Angeles, 1955.

1457. Roca, Pablo. "Problems of Adapting Intelligence Scales from One Culture to Another." *High School Journal* 38, no. 4 (January 1955): 124-31.

1458. Roden, Paula. "A Study of the Relationships among Various Intelligence Tests and Reading Test Results Obtained with Latin American Second Grade Children." Master's thesis, University of Texas at Austin, 1955.

1459. Knapp, Robert R. "The Effects of Time Limits on the Intelligence Test Performance of Mexican and American Subjects." *Journal of Educational Psychology* 51, no. 1 (February 1960): 14-20.

1460. Kittel, Jack E. "Intelligence-Test Performance of Children from Bilingual Environments." *Elementary School Journal* 64, no. 2 (November 1963): 76-83.

1461. Manuel, Herschel T. *Tests of General Ability and Reading, Inter-American Series.* Austin: University of Texas Press, 1963.

1462. Palomares, Uvaldo Hill. "A Critical Analysis of the Research on the Intellectual Evaluation of Mexican-American Children." Los Angeles: University of Southern California, School of Education, May 1965. ERIC ED 027 097.

1463. Rozynko, Vitali, and Wenk, Ernest. "Intellectual Performance of Three Delinquent Groups of Different Ethnic Origin." *Journal of Consulting Psychology* 29, no. 3 (June 1965): 282.

1464. Bransford, Louis A. "A Comparative Investigation of Verbal and Performance Intelligence Measures at Different Age Levels with Bilingual Spanish-Speaking Children in Special Classes for the Mentally Retarded." Doctoral dissertation, Colorado State College, 1966.

1465. Henderson, Ronald Wilbur. "Environmental Stimulation and Intellectual Development of Mexican-American Children: An Exploratory Study." Doctoral dissertation, University of Arizona, 1966.

1466. Palomares, Uvaldo Hill, and Johnson, Laverne C. "Evaluation of Mexican American Pupils for EMR Classes." *California Education* 3 (April 1966): 27-29.

1467. Messeneo, Joseph F. "The Environmental Utilization of Psycholinguistic Abilities of Disadvantaged Slow Learners in Relation to the Ecology of Test Intelligence." Doctoral dissertation, University of Rochester, 1967.

1468. Rieber, Morton, and Womack, Marceleete. "The Intelligence of Preschool Children as Related to Ethnic and Demographic Variables." In *Chicanos: Social and Psychological Perspectives,* pp. 237-43. Edited by Nathaniel L. Wagner and Marsha J. Haug. Saint Louis: The C.V. Mosby Company, 1971; reprint from: *Exceptional Children* 34, no. 4 (1968): 609-14.

1469. Vogler, James Donald. "The Influence of Ethnicity and Socio-Economic Status on the Pictorial Test of Intelligence." Doctoral dissertation, University of Arizona, 1968.

1470. Jensen, Arthur R. "Intelligence, Learning Ability and Socio-Economic Status." *Journal of Special Education* 3, no. 1 (1969): 23-35.

1471. Anderson, Gordon V., and Anderson, H.T. "Comparison of Performance on a Mental Ability Test of English Speaking and Spanish Speaking Children in Grades Two and Three. A Study." 1970. ERIC ED 090 335.

1472. Leary, Mary Ellen. "Children Who Are Tested in an Alien Language: Mentally Retarded?" *New Republic* 162, no. 22 (30 May 1970): 17-18.

1473. Simpson, Robert L. "Study of the Comparability of the WISC and the WAIS." *Journal of Consulting and Clinical Psychology* 34, no. 2 (April 1970): 156-58.

1474. Killian, L.R. "WISC, Illinois Test of Psycholinguistic Abilities and Bender Visual-Motor Gestalt Test Performance of Spanish-American Kindergarten and First-Grade School Children." *Journal of Consulting and Clinical Psychology* 37, no. 1 (August 1971): 38-43.

1475. Price, James David. "Analysis of Changes in Intelligence Test Scores of Mexican-American Youth Assigned to Special Classes in Relation to Jensen's Two-Level Theory of Mental Abilities." Doctoral dissertation, University of Arizona, 1971.

1476. Swanson, Elinor Naumann, and DeBlassie, Richard. "Interpreter Effects on the WISC Performance of Mexican-American Children." *Measurement and Evaluation in Guidance* 4, no. 3 (October 1971): 172-75.

1477. Armstrong, Roy Anthony. "Test Bias from the Non-Anglo Viewpoint: A Critical Evaluation of Intelligence Test Items by Members of Three Cultural Minorities." Doctoral dissertation, University of Arizona, 1972.

1478. García, John. "IQ: The Conspiracy." *Psychology Today* 6, no. 4 (September 1972): 40, 42-43, 92, 94.

1479. Mercer, Jane R. "IQ: The Lethal Label." *Psychology Today* 6, no. 4 (September 1972): 44, 46-47, 95-96.

1480. Ramírez, Manuel, III, and González, Alex. "Mexican Americans and Intelligence Testing." In *La Causa Chicana: The Movement for Justice*, pp. 137-47. Edited by Margaret M. Mangold. New York: Family Service Association of America, 1972.

1481. Jensen, Arthur R. "Level I and Level II Abilities in Three Ethnic Groups." Berkeley: University of California at Berkeley, 1973. ERIC ED 080 646.

1482. Meeker, Mary, and Meeker, Robert. "Strategies for Assessing Intellectual Patterns in Black, Anglo, and Mexican American Boys—Or Any Other Children—And Implications for Education." *Journal of School Psychology* 11, no. 4 (1973): 341-50.

1483. Schroth, Marvin L. "The Use of IQ as a Measure of Learning Rate with Minority Children. Final Report." Santa Clara, California: Santa Clara University, May 1973. ERIC ED 080 590.

1484. Benson, Gerald P., and Kuipers, Judith L. "Personality Correlates of Intellectual Performance among Head Start Children." 1974. ERIC ED 097 121.

1485. de Avila, Edward A., and Havassy, Barbara. *Intelligence of Mexican American Children: A Field Study Comparing Neo-Piagetian and Traditional Capacity and Achievement Measures.* Austin, Texas: Education Service Center Region 13, January 1974. ERIC ED 106 042.

1486. de Avila, Edward A., and Havassy, Barbara. "Testing of Minority Children—A Neo-Piagetian Approach." *Today's Education* 63, no. 4 (1974): 72-75.

1487. Henzlik, Wilma Louise Bartels. "A Comparison of Migrant and Ex-Migrant Mexican-American Children on Locus-of-Control, Intelligence Test Performance, Self-Concept, and Personality." Doctoral dissertation, Purdue University, 1974.

1488. Milne, Nidia Dora Moreno. "Relationships among Scores Obtained on the Wechsler Intelligence Scale for Children, Columbia Mental Maturity Scale and Leiter International Performance Scale by Mexican-American Children." Doctoral dissertation, Texas Woman's University, 1974.

1489. Swanson, Elinor Naumann. "Interpreter and Spanish Administration Effects on the WISC Performance of Mexican-American Children." Doctoral dissertation, New Mexico State University, 1975.

1490. U.S. Department of Health, Education, and Welfare. Office of Education. *Item Analyses of Amerindian and Chicano Responses on the Vocabulary Scales of the Stanford, Binet LM and Wechsler Batteries. Final Report,* by Clark I. Guilliams. Washington, D.C.: Government Printing Office, 1975. ERIC ED 111 878.

3.6 Achievement

3.6.1 General

1491. Drake, Rollen H. *A Comparative Study of the Mentality and Achievement of Mexican and White Children.* San Francisco: R and E Research Associates, 1972; master's thesis, University of Southern California, 1927.

1492. Peak, George Joseph. "Relative Achievement of English Speaking and Spanish Speaking." Master's thesis, University of Arizona, 1931.

1493. Sánchez, George I. "A Study of the Scores of Spanish Speaking Children on Repeated Tests." Master's thesis, University of Texas at Austin, 1931.

1494. Cobb, Wilbur K. "Retardation in Elementary Schools of Children of Migratory Laborers in Ventura County, California." Master's thesis, University of Southern California, 1932.

1495. Kelsey, Ruth. "The Comparison of Scholastic Standing among Children of Native Born Parents with Children of Foreign Parents." Master's thesis, University of Denver, 1932.

1496. Caldwell, Floyd F., and Mowry, Mary D. "Teachers' Grades as Criteria of Achievement of Bilingual Children." *Journal of Applied Psychology* 18, no. 3 (1934): 288-92.

1497. Hogan, Milo Arthur Van Norman. "A Study of the School Progress of Mexican Children in Imperial County." Master's thesis, University of Southern California, 1934.

1498. Coers, Walter C. "Comparative Achievement of White and Mexican Junior High School Pupils." *Peabody Journal of Education* 12, no. 4 (January 1935): 157-62.

1499. Coan, Barlett E. "A Comparative Study of the American and Mexican Children in the 'Big Bend' Area for 1935-36." Master's thesis, University of Texas at Austin, 1936.

1500. Finney, Gladys Cline. "A Comparative Study of the Relative Achievement of English and Spanish Transient and Non-Transient Sixth Grade Groups." Master's thesis, University of Arizona, 1936.

1501. Kensey, Lura. "A Comparison of the Achievement of American and Mexican Seventh and Eighth Grade Pupils." Master's thesis, University of Arizona, 1936.

1502. McLennan, LeRoy. "A Comparison of the Spanish-Speaking and English-Speaking Children in Nine Schools over a Five-Year-Period." Master's thesis, University of Texas at Austin, 1936.

1503. Smith, J.B., Jr. "A Survey of Pupil Failure in the La Feria School with Suggested Remedial Measures." Master's thesis, University of Texas at Austin, 1939.

1504. Browning, Horace Noel. "A Comparison of the Spanish-Speaking and English-Speaking Children in Nine Schools over a Four-Year Period." Master's thesis, University of Texas at Austin, 1944.

1505. Yarbrough, C.L. "Age-Grade Status of Texas Children of Latin-American Descent." *Journal of Educational Research* 40, no. 1 (September 1946): 14-27.

1506. Hart, Robert Newton. "A Comparison of the Academic Achievements of Mexican American Children with Those of Anglo American Children in the Fourth, Fifth, and Sixth Grades of Chino Elementary Schools." Master's thesis, Claremont Graduate School, 1949.

1507. McLean, Robert Jack. "A Comparative Study of the Anglo-American and Spanish-Name Children in the Austin Public Schools over a Seven-Year Period." Master's thesis, University of Texas at Austin, 1950.

1508. Rock, Beryl. "Children's Achievement in the Amanda Burks Elementary School, 1937 to 1951." Master's thesis, University of Texas at Austin, 1951.

1509. Jackson, Doris Elaine. "Educational Status of Mexican Children in a Texas Elementary School." Master's thesis, University of Texas at Austin, 1952.

1510. U.S. Department of Labor. Wage and Hour and Public Contracts Division. *Study of Educational Achievement of a Group of Children Working in Agriculture during School Hours, October-December, 1951.* Washington, D.C.: Government Printing Office, 1952.

1511. Atkinson, Rosa M. "The Educational Retardation of the Spanish Speaking Child and Recommendation for Remediation." Master's thesis, University of Texas at Austin, 1953.

1512. Kilfoyle, John Grant. "Educational Differences of Mexican American Children." Master's thesis, University of Utah, 1955.

1513. Clark, George. "A Study of the Achievement of the Spanish-Speaking Child." Master's thesis, University of Texas at Austin, 1956.

1514. Martínez, Domingo. "A Comparative Study of the Academic Achievement of the Mexican American Students in the Wilson Junior High School, Oxnard, California." Master's thesis, Claremont Graduate School, 1956.

1515. Ynigo, Alexander. *Mexican-American Children in an Integrated Elementary School: An Investigation of Their Academic Performance and Social Adjustment.* San Francisco: R & E Research Associates, 1974; master's thesis, University of Southern California, 1957.

1516. Brady, Fay Alyeen. "A Study of the Scholastic Achievement of Migrant and Permanent-Resident Students." Master's thesis, University of Texas at Austin, 1958.

1517. Henderson, Stanley S. "Social and Academic Problems of Spanish-Speaking Students in Davis County, Central Junior High School." Master's thesis, University of Utah, 1958.

1518. Mitchell, Q.B. "Comparative Achievements of White, Mexican and Colored Children in Elementary Public School." Master's thesis, University of Kansas, 1959.

1519. Stevens, Deon Orlo. "A Status Study of a Group of Mexican-American Children in Elementary School." Master's thesis, University of Utah, 1962.

1520. Bishop, Russell Harold. "A Status Study of Spanish-Speaking Students at Midvale Junior High School." Master's thesis, University of Utah, 1964.

1521. Donahue, Mary P. "A Suggested Plan for Improving Academic Achievement of Mexican-American Students in a Specific High School." Doctoral dissertation, University of Southern California, 1965.

1522. Jacobson, Lenore Francis. "Explorations of Variations in Educational Achievement among Mexican Children, Grades One to Six." Doctoral dissertation, University of California at Berkeley, 1966.

1523. McDowell, Neil Allen. "A Status Study of the Academic Capabilities and Achievements of Three Ethnic Groups: Anglo, Negro, and Spanish Surname, in San Antonio, Texas." Doctoral dissertation, University of Texas at Austin, 1966. ERIC ED 049 861.

1524. Lewis, Eva Pearl. "A Comparison of the Academic Achievement of Head Start Pupils with Non-Head Start Pupils." Doctoral dissertation, Northern Texas State University, 1967.

1525. Palomares, Uvaldo. "Assessment of Rural Mexican-American Students in Grades Pre-School through Twelfth." 29 April 1967. ERIC ED 013 690.

1526. U.S. Department of Health, Education, and Welfare. National Center for Educational Statistics. *Educational Achievement among Mexican-Americans—A Special Report from the Educational Opportunities Survey. Working Paper,* by George W. Mayeske. Washington, D.C.: Government Printing Office, 19 January 1967.

1527. California. State Department of Education. *Assessment of Rural Mexican-American Pupils, Preschool and Grades One through Six, San Ysidro, California,* by Uvaldo H. Palomares and Emery J. Cummins. Sacramento: California State Department of Education, April 1968. ERIC ED 020 845.

1528. California. State Department of Education. *Assessment of Rural Mexican-American Pupils, Preschool and Grades One through Twelve, Wasco, California,* by Uvaldo H. Palomares and Emery J. Cummins. Sacramento: California State Department of Education, April 1968. ERIC ED 020 846.

1529. Gordon, C. Wayne, et al. "Educational Achievement and Aspirations of Mexican-American Youth in a Metropolitan Context." Los Angeles: University of California at Los Angeles, October 1968. ERIC ED 028 012.

1530. Melaragno, Ralph J., and Newmark, Gerald. *A Pilot Study to Apply Evaluation-Revision Procedures in First-Grade Mexican-American Classrooms. Final Report. Technical Memorandum Series.* Santa Monica, California: System Development Corporation, 17 May 1968. ERIC ED 026 170.

1531. Dreyer, Harold B., et al. "A Study of Ability and Academic Achievement Levels of Mexican-American Children Ages Four through Eight in Selected Summer Migrant Programs in Minnesota and North Dakota." Minnesota: Mankato State College, 1969. ERIC ED 037 270.

1532. Gallegos, Ruben. "A Comparative Study of Achievement and Adjustment of Mexican-American Migrant and Non-Migrant Children in the Elementary School." Doctoral dissertation, East Texas State University, 1970.

1533. U.S. Department of Health, Education, and Welfare. National Institute of Mental Health, Alcohol, Drug Abuse, and Mental Health Administration. *Programmed Reinforcement in the Classroom: The Effects of Tangible and Social Rewards on the Educational Achievement of Mexican-American and Black Children. Final Report, NIMH Grant MH-14497, 1970,* by Robert C. Day and Bruce A. Chadwick. Washington, D.C.: Government Printing Office, 1970.

1534. Connecticut. State Department of Education. *The Academic Achievement of Spanish-Speaking First Graders in Connecticut,* by Perry Alan Zirkel. Hartford: Connecticut State Department of Education, April 1971. ERIC ED 054 275.

1535. Karadenes, Mark. "A Comparison of Differences in Achievement and Learning Abilities between Anglo and Mexican-American Children When the Two Groups Are Equated by Intelligence." Doctoral dissertation, University of Virginia, 1971.

1536. Killian, L.R. "Cognitive Test Performance of Spanish-American Primary School Children: A Longitudinal Study. Final Study." Kent, Ohio: Kent State University, November 1971. ERIC ED 060 156.

1537. Luke, Douglas Bowen. "Academic and Social Differences Study between Mexican and Non-Mexican Students at Layton High School." Master's thesis, University of Utah, 1971.

1538. Wolfson, Sara Crawford. "A Comparative Study of the Prediction of Academic Achievement of Anglo-American, Mexican-American and Negro Students in Junior High School." Doctoral dissertation, University of Houston, 1971.

1539. Turner, Paul R. "Academic Performance of Mexican-Americans." *Integrated Education* 11, no. 3 (May 1973): 3-6.

1540. Bianchini, John C., and Loret, Peter G. "Anchor Test Study. Final Report. Volume 18, Subgroup Equating Tables. Spanish Surnamed Children, Grades 4, 5, and 6." Berkeley, California: Educational Testing Service, 1974. ERIC ED 092 619.

1541. Levario, Matthew. "Difference in Achievement among Three Groups of Mexican-American Children Having Different Linguistic Backgrounds." Doctoral dissertation, University of Arizona, 1974.

1542. López, Rodolfo S., and Piper, Richard. "The Mexican-American Child Evaluation Report, 1973-74." Los Angeles, California: Hispanic Urban Center, 1974. ERIC ED 097 169.

. McGuigan, Donald Edward. "Academic Underachievement of Mexican-American Secondary Students." Doctoral dissertation, University of California at Los Angeles, 1976.

3.6.2 Factors

1544. Garretson, Oliver K. "Causes of Retardation of Mexican Children in American Schools." Master's thesis, University of Texas at Austin, 1926.
1545. Taylor, M.C. "Retardation of Mexican Children in the Albuquerque Schools." Master's thesis, Stanford University, 1927.
1546. Garretson, Oliver K. "A Study of the Causes of Retardation among Mexican Children in a Small Public School System in Arizona." *Journal of Educational Psychology* 19, no. 1 (January 1928): 31-40.
1547. Ellis, Christine Evangeline. "The Relation of Socio-Economic Status to the Intellectual and School Success of Mexican Children." Master's thesis, University of Texas at Austin, 1932.
1548. Caldwell, Floyd F., and Mowry, Mary Davis. "Sex Difference in School Achievement among Spanish-American and Anglo-American Children." *Journal of Educational Sociology* 8, no. 3 (November 1934): 168-73.
1549. Mendenhall, W. C. "A Comparative Study of Achievement and Ability of the Children in Two Segregated Mexican Schools." Master's thesis, University of Southern California, 1937.
1550. Cornelius, John Scott. "The Effects of Certain Changes of Curriculum and Methods on the School Achievement of Mexican Children in a Segregated School." Master's thesis, University of Southern California, 1941.
1551. Cromer, Sturgeon. "Transiency and Its Effect upon the Progress of Pupils. . . ." Master's thesis, University of Arizona, 1941.
1552. Dailey, Mauryne Phelps. "A Study of Achievement in Spanish in Relation to Intelligence and Other Traits." Master's thesis, University of Texas at Austin, 1942.
1553. González de los Santos, María de Jesús. "Factors Affecting the Education of Twenty-Five Migrant Spanish-Speaking Children." Master's thesis, University of Texas at Austin, 1951.
1554. Villarreal, Dora. "Relationships between Over-Ageness and Scholastic Achievement." Master's thesis, University of Texas at Austin, 1951.
1555. Smith, Alva Louis. "A Comparative Study of the Facts and Factors Affecting and Effecting the Retardation of Bilingual Pupils." Master's thesis, University of Texas at Austin, 1952.
1556. Whitehead, James E. "Socio-Economic Background as Related to School Readiness and Subsequent Achievement of First-Grade Pupils." Master's thesis, University of Texas at Austin, 1954.
1557. Chernosky, Adelma Shirley. "Educational Enrichment of Spanish Speaking Children in the Third Grade and Its Effect upon Intelligence and Achievement Test Scores." Master's thesis, University of Texas at Austin, 1955.
1558. McNiel, Guy Brett. "A Pre-First-Grade Oral-English Program as Related to the Scholastic Achievement of Spanish-Speaking Children." Doctoral dissertation, University of Colorado, 1958.
1559. Deutsch, M. *Minority Group and Class Status as Related to Social and Personality Factors in Scholastic Achievement.* Ithaca, New York: Society for Applied Anthropology, 1960.

1560. Móntez, Philip. *Some Differences in Factors Related to Educational Achievement of Two Mexican-American Groups*. San Francisco: R and E Research Associates, 1974; doctoral dissertation, University of Southern California, 1960.

1561. Cline, Marion, Jr. "Achievement of Bilinguals in Seventh Grade by Socioeconomic Levels." Doctoral dissertation, University of Southern California, 1961.

1562. Gill, Lois J. "Some Non-Intellectual Factors Related to the Academic Achievement of Spanish-American Secondary School Students." Doctoral dissertation, University of Denver, 1961.

1563. Marcoux, Fred Wesley. *Handicaps of Bilingual Mexican Children*. San Francisco: R and E Research Associates, 1973; master's thesis, University of Southern California, 1961.

1564. Gill, Lois J., and Spilka, B. "Some Non-Intellectual Correlates of Academic Achievement among Mexican American Secondary School Students." *Journal of Educational Psychology* 53, no. 3 (June 1962): 144-49.

1565. Hobart, Charles W. "Underachievement among Minority Group Students: An Analysis and a Proposal." *Phylon* 24, no. 2 (summer 1963): 184-96.

1566. Caplan, Stanley W., and Ruble, Ronald A. "Study of Culturally Imposed Factors on School Achievement in a Metropolitan Area." *Journal of Educational Research* 58, no. 1 (September 1964): 16-21.

1567. Metessel, Newton S. "An Investigation of Attitudinal and Creativity Factors Related to Achieving and Nonachieving Culturally Disadvantaged Youth. Project Potential Preliminary Documentation, Vol. 1." Los Angeles: University of Southern California, 15 August 1965. ERIC ED 012 741.

1568. Spilka, Bernard, and Gill, Lois J. "Some Nonintellectual Correlates of Academic Achievement among Spanish-American Students." *School Counselor* 12, no. 4 (May 1965): 218-21.

1569. MacMillan, Robert Wilson. "A Study of the Effect of Socioeconomic Factors on the School Achievement of Spanish-Speaking School Beginners." Doctoral dissertation, University of Texas at Austin, 1966. ERIC ED 049 864.

1570. Morper, Jack. "An Investigation of the Relationship of Certain Predictive Variables and Academic Achievement of Spanish-American and Anglo Pupils in Junior High School." Doctoral dissertation, Oklahoma State University, 1966.

1571. Steen, Margaret Trotter. "The Effects of Immediate and Delayed Reinforcement on the Achievement Behavior of Mexican-American Children of Low Socioeconomic Status." Doctoral dissertation, Stanford University, 1966.

1572. Barberio, Ricky. "The Relationship between Achievement Motivation and Ethnicity in Anglo-American and Mexican-American Junior High School Students." *Psychological Record* 17, no. 2 (January-October 1967): 263-66.

1573. Davies, Walter L. "A Comparative Study of the Performance of Pupils from Low, High and Economically Diversified Socio-Economic Areas on Test Items from a Social Studies Achievement Battery." Doctoral dissertation, University of Kansas, 1967.

1574. Eitelgeorge, Charles William. "A Study to Compare the Self-Concept Ratings with the Achievement Scores of Mexican-American and Caucasian Pupils." Master's thesis, Sacramento State College, 1967.

1575. Fennessey, James. "An Exploratory Study of Non-English Speaking Homes and Academic Performance." Baltimore: Johns Hopkins University, May 1967. ERIC ED 011 613.

1576. Philippus, M.J. "Test Prediction of School Success of Bilingual Hispanoamerican Children." Denver, Colorado: Denver Department of Health and Hospitals, October 1967. ERIC ED 036 577.

1577. Rapier, Jacqueline L. "Effects of Verbal Mediation upon the Learning of Mexican-American Children." *California Journal of Educational Research* 18, no. 1 (January 1967): 40-48.

1578. Schwartz, Audrey James. "Affectivity Orientations and Academic Achievement of Mexican-American Youth." Doctoral dissertation, University of California at Los Angeles, 1967.

1579. Anderson, James G., and Johnson, William H. "Socio-Cultural Determinants of Achievement among Mexican-American Students." Las Cruces: New Mexico State University, Educational Resources Information Center, 1968. ERIC ED 017 394.

1580. Bryant, James Chester. "Some Effects of Racial Integration of High School Students on Standardized Achievement Test Scores, Teacher Grades, and Dropout Rates in Angleton, Texas." Doctoral dissertation, University of Houston, 1968:

1581. Henderson, Ronald W., and Merritt, C.B. "Environmental Backgrounds of Mexican-American Children with Different Potentials for School Success." *Journal of Social Psychology* 75 (June 1968): 101-6.

1582. Kimball, William Lloyd. "Parent and Family Influence on Academic Achievement among Mexican American Students." Doctoral dissertation, University of California at Los Angeles, 1968.

1583. Thiel, Richard H. "An Analysis of Socio-Cultural Factors and Performance of Primary Grade Children." Doctoral dissertation, University of Southern California, 1968.

1584. Anderson, James G. *Factors Affecting Achievement among Mexican-Americans in a Metropolitan Context. Final Report, Mathematics Education Program.* Las Cruces: New Mexico State University, Southwest Educational Development Laboratory, December 1969.

1585. Evans, Francis Benjamin. "A Study of Sociocultural Characteristics of Mexican-American and Anglo Junior High School Students and the Relation of These Characteristics to Achievement." Doctoral dissertation, New Mexico State University, 1969. ERIC ED 039 999.

1586. Gillman, Geneva Blackwell. "The Relationship between Self-Concept, Intellectual Ability, Achievement, and Manifest Anxiety among Select Groups of Spanish-Surname Migrant Students in New Mexico." Doctoral dissertation, University of New Mexico, 1969. ERIC ED 029 723.

1587. Henderson, Ronald W. "Environmental Variables as Predictors of Academic Performance." Paper presented at the annual meetings of the Western Psychological Association, Vancouver, British Columbia, Canada, 20 June 1969. ERIC ED 036 592.

1588. Hill, Floyd Williams. "A Study of the Influence of Socialization Anxiety on the Achievement of First-Grade Mexican-American Children." Doctoral dissertation, University of Texas at Austin, 1969.

1589. Justin, Neal E. "The Relationship of Certain Socio-Cultural Factors to the Academic Achievement of Male Mexican-American High School Seniors." Doctoral dissertation, University of Arizona, 1969.

1590. La Belle, Thomas Jeffrey. "Attitudes and Academic Achievement among Male and Female Anglo and Spanish American Fifth Grade Students." Doctoral dissertation, University of New Mexico, 1969.

1591. Ruesink, David C., et al. "Relocating Mexican-Americans Who Have Been Retrained." College Station: Texas Agricultural Experiment Station, 28 August 1969. ERIC ED 032 157.

1592. Schwartz, Audrey James. "Comparative Values and Achievement of Mexican American and Anglo Pupils. Report No. 37." Los Angeles: University of California at Los Angeles, Center for the Study of Evaluation, February 1969. ERIC ED 028 873.

1593. Smith, George Worth. "Correlates of Academic Achievement for Mexican American Students." Doctoral dissertation, Texas Tech University, 1969.

1594. Age, Clifford. "The Prediction of Academic Achievement of Mexican-American Students." Doctoral dissertation, University of Arizona, 1970.

1595. Allen, Gerald Gordon. "The Influence of Group Counseling on the School Performance and Self Concept of Junior High School Students of Mexican Descent." Master's thesis, University of Utah, 1970.

1596. Cain, Mary Alexander. "A Study of Relationships between Selected Factors and the School Achievement of Mexican-American Migrant Children." Doctoral dissertation, Michigan State University, 1970.

1597. California. State Department of Education. *Educational and Cultural Values of Mexican-American Parents; How They Influence the School Achievement of Their Children*, by Marie E. Taylor. Sacramento: California State Department of Education, 1970. ERIC ED 050 842.

1598. California. State Department of Education. Office of Compensatory Education. *Effect of Integration on Achievement of Anglos, Blacks, and Mexican-Americans*, by Harry Singer. Sacramento: California State Department of Education, 3 March 1970. ERIC ED 041 975.

1599. Casavantes, Edward J. *Variables Which Tend to Affect (Impede or Retard) Learning of the Mexican-American Student in American Education. A Position Paper.* Albuquerque, New Mexico: Southwestern Cooperative Education Lab., August 1970. ERIC ED 060 990.

1600. Flynn, Timothy M., et al. "Traits Related to Achievement Motivation in Migrant Pre-School Children." Tallahassee: Florida State University, August 1970. ERIC ED 049 870.

1601. Gargiulo, R. "A Field Study to Effect Changes in Academic Achievement Levels of Under Achieving Seventh Grade Students." Doctoral dissertation, University of New Mexico, 1970.

1602. Justin, Neal E. "Culture Conflict and Mexican American Achievement." *School and Society* 98 (January 1970): 27-28.

1603. Linton, Thomas Harvey. "Sociocultural Characteristics, Alienation from School and Achievement among Mexican-American and Anglo Sixth Grade Students." Doctoral dissertation, New Mexico State University, 1970.

1604. Mangano, James F., and Towne, Richard C. "Improving Migrant Students' Academic Achievement through Self-Concept Enhancement." Geneseo: State University of New York College at Geneseo, Center for Migrant Studies, 1970. ERIC ED 049 868.

1605. Mercer, Jane R. "Current Retardation Procedures and the Psychological and Social Implications on the Mexican-American. A Position Paper." Albuquerque, New Mexico: Southwestern Cooperative Educational Lab., April 1970. ERIC ED 052 848.

1606. Plant, Walter T., and Southern, Mara L. "Effects of Preschool Performance among the Culturally Disadvantaged." California: San Jose State College, Department of Psychology, 30 September 1970. ERIC ED 046 545.

1607. Taylor, Marie E. "Investigation of Parent Factors Affecting Achievement of Mexican American Children." Doctoral dissertation, University of Southern California, 1970.

1608. Anderson, James G., and Johnson, William H. "Stability and Change among Three Generations of Mexican Americans: Factors Affecting Achievement." *American Educational Research Journal* 8, no. 2 (March 1971): 285-309.

1609. Gabet, Yvonne Helen Yadon. "Birth Order and Achievement in Anglo, Mexican-American, and Black Americans." Doctoral dissertation, University of Texas at Austin, 1971.

1610. Massarotti, M.C. "Effect of the Spanish Language as Auditory Stimulation during Test Administration on the Measured Achievement of Fifth Grade Spanish-Surnamed Pupils." Doctoral dissertation, University of Denver, 1971.

1611. Ramirez, Manuel, III. "The Relationship of Acculturation to Educational Achievement and Psychological Adjustment in Chicano Children and Adolescents: A Review of the Literature." *El Grito* 4, no. 4 (summer 1971): 21-28.

1612. Rogers, Dorothy Patricia Brady. "Personality Traits and Academic Achievement among Mexican-American Students." Doctoral dissertation, University of Texas at Austin, 1971. ERIC ED 052 884.

1613. Schwartz, Audrey James. "A Comparative Study of Value and Achievement: Mexican-American and Anglo Youth." *Sociology of Education* 44, no. 4 (fall 1971): 438-62.

1614. Singhal, Sushila, and Crago, Priscilla H. "Sex Differences in the School Gains of Migrant Children." *Journal of Educational Research* 64, no. 9 (May-June 1971): 417-19.

1615. Stone, Paula C., and Ruiz, Rene A. "Race and Class as Differential Determinants of Underachievement and Underaspiration among Mexican-Americans." Paper presented at the annual convention of the American Psychological Association, n.p., September 1971. ERIC ED 077 612.

1616. Valenzuela, Alvaro Miguel. "The Relationships between Self-Concept, Intelligence, Socio-Economic Status and School Achievement among Spanish American Children in Omaha." Omaha: University of Nebraska, August 1971. ERIC ED 056 785.

1617. Campbell, Wallace. "Parents' Perceptions of Their Powerlessness in Lower Class White, Middle Class White, and Lower Class Mexican American Homes, and the Resulting Influence on Student Achievement." Doctoral dissertation, University of Toledo, 1972.

1618. Friend, Ras Roland. "The Relationship between Academic Achievement and Locus-of-Control in Middle and Lower Socioeconomic Level Black, White, and Mexican-American High School Students in an Urban School Setting." Doctoral dissertation, University of Houston, 1972.

1619. García, Angela B., and Zimmerman, Barry J. "The Effect of Examiner Ethnicity and Language on the Performance of Bilingual Mexican-American First Graders." *Journal of Social Psychology* 87, no. 1 (June 1972): 3-11.

1620. Henderson, Ronald W. "Environmental Predictors of Academic Performance of Disadvantaged Mexican-American Children." *Journal of Consulting and Clinical Psychology* 38, no. 2 (April 1972): 297.

1621. Manaster, G.J., and King, M.R. "Mexican-American Group Cohesiveness and Academic Achievement." *Urban Education* 7, no. 3 (October 1972): 235-40.

1622. Mech, Edmund V. "Achievement-Motivation Patterns among Low-Income Anglo-American, Mexican-American, and Negro Youth." Paper presented at the annual meeting of the American Psychological Association, Honolulu, Hawaii, 2 September 1972. ERIC ED 073 210.

1623. Miller, Max Donald. "Patterns of Relationships of Fluid and Crystallized Mental Abilities of Achievement in Different Ethnic Groups." Doctoral dissertation, University of Houston, 1972.

1624. Morrison, Grant Albert, Jr. "An Analysis of Academic Achievement Trends for Anglo-American, Mexican-American, and Negro-American Students in a Desegregated School Environment." Doctoral dissertation, University of Houston, 1972.

1625. Stedman, James M., and Adams, Russell L. "Achievement as a Function of Language Competence, Behavior Adjustment, and Sex in Young, Disadvantaged Mexican-American Children." *Journal of Educational Psychology* 63, no. 5 (October 1972): 411-17.

1626. U.S. Department of Health, Education, and Welfare. Office of Education. *The Effects of Two Types of Group Counseling upon the Academic Achievement and Self-Concept of Mexican-American Pupils in Elementary School.* Washington, D.C.: Government Printing Office, January 1972. ERIC ED 059 002.

1627. Anderson, James G., and Evans, Francis B. "Family Socialization and Educational Achievement in Two Cultures: Mexican-American and Anglo-American. Working Paper No. 58." Paper presented at the American Educational Research Association, New Orleans, Louisiana, 25 February-1 March 1973. ERIC ED 077 813.

1628. Boyd, William E., Jr. "Achievement Motivation as Related to Level of Achievement and Selected Personality Variables." Master's thesis, Texas A&I University at Kingsville, 1973.

1629. Brawner, Marlyn R. "Migration and Educational Achievement of Mexican Americans." *Social Science Quarterly* 53, no. 4 (March 1973): 727-37.

1630. Cron, Cyril Thomas. "The Relationship between Attitudes toward School and Academic Achievement of Fourth-, Fifth- and Sixth-Grade Mexican American Pupils Attending Schools in Areas of Different Levels of Economic Affluençe." Doctoral dissertation, University of Houston, 1973.

1631. Evans, Francis Benjamin, and Anderson, James G. "Psychocultural Origins of Achievement and Achievement Motivation: The Mexican-American Family." *Sociology of Education* 46, no. 4 (fall 1973): 396-416.

1632. Hernández, Norma G. "Variables Affecting Achievement of Middle School Mexican-American Students." *Review of Educational Research* 43, no. 1 (winter 1973): 1-39.

1633. Montgomery, Robert Lawrence. "A Study of Relationships between Group Test of Creativity (GTOC) Scores and Achievement Test Scores of Students with Spanish and Non-Spanish Surnames." Doctoral dissertation, University of Southern California, 1973.

1634. Pruneda, Manuela C. "Acculturation, Self-Concept, and Achievement of Mexican-American Students." Doctoral dissertation, East Texas State University, 1973.

1635. Ramírez, Inez Ruiz. "The Effect of English as a Second Language Instruction on Oral Proficiency, Self-Concept and Scholastic Achievement of Kindergarten-Age Mexican-American Students." Doctoral dissertation, East Texas State University, 1973.

1636. Veaco, Lelia. "The Effect of Paraprofessional Assistance on the Academic Achievement of Migrant Children." Doctoral dissertation, Pacific College, 1973. ERIC ED 086 380.

1637. Archer, Helen Morgan. "Achievement Motivation Relating to Attitudes, Sex, and Level of Achievement." Master's thesis, Texas A&I University at Kingsville, 1974.

1638. Bender, Paula Stone, and Ruiz, Rene A. "Race and Class as Differential Determinants of Underachievement and Underaspiration among Mexican-Americans and Anglos." *Journal of Educational Research* 68, no. 2 (October 1974): 51-55.

1639. Cornett, Joe D.; Ainsworth, Len; and Askins, Bill. "Effect of an Intervention Program on 'High Risk' Spanish American Children." *Journal of Educational Research* 67, no. 8 (April 1974): 342-43.

1640. Guynn, Kenneth Paul. "Effects of Ethnicity and Socioeconomic Status on Learning Achievement of Ninth- and Eleventh-Grade Students." Master's thesis, New Mexico State University, 1974. ERIC ED 088 655.

1641. Marsh, Linda Kessler. "Self-Esteem, Achievement of Lower Class Black, White, and Hispanic Seventh-Grade Boys." Doctoral dissertation, New York University, 1974.

1642. Ortiz, Flora Ida, and Morelan, Steve J. "Effect of Personal and Impersonal Rewards on the Learning Performance of Field Independent-Dependent Mexican-American Children." Paper presented at the annual meeting of the American Educational Research Association, Chicago, Illinois, 15-19 April 1974. ERIC ED 091 094.

1643. Santana, Henry A. "A Study of the Scholastic Performance and Attitudes of Mexican-American Students under the Majority to Minority Voluntary Transfer Policy within a Major South Texas School District." Doctoral dissertation, University of Houston, 1974.

1644. Thorne, Joyce Holley. "An Analysis of the WISC and ITPA and Their Relationships to School Achievement, Socio-Economic Status, and Ethnicity." Master's thesis, University of Houston, 1974.

1645. Baral, David Parsons. "Achievement Levels among Foreign-Born and Native-Born Mexican American Students." Doctoral dissertation, University of Arizona, 1975.

1646. Cantú, Ismael Sierra. "The Effects of Family Characteristics, Parental Influence, Language Spoken, School Experience, and Self-Motivation on the Level of Educational Attainment of Mexican Americans." Doctoral dissertation, University of Michigan, 1975.

1647. Carter, Melba Constant. "An Examination of the Relationship between Educationally Supportive Home Environmental Factors and Academic Performance of Socially Disadvantaged Anglo, Black, and Chicano Children in Selected Parochial Elementary Schools." Doctoral dissertation, University of Missouri at Kansas City, 1975.

1648. Espinosa, Gilbert. "An Evaluation of the Effects of Ethnic Minority and Majority Teachers on the Attitudes and Academic Achievement of Ethnic Minority and Majority Students." Doctoral dissertation, University of Southern California, 1975.

1649. Espinosa, Ruben William. "The Impact of Evaluation Processes upon Student Effort in Ethnic Groups Which Vary in Academic Preparation." Doctoral dissertation, Stanford University, 1975.

1650. Fernández, Celestino, et al. "Factors Perpetuating the Low Academic Status of Chicano High School Students. Research and Development Memorandum No. 138." Palo Alto, California: Stanford University, Stanford Center for Research and Development in Teaching, July 1975. ERIC ED 110 241.

1651. Flynn, Timothy M. "Personality Factors Related to Intellectual Achievement in Migrant Preschool Children." Paper presented at the biennial meeting of the Society for Research in Child Development, Denver, Colorado, April 1975. ERIC ED 111 509.

1652. Mintz, Richard Lawrence. "The Relationship between Specific and Global Measures of Self-Concept and Academic Achievement in Fourth and Sixth Grade Students." Doctoral dissertation, New Mexico State University, 1975.

1653. Morales, Ardiccio Daniel. "Minority Children's Beliefs Concerning Control of Reinforcements in Intellectual-Academic Achievement Situations." Doctoral dissertation, Michigan State University, 1975.

1654. Pirofski, Florence Goodman. "Individual Differences in Cognitive Competence among Mexican-American Children from Low-Income Families." Doctoral dissertation, Stanford University, 1975.

1655. Shawver, Jenny Heinz. "Achievement Motivation as Related to Sex and Level of Achievement among Adolescent Boys and Girls." Master's thesis, Texas A&I University at Kingsville, 1975.

1656. Tsai, Yung-Mei, and Perry, Floyd, Jr. "Factors Affecting Academic Performance and Persistence among the Mexican-American, the Black and the Anglo Students in a Southwestern University." Paper presented at the annual meeting of the Southwestern Sociological Association, San Antonio, Texas, 26-29 March 1975. ERIC ED 104 613.

1657. Guzman-Mejias, Virginia. "Initial School Achievement of Spanish Dominant and Bilingual Mexican American Children." Master's thesis, Texas A&I University at Kingsville, 1976.

3.6.3 Reading

1658. Kelley, Victor H. "Reading Abilities of Spanish and English-Speaking Pupils." *Journal of Educational Research* 29, no. 3 (November 1935): 209-11.

1659. Manuel, Herschel T. "Comparison of Spanish-Speaking and English-Speaking Children in Reading and Arithmetic." *Journal of Applied Psychology* 19 (April 1935): 189-202.

1660. Drennan, Davy Deolece. "The Progress in Reading of Fourth-Grade Spanish-Speaking and English-Speaking Pupils." Master's thesis, University of Texas at Austin, 1937.

1661. O'Brien, Mary Ross. "A Comparison of the Reading Ability of Spanish Speaking with Non-Spanish-Speaking Pupils in Grade 6A of the Denver Public Schools." Master's thesis, University of Denver, 1937.

1662. Drennan, Orlena Pink. "The Progress in Reading of Second-Grade Spanish-Speaking Pupils." Master's thesis, University of Texas at Austin, 1939.

1663. Stueber, Josephine. "Racial Differences in Reading Achievement." *Texas Outlook* 24, no. 1 (January 1940): 32.

1664. Broom, M. Eustace. "A Study of Race and Sex Differences in Reading Comprehension." *Journal of Educational Research* 34 (April 1941): 587-93.

1665. East, Mary Elizabeth. "A Comparison of the Reading Achievement of Mexican and American Children on the Gates Silent Reading Tests." Master's thesis, University of Southern California, 1942.

1666. Herr, Selma E. "The Effect of Pre-First Grade Training upon Reading Readiness and Achievement among Spanish American Children in the First Grade." Doctoral dissertation, University of Texas at Austin, 1944.

1667. Herr, Selma E. "The Effect of Pre-First-Grade Training upon Reading Readiness and Reading Achievement among Spanish American Children." *Journal of Educational Psychology* 37, no. 2 (February 1946): 87-102.

1668. Glass, Nellie May. "A Study of Reading Performance of Anglo and Latin American Children." Master's thesis, University of Texas at Austin, 1949.

1669. Davenport, Mary Elizabeth. "Spanish-Name Children's Difficulties with Third Grade Basal Reader Vocabulary." Master's thesis, University of Texas at Austin, 1951.

1670. Richter, Tellmond Herder. "Comparison of Latin-Americans and Anglo-Americans with Reference to Chronological Age, Reading Comprehension, and Arithmetic Computation in the Upper Elementary Grades in the Pearsall and Charlotte, Texas, Schools." Master's thesis, Southwest Texas State University, 1951.

1671. Clayton, Frances. "A Study of the Reading of Latin and Anglo Students at Texas Western College." Master's thesis, University of Texas at Austin, 1954.

1672. Hernández, Elias Vega. "Reading Retardation of Children in Zavala School." Master's thesis, University of Texas at Austin, 1954.

1673. Criscuolo, Nicholas Paul. "A Comparison of the Enrichment and Acceleration Approaches with Children of Different Socio-Economic Backgrounds and Their Effect on Reading Achievement." Doctoral dissertation, University of Connecticut, 1967.

1674. Kaufman, Maurice. "The Effect of Instruction in Reading Spanish on Reading Ability in English of Spanish-Speaking Retarded Readers." Doctoral dissertation, New York University, 1967.

1675. Pauck, Frederick Glen. "An Evaluation of the Self-Test as a Predictor of Reading Achievement of Spanish-Speaking First Grade Children." Doctoral dissertation, University of Texas at Austin, 1968.

1676. Knight, Lester Neal. "A Comparison of the Effectiveness of Intensive Oral-Aural English Instruction, Intensive Oral-Aural Spanish Instruction, and Non-Oral-Aural Instruction on the Reading Achievement of Spanish-Speaking Second- and Third-Grade Pupils. 1966-67 Findings." Doctoral dissertation, University of Texas at Austin, 1969.

1677. Padelford, William B. "The Influence of Socioeconomic Level, Sex, and Ethnic Background upon the Relationship between Reading Achievement and Self-Concept." Doctoral dissertation, University of California at Los Angeles, 1969.

1678. Watson, Billy L. "Field Dependence and Early Reading Achievement." Doctoral dissertation, University of California at Los Angeles, 1969.

1679. Pomerantz, Norman E. "An Investigation of the Relationship between Intelligence and Reading Achievement for Various Samples of Bilingual Spanish-Speaking Children." Doctoral dissertation, New Mexico State University, 1970.

1680. Acosta, Robert Torres. "Factors Contributing to the Successful Remediation of Reading Disabilities in Mexican American Third Graders." Doctoral dissertation, University of California at Los Angeles, 1971.

1681. Arnold, Richard D. "Reading Skills of Afro- and Mexican-American Students." Paper presented at the meeting of the International Reading Association, Atlantic City, New Jersey, 19-23 April 1971. ERIC ED 055 727.

1682. Poulsen, Marie Kanne. "Automatic Patterning of Grammatical Structures and Auditory and Visual Stimuli as Related to Reading in Disadvantaged Mexican-American Children." Doctoral dissertation, University of Southern California, 1971.

1683. Stevens, Frances Ann Bennett. "Predicting Third Grade Reading Achievement for Mexican-American Students from Lower Socioeconomic Levels." Doctoral dissertation, New Mexico State University, 1971. ERIC ED 068 240.

1684. Bowles, Stephen Anthony. "Effectiveness of Reinforcement Means in Promoting Reading Behaviors among Spanish and Non-Spanish Surname Students." Doctoral thesis, University of California at Santa Barbara, 1972.

1685. Easterling, Ross E., and Stevens, Francis A. "Reading Achievement of Lower Socioeconomic Level Mexican American Students." Las Cruces: New Mexico State University, November 1972. ERIC ED 068 221.

1686. Knight, Lester Neal. "Oral-Aural Language Instruction and Reading Achievement of Selected Spanish-Speaking Children." *California Journal of Educational Research* 23, no. 4 (September 1972): 188-97.

1687. Solís, Juan S. "Exploring the Relationship between Spanish Reading Achievement and English Reading Achievement." Master's thesis, Texas A&I University at Kingsville, 1972.

1688. Baecher, Richard Emeram. "An Exploratory Study to Determine Levels of Educational Development, Reading Levels, and the Cognitive Styles of Mexican-American and Puerto Rican American Students in Michigan." Doctoral dissertation, University of Michigan, 1973.

1689. Bedotto, M. Jean Rosaire. "The Effect of Non-Native Speech upon the Reading Achievement of Spanish-Speaking Students at Different Levels of Intelligence and upon Their Ability to Use Syntactic Clues to Meaning in Reading English." Doctoral dissertation, New York University, 1973. ERIC ED 089 212.

1690. Casavantes, Edward J. "Reading Achievement and In-Grade Retention Rate Differentials for Mexican-American and Black Students in Selected States of the Southwest." Doctoral dissertation, University of Southern California, 1973.

1691. Lucas, Marilyn S., and Singer, Harry. "Dialect in Relation to Reading Achievement: Recording, Encoding, or Merely a Code?" Paper presented at the annual meeting of the American Educational Research Association, New Orleans, Louisiana, 25 February-1 March 1973. ERIC ED 078 374.

1692. Mendenhall, Betty Joan. "Developing Self-Acceptance and Reading Achievement among Second Grade Chicano Children." Doctoral dissertation, University of Colorado, 1973.

1693. Gentile, Lance Michael. "The Influence of Tutor Sex on the Reading Achievement of Spanish Surname Boys." Doctoral dissertation, Arizona State University, 1974.

1694. Gurecki, Karen J., and Wurster, Stanley R. "A Study of the Relationship of the Length of Continuous Attendance at a Single School to Reading and Arithmetic Achievement Test Scores." Arizona: University of Arizona, July 1974. ERIC ED 093 511.

1695. Parrish, Bert Wiley. "The Effects of Experimental Background upon the Informal Reading Inventory Diagnosis of Anglo-American and Mexican-American Ninth-Grade Students." Doctoral dissertation, Arizona State University, 1974.

1696. Bill, Elizabeth J. "A Comparison of Reading Achievement of Disadvantaged Children Using Montessori-Based Structural Reading Instruction and Basal Reading Instruction." Master's thesis, University of Texas at Austin, 1975.

1697. Carline, Donald E., et al. "Relationships between Spanish and English Reading Skill and Concept Usage in Spanish and English by Mexican-American Bilingual Migrant Children." Boulder: University of Colorado, Bureau of Educational Field Services, 1975. ERIC ED 119 177.

1698. Frieder-Vierra, Andrea. "School-Year and Summer Reading Growth of Minority and Non-Minority Children in Albuquerque, New Mexico." Doctoral dissertation, University of New Mexico, 1975.

1699. Froyen, Richard Gordon. "A Comparative Study of the Relationship between Reading Achievement Scores of Anglo and Spanish Surname Students in Hueneme School District, California." Doctoral dissertation, Brigham Young University, 1975.

1700. Sherfey, Richard Wayne. "Relationship of Attention Span to Reading Performance in Mexican-American Children." Doctoral dissertation, University of Arizona, 1975.

1701. Trepper, Terry Steven. "A Two Year Report on an Inner City School's Reading Achievement Center." Northridge: California State University at Northridge, 1975. ERIC ED 110 956.

1702. Trinidad, Reuben Salistino. "An Analysis of the Reading Abilities of Spanish Surnamed Students in the Redwood City School District as Related to Educational Success." Doctoral dissertation, University of Northern Colorado, 1975.

1703. Bronfeld, Evelyne Phyllis. "Auditory Discrimination Training and Reading Performance of Spanish- and English-Speaking Children." Master's thesis, University of California at Long Beach, 1976.

3.6.4 Other Areas

1704. Parry, Esther Louise. "A Comparison of the Abilities of Spanish-Speaking and English-Speaking Children in Ninth Grade Algebra." Master's thesis, University of Texas at Austin, 1933.

1705. Swalestuen, E.D. "A Comparative Study of the Mexican and White Child in Ninth Grade Albegra." Master's thesis, University of Southern California, 1933.

1706. Vincent, Henrietta H. "A Study of Performance of Spanish Speaking Pupils on Spanish Tests." Master's thesis, New Mexico State Teachers College, 1933.

1707. "We Learn English: A Preliminary Report of the Achievement of Spanish-Speaking Pupils in New Mexico." Albuquerque: University of New Mexico, 1936.

1708. Clark, Daniel Hendricks. "A Comparison of the Factors Related to Success in Problem Solving in Mathematics for Latin American and Anglo American Students in the Junior High School." Master's thesis, University of Texas at Austin, 1938.

1709. Manzo, Ricardo. "Difficulties of Spanish-Speaking Children in the Fundamental Number Combinations." Master's thesis, University of Arizona, 1939.

1710. Miller, Mrs. Willie. "Latin-American Child and Music." *Texas Outlook* 31, no. 10 (October 1947): 26-27.

1711. Craddock, Vina Marie. "A Comparative Study of Anglo-American and Latin-American Children in Preference and Performance of Arithmetic Problems." Master's thesis, University of Texas at Austin, 1949.

1712. Morrison, Charlotte Amos. "A Comparison of the Achievement of Mexican Pupils Learning English in a Segregated School and in a Non-Segregated School, 1952."Master's thesis, University of Oregon, 1952.

1713. Jarvis, Gertrude O. "A Study of the Relation of Achievement in Spanish to Achievement in English." Master's thesis, University of Texas at Austin, 1953.

1714. Washington, Thomas Pratt. "A Study of Sex, Language Background, and Measured Proficiency in English as Related to Grades and Test Scores." Master's thesis, University of Texas at Austin, 1953.

1715. Putchkoff, Benjamin H. "A Comparison of the Spelling Achievement of Bilingual Children with That of Monoglot Children." Master's thesis, Arizona State University, 1954.

1716. López, Mary Louise. "The Relationship of Kindergarten Experience to the Learning of English by the Spanish Speaking Child." Master's thesis, Southwest Texas State University, 1956.

1717. Anglin, Stella Campbell Glass. "A Study for the Improvement of Spanish-Speaking Children's Problem-Solving Ability in Third-Grade Arithmetic." Master's thesis, University of Texas at Austin, 1957.

1718. Love, Harold D. "Auditory Discrimination, Spelling and Reading with Bilingual and Monolingual Children." *Journal of Reading* 6 (spring 1963): 212-14.

1719. Charles, C.M. "Bicultural Children and Science Achievement." *Science Education* 48, no. 1 (February 1964): 93-96.

1720. Fitch, Michael John. "Verbal and Performance Test Scores in Bilingual Children." Doctoral dissertation, Colorado State College, 1966.

1721. Swan, Dorothy Louise. "The Effect of Ethnic Background on Attitude and Achievement in Physical Education." Master's thesis, California State College, 1968.

1722. Anderson, James G. *Patterns of Achievement among Mexican-American Students. Interim Report, Mathematics Education Program.* Las Cruces: New Mexico State University, Southwest Educational Development Laboratory, Research Center, October 1969.

1723. Arnold, Richard D., and Taylor, Thomasine H. "Mexican-Americans and Language Learning." *Childhood Education* 46, no. 3 (December 1969): 149-54.

1724. Johnson, Louise Henrietta. "Elementary School Geometry: A Study of Achievement on Selected Objectives of Geometry of Mexican American and Anglo American Second Grade Children." Doctoral dissertation, University of Northern Colorado, 1971.

1725. Dickson, J.M.T. "A Comparison of Mathematical Achievement of Selected Objectives by Ethnically Unequal Students of a Low SES Background." Master's thesis, University of Texas at Austin, 1972.

1726. Shachter, Jaqueline N. "Effect of Studying Literary Translations on Sixth-Grade Pupils' Knowledge of Mexican Culture." *Social Education* 36, no. 2 (February 1972): 162-67, 179.

1727. Fisher, M.D., et al. "Student Control and Choice: Their Effects on Student Engagement in a CAI Arithmetic Task in a Low-Income School. Technical Report No. 41." Palo Alto, California: Stanford University, Stanford Center for Research and Development in Teaching, August 1974.

1728. Begle, E.G., et al. "SMESG Working Paper No. 9: The Effect of Review of Prerequisite Skills and Concepts on Learning a Topic in Mathematics for Chicano Students." Mimeographed. California: Stanford University, Stanford Mathematics Education Study Group, February 1975.

1729. Begle, E.G., et al. "SMESG Working Paper No. 10: Test Factors, Instructional Programs, and Socio-Cultural-Economic Factors Related to Mathematics Achievement of Chicano Students: A Review of the Literature." Mimeographed. California: Stanford University, Stanford Mathematics Education Study Group, March 1975.

1730. Fournier, James Francis, Jr. "An Investigation on the Correlation Differences in Science Concepts Held by Fifth-Grade Mexican and Anglo-American Students: A Cross Cultural Study." Doctoral dissertation, University of Northern Colorado, 1975.

1731. Ginther, Joan R., and Begle, E.G. "SMESG Working Paper No. 14: The Effect of Pretraining Chicano Students on Parallel Test Items before Administration of a Mathematics Predictor Test." Mimeographed. Palo Alto, California: Stanford University, Stanford Mathematics Education Study Group, August 1975.

1732. Ginther, Joan R., and Tsang, Sau-Lim. "SMESG Working Paper No. 8: Correlation, for Chicano Students, of Two Scoring Methods for the Missing Words Test." Mimeographed. Palo Alto, California: Stanford University, Stanford Mathematics Education Study Group, February 1975.

1733. Rodríguez, Edgar Hugo. "The Effect of Instruction on the Learning of Social Studies Time Concepts by Mexican American and Anglo American Pupils in Grades Five and Six." Doctoral dissertation, University of Texas at Austin, 1975.

1734. Tsang, Sau-Lim. "SMESG Working Paper No. 15: The Effects of Language Factor and the Cultural Content Factor of a Mathematics Test on the Chinese and the Chicano Students." Palo Alto, California: Stanford University, Stanford Mathematics Education Study Group, August 1975.

3.6.5 Testing

1735. Caldwell, F., and Mowry, M. "The Essay Versus the Objective Examination as Measures of the Achievement of Bi-Lingual Children." *Journal of Educational Psychology* 24, no. 9 (December 1933): 696-702.

1736. Callicutt, Laurie T. "The Construction and Evaluation of Parallel Tests of Reading in English and Spanish." Doctoral dissertation, University of Texas at Austin, 1942.

1737. Ammons, Robert B., and Aguero, Abelardo. "The Full-Range Picture Vocabulary Test: VII. Results for a Spanish-American School-Age Population." *Journal of Social Psychology* 32 (August 1950): 3-10.

1738. Manuel, Herschel T. "The Use of Parallel Tests in the Study of Foreign Language Teaching." *Educational and Psychological Measurement* 13, no. 3 (autumn 1953): 431-36.

1739. Santos, Beatriz N. "Special Achievement Testing Needs of the Educationally Disadvantaged." Doctoral dissertation, University of Iowa, 1967.

1740. U.S. Civil Service Commission. Bureau of Policies and Standards. *Effects on Test Score of Presenting Verbal Test Questions in an English-Spanish Format to a Predominantly Spanish-American Group; San Antonio, Texas, May, 1968*, by Albert P. Maslow and David L. Futransky. Washington, D.C.: Government Printing Office, July 1968. ERIC ED 045 265.

1741. Arnold, Richard D. "Reliability of Test Scores for the Young Bilingual Disadvantaged." *Reading Teacher* 22, no. 2 (January 1969): 341-45.

1742. Personke, C.R., Jr., and Davis, O.L., Jr. "Predictive Validity of English and Spanish Versions of a Readiness Test." *Elementary School Journal* 70, no. 2 (November 1969): 79-85.

1743. Hurt, Maure, Jr., and Mishra, Shitala P. "Reliability and Validity of the Metropolitan Achievement Tests for Mexican-American and Anglo Children." *Educational and Psychological Measurement* 30, no. 4 (winter 1970): 989-92.

1744. Merz, William R. "A Factor Analysis of the Goodenough-Harris Drawing Test Across Four Ethnic Groups." Doctoral dissertation, University of New Mexico, 1970.

1745. California. State Department of Education. *Pluralistic Diagnosis in the Evaluation of Black and Chicano Children: A Procedure for Taking Sociocultural Variables into Account in Clinical Assessment,* by Jane R. Mercer. Sacramento: California State Department of Education, September 1971. ERIC ED 055 145.

1746. Flynn, Timothy M. "Convergent-Discriminant Validation of Behavioral Ratings." Paper presented at the annual meeting of the American Educational Research Association, New York, February 1971. ERIC ED 049 282.

1747. Green, Donald Ross. *Racial and Ethnic Bias in Test Construction. Final Report.* Monterey, California: CTB/McGraw Hill, 24 September 1971. ERIC ED 056 090.

1748. Hartigan, Robert R. "A Temporal-Spatial Concept Scale: A Developmental Study." *Journal of Clinical Psychology* 27, no. 2 (April 1971): 221-23.

1749. Henderson, R.W., and Rankin, R.J. "WPPSI Reliability and Predictive Validity with Disadvantaged Mexican-American Children." *Journal of School Psychology* 11, no. 1 (March 1972): 16-20.

1750. Sciara, Frank J. "Criterion-Referenced Tests—A New Promise for Old Problems in Migrant Education." Paper presented at the Indiana Migrant Education Evaluation Conference, Anderson, Indiana, 22 January 1972. ERIC ED 057 984.

1751. Texas. Education Agency. *The Use of Norm-Referenced Survey Achievement Tests with Mexican-American Migrant Students: A Literature Review and Analysis of Implications for Evaluation of the Texas Migrant Education Program,* by John H. Littlefield. Austin: Texas Education Agency, 1972. ERIC ED 063 983.

1752. Jensen, Arthur R. "How Biased Are Culture-Loaded Tests?" Berkeley: University of California at Berkeley, 1973. ERIC ED 080 644.

1753. Calhoun, Jo Anne P. "Developmental and Sociocultural Aspects of Imagery in the Picture-Word Paired-Associate Learning of Children." *Developmental Psychology* 10, no. 3 (May 1974): 357-66.

1754. Cervantes, Robert. "Problems and Alternatives in Testing Mexican-American Students." *Integrated Education* 12, no. 3 (May-June 1974): 33-37.

1755. Kissinger, Joan Brunswick. "A Category System to Measure the Development of Affection in Young Children between the Ages of One and Five." Doctoral dissertation, University of Texas at Austin, 1974.

3.7 Gifted

1756. Stolz, Alberta, and Manuel, H.T. "Art Ability of Mexican Children." *School and Society* 34 (12 September 1931): 379-80.

1757. Shulman, Dawn Smith. "Identification of Giftedness in Disadvantaged School Children." Master's thesis, United States International University, 1973.

1758. Bernal, Ernest M., Jr. "Gifted Mexican American Children: An Ethnico-Scientific Perspective." Paper presented at the annual meeting of the American Educational Research Association, Chicago, Illinios, April 1974. ERIC ED 091 411.
1759. Bernal, Ernest, M., Jr., and Reyna, Josephine. *Analysis of Giftedness in Mexican American Children and Design of a Prototype Identification Instrument.* Austin, Texas: Southwest Educational Development Lab., March 1974. ERIC ED 090 743.

3.8 Handicapped

1760. Hernández, Arcadia. "A Study of Retarded Spanish Speaking Children in Second Grade." Master's thesis, University of Texas at Austin, 1938.
1761. Shotwell, Anna M. "Arthur Performance Ratings of Mexican and American High-Grade Mental Defectives." *American Journal of Mental Deficiency* 49, no. 4 (April 1945): 445-49.
1762. Smith, Sue Ida. "Three Studies of Retarded Spanish-Culture Beginners, Edinburg, Texas." Master's thesis, Texas A&I University at Kingsville, 1947.
1763. Swickard, Don L., and Spilka, Bernard. "Hostility Expression among Delinquents of Minority and Majority Groups." *Journal of Consulting Psychology* 25, no. 3 (June 1961): 216-20.
1764. Silverstein, A.B., et al. "Cultural Factors in the Intellectual Functioning of the Mentally Retarded." *American Journal of Mental Deficiency* 67, no. 3 (November 1962): 396-401.
1765. Arena, John I., ed. *Teaching Educationally Handicapped Children.* San Rafael, California: Academy Therapy Publications, 1967.
1766. Thomas, Glen E. "A Comparison of Language Concept Development among Spanish-American and Caucasian Average and Mentally Retarded Children." Doctoral dissertation, Colorado State College, 1968.
1767. U.S. Department of Health, Education, and Welfare. Office of Education. *Improving Educational Opportunities for Mexican-American Handicapped Children,* by Jane Case Williams. Washington, D.C.: Government Printing Office, April 1968. ERIC ED 018 326.
1768. California. State Department of Education. *Spanish-Speaking Pupils Classified as Educable Mentally Retarded.* Sacramento: California State Department of Education, 1969.
1769. California. State Department of Education. Division of Instruction. *Spanish-Speaking Pupils Classified as Educable Mentally Retarded,* by John T. Chandler and John Plakos. Sacramento: California State Department of Education, 1969. ERIC ED 050 845.
1770. Rosenquist, Carl M., and Megargee, Edwin I. *Delinquency in Three Cultures.* Austin: University of Texas Press, 1969.
1771. Cordova, José. "Television Viewing Habits of Selected Special Education and Regular Education Children in Five New Mexico School Districts." Doctoral dissertation, University of New Mexico, 1973.
1772. Hoernicke, Placido Arturo. "The Morphological Development of Language in School Age Chicano Educable Mentally Retarded." Doctoral dissertation, University of Northern Colorado, 1974.
1773. Morrison, Violet Thompson. "A Study of Human Birth Defects with Emphasis on Environmental Influences in the Lower Rio Grande Valley of South Texas." Master's thesis, Pan American University, August 1974.

1774. Baca, Gilberto Matias. "Forty Families: A Comparative Study of Mexican-American and Anglo Parents of an Institutionalized Retarded Child." Doctoral dissertation, University of Denver, 1975.

1775. Hill, Wille Kiah. "Variations in the Rationale of Referrals Leading to Educable Mentally Retarded Placement of Anglo, Black and Spanish-Speaking Students." Doctoral dissertation, Rutgers University, 1975.

1776. Mangum, Melvin Earl, Jr. "Familial Identification in Black, Anglo and Chicano Mentally Retarded Children Using Kinetic Family Drawing." Doctoral dissertation, University of Northern Colorado, 1975.

1777. Velez-Serra, Damian. "Effects of Extraneous Information on the Solving of Arithmetic Word Problems by the Spanish-Speaking Mentally Handicapped." Doctoral dissertation, University of Connecticut, 1975.

3.9 Delinquent

1778. U.S. President. Committee on Juvenile Delinquency and Youth Crime. *The Spanish-Speaking People in the United States*, by Eleanor B. Rubin. Washington, D.C.: Government Printing Office, n.d. ERIC ED 002 507.

1779. U.S. National Commission on Law Observance and Enforcement. "Crime and Justice among the Mexicans of Illinois," by Paul Livingstone Warnshuis. In *Report on Crime and the Foreign Born*, pp. 265-320. Vol. 10. Washington, D.C.: Government Printing Office, 1931.

1780. Baur, Edward Jackson. "Delinquency among Mexican Boys in South Chicago." Master's thesis, University of Chicago, 1938.

1781. Saint John, Berea Edith. "Spanish-Speaking Delinquents of the Denver Juvenile Court." Master's thesis, University of Denver, 1939.

1782. McWilliams, Carey. "Los Angeles' Pachuco Gangs." *New Republic* 108, no. 3 (18 January 1943): 76-77.

1783. McWilliams, Carey. "Zoot Suit Riots." *New Republic* 108, no. 25 (21 June 1943): 818-20.

1784. Gray, Lillian. "Zoot-Suit Youth; or What Happened to Juan García." *Childhood Education* 23, no. 2 (October 1946): 67-74.

1785. Harvey, Louise F. "The Delinquent Mexican Boy in an Urban Area, 1945." Master's thesis, University of California at Los Angeles, 1947.

1786. Crasilneck, Harold B. "A Study of One Hundred Male Latin-American Juvenile Delinquents in San Antonio, Texas." Master's thesis, University of Texas at Austin, 1948.

1787. Kresselman, Harold B. "A Study of 100 Male Latin-American Juvenile Delinquents in San Antonio." Master's thesis, University of Texas at Austin, 1948.

1788. Harvey, Louise F. "Delinquent Mexican Boy." *Journal of Educational Research* 42 (April 1949): 573-83.

1789. McWilliams, Carey. "Nervous Los Angeles. [Juvenile Mexican American Delinquents.]" *Nation* 170 (10 June 1950): 570-72.

1790. Palace, Arthur Lawrence. "A Comparative Description of Anglo-White and Mexican-White Boys Committed to Pacific Colony." Master's thesis, University of Southern California, 1950.

1791. Sion, Alvin P. "Mentally Deficient Mexican American Delinquent Boys Who Made Good after Institutional Care: An Analysis of Six Cases." Master's thesis, University of Southern California, 1951.

1792. Ranker, Jesse E., Jr. "A Study of Juvenile Gangs in the Hollenbeck Area of East Los Angeles." Master's thesis, University of Southern California, 1958.

1793. Eaton, Joseph W. *Measuring Delinquency: A Study of Probation Department Referrals.* Pittsburgh: University of Pittsburgh Press, 1961.

1794. Heller, Celia Stopnica. *The Pattern of Offenses among Juveniles of Mexican Descent.* Pittsburgh: University of Pittsburgh Press, 1961.

1795. Jackson, Ralph Myron. "Characteristics of Students Released from the Utah State Industrial School 1961. Part IV: Spanish American Boys." Master's thesis, University of Utah, 1963.

1796. Roberts, Mary Marshall. "Comparison of the Physical Status, Physical Abilities and Physical Self Concepts of Delinquent and Non-Delinquent Boys." Doctoral dissertation, University of Colorado, 1964.

1797. Meadow, Arnold, and Bronson, Louise. "Religious Affiliation and Psychopathology in a Mexican American Population." *Journal of Abnormal Psychology* 74, no. 2 (April 1969): 177-80.

1798. Rusk, Marian Terry. "A Study of Delinquency among Urban Mexican-American Youth." Doctoral dissertation, University of Southern California, 1969.

1799. Casavantes, Edward J. "Deviant Behavior in the Mexican-American Student and Its Relation to Education. A Position Paper." Albuquerque, New Mexico: Southwestern Cooperative Educational Lab., August 1970. ERIC ED 060 989.

1800. Woods, Richard G., and Harkins, Arthur M. "Indians and Other Americans in Minnesota Correctional Institutions. The National Study of American Indian Education." Minneapolis: University of Minnesota, Training Center for Community Programs, March 1970. ERIC ED 042 189.

1801. Aumann, Jon, et al. *The Chicano Addict: An Analysis of Factors Influencing Rehabilitation in a Treatment and Prevention Program.* Phoenix, Arizona: Valle Del Sol, Inc., 1972. ERIC ED 064 007.

1802. Lee, David López. "Cultural Identity: An Approach to Preventing Delinquency among Chicanos." Los Angeles, California: Special Services for Groups, Inc., 1972. ERIC ED 075 136.

1803. Dieppa, Ismael. "The Zoot-Suit Riots Revisited: The Role of Private Philanthropy in Youth Problems of Mexican-Americans." Doctoral dissertation, University of Southern California, 1973.

1804. Hunter, Michael Nathan. "A Comparison of Mexican-American and Caucasian Male Juvenile Detainees." Doctoral dissertation, University of Utah, 1973.

1805. Guinn, Robert Kenneth, Jr. "Characteristics of Drug Use among Mexican-American Students of the Lower Rio Grande Valley." Doctoral dissertation, Texas A&M University, 1974.

1806. Yiannakis, Andrew. "Psychological Profiles of Delinquent and Nondelinquent Participants in a Sports Program." Paper presented at the annual convention of the American Alliance for Health, Physical Education, and Recreation, Anaheim, California, 1974. ERIC ED 098 152.

3.10 Dropout

1807. Buckner, H.A. "A Study of Pupil Elimination and Failure among Mexicans." Master's thesis, University of Southern California, 1935.

1808. Doerr, Marvin Ferdinand. "Problems of the Elimination of Mexican Pupils from School." Master's thesis, University of Texas at Austin, 1938.

1809. McGregor, Mrs. R.P. "The Elimination of Eighth Grade Graduates among the Mexicans from the High Schools of a Certain Small City in California." Master's thesis, University of Southern California, 1940.

1810. Pipes, Karl M. "A Study of the Failures and Drop-Outs in the San Benito High School." Master's thesis, University of Texas at Austin, 1950.

1811. Frenzel, Rufus Emil. "Factors That Contribute to Non-Attendance in School of Latin-American Children and to Withdrawal after Entering the Ninth Grade in Big Wells Independent School District." Master's thesis, Southwest Texas State University, 1951.

1812. Hayes, James V. "An Analysis of Latin-American Partial Attendance and Drop-Outs in the Elementary Schools of Eagle Pass, Texas, in Recent Years." Master's thesis, University of Texas at Austin, 1952.

1813. Wilson, Joe Harvey. "Secondary School Dropouts with Special Reference to Spanish-Speaking Youth in Texas." Doctoral dissertation, University of Texas at Austin, 1953.

1814. Low, Wilson E. "A Study of the Failures and Withdrawals of Martin High School, Laredo, Texas." Master's thesis, University of Texas at Austin, 1954.

1815. Ybarra, Jesse R. "A Study to Determine Why Spanish-Speaking Children Drop Out of School in Junior and Senior School in a Particular Community in San Antonio, Texas." Master's thesis, Trinity University, 1955.

1816. Luján, Juan R. "Fourteen-Year-Old Drop-Outs in the Harlingen School System." Master's thesis, University of Texas at Austin, 1956.

1817. Muñoz, Rosalio Florian. "Differences in Drop-Out and Other School Behavior between Two Groups of Tenth Grade Boys in an Urban High School." Doctoral dissertation, University of Southern California, 1957.

1818. Whitaker, Neely, and Burk, Carl J. *Summary Report of the Study of Drop-Outs in the Three Senior High Schools, Compton Union High School District.* California: Office of the Los Angeles County Superintendent of Schools, 1960.

1819. Baker, William Pitt. "1961 Follow-up Study of Drop-Outs and Graduates of 1957-58 and 1959-60: With Special Reference to Problems Encountered by Bilingual (Mexican-American) Leavers." San Jose, California: San Jose East Side Union High School District, December 1962. ERIC ED 039 088.

1820. Bullock, Paul, and Singleton, Robert. "What to Do with the Drop-Out?" *New Republic* 147, no. 16 (20 October 1962): 17-18.

1821. Grimm, Louis. "School Dropouts: A Comparison of Interests in School with Peer and Authority Relationships." Master's thesis, Our Lady of the Lake College, 1964.

1822. Whitworth, Wallace. "School Drop-Outs: A Comparison of Interest in School with Peer and Authority Relationship." Master's thesis, Our Lady of the Lake College, Worden School of Social Service, 1964.

1823. Takesian, Sarkis Armen. *A Comparative Study of the Mexican American Graduate and Dropout.* San Francisco: R and E Research Associates, 1971; doctoral dissertation, University of Southern California, 1967.

1824. Baker, William Pitt. "1969 Follow-Up Study of Dropouts and Graduates of 1962-63 and 1964-65; With Special Reference to Problems Encountered by Mexican-American Leavers." California: San Jose East Side Union High School District, March 1969. ERIC ED 039 089.

1825. Wages, Sherry D., et al. "Mexican American Teen-Age School Dropouts: Reasons for Leaving School and Orientations toward Subsequent Educational Attainment." Paper presented at the meeting of the Southwestern Sociological Association, Houston, Texas, April 1969. ERIC ED 028 854.

1826. Kuvlesky, William P., and Wages, Sherry. "Differences in the Occupational and Educational Projections of Mexican American High School Students and Dropout Age Peers." Paper read before the Southwestern Sociological Association meeting, Dallas, Texas, March 1970. ERIC ED 039 989.

1827. Blair, Philip M. "Rates of Return to Schooling of Majority and Minority Groups in Santa Clara County, California." Doctoral dissertation, Stanford University, 1971.

1828. Brawner, Marlyn R. "Factors in the School Completion Rates of Mexican-American Children in Racine, Wisconsin." Doctoral dissertation, University of Iowa, 1971.

1829. Wages, Sherry D. "Mexican American Dropouts in the Valley—Their Reasons for Leaving School and Their Educational and Occupational Status Projections." Master's thesis, Texas A&M University, 1971. ERIC ED 078 983.

1830. Baker, William P., and Jenson, Henry C. "Mexican American, Black and Other Graduates and Dropouts. A Follow-Up Study Covering 15 Years of Change, 1956-1971. Fourth in a Five-Year Series of Follow-Up Studies of School Leavers of East Side Union High School District." California: San Jose East Side Union High School District, September 1973. ERIC ED 091 091.

1831. Blair, Philip M. "Rates of Return to Education of Mexican-Americans and European-Americans in Santa Clara County, California." *Comparative Education Review* 17, no. 1 (February 1973): 26-43.

1832. Blevins, Hubert W., Jr. "A Comparative Study of Mexican American and Anglo Dropouts in a Large Metropolitan School District in Texas." Doctoral dissertation, North Texas State University, 1975.

1833. Cordova, Charles Gilbert. "A Comparison of Educational Characteristics of Mexican-American and Anglo Graduates and Dropouts in Greeley, Colorado." Doctoral dissertation, University of Northern Colorado, 1975.

1834. Rosales, Raul G. "General Educational Development Certification: Effects of G.E.D. Certification on Migrant Recipients as Compared to Migrant Dropouts in South Texas." Doctoral dissertation, University of Houston, 1975.

4. SCHOOLS

4.1 Administration

1835. Holliday, Jay Newton. "A Study of Non-Attendance in Miguel Hidalgo School of Brawley, California." Master's thesis, University of Southern California, 1935.

1836. Graeber, Llian Kernaghan. "A Study of Attendance at Thomas Jefferson High School, Los Angeles, California." Master's thesis, University of Southern California, 1938.

1837. Merriot, M.E. "Administrative Responsibilities for Minorities." *California Journal of Secondary Education* 18, no . 6 (October 1943): 362-64.

1838. Powell, Mrs. Sadie Ray (Graham). "How to Increase Attendance in a Mexican School." Master's thesis, Southwest Texas State University, 1943.

1839. Parada, Mrs. Stella (Garza). "School Attendance of Southside School (Latin-American), San Marcos, Texas." Master's thesis, Southwest Texas State University, 1945.

1840. Brameld, Theodore. *Minority Problems in the Public Schools: A Study of Administrative Policies and Practices in Seven School Systems.* New York: Harper, 1946.

1841. Elms, James Edwin. "Attendance of Mexican and Anglo Students in Two Austin, Texas Schools." Master's thesis, University of Texas at Austin, 1950.

1842. Partridge, Donnie Lee. "An Analysis of Pupil Personnel Factors in an Elementary School." Master's thesis, University of Texas at Austin, 1951.

1843. Young, Mary Winkle. "A Proposed Program of Supervision for Teaching Non-English Speaking Six-Year-Old Beginners in Edinburg Schools." Master's thesis, Texas A&I University at Kingsville, 1952.

1844. Box, W.J. "To Determine the Factors Influencing the Attendance of Spanish-Culture Children in Raymondville Elementary Schools." Master's thesis, Texas A&I University at Kingsville, 1952.

1845. Gutiérrez, Emeterio, Jr. "A Study of School Attendance of Migrant Students in Grulla, Texas." Master's thesis, University of Texas at Austin, 1952.

1846. Daly, Mary Ann (Beck). "The Educational Problem of the Mexican Migrants of Texas with Specific Reference to Average Daily Attendance." Master's thesis, Southwest Texas State University, 1955.

1847. Uslan, David T. "Educational Regionalism in Northern California: A Cooperative Study of the Organizational Structure of Emerging Educational Regionalism by the Offices of Northern California County Superintendent of Schools." n.p.: Northern California County Superintendent of Schools Office, 1967.

1848. Lynch, Patrick D. "Training Mexican American School Principals: An Analysis of a Program's Hits and Misses." University Park: New Mexico State University, February 1969. ERIC ED 025 371.

1849. Managers, Dennis H. "Education in the Grapes of Wrath; Problems of an Elementary School Principal." *National Elementary Principal* 50, no. 2 (November 1970): 34-40.

1850. Yamamoto, David Hiroshi. "Role Conflict Resolution: An Exploratory Study of Minority Group School Principals." Doctoral dissertation, Stanford University, 1970.

1851. Gustafson, Richard A., et al. "The Organizational Climate in Schools Having High Concentrations of Mexican-Americans." Paper presented at the 51st annual meeting of the Western Psychological Association, San Francisco, California, 24 April 1971. ERIC ED 053 849.

1852. Franc, Max B. "Communication, Administration, and Mexican-American Administrators." Paper presented at the Rocky Mountain Social Science Association meeting, Salt Lake City, Utah, 28-29 April 1972. ERIC ED 076 283.

1853. Franc, Max B. "Minority Attitudes and Opinions That Have Impacts on Administration of Minority-Oriented Programs." Paper presented at the Pacific Chapter of the American Association for Public Opinion Research meeting, Asilomar, California, 3-5 March 1972. ERIC ED 076 282.

1854. Arrévalo, Rodolfo. "A Comparative Study of Mexican-American and Anglo-American School Administrators' Perceptions of Responsibility, Authority and Delegation." Doctoral dissertation, University of Michigan, 1973.

1855. Ballesteros, Octavio Antonio. "The Effectiveness of Public School Education for Mexican-American Students as Perceived by Principals of Elementary Schools of Predominantly Mexican-American Enrollment." Doctoral dissertation, East Texas State University, 1974.

1856. Franc, Max B. "Improving Ethics and Morality in the Public Service: Looking to Mexican-American Administrators." Paper presented at the Rocky Mountain Council for Latin American Studies, Lubbock, Texas, 15-16 March 1974. ERIC ED 114 214.

1857. García, Tony. "The Role of the Principal Who Supervises a Bilingual Education Program within His School in Regard to Planning, Program Operations, In-Service Training, Community Development and Evaluation." Doctoral dissertation, University of Houston, 1974.

1858. Ramírez, Augustine. "Correlates of Success of Selected Mexican-American Educational Leaders in California." Doctoral dissertation, University of Southern California, 1974.

1859. Adams, Joe A. "Anglo American Elementary School Principals' Perceptions of the Behavior of Mexican American Students." Doctoral dissertation, University of Toledo, 1975.

1860. Kemper, Lawrence Bartlett. "Morale of Elementary Principals in Mexican-American Poverty Schools." Doctoral dissertation, University of Southern California, 1975.

1861. Nectoux, Joseph J. "An Investigation of Perceptions Held by Elementary School Principals, Teachers, and Teacher Aides of Collier County, Florida, toward Elementary School-Aged Migrant Children of Mexican-American Heritage." Doctoral dissertation, University of Southern Mississippi, 1975.

4.2 Teachers

1862. West, Guy A. "Race Attitudes among Teachers in the Southwest." *Journal of Abnormal and Social Psychology* 31, no. 3 (1936/1937): 331-37.

1863. Shannon, Fain Gillock. "A Comparative Study of De irable Teacher Traits as Listed by Anglo American and Latin American Pupils." Master's thesis, University of Texas at Austin, 1939.

1864. Abraham, Willard. "The Bi-Lingual Child and His Teacher." *Elementary English* 34, no. 7 (November 1957): 474-78.

1865. Ulibarri, Horacio. "Teacher Awareness of Socio-Cultural Differences in Multicultural Classrooms." Master's thesis, University of New Mexico, 1959.

1866. Ulibarri, Horacio. "Teacher Awareness of Sociocultural Differences in Multicultural Classrooms." *Sociology and Social Research* 45, no. 1 (October 1960): 49-55.

1867. Garner, M.V. "A Study of the Educational Backgrounds and Attitudes of Teachers toward Algebra as Related to the Attitudes and Achievement of Their Anglo-American and Latin-American Pupils in First-Year Algebra Classes of Texas." Doctoral dissertation, North Texas State University, 1963.

1868. Gemar, Robert A. "An Investigation into the Relationship of the Selected Personal Attitudes of Teachers and Students of the Seventh and Eighth Grades in a Particular School of Differing Ethnic Backgrounds." Master's thesis, Sacramento State College, 1965.

1869. Stocks, William D. "Searching for Teachers within Subcultures." *Childhood Education* 42, no. 2 (October 1965): 86-88.

1870. Wonder, John P. "The Bilingual Mexican-American as a Potential Teacher of Spanish." *Hispania* 48, no. 1 (March 1965): 97-99.

1871. Arnez, Nancy L. "The Effect of Teacher Attitudes upon the Culturally Different." *School and Society* 94 (19 March 1966): 149-52.

1872. Cooke, E.D., Jr. "Interpersonal Orientation of Elementary Teachers with Mexican-American Pupils." Doctoral dissertation, University of California at Los Angeles, 1967.

1873. Geis, Sally Ann Brown. "The Teacher-Student Role Relationship in Junior High Schools Serving Significant Numbers of Disadvantaged." Doctoral dissertation, University of Denver, 1967.

1874. Adler, Elaine France. "A Study of Teachers' Attitudes towards the Theory and Methods of Teaching English." Master's thesis, University of California at Los Angeles, 1968.

1875. Richards, Catharine V. "Migrant Teacher." *Instructor* 77, no. 10 (1968): 73.

1876. Anderson, James G. "Teachers of Minority Groups: The Origins of Their Attitudes and Instructional Practices." Las Cruces: New Mexico State University, January 1969. ERIC ED 026 192.

1877. Jones, James C., and Hempstead, R. Ross. *Teachers for the Disadvantaged.* San Francisco, California: Jossey-Bass, Inc., Publishers, 1969.

1878. Cordova, R. Rudy. "Assessing Attitudes and Performance of Student Teachers in Mexican American Schools." Doctoral dissertation, University of California at Los Angeles, 1970.

1879. García, Ernesto F. "Modification of Teacher Behavior in Teaching the Mexican-Americans." Albuquerque, New Mexico: Southwestern Cooperative Educational Lab., 1970. ERIC ED 057 971.

1880. Oliveira, Arnulfo Luis. "A Comparison of the Verbal Teaching Behaviors of Junior High School Mexican American and Anglo American Teachers of Social Studies and Mathematics with Classes of Predominantly Spanish-Speaking Children." Doctoral dissertation, University of Texas at Austin, 1970.

1881. DeHart, Ruth S. "An Investigation of the Congruence between Selected Values of Fifth Grade Teachers and Pupils from Varied Ethnic and Socioeconomic Backgrounds in an Urban School Setting." Doctoral dissertation, University of Houston, 1971.

1882. Fielder, William; Cohen, Ronald; and Feeney, Stephanie. "An Attempt to Replicate the Teacher Expectancy Effect." *Psychological Reports* 29, no. 3, part 2 (December 1971): 1223-28.

1883. Haro, Carlos Manuel. "Correlation Study of Interpersonal Attitudes of Teachers and Chicano Students and Achievement." Master's thesis, University of California at Los Angeles, 1971.

1884. Baca, Joseph Donald. "A Comparative Study of Differences in Perception of Mexican American Students between Anglo and Mexican American Secondary School Teachers in Dona Ana County (New Mexico)." Master's thesis, New Mexico State University, 1972. ERIC ED 065 218.

1885. Blubaugh, Richard E. "Teachers in the Fields." *American Education* 8, no. 4 (May 1972): 24-29.

1886. Klingstedt, Joe Lars. "Teachers of Middle School Mexican American Children: Indicators of Effectiveness and Implications for Teacher Education." El Paso: University of Texas at El Paso, 1972. ERIC ED 059 828.

1887. Miller, Leslie M. "Evaluational Reactions of Mexican-American and Anglo Teachers to Children's Speech." *Western Speech* 36, no. 2 (spring 1972): 109-14.

1888. Sánchez, Richard Monarrez. "Verbal Interaction Patterns, Student Opinions, and Teacher Perceptions in Classrooms with Mexican-American Student Enrollment." Doctoral dissertation, Western Michigan University, 1972.

1889. Sebastian, Carolyn Bryan. "Teachers' Understandings of the Behavior of Mexican-American Children." Doctoral dissertation, University of Southern California, 1972.

1890. Tyo, Alexina M. "A Comparison of the Verbal Behaviors of Teachers in Interaction with Migrant and Non-Migrant Students." Geneseo: State University of New York College at Geneseo, Center for Migrant Studies, 1972. ERIC ED 075 160.

1891. Ward, James H. "Spanish Teachers and Spanish Speaking Minorities." *Hispania* 55, no. 4 (December 1972): 893-95.

1892. Drake, Diana M. "Anglo American Teachers, Mexican American Students, and Dissonance in Our Schools." *Elementary School Journal* 73, no. 4 (January 1973): 207-12.

1893. Rosenfeld, Lawrence B. "An Investigation of Teachers' Stereotyping Behavior: The Influence of Mode of Presentation, Ethnicity, and Social Class on Teachers' Evaluations of Students." Albuquerque: University of New Mexico, Department of Speech Communication, October 1973. ERIC ED 090 172.

1894. U.S. Commission on Civil Rights. *Teachers and Students: Differences in Teacher Interaction with Mexican American and Anglo Students. Report V: Mexican American Education Study.* Washington, D.C.: Government Printing Office, March 1973. ERIC ED 073 881.

1895. Alfaro, Manuel Rios, Jr. "A Study of the Attitudes and Task Assignments of Mexican-American and Non-Mexican-American Teacher Aides in the Michigan Migrant Educational Program." Doctoral dissertation, Michigan State University, 1974.

1896. Andersson, Theodore. "The Role of the Teacher in a Bilingual Bicultural Community." *Hispania* 57, no. 4 (December 1974): 927-32.

1897. Castillo, Max S., and Cruz, Josue, Jr. "Special Competencies for Teachers of Pre-school Chicano Children: Rationale, Content, and Assessment." *Young Children* 29, no. 6 (September 1974): 341-47.

1898. Chacon, Gloria, and Bowman, James, eds. *The Recruitment, Channeling, and Place-ment of Chicano Teachers.* Lincoln, Nebraska: University of Nebraska Printing and Duplicating Service, 1974. ERIC ED 107 430.

1899. Copeland, Robert McDaniel. "A Comparative Study of Visually Perceived Teacher Nonverbal Behavior and the Formation of Student Affect among Members of Three Different Ethnic Groups." Doctoral dissertation, Oregon State University, 1974.

1900. Flores, Alfredo Rodríguez. "A Study of Mexican-American and Anglo Teachers' Attitudes and Behaviors toward Mexican-American Children." Doctoral disserta-tion, Northern Illinios University, 1974.

1901. Johnson, David L. "Teacher-Pupil Interaction in Bilingual Elementary School Classrooms." Paper presented at the Southwestern Social Science Association meetings, Dallas, Texas, 28 March 1974. ERIC ED 089 900.

1902. Strom, Rober D., and Engelbrecht, Guillermina. "Creative Peer Teaching." *Journal of Creative Behavior* 8, no. 2 (1974): 93-100.

1903. Vásquez, Jo Ann. "Reaction Patterns of Anglo Student-Teachers toward Anglo Compared with Mexican-American Elementary School Students." Doctoral dis-sertation, Claremont Graduate School, 1974.

1904. Wahab, Zaher. "Teacher-Pupil Transaction in Bi-Racial Classrooms; Implications for Instruction." Paper presented at the annual convention of the Pacific Socio-logical Association, San Jose, California, March 1974. ERIC ED 092 294.

1905. García, Soledad Sotres. "The Mexican-American Educator in the Los Angeles Uni-fied School District: A Descriptive Study of His Professional Status, His Aspira-tions, and His Image." Doctoral dissertation, University of Southern California, 1975.

4.3 Teacher Training

1906. U.S. Department of Interior. Bureau of Education. *Opportunities for the Prepara-tion of Teachers of Children of Native and Minority Groups,* by Katherine M. Cook. Washington, D.C.: Government Printing Office, 1937.

1907. Jonson, Carl R. "A Study of the Spanish American Normal School at El Rito." Master's thesis, University of New Mexico, 1939.

1908. England, Byron. "El Paso Develops Aids for Teachers of Bilinguals." *Texas Out-look* 29, no. 10 (October 1945): 42, 44.

1909. Tinsley, Willa Vaughn, director. "Inter-American Teacher Education Program in the Southwest; School and Community Cooperation; Final Report." San Marcos: Southwest Texas State Teachers College, 1945.

1910. Chang, D.K. *A Guide of Understanding and Teaching of Mexican-American Adolescents.* San Francisco: R and E Research Associates, 1973; master's thesis, University of Southern California, 1957.

1911. Prichard, Michael T. "A Resource Guide for Grant Union High School District Teachers Seeking to Promote an Understanding of Mexican-American Culture." Master's thesis, Sacramento State College, 1964.

1912. Past, Ray. "Bilingualism—From the Viewpoint of Recruitment and Preparation of Bilingual Teachers." Paper presented at the annual conference of the Southwest Council of Foreign Language Teachers, El Paso, Texas, 4 November 1966. ERIC ED 018 297.

1913. Willey, Darrell S. "An Interdisciplinary Institute for the In-Service Training of Teachers and Other School Personnel to Accelerate the School Acceptance of Indian, Negro, and Spanish-Speaking Pupils of the Southwest. Interim Report No. 2." University Park: New Mexico State University, December 1966. ERIC ED 015 033.

1914. Burger, Henry G. *Ethno-Pedagogy: A Manual in Cultural Sensitivity, with Techniques for Improving Cross-Cultural Teaching by Fitting Ethnic Patterns.* Albuquerque, New Mexico: Southwestern Cooperative Educational Laboratory, 1968. ERIC ED 091 109.

1915. "Ethno-Pedagogy: A Manual in Cultural Sensitivity with Techniques for Improving Cross-Cultural Teaching by Fitting Ethnic Patterns." Albuquerque, New Mexico: Southwestern Cooperative Educational Laboratory, 1968.

1916. Manuel, Hershel T. "Recruiting and Training Teachers for Spanish-Speaking Children in the Southwest." *School and Society* 96 (30 March 1968): 211-14.

1917. Carter, Thomas P. "Preparing Teachers for Mexican American Children." Washington, D.C.: National Education Association, February 1969. ERIC ED 025 367.

1918. Holland, Thomas R., and Lee, Catherine M., eds. "The Alternative of Radicalism: Radical and Conservative Possibilities for Teaching the Teachers of America's Young Children; Proceedings of the National Conference of the Tri-University Project. Fifth Project, New Orleans, January 29-31, 1969." Lincoln: University of Nebraska, Curriculum Development Center, January 1969. ERIC ED 046 941.

1919. Karr, Ken, and McGuire, Esther. "Mexican Americans on the Move—Are Teacher Preparation Programs in Higher Education Ready?" 1969. ERIC ED 031 348.

1920. Ramírez, Manuel, III. "Potential Contributions by the Behavioral Sciences to Effective Preparation Programs for Teachers of Mexican American Children." University Park: New Mexico State University, February 1969. ERIC ED 025 370.

1921. Saunders, Jack O.L. "The Blueprint Potentials of the Cooperative Teacher Education Preparation; Utilizing the Talented Mexican American." University Park: New Mexico State University, February 1969. ERIC ED 025 372.

1922. Van Meter, Ed., and Barba, Alma, eds. "Regional Conference on Teacher Education for Mexican-Americans (New Mexico State University, February 13-15, 1969). Conference Proceedings." University Park: New Mexico State University, March 1969. ERIC ED 027 444.

1923. Baty, Roger Mendenhall. "The Effect of Cross-Cultural Inservice Training on Selected Attitudes of Elementary School Teacher Volunteers: A Field Experiment." Palo Alto: Stanford University, Stanford International Development Education Center, 1970. ERIC ED 046 902.

1924. Tallant, Weldon J. "Changes in Pre-Service Teachers Involved in a Multicultural Training Program Utilizing Formal Presentations, Sensitivity Training, Planned Social Activities, and a Cooperative Living Arrangement." Doctoral dissertation, East Texas State University, 1970.

1925. "Tri-Cultural Sensitivity In-Service Training Program. Sample Teaching Units through Cultural Awareness." Bernalillo, New Mexico: Bernalillo Public Schools, April 1970. ERIC ED 051 327.

1926. Ulibarri, Mari-Luci. "In-Service Teacher Education in a Tri-Ethnic Community: A Participant Observer Study." Doctoral dissertation, University of New Mexico, May 1970. ERIC ED 044 680.

1927. Cabello-Argandoña, Robert; Gómez-Quinones, Juan; and Tamayo, William. "Library Services and Chicano Periodicals: A Critical Look at Librarianship." *Aztlán* 2, no. 2 (fall 1971): 151-72.

1928. Zintz, Miles V., et al. "The Implications of Bilingual Education for Developing Multicultural Sensitivity through Teacher Education." September 1971. ERIC ED 054 071.

1929. Baty, Roger M. *Reeducating Teachers for Cultural Awareness: Preparation for Educating Mexican-American Children in Northern California. Praeger Special Studies in U.S. Economic and Social Development Series.* New York: Praeger Publishers, 1972.

1930. Epstein, Erwin H., and Pizzillo, Joseph J., eds. "A Human Relations Guide for Teachers: Linguistic Minorities in the Classroom." 1972. ERIC ED 066 417.

1931. Grant, June. "Proceedings of a Workshop on the Preparation of Personnel in Education of Bilingual Hearing-Impaired Children Ages 0-4." San Antonio, Texas: Trinity University, November 1972. ERIC ED 113 908.

1932. Lingstedt, Joe Lars. "Teachers of Middle School Mexican American Children: Indicators of Effectiveness and Implications for Teacher Education." 1972. ERIC ED 059 828.

1933. Magee, Bettie, et al. "A Description of Simulation Technique to Develop Teacher and Counselor Empathy with the Spanish Speaking Student." 1972. ERIC ED 065 254.

1934. Piper, Richard, comp. "Program of In-Service Education for Teachers. Hispanic Urban Center Evaluation Report." Los Angeles, California: Los Angeles Unified School District, 10 July 1972. ERIC ED 067 184.

1935. Terry, Dewayne. "Orientation and Inservice Education for Teachers of Mexican-American Pupils." Doctoral dissertation, University of California at Los Angeles, 1972.

1936. Bartley, Diana E. "Staff Development Microteaching Workshop in Adult Basic Education-TESOL: A Region V Project. Final Report." Milwaukee: University of Wisconsin, Tri-State Adult Basic Education Workshop, 1973. ERIC ED 090 417.

1937. U.S. Department of Health, Education, and Welfare. Office of Education. *A Model Program for Training Personnel to Develop Solutions to Major Educational Problems in the Indian and Mexican-American Communities. Final Report,* by James A. Hale. Washington, D.C.: Government Printing Office, December 1973. ERIC ED 101 896.

1938. Escobedo, Theresa Herrera. "The Impact of a Mexican American Cultural Awareness Model on the Attitudes of Prospective Teachers." Doctoral dissertation, Texas Tech University, 1974.

1939. García, Ernest F. "Chicano Cultural Diversity: Implication for Competency-Based Teacher Education." 1974. ERIC ED 091 375.

1940. Pérez, Bertha G. "A Process Model for Inservice Education for Teachers of Mexican-American Students." Doctoral dissertation, University of Massachusetts, 1974.

1941. Pearce, Consuelo Q. de. "Title I Instructional Aides' Training Sessions (Nampa, Idaho, School District 131, November 21, 1974-January 2, 1975)." Nampa, Idaho: Migrant Education Resource Center, 1975. ERIC ED 119 881.

1942. Ruiz, Eliseo, Jr. "A Training Component Designed to Affect the Attitudes and Behavior of Educational Practitioners toward Mexican-American Students." Doctoral dissertation, University of Texas at Austin, 1975.

1943. McConnell, Beverly. "Training Migrant Paraprofessionals in Bilingual Mini Head Start. Mid-Year Evaluation, 1975-76 Program Year. Evaluation of Progress No. 8." Ephrata, Washington: Washington State Intermediate School District 104, January 1976. ERIC ED 121 496.

4.4 Counseling

1944. Broom, Perry Morris. "An Interpretative Analysis of the Economic and Educational Status of Latin Americans in Texas, with Emphasis upon the Basic Factors Underlying an Approach to an Improved Program of Occupational Guidance, Training and Adjustment for Secondary Schools." Doctoral dissertation, University of Texas at Austin, 1942.

1945. Hill, Marguerite W. "A Proposed Guidance Program for Mexican Youth in the Junior High Schools." Master's thesis, Claremont Graduate School, 1945.

1946. "Teachers and Counselors for Mexican American Children." Austin, Texas: Southwest Educational Development Lab., 1959.

1947. California. State Department of Education. *References on Counseling Minority Youth: A Four Part Series,* by Ruth B. Love. Sacramento: California State Department of Education, June 1964. ERIC ED 034 232.

1948. Caskey, Owen L., ed. "Guidance Needs of Mexican American Youth. Proceedings of the Invitational Conference (First, November 10, 1967, Lubbock, Texas)." Austin, Texas: Southwest Educational Development Lab., 1967. ERIC ED 036 347.

1949. Rippee, Billy Dean. "An Investigation of Anglo-American and Spanish-American Students' Expectations of the Counseling Relationship." Doctoral dissertation, New Mexico State University, 1967.

1950. Vontress, Clemont E. "Cultural Differences: Implications for Counseling." Paper presented before the American Personnel and Guidance Association, Washington, D.C., 10 April 1968. ERIC ED 023 105.

1951. Ainsworth, C.L., ed. "Teachers and Counselors for Mexican American Children." Austin, Texas: Southwest Educational Development Laboratory, 1969. ERIC ED 029 728.

1952. Caskey, Owen L., ed. "Community Responsibilities and School Guidance Programs for Mexican American Youth. A Report on the Proceedings of the Second Invitational Conference on Guidance Needs of Mexican American Youth, Lubbock, Texas, February 7, 1969." Austin, Texas: Southwest Educational Development Lab., February 1969. ERIC ED 041 646.

1953. Moore, Marilyn. "Counseling in Mexican American Schools as Perceived by Administrators, Counselors, Teachers, Students, and Community Leaders." Master's thesis, University of California, 1969.

1954. Webb, Doris. " 'No High Adobe!' Counseling with Mexican-American Children." *School Counselor* 17, no. 4 (March 1969): 251-54.

1955. McGehearty, Loyce, and Womble, Mary. "Case Analysis: Consultation and Counseling." *Elementary School Guidance and Counseling* 5, no. 2 (December 1970): 141-44, 147.

1956. Acevedo, Homero. "An Approach for Counseling Mexican-American Parents of Mentally Retarded Children. Vol. 1, No. 4." Austin: University of Texas at Austin, Department of Special Education, 1971. ERIC ED 055 385.

1957. Cross, William C., and Maldonado, Bonnie. "Counselor, the Mexican-American and the Stereotype." *Elementary School Guidance and Counseling* 6 (October 1971): 27-31.

1958. McCoy, Georgia. "Cause Analysis: Consultation and Counseling." *Elementary School Guidance and Counseling,* 5, no. 3 (March 1971): 221-25.

1959. Palomares, Uvaldo H.; Welch, Janet; and Curren, James. "Portrait of a Counselor: A Group Interview." *Personnel and Guidance Journal* 50, no. 2 (October 1971): 130-35.

1960. Pollack, Erwin W. *Spanish-Speaking Students and Guidance.* New York: Houghton Mifflin Company, 1971.

1961. González, Carlos, et al. "Counseling the Mexican-American Student: A Position Paper." March 1972. ERIC ED 101 259.

1962. Leo, Paul Frank. "The Effects of Two Types of Group Counseling upon the Academic Achievement and Self-Concept of Mexican-American Pupils in the Elementary School." Doctoral dissertation, University of the Pacific, 1972. ERIC ED 059 002.

1963. Mansfield, Carl Clinton. "Black, Mexican-American, and Anglo Graduates' Perceptions of Their Secondary School Counselor." Doctoral dissertation, University of Arizona, 1972.

1964. McCoy, R.D. "Migrant Counseling: The Oyster Method." *School Counselor* 19 (May 1972): 349-53.

1965. Senour, Maria Nieto. "The Needs of Mexican-American Elementary School Students and Their Implications for Counselor Preparation." Doctoral dissertation, Wayne State University, 1972.

1966. Fowler, Nelva D'Orsay. "Characteristics of Mexican-American, Black, and Anglo Counselors in Texas Public Schools." Doctoral dissertation, East Texas State University, 1973.

1967. Mullen, Frances A. "Psychological Services to Spanish Speaking Children in the Schools of Chicago." Paper presented at the 14th Interamerican Congress on Psychology, São Paulo, Brazil, April 1973. ERIC ED 091 451.

1968. Alemán, Ramón. "Chicano Counselor Training: Curriculum and beyond Curriculum." Paper presented at the American Personnel and Guidance Association Convention, New Orleans, Louisiana, April 1974. ERIC ED 094 273.

1969. Escobedo, Arturo E. *Chicano Counselor.* Lubbock, Texas: Trucha Publications, 1974.

1970. Etchegoinberry, Paul Leon. "The Effects of Group-Centered Counseling on the Attitudes, Feelings and Behavior of Chicano Inner City EMRT Students." Doctoral dissertation, University of Southern California, 1974.

1971. Gares, Vaughn Dale. "A Comparative Investigation of the Occupational Counseling Given to Mexican-American and Anglo-American Students upon Entering the Community College." Doctoral dissertation, United States International University, 1974.

1972. Maes, Wayne R., and Rinaldi, John R. "Counseling the Chicano Child." *Elementary School Guidance and Counseling* 8, no. 4 (May 1974): 279-84.

1973. Tumlinson, Mildred Yates. "Personality Characteristics in Relation to Preference of Computerized Counseling and Concept of Others." Master's thesis, Texas A&I University at Kingsville, 1974.

1974. Casaus, Luis. "Training Chicano Counselors To Be Change Agents in Resolving Community and School Conflicts." Paper presented at the annual meeting of the American Educational Research Association, Washington, D.C., 30 March-3 April 1975. ERIC ED 104 592.

1975. Goolsby, Irene G. "The Effects of Individual Counseling on the Self-Concept of the Disadvantaged Student." Master's thesis, California State University at Long Beach, 1975.

1976. Hodges, William Edward. "The Effects of an Intensive Group Counselling Process on Failing Chicano Males." Doctoral dissertation, University of Utah, 1975.

1977. Masterman, Leslie John. "Effects of Modeling on Self-Referent Talk of Mexican-American Girls with Culturally Similar and Dissimilar Counselors." Doctoral dissertation, Arizona State University, 1975.

1978. Schraer, Ronald Gene. "The Effects of Two Modeling Methods on Mexican-American Counselees' Self-Referent Affective Statements, Time Perspective, Degree of Concreteness and Content of Verbalizations in the Initial Counseling Interview." Doctoral dissertation, University of Missouri, Kansas City, 1975.

1979. DeBlassie, Richard R. *Counseling with Mexican American Youth: Preconceptions and Processes.* Austin, Texas: Learning Concepts, 1976.

1980. Ragusa, Sister Rosalie Ann, F.M.A. "A Guide for Teachers in Multicultural Education at Corpus Christi School, San Francisco, California." Master's thesis, California State University at Long Beach, 1976.

4.5 Libraries

1981. Darling, Richard L. "School Library Services for the Culturally Deprived Child." *School Life* 46, no. 1 (October 1963): 18-20.

1982. Burr, Elizabeth. "Along the Migrant Stream." *Library Journal* 91, no. 2 (15 January 1966): 335-36.

1983. Dudley, Miriam Sue. "Chicano Library Program, Based on the 'Research Skills in the Library Context' Program Developed for Chicano High Potential Students in the Department of Special Educational Programs." Los Angeles: University of California at Los Angeles Library, 1970. ERIC ED 045 105.

1984. Haro, Robert P. "Chicanos and Libraries." *American Libraries* 1, no. 10 (November 1970): 932-33.

1985. Haro, Robert P. "How Mexican-Americans View Libraries; East Los Angeles and Sacramento, California." *Wilson Library Bulletin* 44, no. 7 (March 1970): 736-42.

1986. Haro, Robert P. "Library Service to Mexican-Americans." *El Grito* 3, no. 3 (spring 1970): 30-37.

1987. Macías, Ysidro R. "Chicano Movement." *Wilson Library Bulletin* 44, no. 7 (March 1970): 731-35.

1988. "Manual for Providing Library Services to Indians and Mexican Americans." Las Cruces: New Mexico State University, Institute to Train School and Public Librarians to Work in Communities with Large Numbers of Mexican Americans and/or Indians, 8 June-3 July 1970. ERIC ED 047 872.

1989. Ramirez, William L. "Libraries and the Spanish-Speaking; Symposium." *Wilson Library Bulletin* 44, no. 7 (March 1970): 714-67.

1990. Reynolds, Mary B. "San Joaquin Valley, California: La biblioteca ambulante." *Wilson Library Bulletin* 44, no. 7 (March 1970): 767.

1991. Shepard, Marietta Daniels. "Reading Resources and Project LEER." *Wilson Library Bulletin* 44, no. 7 (March 1970): 743-50.

1992. Vadala, Julia, ed. "Hispano Library Services for Arizona, Colorado and New Mexico; A Workshop Held in Santa Fe, New Mexico, April 30, May 1-2, 1970." Boulder, Colorado: Western Interstate Commission for Higher Education, August 1970. ERIC ED 043 360.

1993. Wynn, Barbara L. "Oakland, California: La biblioteca Latino Americana." *Wilson Library Bulletin* 44, no. 7 (March 1970): 751-56.

1994. Zonligt, Martin J. "Library Services to Migrants." *Library Journal* 97, no. 4 (15 February 1972): 735-36.

1995. Freudenthal, Juan R. "Special Report: SALALM in Texas." *Wilson Library Bulletin* 49, no. 1 (September 1974): 80.

1996. Smith, Joshua I., ed. *Library and Information Services for Special Groups.* New York: Science Associates/International, Inc., 1974.

5. CURRICULUM

5.1 General

1997. Chávez, David J. "Civic Education of the Spanish American." Master's thesis, University of Texas at Austin, 1923.

1998. Allstrom, Eric W. "A Program of Social Education for a Mexican Community in the U.S." Master's thesis, University of Arizona, 1929.

1999. Wilder, L.A., Mrs. "Problems in the Teaching of Mexican Children." *Texas Outlook* 20, no. 8 (August 1936): 9-10.

2000. Rowan, Bob; Kendall, Ellis; and Stroud, Mary. "The Teaching of Bilingual Children." *Education* 70, no. 7 (March 1950): 423-26.

2001. Collings, Robert L. "A Program for Better Understanding of Bilingual Children at Washington." Master's thesis, Arizona State University, 1951.

2002. Saenz, Alfredo N. "A Field Study of Two Programs Designed for Preparing the Resident, Non-English Speaking Child of Spanish Culture to Meet First-Grade Requirements in One Year." Doctoral dissertation, University of Houston, 1957.

2003. "The Invisible Minority. Report of the NEA-Tucson Survey on the Teaching of Spanish to the Spanish-Speaking." Washington, D.C.: National Education Association, 1966. ERIC ED 017 222.

2004. California. State Department of Education. *Mexican-American Education Research Project. Progress Report, 1967,* by John Plakos. Los Angeles, California: California State Department of Education, 13 July 1967. ERIC ED 018 281.

2005. Angel, Frank. "Program Content to Meet the Educational Needs of Mexican Americans." University Park: New Mexico State University, 1968.

2006. Kniefel, Tanya Suarez. "Programs Available for Strengthening Education of Spanish-Speaking Students." Las Cruces, New Mexico: 1968. ERIC ED 025 366.

2007. Passow, A. Harry, ed. *Developing Programs for the Educationally Disadvantaged.* New York: Teachers College Press, 1968.

2008. Wilson, Herbert B. "Evaluation of the Influence of Educational Programs on Mexican-Americans." University Park: New Mexico State University, March 1968. ERIC ED 016 561.

2009. "Language and Area Studies Programs and the Participation of Spanish and Portuguese Speaking Minorities in American Society. Report of a Meeting Held at Miami, Florida, May 1-3, 1969." Washington, D.C.: Hispanic Foundation, October 1969. ERIC ED 036 599.

2010. Campbell, Duane E., and Salas, Rudolph M. "Teaching about the Chicano." *Social Education* 34, no. 6 (October 1970): 667-69, 672.

2011. Massad, Carolyn Emrick; Yamamoto, Kaoru; and Davis, O.L., Jr. "Stimulus Modes and Language Media: A Study of Bilinguals." *Psychology in the Schools* 7, no. 1 (1970): 38-42.

2012. Rocco, Raymond A. "The Chicano in the Social Sciences: Traditional Concepts, Myths, and Images." *Aztlán* 1, no. 2 (fall 1970): 75-98.

2013. Vaca, Nick C. "The Mexican-American in the Social Sciences; 1912-1970. Part I: 1912-1935." *El Grito* 3, no. 3 (spring 1970): 3-24.

2014. Vaca, Nick C. "The Mexican-American in the Social Sciences. Part II: 1936-1970." *El Grito* 4, no. 1 (fall 1970): 17-51.

2015. Crespin, Benjamin J. "Means of Facilitating Education Sought." *Education* 92, no. 2 (November 1971): 36-37.

2016. Gerry, Martin H. "Cultural Freedom in the Schools: The Right of Mexican-American Children to Succeed." 21 May 1971. ERIC ED 104 575.

2017. Lakin, David Schoonmaker. "Cross Age Tutoring with Mexican-American Pupils." Doctoral dissertation, University of California at Los Angeles, 1971.

2018. Ortega, Frank. "Special Education and Mexican Americans." *El Grito* 4, no. 4 (summer 1971): 29-35.

2019. Ortego, Philip D. "Schools for Mexican Americans: Between Two Cultures." *Saturday Review* 54 (17 April 1971): 62-64, 80-81.

2020. Rosen, Carl L., and Ortego, Philip D. "Resources: Teaching Spanish-Speaking Children." *The Reading Teacher* 25, no. 1 (October 1971): 11-13.

2021. Samora, Julian, and Galarza, Ernesto. "Research and Scholarly Activity." *Epoca: The National Concilio for Chicano Studies Journal* 1, no. 2 (winter 1971): 51-54.

2022. Estupinian, Rafael. "A Tri-Partite Development for the Cultural Arts in the Education of the Mexican-American." In *Adelante: An Emerging Design for Mexican-American Education*. Edited by Manuel Reyes Mazon. Austin: University of Texas at Austin, Center for Communication Research, 1972.

2023. Rosenthal, Ted L., and Zimmerman, Barry J. "Modeling by Exemplification and Instruction in Training Conservation." *Developmental Psychology* 6, no. 3 (May 1972): 392-401.

2024. Sánchez, Rodolfo B. "A Chicano Perspective on Social Work Curriculum Development. Social Work Education for Economically Disadvantaged Groups in Texas. An Occasional Paper of the Consortium of Texas Schools of Social Work." Paper presented at the Social Work Workshop, Houston, Texas, 13-14 April 1972. ERIC ED 072 892.

2025. Smith, George W., and Caskey, Owen L., eds. "Promising School Practices for Mexican Americans." Austin, Texas: Southwest Educational Development Lab., 1972. ERIC ED 064 003.

2026. Tindall, Lloyd W., et al. "An Examination of the Receptivity of Mexican-American and Anglo Rural Disadvantaged to Educational Programs." East Lansing: Michigan State University, Center for Rural Manpower and Public Affairs, March 1972. ERIC ED 060 974.

2027. Armendáriz, Juan. "Social Work Education for Economically Disadvantaged Groups in Texas. Final Report, July 1, 1970-August 31, 1973." Austin: University of Texas at Austin, Graduate School of Social Work, 1973. ERIC ED 080 255.

2028. Franc, Max B. "Broad Applications of Research on Programs Involving Mexican-Americans." Paper presented at the Rocky Mountain Council for Latin American Studies, Missoula, Montana, spring 1973. ERIC ED 076 284.

2029. Larez, Manuel. "Statement before the Federal Communications Commission." Paper presented to the Federal Communications Commission's Hearings on Children's Television, Washington, D.C., 8-10 January 1973. ERIC ED 071 441.

2030. Rodrigues, R.J. "A Few Directions in Chicano Literature." *English Journal* 62, no. 5 (May 1973): 724-29.

2031. Smith, Ian D. "Impact of Computer-Assisted Instruction on Student Attitudes." *Journal of Educational Psychology* 64, no. 3 (June 1973): 366-72.

2032. Wahab, Zaher. "Barrio School: White School in a Brown Community." Paper presented at the annual convention of the American Anthropological Association, New Orleans, Louisiana, 28 November-2 December 1973. ERIC ED 092 295.

2033. Keogh, Barbara K.; Becker, Lawrence D.; Kukic, Maurine, et al. "Programs for EH and EMR Pupils: Review and Recommendations, Part I." *Academic Therapy* 9, no. 3 (winter 1973-74): 187-98.

2034. Hosford, Ray E., and Bowles, Stephen A. "Determining Culturally Appropriate Reinforces for Anglo and Chicano Students." *Elementary School Guidance and Counseling* 8, no. 4 (May 1974): 290-300.

2035. Konstam, Patricia S. "Pioneering Media for Mexican Americans: Oblate College Television Productions." *America* 131, no. 20 (21 December 1974): 408-10.

2036. Molina, Huberto. "Evaluating the Effectiveness of a Program Used in School Situations Characterized by High Pupil Absenteeism and Attrition." Paper presented at the annual meeting of the American Educational Research Association, Chicago, Illinois, April 1974. ERIC ED 091 407.

2037. Sotomayor, Marta, and Ortego y Gasca, Philip D., eds. "Chicano Content and Social Work Education." New York: Council on Social Work Education, 1975. ERIC ED 113 999.

2038. Texas. Education Agency. *Reaching Each Child—Programs for Texas Minority Students.* Austin: Texas Education Agency, February 1975. ERIC ED 104 614.

5.2 Preschool

2039. New Mexico. State Board of Education. *Handbook for Pre-Primary School for Non-English Speaking Children.* Santa Fe: New Mexico State Board of Education, 1938.

2040. Texas. Education Agency. *Pre-School Instruction Program for Non-English Speaking Children.* Austin: Texas Education Agency, 1961.

2041. Siegel, Earl. "Health and Day Care for Children of Migrant Workers." *Public Health Reports* 79 (October 1964): 847-52.

2042. Texas. Education Agency. *Preschool Instructional Programme for Non-English Speaking Children.* Bulletin 642. Austin: Texas Education Agency, 1964.

2043. Foster, Florence P. "The Song within: Music and the Disadvantaged Preschool Child." *Young Children* 20, no. 6 (September 1965): 373-76.

2044. Jean Marie, Sister. "A Summer School for Pre-First Grade for Mexican American Children." *Catholic School Journal* 65, no. 6 (June 1965): 34-35.

2045. Olmsted, Cameron B., and Zinser, Melvin. "Project Head Start in Central Arizona, Summer, 1965. Report." Tempe: Arizona State University, Bureau of Educational Research and Services, 1965. ERIC ED 024 487.

2046. King, Paul E. "Bilingual Readiness in Primary Grades; An Early Childhood Demonstration Project." December 1966. ERIC ED 042 999.

2047. Lancaster, Louise. *Introducing English; An Oral Pre-Reading Program for Spanish-Speaking Pupils.* Boston: Houghton Mifflin Co., 1966.

2048. Móntez, Philip, et al. "An Evaluation of Operation Head Start Bilingual Children, Summer, 1965." n.p.: Foundation for Mexican-American Studies, August 1966. ERIC ED 013 667.

2049. Texas. Education Agency. *Pre-School Oral English Program*, by Carlos Rivera. Austin: Texas Education Agency, Educational Information Center, 16 September 1966.

2050. Weil, David Wayne. "An Experimental Project Involving a Male-Female Teaching Team with Kindergarten-Primary Children Living in a Culturally Deprived Area." Master's thesis, Sacramento College, 1966.

2051. Whitten, Marjorie Birch. "An Internal Descriptive Analysis of an 'Operational Headstart' Program (With Recommendations for Changes and Further Study)." Master's thesis, Sacramento State College, 1966.

2052. Fratto, Nicholas. "A Study of the Effect of Head Start on the Vocabulary Development of Economically Deprived Preschool Children." Doctoral dissertation, University of Pittsburgh, 1967.

2053. Hodges, Walter L, and Spicker, Howard H. "The Effects of Preschool Experiences on Culturally Deprived Children." *Young Children* 23, no. 1 (October 1967): 23-43.

2054. Nedler, Shari. "An Early Childhood Education Model: A Bilingual Approach." Austin, Texas: Southwest Educational Development Lab., 1967. ERIC ED 038 167.

2055. Ott, Elizabeth. "The Language and Reading Education Program of the Southwest Educational Development Laboratory." Address at a working conference on Research and Activity in the Language Arts for the Pre-Primary/Primary Culturally Diverse Non-English Speaking Child, Albuquerque, New Mexico, 4-6 June 1967. ERIC ED 016 542.

2056. Rupp, Louise Mathias. "An Educational Program for Culturally Distinctive Young Children (Including) an Educational Guide for Culturally Distinctive Young Children." Doctoral dissertation, Arizona State University, 1967.

2057. Vance, Barbara Jane. "The Effect of Preschool Group Experience on Various Language and Social Skills of Disadvantaged Children." Doctoral dissertation, Stanford University, 1967.

2058. Blackman, Clyde Thomas. "A Study Using a Structured Audio-Lingual Approach to the Teaching of English to Spanish Speaking Kindergarten Pupils in Two Elementary Schools." Doctoral dissertation, University of Houston, 1968.

2059. Brussell, Charles B. "Disadvantaged Mexican American Children and Early Educational Experience." Austin, Texas: Southwest Educational Development Corp., 1968. ERIC ED 030 517.

2060. Cervenka, E.J. "Administration Manual for the Inventory of Socialization of Bilingual Children Ages Three to Ten." In *Final Report on Head Start Evaluation and Research 1966-1967 to the Institute for Educational Development*, pp. 1-75. Austin: University of Texas, Child Development Evaluation and Research Center, 1968. ERIC ED 027 062.

2061. Barclay, Lisa Frances Kurcz. "The Comparative Efficacies of Spanish, English, and Bilingual Cognitive Verbal Instruction with Mexican American Head Start Children." Doctoral dissertation, Stanford University, 1969. Also: as a final report; Union City, California: New Haven Unified School District, January 1969. ERIC ED 030 473.

2062. Kuzma, Kay Judeen. "The Effects of Three Preschool Intervention Programs on the Development of Autonomy in Mexican-American and Negro Children." Doctoral dissertation, University of California at Los Angeles, 1970.

2063. "The Micro-Social Preschool Learning System, Vineland, New Jersey; Childhood Education. Model Programs." Palo Alto, California: American Institute for Research, 1970. ERIC ED 045 254.

2064. Nedler, Shari. "The Status and Educational Effect of Head Start Programs on Mexican American Children." Albuquerque, New Mexico: Southwestern Cooperative Educational Lab., 1970. ERIC ED 056 804.

2065. Stern, Carolyn, and Ruble, Diane. "Teaching New Concepts to Non-English Speaking Preschool Children." Los Angeles: University of California at Los Angeles, August 1970. ERIC ED 054 903.

2066. U.S. Department of Health, Education, and Welfare. Office of Education. *Bilingual Early Education Program, San Antonio, Texas.* Washington, D.C.: Government Printing Office, 1970.

2067. Aaronson, May, and Moberg, Patricia E. "Home-Type Activities at the Day Care Center. (Tipos de actividades del hogar en el centro de cuidado diario)." New York: Institute for the Development of Human Resources; Billings, Montana: Billings School District 2, 1971. ERIC ED 118 215.

2068. Dreher, Barbara B. "Language Training in a Preschool for Spanish-Speaking Migrant Children." *Speech Teacher* 20, no. 1 (January 1971): 64-65.

2069. Durrett, Mary Ellen, and Pirofski, Florence. "A Pilot Study of the Effects of Heterogeneous and Homogeneous Grouping on Mexican-American and Anglo Children Attending Prekindergarten Programs." Paper presented at the annual meeting of the American Research Association, New York City, February 1971. ERIC ED 047 862.

2070. Hagen, John W., and Hallahan, Daniel P. "Language Training Program for Preschool Migrant Children." *Exceptional Children* 37, no. 8 (April 1971): 606-7.

2071. Leslie, Judith W., and Leslie, Larry L. "Preschools for Mexican Americans: Some Required Characteristics." University Park: Pennsylvania State University, 1971. ERIC ED 089 864.

2072. Nedler, Shari, and Sebera, Peggy. "Intervention Strategies for Spanish-Speaking Preschool Children." *Child Development* 42, no. 1 (March 1971): 259-67.

2073. Arizona. State Training Office. *National Conference—Early Childhood Education and the Chicanito. Pima Community College, August 3, 4, 5, 1972, Tucson, Arizona,* edited by Rafael Chávez. Tucson: Arizona State Training Office, 1972.

2074. Bernbaum, Marcia. "Early Childhood Programs for Non-English-Speaking Children. PREP. 31." 1972. ERIC ED 060 397.

2075. Leslie, Judith W. "Preschools for Mexican Americans: Research and Curriculum." University Park: Pennsylvania State University, 1972. ERIC ED 080 186.

2076. McConnell, Beverly. "Evaluation of Progress in Bilingual Mini-Head Start, October 1972." Ephrata, Washington: Washington State Intermediate School District 104, 1972.

2077. "Programs of Model Day Care Child Development Centers for Mexican Americans, Native Americans, and Puerto Ricans. Report." September 1972. ERIC ED 091 073.

2078. Castillo, Max. "CDA Developmental Instruments: An Assessment into Competencies and Skills Needed by CDA's Working with Pre-School Mexican-American Children." Washington, D.C.: Child Development Associate Consortium, Inc., September 1973. ERIC ED 121 462.

2079. Dall Armi, Lorenzo. "Infant Development through Enriching Activities at Home. Project I.D.E.A. Final Project Report." Santa Barbara, California: Santa Barbara County Schools, 30 June 1973. ERIC ED 101 851.

2080. McConnell, Beverly. "Evaluation of Progress, Bilingual Mini-Head Start, November 1973." Ephrata, Washington: Washington State Intermediate School District 104, November 1973. ERIC ED 116 870.

2081. Evans, Joyce S. *A Project to Develop Curriculum for Four-Year-Old Handicapped Mexican American Children. Final Report.* 2 vols. Austin, Texas: Southwest Educational Development Lab., November 1974. ERIC EDS 121 046, 121 047.

2082. González, Gustavo. "The Identification of Competencies for Child Development Associates Working with Chicano Children. Final Report." Washington, D.C.: Child Development Associate Consortium, Inc., December 1974. ERIC ED 118 231.

2083. McConnell, Beverly. "Evaluation of Progress, Bilingual Mini-Head Start. Final Evaluation, 1973-1974 Program Year." Ephrata, Washington: Washington State Intermediate School District 104, 1974. ERIC ED 116 871.

2084. Micotti, Toni, et al. "Daily Curriculum Supplement. A Preschool Program for the Spanish-Speaking Child." San Jose, California: Spanish Dame Bilingual Bicultural Project; Austin, Texas: Dissemination Center for Bilingual Bicultural Education, October 1974. ERIC ED 108 501.

2085. Andersson, Theodore. "A Proposed Investigation of Preschool Biliteracy." Austin: University of Texas at Austin, 25 May 1975. ERIC ED 112 668.

2086. Christman, Myrna Lee. "A Study of Sociodramatic Play among Three and Four Year Old Mexican-American Children." Doctoral dissertation, Ball State University, 1975.

2087. Hahn, Joyce, and Dunstan, Virginia. "The Child's Whole World: A Bilingual Preschool That Includes Parent Training in the Home." *Young Children* 30, no. 4 (May 1975): 281-88.

2088. Tindol, Judith Ann. "Pilot Project: An Assessment Program for the Development of Oral Language with Mexican-American Children in the Alpine Kindergarten." Doctoral dissertation, East Texas State University, 1975.

2089. Zinnecker, Paola Gordon. "Descriptive Research to Determine Educational Criteria for Developing a Curriculum for Four-Year-Old Economically Disadvantaged Mexican American Children." Doctoral dissertation, University of Texas at Austin, 1975.

2090. Grubb, Susan A. " 'Back of the Yards' Goes Bilingual; Preschool Program." *American Education* 12, no. 2 (March 1976): 15-18.

5.3 Elementary

5.3.1 General

2091. Harris, James K. "A Sociological Study of a Mexican School in San Antonio, Texas." Master's thesis, University of Texas at Austin, 1927.

2092. Neal, E.A. "Adapting the Curriculum to Non-English Speaking Children." *Elementary English* 6, no. 7 (September 1929): 183-85.

2093. Gould, Betty. "Methods of Teaching Mexicans." Master's thesis, University of Southern California, 1932.

2094. Lozano, Amparo. "An Experiment in Teaching Spanish and English to Spanish-Speaking Children." Master's thesis, University of Texas at Austin, 1932.

2095. Meriam, Junius L. "Activity Curriculum in a School of Mexican Children." *Journal of Experimental Education* 1 (June 1933): 304-8.

2096. Hayden, Jessie. "The La Habra Experiment in Mexican Social Education." Master's thesis, Claremont Graduate School, 1934.

2097. Robertson, Clyde Reeves. "A Comparative Study of the Program of American and Mexican Pupils in Certain Elementary Schools in Texas." Master's thesis, University of Texas at Austin, 1935.

2098. Johnson, C.G. "The Effectiveness of Light Singing Instruction for Mexican and Negro Children." Master's thesis, University of Southern California, 1938.

2099. Meguire, Katherine Hollier. *Educating the Mexican Child in the Elementary School.* San Francisco: R and E Research Associates, 1973; master's thesis, University of Southern California, 1938.

2100. Summers, Helen. "An Evaluation of Certain Procedures in the Teaching of Non-English-Speaking Mexican Children." Master's thesis, University of California at Los Angeles, 1939.

2101. Whitten, Chester Irwin. "An Experimental Study of the Comparison of 'Formal' and 'Progressive' Methods of Teaching Mexican Children." Master's thesis, University of Southern California, 1939.

2102. Curran, Harriett Edgar. "New Approach to Health and Physical Education Instruction for Mexican Children." Master's thesis, Southern Methodist University, 1940.

2103. Ebel, Clara Peterson. "Developing an Experience Curriculum in a Mexican First Grade." Master's thesis, Arizona State Teachers College, 1940.

2104. Gibson, Mary Ellen. "Some Important Problems in Teaching Spanish-Culture Children." Master's thesis, Texas A&I University at Kingsville, 1940.

2105. Netzer, Helen E. "Teaching Mexican Children in the First Grade." *Modern Language Journal* 25, no. 4 (January 1941): 322-25.

2106. Ortega, Joaquín. *The Compulsory Teaching of Spanish in the Grade Schools of New Mexico: An Expression of Opinion.* Albuquerque: University of New Mexico Press, 1941.

2107. Ballard, Josephine (Galloway). "Planning a Curriculum Which is Conductive [sic] to the Optimum Organismic Development of the First Grade Non-English Speaking Mexicans." Master's thesis, Southwest Texas State University, 1945.

2108. Milligan, Mrs. Carmen Irene (Tombaugh). "An Integration of Instructional Methods for Teaching Children of Latin-American Descent." Master's thesis, Southwest Texas State University, 1945.

2109. Johnson, Claudia Loris. "The Re-Organization of an Elementary School for Spanish Speaking Children." Master's thesis, University of Texas at Austin, 1946.

2110. Mitchell, Nan J. "An Evaluation of Provisions for the Education of Spanish Speaking Children in San Marcos, Texas." Master's thesis, University of Texas at Austin, 1946.

2111. Booth, Jonathan L. "Meeting a Bilingual Problem: Elementary Spanish in the Tucson Public Schools." *American School Board Journal* 117, no. 1 (July 1948): 15-17.

2112. Furnirall, Fred. "A Proposed Program for the Teaching of Mexican American Children Based upon a Survey of a Mexican Rural Community and a Mexican Urban Community." Master's thesis, Claremont Graduate School, 1948.

2113. Tireman, L.S., and Watson, Mary. *A Community School in a Spanish-Speaking Village*. Albuquerque: University of New Mexico Press, 1948.

2114. Way, Robert Ves. *Adapting the Curriculum of an Elementary School to Serve the Language Needs of Spanish Speaking Children*. San Francisco: R and E Research Associates, 1974; master's thesis, University of Southern California, 1948.

2115. Brand, Vera Owens. "An Attempt to Show That the Activities Program Contributes to the Developmental Growth of Beginning Latin-American Children in Austin Elementary School, Corpus Christi, Texas." Master's thesis, Texas A&I University at Kingsville, 1950.

2116. Calderón, Carlos I. "The Education of Spanish Speaking Children in Edcouch-Elsa, Texas." Master's thesis, University of Texas at Austin, 1950.

2117. Hale, Jessie Scott. "An Evaluation of the Use of Speech Exercises and Mechanical Devices as Aides in Overcoming the Language Handicap of the Latin-American Youth, Thereby Improving Reading Readiness." Master's thesis, Southwest Texas State University, 1950.

2118. Davis, Treva Tongate. "Building Word Concepts through Music." Master's thesis, Texas A&I University at Kingsville, 1951.

2119. Ferges, Mildred Louise. "Music; An Essential in Teaching Non-English Speaking First-Grade Children." Master's thesis, Texas A&I University at Kingsville, 1951.

2120. California. State Department of Education. "Teacher Guide to the Education of Spanish Speaking Children," edited by Helen Heffernan. *Bulletin of the California State Department of Education* 21, no. 14 (1952).

2121. Clark, Harriet Katherine. "Fostering Better Human Relationships among First Grade Children of Rafael Gonzales Elementary School, San Antonio." Master's thesis, Southwest Texas State University, 1952.

2122. Howe, Anna L. "Proposals for the Organization and Administration of a Program of Special Education to Improve the English Speech of Certain Spanish-Speaking Pupils, Eagle Pass, Texas." Master's thesis, University of Texas at Austin, 1952.

2123. Johnson, Vally Lou. "A Study to Determine the Levels in Curriculum Areas Where Remedial Work Is Needed Most, in an Elementary School for Spanish-Speaking Children, Shown by Correlation of Mental Age and Educational Age." Doctoral dissertation, Colorado State College of Education, 1952.

2124. Hancock, Mildred. "Teaching Numbers in the Range from One to Six to Latin-American Beginners." Master's thesis, Southwest Texas State University, 1954.

2125. Wallace, Margaret Adelle. "Creative Dramatic, Graphic, and Craft Activities in an Enrichment Program for the Primary Spanish Speaking Child." Master's thesis, University of Texas at Austin, 1954.

2126. Akery, Nicholas. "An Exploratory Study of the Education of Spanish Speaking Children in the Primary Grades in Edinburg, Texas." Master's thesis, University of Texas at Austin, 1955.

2127. Fuller, Jerome Elmer. "School Program of Children of Migratory and Non-Migratory Families." Master's thesis, University of Texas at Austin, 1955.

2128. Martin, Mary M. "Story of Toltec School, Eloy, Arizona." *School Life* 37, no. 7 (April 1955): 109-12.

2129. Garner, Mrs. Veldron R. "Development Tasks and Television Choices of Latin American and Anglo American School Children." Master's thesis, University of Texas at Austin, 1956.

2130. Lowe, Emma Louise. "A Study of a Changing School Community and Its Educational Program." Master's thesis, University of Texas at Austin, 1958.

2131. Gerdes, Frances Dolores (Stephenson). "An Experiment in Methods for Developing Time Concepts in Latin-American Beginners." Master's thesis, Texas A&I University at Kingsville, 1959.

2132. Wheeler, Hattie Beth. "A Comparative Study of Two Methods of Teaching First Grade." Master's thesis, University of Texas at Austin, 1959.

2133. Alexander, William Peddie. "Hispanic Folk Music in Intercultural Education in New Mexico." Doctoral dissertation, George Peabody College for Teachers, 1961.

2134. Andersson, Theodore. "An FL Blueprint in Focus." Modern Language Journal 46, no. 3 (March 1962): 116-17.

2135. Schulze, Ruth. "A Study of the Education of 621 Children at Govalle School, Austin, Texas, 1959-60." Master's thesis, University of Texas at Austin, 1962.

2136. Brault, G.J. "Some Misconceptions about Teaching American Ethnic Children Their Mother Tongue." Modern Language Journal 48, no. 2 (February 1964): 67-71.

2137. Valette, Rebecca M. "Some Reflections on Second-Language Learning in Young Children." Language Learning 14, no. 3 (1964): 91-98.

2138. "Spanish Program for Spanish Speaking Students, Merced City School District." Merced City, California: Merced City School District, June 1965. ERIC ED 032 951.

2139. Masella, Aristide B. "Help for Newly-Arrived Spanish-Speaking Students." High Points 48 (December 1966): 64-67.

2140. U.S. Department of Health, Education, and Welfare. Office of Education. Summer Education for Children of Poverty, Report of National Advisory Council on Education for Disadvantaged Children. Washington, D.C.: Government Printing Office, 1966.

2141. Arizona. State Department of Public Instruction. State of Arizona Annual Evaluation Report, Fiscal Year 1967, Title 1, P.L. 89-10, Elementary and Secondary Education Act of 1965. Phoenix: Arizona State Department of Public Instruction, 1967. ERIC ED 017 613.

2142. Castañeda, Alberta Maxine Mondor. "The Differential Effectiveness of Two First Grade Mathematics Programs for Disadvantaged Mexican-American Children." Doctoral dissertation, University of Texas at Austin, 1967.

2143. Cheyney, Arnold B. Teaching Culturally Disadvantaged in the Elementary School. Columbus, Ohio: Charles E. Merrill Books, Inc., 1967.

2144. Davidson, Margaret Ruth Ashe. "A Comparative Pilot Study of Two First-Grade Programs for Culturally Deprived Mexican-American Children." Doctoral dissertation, University of Texas at Austin, 1967.

2145. Howe, E.C. "Programs for Bilingual Students of Utah." In Reports to the Annual Conference of the Southwest Council of Foreign Language Teachers, El Paso, November 10-11, 1967, pp. 78-81. El Paso, Texas: Southwest Council of Foreign Language Teachers, 1967.

2146. Liddle, Gordon Philip. Education Improvement for the Disadvantaged in an Elementary Setting. Springfield, Illinois: Charles C. Thomas, Publisher, 1967.

2147. McDonald, Christina R. "Language Development through Literature: A Program for Young Spanish-Speaking Children." *Claremont Reading Conference Yearbook* 31 (1967): 121-34.

2148. Castañeda, Alberta Maxine Mondor. "Mathematics Program for Disadvantaged Mexican American First Grade Children." *Arithmetic Teacher* 15, no. 5 (May 1968): 413-19.

2149. Hill, Bera Brown. "Teaching Non-English-Speaking Beginners: A Supervisor's Study." Master's thesis, Texas A&I University at Kingsville, 1968.

2150. "A Project for Educational Opportunities through Enriched and Improved Education Programs. ESEA Title I Evaluation Report, 1967-1968." Denver, Colorado: Denver School District Number 1, 1968. ERIC ED 038 455.

2151. Sarthory, J.A. "The Effect of Ability Grouping in Multi-Cultural School Situations." Doctoral dissertation, University of New Mexico, 1968.

2152. Andersson, Theodore. *Foreign Languages in the Elementary School: A Struggle against Mediocrity.* Austin: University of Texas Press, 1969.

2153. Arnold, Richard D. "Social Studies for the Culturally and Linguistically Different Learner." *Social Education* 33, no. 1 (January 1969): 73-76.

2154. Perales, Alonso M., and Howard, Lester B. "On Teaching the Disciplines to Disadvantaged Mexican-Americans: A Linguistic Approach." Paper presented at the third annual TESOL Convention, Chicago, Illinois, 5-8 March 1969. ERIC ED 031 689.

2155. U.S. Department of Health, Education, and Welfare. Office of Education. *Teaching the Educationally Disadvantaged Hispano Child at the K-3 Level,* by Betty R. Sepulveda. Washington, D.C.: Government Printing Office, 1969. ERIC ED 036 807.

2156. Adkins, Patricia G. "Speech for the Spanish-Speaking Student." *National Association of Secondary School Principals* 54 (6 November 1970): 108-13.

2157. "Basic Program Plan for Communications Arts Program." Albuquerque, New Mexico: Southwestern Cooperative Educational Laboratory, 15 April 1970. ERIC ED 050 888.

2158. Brandt, Larry Jacob. "The Effect of Token Reinforcement without Backup on the Rate of Question asking Behavior of a Fifth Grade Science Class." Master's thesis, University of Arizona, 1970.

2159. Green, J.F. "Use of the Mother Tongue and the Teaching of Translations." *English Language Teaching* 24, no. 3 (May 1970): 217-23.

2160. Hillerby, Robert Webster. "Teaching First Grade Math to Spanish Speaking Students." Doctoral dissertation, University of California at Los Angeles, 1970.

2161. U.S. Department of Health, Education, and Welfare. Office of Education. *The Schools and the Minority Child's Language,* by Richard L. Light. Washington, D.C.: Government Printing Office, November 1970. ERIC ED 047 320.

2162. Adkins, Patricia G. "Effective Classroom Climate for Mexican-American Students." *Education* 92, no. 2 (November 1971): 26-27.

2163. Banks, James A., and Joyce, William W., eds. *Teaching Social Studies to Culturally Different Children.* Reading, Massachusetts: Addison-Wesley Publishing Company, 1971.

2164. California. State Department of Education. *Evaluating the Effectiveness of Programs Designed to Improve the Education of Mexican-American Pupils,* by Eleanor Wall Thonis. Sacramento: California State Department of Education, 1971. ERIC ED 062 047.

2165. "The Garfield Educational Complex: An Innovative Idea. Summary of Three Years of Experiments in Curriculum Relevancy in East Los Angeles." Los Angeles, California: Los Angeles Unified School District, 22 April 1971. ERIC ED 053 227.

2166. Hepner, Ethel M. "The American Elementary School Versus the Values and Needs of Mexican-American Boys. Final Report." Lynwood, California: Lynwood Unified School District, May 1971. ERIC ED 052 860.

2167. Kennedy, Dora F. "Mexican Americans. An Appendix to 'A Curriculum Guide in Spanish (Levels III-V).' " Upper Marlboro, Maryland: Prince George's County Board of Education, 1971. ERIC ED 096 834.

2168. MacCoby, Eleanor E., and Zellner, Miriam. *Experiments in Primary Education: Aspects of Project Follow-Through.* New York: Harcourt, Brace and Jovanovich, Inc., 1971.

2169. Muckley, Robert L. "After Childhood, Then What? An Overview of Ethnic Language Retention (ELRET) Programs in the United States." Quebec, Canada: Laval University, International Center on Bilingualism, November 1971. ERIC ED 061 808.

2170. Ramírez, María Irene. "A Comparison of Three Methods of Teaching the Spanish-Speaking Student." Doctoral dissertation, East Texas State University, 1971.

2171. Rivera, Hugo H. "Ascertaining Language and Computational Curriculum Needs for Economically Disadvantaged Mexican-American Elementary Students." Doctoral dissertation, Arizona State University, 1971.

2172. Brennan, Pamela, and Donoghue, Anna Acitelli. "Biculturalism through Experimental Language Learning." Paper presented at the Inter-American Seminar on Literacy in Social and Economic Development, Key Biscayne, Florida, April 1972. ERIC ED 064 603.

2173. Hernández, Norma G. "Mathematics for the Bicultural Student." Paper presented at the Mathematics Colloquium, Las Cruces, New Mexico, 5 April 1972. ERIC ED 060 987.

2174. Kaplan, Jerome. "The Triangle Program Planning Project. Final Report." January 1972. ERIC ED 072 879.

2175. Nevárez, Miguel Angel. "A Comparison of Three Methods of Oral Presentation of Science Activities to Fourth Grade Spanish-Speaking Children." Doctoral dissertation, New York University, 1972.

2176. Spolsky, Bernard. "The Language Education of Minority Children." In *The Language Education of Minority Children: Selected Readings,* pp. 1-10. Edited by Bernard Spolsky. Rowley, Massachusetts: Newbury House, 1972.

2177. Aguilar, Joe Vargas. "A Comparative Study of Teaching Methods for Developing More Positive Attitudes in Elementary School Children toward Ethnic Minority Groups." Doctoral dissertation, University of Nebraska, 1973.

2178. Archuleta, Lena, comp. "The Magic of Names—Their Origin and Meaning. A Bilingual-Bicultural Resource Booklet for Teachers, Pre-School through Grade Six." Denver, Colorado: Denver Public Schools, 1973. ERIC ED 100 736.

2179. Ceja, Manuel Valencia. *Methods of Orientation of Spanish-Speaking Children to an American School; A Project.* San Francisco: R and E Research Associates, 1973. [A report prepared in 1957.]

2180. Harris, Mary B., and Stockton, S.J. "A Comparison of Bilingual and Monolingual Physical Education Instruction with Elementary School Students." *Journal of Educational Research* 67, no. 2 (1973): 53-54, 56.

2181. Wubbena, Richard Lee. "An Experiment with the Neurological Impress Reading Method Utilizing Pupil-Aides." Master's thesis, Pan American University, 1973.

2182. Aylor, Kay E. "Plus Four: Individualized Instruction Unit, Rocky Ford, Colorado." *American Education* 10, no. 3 (April 1974): 24-29.
2183. *Chicano Alternative Education.* Hayward, California: Southwest Network, 1974.
2184. Evans, Joyce, and Guevara, A.E. "Classroom Instruction for Young Spanish Speakers." *Exceptional Children* 41, no. 1 (September 1974): 16-19.
2185. Gallegos, Leovigildo López. "A Comparison of Social Studies Curriculum Needs as Perceived by Urban Mexican American Parents, Students, and Teachers." Doctoral dissertation, University of Houston, 1974.
2186. González, Josue M. "A Developmental and Sociological Rationale for Culture-Based Curricula and Cultural Context Teaching in the Early Instruction of Mexican-American Children." Doctoral dissertation, University of Massachusetts, 1974.
2187. Hunter, William A., ed. "Multicultural Education through Competency-Based Teacher Education." Washington, D.C.: American Association of Colleges for Teacher Education, 1974. ERIC ED 098 226.
2188. Reyes, Donald J. "Spanish Language Teaching and Teaching the Spanish Language." *Contemporary Education* 45, no. 2 (winter 1974): 147-48.
2189. Smith, Lehi T., and Bitter, Gary G. "Cultural Considerations in Mathematics Education in Arizona." *Arithmetic Teacher* 21, no. 2 (February 1974): 86-89.
2190. Hamilton, Andrew. "Old Equalizer: Program in Huntington Drive Elementary School, Los Angeles." *American Education* 11, no. 2 (March 1975): 6-10.
2191. Larson, Anna Marie Gustafson. "Instruction by Tutoring of Third Grade, Bilingual, Inner-City Children in Meaning Vocabulary." Doctoral dissertation, University of Illinois, 1975.
2192. McKay, Maryann. "Spoken Spanish of Mexican American Children: A Monolingual and Bilingual School Program." Doctoral dissertation, Stanford University, 1975.
2193. Reeder, Alfred Wayne. "A Comparative Study of Mexican-American Elementary Students in Open and Traditional Classrooms." Doctoral dissertation, New Mexico State University, 1975.
2194. Sisca, Nancy B. "The Effect of a Career Education Program on the Career Awareness of Mexican American Children in Upper Elementary Grades." Doctoral dissertation, Brigham Young University, 1976.

5.3.2 English

2195. Vito, Lawrence. "The Teaching of English to Non-English-Speaking Migrants." Naples, Florida: Collier County Board of Public Instruction, n.d. ERIC ED 010 746.
2196. Meriam, Junius L. "Play and the English Language for Foreign Children." *Journal of Educational Sociology* 4 (November 1930): 129-33.
2197. Montoya, Atanasio. "Removing the Language Difficulty." *American Childhood* 17, no. 7 (March 1932): 12-15, 55.
2198. Hoard, L.C. "Teaching English to the Spanish-Speaking Child in the Primary Grades." El Paso, Texas: El Paso Public Schools, 1936.
2199. U.S. Department of Interior. Bureau of Education. *Learning English Incidentally: A Study of Bilingual Children. Bulletin No. 15.* Washington, D.C.: Government Printing Office, 1937.

2200. U.S. Department of Interior. Bureau of Education. *Successful Methods of Teaching English to Bilingual Children in Seattle Public Schools, Pamphlet Number 76,* by Francis F. Powers and Marjorie Hetzler. Washington, D.C.: Government Printing Office, 1937.

2201. Rogde, Margaret. "Learning to Speak English in First Grade." *Texas Outlook* 22, no. 9 (September 1938): 40-41.

2202. Johnston, Marjorie Cecil. "Cognate Relationships between English and Spanish Vocabularies as a Basis for Instruction." Doctoral dissertation, University of Texas at Austin, 1939.

2203. Tireman, Lloyd S., and Woods, Velma E. "Aural and Visual Comprehension of English by Spanish-Speaking Children." *Elementary School Journal* 40, no. 3 (November 1939): 204-11.

2204. Brown, Esther. "Some Aspects of Teaching Languages in the Grades in the Southwest." *Hispania* 23, no. 2 (May 1940): 171-74.

2205. Coleman, Algerono, and King, Clara B. *English Teaching in the Southwest: Organization and Materials for Instructing Spanish-Speaking Children.* Washington, D.C.: American Council on Education, 1940.

2206. Wedberg, Alma. "Teaching of Speech to Mexican Children." *California Journal of Elementary Education* 10 (May 1942): 216-22.

2207. Arredondo, Santos Torres. "A Survey of Special Methods and Procedures for Teaching English to Spanish-Speaking Children." Master's thesis, Southwest Texas State University, 1943.

2208. Hyland, Eunice D. "Using Music to Teach English to Spanish-Speaking Beginners." *Texas Outlook* 29, no. 5 (May 1945): 30.

2209. Jones, Katherine (Greenawalt). "A Program for First Grade Spanish American Children Based on Language Experiences." Master's thesis, Arizona State University, 1945.

2210. Williams, Mrs. Luella (Daniell). "Story Telling as an Aid to Teaching English to Latin American Children." Master's thesis, Southwest Texas State University, 1945.

2211. Coindreau, Josephine. "Teaching English to Spanish-Speaking Children." *National Elementary Principal* 25, no. 6 (June 1946): 40-44.

2212. O'Bryant, Mrs. Audrey. "Teaching Oral English to Latin-American Beginners." Master's thesis, Southwest Texas State University, 1950.

2213. Aimone, Virginia Meyer. "A Program in the English for Spanish-Speaking Children in the Third Grade." Master's thesis, University of Texas at El Paso, 1953.

2214. Garza, María A. "The Teaching of English to Spanish Speaking Beginners." Master's thesis, University of Texas at Austin, 1953.

2215. Koenig, Frances B. "Improving the Language Abilities of Bilingual Children." *Exceptional Children* 19, no. 5 (February 1953): 183-86.

2216. Stohl, Darthula D. "A Study Treating the Teaching of Language Skills through Music to Spanish Speaking Children." Master's thesis, University of Texas at Austin, 1954.

2217. Dauchy, Norma (Myers). "A Social-Living School Program for Beginner Spanish-Speaking Children Emphasizing Experiences with Language." Master's thesis, Southwest Texas State University, 1955.

2218. Johnson, J.T.; Blanco, Alma; Winton, Tulia, et al. "Teaching the English Language to Non-English Speaking Children." *National Elementary Principal Yearbook* 36, no. 1 (September 1956): 58-61.

2219. Taylor, Julia Hamilton. "Critical Review of the Literature of Teaching English to Foreign Home-Language Children." Master's thesis, University of Texas at Austin, 1956.

2220. Arizona. State Department of Public Instruction. *A New Approach to Second Language Teaching*, by Mamie Sizemore. Phoenix: Arizona State Department of Public Instruction, 1962.

2221. Frazee, Naomi Burks. "An Experiment in English to Spanish Speaking Beginners through the Use of a Series of Original Pictures." Doctoral dissertation, University of Houston, 1964.

2222. Allen, Harold B., ed. *Teaching English as a Second Language; A Book of Readings*. New York: McGraw-Hill, 1965.

2223. Allen, Virginia French. "On Teaching English to Speakers of Other Languages, Series I. Papers Read at the TESOL Conference." Champaign, Illinois: National Council of Teachers of English, 1965.

2224. Kerr, Patrick Joseph. "A Detailed Guide in Oral-Aural English Instruction for Teachers of Bilingual Students at Secondary Level." Master's thesis, University of Texas at El Paso, 1965.

2225. Brengleman, Frederick H., and Manning, John C. "A Linguistic Approach to the Teaching of English as a Foreign Language to Kindergarten Pupils Whose Primary Language Is Spanish." Fresno, California: Fresno State College, 1966. ERIC ED 010 034.

2226. Horn, Thomas D. "A Study of the Effects of Intensive Oral-Aural English Language Instruction, Oral-Aural Spanish Language Instruction and Non-Oral-Aural Instruction on Reading Readiness in Grade One." Austin: University of Texas at Austin, 1966. ERIC ED 101 048.

2227. Rubel, Arthur J. "Some Cultural Anthropological Aspects of English as a Second Language." Address at the annual meeting of the American Educational Research Association, Chicago, Illinois, February 1966. ERIC ED 011 609.

2228. Stemmler, Anne O. "The Psychological and Cognitive Aspects of Teaching English as a Second Language; San Antonio, Texas, Research Project." Paper presented at the annual meeting of the American Educational Research Association, Chicago, Illinois, February 1966. ERIC ED 011 606.

2229. Atkins, Elsa. "Teaching Special English to Spanish-Speaking Children in First Grade." *Illinois Education* 55, no. 5 (January 1967): 219-20.

2230. Condie, Le Roy. "A Decade of Experimentation in Teaching English to Spanish-Speaking Children in the Southwest." *TESOL Quarterly* 1, no. 1 (March 1967): 38-43.

2231. *English as a Second Language in Elementary Schools: Background and Text Materials*. Arlington, Virginia: Center for Applied Linguistics, 1967.

2232. Hernández, Luis F., and Johnson, Kenneth R. "Teaching Standard Oral English to Mexican American and Negro Students for Better Vocational Opportunities." *Journal of Secondary Education* 42, no. 4 (April 1967): 151-55.

2233. Krear, Morris L., and Boucher, Charles R. "Comparison of Special Programs or Classes in English for Elementary School Pupils." *Modern Language Journal* 51, no. 6 (October 1967): 335-37.

2234. MacAdam, M. Evalyn. "Happiness Is English." *The Instructor* 77, no. 2 (October 1967): 25-26.

2235. Adkins, Patricia G. "Teaching Idioms and Figures of Speech to Non-Native Speakers of English." *Modern Language Journal* 52, no. 3 (March 1968): 148-52.

2236. Arnold, Richard D. "English as a Second Language." *Reading Teacher* 21, no. 7 (April 1968): 634-39.

2237. Cooksey, Robbie C. "Priorities in Instituting the Teaching of English as a Second Language in a Southwest Texas School." *TESOL Quarterly* 2, no. 3 (September 1968): 181-86.

2238. *English Via Television.* Albuquerque, New Mexico: Southwestern Cooperative Educational Laboratory, 1968.

2239. Hernández, Luis F. "Teaching English to the Culturally Disadvantaged Mexican American Student." *English Journal* 47, no. 1 (January 1968): 87-92, 122.

2240. Levin, Richard H. "Learn a 'Lito Englich.' " *American Education* 4, no. 1 (December 1967-January 1968): 24-25.

2241. Oklahoma. State Department of Education. *Classroom Projects and Linguistic Laboratory for Non-English Speaking Children of Oklahoma.* Oklahoma City: Oklahoma State Department of Education, 1968. ERIC ED 026 176.

2242. Perales, Alonso M., et al. "Guidelines for Implementing an Effective Language Program for Disadvantaged Mexican-Americans in the Elementary School; Guidelines for Implementing an Effective Workshop on ESOL." San Antonio, Texas: Our Lady of the Lake College, 1968. ERIC ED 027 984.

2243. Rubel, Arthur J. "Some Cultural Aspects of Learning English in Mexican-American Communities." In *Schools in Transition: Essays in Comparative Education,* pp. 370-82. Edited by Andreas M. Kazamias and Erwin H. Epstein. Boston, Massachusetts: Allyn and Bacon, Inc., 1968.

2244. Scarth, Peter, and Regan, Timothy F. "TESOL and the Mexican-American." *Linguistic Reporter* 10, no. 2 (April 1968): 1-2.

2245. "Exemplary Programs in English as a Second Language, San Diego County. Final Report." San Diego, California: San Diego City Schools, April 1969. ERIC ED 032 244.

2246. Rosen, Carl L., and Ortego, Philip D. "Problems and Strategies in Teaching the Language Arts to Spanish-Speaking Mexican American Children." University Park: New Mexico State University, February 1969. ERIC ED 025 368.

2247. Turner, Pearl; Karr, Ken; and Jameson, Gloria. *The Education of Mexican American Children and Teaching English as a Second Language.* San Luis Obispo: California State College Library, 1969.

2248. Garza, Nick E., comp. "Un paso hacia el futuro: the San Antonio Language Research Project." Austin, Texas: Southwest Educational Development Laboratory, [1970?]

2249. Arizona. State Department of Public Instruction. Division of Migrant Child Education. *House Bill No. 1 Special English Classes: Evaluation. Report,* by J.O. Maynes, Jr. Phoenix: Arizona State Department of Public Instruction, September 1970. ERIC ED 044 192.

2250. Gardner, Rosemary, and Ingram, Carolyn. "The Yettem School Visual Literacy Project English as a Second Language." Paper presented at the fourth annual TESOL Convention, San Francisco, California, 18-21 March 1970. ERIC ED 041 257.

2251. Stafferton, Patricia Mae. "Specific Methods for Helping the Mexican-American Bilingual Child Improve Final Sounds in English." Master's thesis, California State College at Fullerton, 1970.

2252. Arizona. State Department of Public Instruction. *House Bill No. 1: Special English Classes. Evaluation,* by J.O. Maynes, Jr. Phoenix: Arizona State Department of Public Instruction, October 1971. ERIC ED 055 703.

2253. Freiheit, Beryle Rae. "Effectiveness of a Daily Auditory Training Program for Spanish-Speaking Children Learning English." Doctoral dissertation, United States International University, 1971.

2254. Taylor, Joseph Alexander. "Teaching English to Chicano Students: A Rationale for Change." Master's thesis, University of California at Los Angeles, 1971.

2255. Valencia, Gilberto. "Three Instructional Modules on Teaching English as a Second Language." Master's thesis, University of Texas at El Paso, 1971.

2256. Verner, Zenobia, and González, Josué. "English Language Teaching in a Texas Bilingual Programme." *English Language Teaching* 25, no. 3 (June 1971): 296-302.

2257. Hendrickson, Richard H., and Gallegos, Frances S. "Using Creative Dramatics to Improve the English Language Skills of Mexican-American Students. Final Report." Rohnert Park: California State College at Sonoma, October 1972. ERIC ED 077 023.

2258. White, Opal Thurow. "The Mexican American Subculture: A Study of Teaching Contrastive Sounds in English and Spanish." Doctoral dissertation, University of Oklahoma, 1972.

2259. Donelson, Ken, ed. "The Many Faces of Language Teaching in the English Classroom." *Arizona English Bulletin* 15, no. 2 (February 1973): 1-130.

2260. Molina, Huberto. "The SWRL English Language and Concepts Program for Spanish-Speaking Children: 1971-1972 Tryout. Technical Report No. 46." March 1973. ERIC ED 097 373.

2261. Ramírez, A.R., and Liberty, Paul G., Jr. "An Evaluative Study of Instructional Strategies and Pupil Cognitive Learning in an English as a Second Language Program of a Spanish-English Bilingual Project." Paper presented at the American Educational Research Association meeting, New Orleans, Louisiana, 25 February-1 March 1973. ERIC ED 075 504.

2262. Cortez, Emilio G. "Lip-Reading: A Viable Approach to Language Teaching in the EFL Classroom." *English Language Teaching Journal* 28, no. 2 (January 1974): 135-38.

2263. Diamond, Glenda Ann. "A Semantic Description of English Models for Use in Teaching English as a Foreign Language." Master's thesis, University of Texas at El Paso, 1974.

2264. Molina, Huberto. "Assessment in an Instructional Program Designed for Spanish-Speaking Children Acquiring English Language Skills." Paper presented at the California Association of Teachers of English to Speakers of Other Languages, San Francisco, California, April 1974. ERIC ED 093 910.

2265. Yawkey, Thomas D.; Aronin, Eugene L.; Street, Michael A., et al. "Teaching Oral Language to Young Mexican-Americans." *Elementary English* 51, no. 2 (February 1974): 198-202, 238.

2266. Frantz, Cecilia Aranda. "An Oral Language Development Program for Mexican-American Children: A Descriptive Study." Doctoral dissertation, Arizona State University, 1975.

5.3.3 Reading

2267. Tireman, Lloyd S. "Reading in the Elementary Schools of New Mexico." *Elementary School Journal* 30, no. 8 (April 1930): 621-26.

2268. McDaniel, Gertrude D. "The Use of Visual Aids in Teaching the Mexican Beginners to Read." Master's thesis, University of Texas at Austin, 1937.

2269. Kuhns, Lulu (Rumbaugh). "An Informal Reading Program for Spanish-Speaking Children in the Primary Grades." Master's thesis, Arizona State University, 1938.

2270. Holland, B.F., and McDaniel, Gertrude. "Teaching Latin Americans to Read by Means of Visual Aids." *Texas Outlook* 26, no. 7 (July 1942): 20-22.

2271. Griggs, Julia F. "Problem of Delayed Reading; How It Was Solved in Our School." *Grade Teacher* 64, no. 4 (December 1946): 28, 74.

2272. Hofman, Mrs. Ernestine (White). "A Method for Teaching the First Sight Vocabulary to a Transient Group of Latin-American Children." Master's thesis, Southwest Texas State University, 1948.

2273. McKnight, Cora. "Reading Materials for Over-Age Mexican Children Second Grade Level." Master's thesis, Southwest Texas State University, 1949.

2274. Dowden, Dora Jean (Mathias). "Utilization of Art in Teaching Reading to Latin-American Primary Children." Master's thesis, Southwest Texas State University, 1950.

2275. Waltrip, Bette N. "Downy Ducks Learn to Read." *Educational Screen* 32, no. 9 (November 1953): 392-94.

2276. Kennedy, Ruby Lucile Imlay. "The Collateral Reading Program in the Bi-Lingual High Schools of South Texas." Master's thesis, Texas A&I University at Kingsville, 1955.

2277. Patterson, William R., and Joyce, Eugenia. "Teaching Reading to the Bilingual Child." *National Elementary Principal* 35, no. 1 (September 1955): 103-6.

2278. Arizona. State Department of Public Instruction. *Teaching Reading to the Bilingual Child.* Phoenix: Arizona State Department of Public Instruction, 1963. ERIC ED 020 029.

2279. Wilkerson, Doxey A. "Programs and Practices in Compensatory Education for Disadvantaged Children: Reading Improvement Program for Migrants." *Review of Educational Research* 35, no. 5 (December 1965): 430-31.

2280. Amsden, Constance. "A Reading Program for Mexican-American Children, First Interim Report." Los Angeles: California State College, 1966. ERIC ED 010 532.

2281. Belliaeff, Alexander. "A Beginning Reading Program for the Linguistically Handicapped." 1966. ERIC ED 014 365.

2282. Horn, Thomas D. "Three Methods of Developing Reading Readiness in Spanish-Speaking Children in First Grade." *Reading Teacher* 20, no. 2 (October 1966): 38-42.

2283. McCanne, Roy. "Approaches to First Grade English Reading Instruction for Children from Spanish-Speaking Homes." *Reading Teacher* 19 (May 1966): 670-75.

2284. McCrossen, John. *The Reading of the Culturally Disadvantaged.* University of Illinois Graduate School of Library Science Occasional Papers, no. 80. Urbana: University of Illinois Press, 1966.

2285. Stemmler, Anne O. "Experimental Approach to the Training of Oral Language and Reading." *Harvard Education Review* 36 (winter 1966): 42-58.

2286. Amsden, Constance; Hartwick, Jacqueline; Liebman, Anita, et al. "Mexican American Children Discover Themselves in the Reading Process: Panel Discussion." *Claremont Reading Conference Yearbook* 31 (1967): 107-20.

2287. Dolan, G. Keith, and Nevárez, Cruz E. "Family Reading Circles." *Clearing House* 41, no. 8 (April 1967): 500-501.

2288. Holmes, Jack A., et al. "The Teaching of Beginning Reading by Use of the Initial Teaching Alphabet." Stockton, California: Stockton Unified School District, 1967. ERIC ED 031 341.

2289. Yoes, Deck, Jr. "Reading Programs for Mexican-American Children of Texas." *Reading Teacher* 20, no. 4 (January 1967): 313-18, 323.

2290. Amsden, Constance. "A Reading Program for Mexican-American Children. Second Interim Report." Los Angeles: California State College, March 1968. ERIC ED 027 347.

2291. McNeil, John D. "Adapting a Beginning Reading Program for Spanish-Speaking Children." Paper read at the annual meeting of the American Educational Research Association, Chicago, Illinois, 6-10 February 1968. ERIC ED 016 602.

2292. Amsden, Constance. "A Reading Program for Mexican-American Children, Third Interim Report. Final Report." Los Angeles: California State College, September 1969. ERIC ED 039 961.

2293. Hillerich, Robert L., and Thorn, Florence H. "ERMAS: Experiment in Reading for Mexican American Students." Glenview, Illinois: Glenview Public Schools, 1969. ERIC ED 035 526.

2294. Holmes, Jack A., and Rose, Ivan M. "Disadvantaged Children and the Effectiveness of I.T.A." *Reading Teacher* 22, no. 4 (January 1969): 350-56.

2295. "Malabar Reading Program for Mexican-American Children, Los Angeles, California. Elementary Program in Compensatory Education, 2." Palo Alto, California: American Institute for Research in Behavioral Sciences, 1969. ERIC ED 038 473.

2296. Arnold, Richard D. "Components of a Reading Program for the Mexican-American Child." Paper read before the International Reading Association Conference, Anaheim, California, 6-9 May 1970. ERIC ED 040 026.

2297. Bowden, Lucinda Louise. "Mexican American Reading Problems: An Assessment of the Problems and Proposed Solutions." Master's thesis, University of Texas at Austin, 1970.

2298. Crawford, Alan Neal. "The Cloze Procedure as a Measure of the Reading Comprehension of Elementary Level Mexican-American and Anglo-American Children." Doctoral dissertation, University of California at Los Angeles, 1970.

2299. Goodman, Lillian. "Juan's Right to Read; Whisman, California, Reading/Learning Clinic." *American Education* 6, no. 6 (July 1970): 3-6.

2300. Green, Cecil Calvert. "A Study of Mexican American Children Taught by a Spelling-Pattern Approach to Reading Instruction." Doctoral dissertation, Texas Tech University, 1970.

2301. Heitzman, J. Andrew. "Effects of a Token Reinforcement System on the Reading and Arithmetic Skills Learning of Migrant Primary School Pupils." *Journal of Educational Research* 63, no. 10 (July-August 1970): 455-58.

2302. Hillerich, Robert L. "ERMAS: A Beginning Reading Program for Mexican American Children." *National Elementary Principal* 50, no. 2 (November 1970): 80-84.

2303. Peña, Albar Antonio. "Spanish-Speakers." In *Reading for the Disadvantaged: Problems of Linguistically Different Learners,* pp. 157-60. Edited by Thomas D. Horn. New York: Harcourt, Brace and World, Inc., 1970.

2304. Rosen, Carl L. "Assessment and Relative Effects of Reading Programs for Mexican Americans. A Position Paper." Albuquerque, New Mexico: Southwestern Co-operative Educational Lab., 1970. ERIC ED 061 000.

2305. Vail, Edward O. "What Will It Be? Reading or Machismo and Soul?" *Clearing House* 45, no. 2 (October 1970): 92-96.

2306. Weber, Lin. "Learning Readiness for Migrant Children; Micro-Social Learning Center, Vineland, New Jersey." *Grade Teacher* 88, no. 4 (December 1970): 36-38.

2307. Lund, Arline. "Reading: Teaching Migrant Children." *Today's Education* 60 (October 1971): 49-51.

2308. Levenson, Stanley. "Language Experience Approach for Teaching Beginning Reading in Bilingual Education Programs." *Hispania* 55, no. 2 (May 1972): 314-19.

2309. Nieto, Consuelo Vásquez. "A Study of Six Spanish Reading Programs: Kindergarten and Level One." Master's thesis, University of Texas at Austin, 1972.

2310. Caballero, Lawrence Manuel. "A Survey of Reading Programs Available to Mexican-American Students in Sample Schools in Selected Districts." Master's thesis, California State University at Long Beach, 1973.

2311. Dahlem, Glenn G. "The Effect of Like Ethnic Qualities upon Reading Tutoring of Third Graders. Final Report." March 1973. ERIC ED 095 488.

2312. García, Ricardo L. "Mexican Americans Learn through Language Experience." *Reading Teacher* 28, no. 3 (December 1974): 301-5.

2313. Chapa, Ricardo Romeo. "English Reading and the Mexican-American Child in a Second Grade Bilingual Program." Doctoral dissertation, Michigan State University, 1975.

2314. Gentile, Lance M. "Effect of Tutor Sex on Learning to Read." *Reading Teacher* 28, no. 8 (May 1975): 726-30.

5.4 Secondary

2315. Lyon, L.L. "Investigation of the Program for the Adjustment of Mexican Girls to the High Schools of San Fernando Valley." Master's thesis, University of Southern California, 1933.

2316. Roots, Floy Eula. "Methods and Materials for Teaching Spanish to Spanish-Speaking Students in Texas High Schools." Master's thesis, University of Texas at Austin, 1939.

2317. Ginsburg, Ruth F. "A New Program in Spanish for Los Angeles." *California Journal of Secondary Education* 18, no. 6 (October 1943): 342-46.

2318. Tucker, Dolores. "Mexican Folk Dancing Class in a Junior High School." *California Journal of Secondary Education* 18, no. 6 (October 1943): 357-58.

2319. Bryant, Katharine Fagan. "A Homemaking Program for Spanish Girls of Kleberg County, Planned in Accordance with Findings from a Study of Their Home Life." Master's thesis, Texas A&I University at Kingsville, 1944.

2320. Johnston, M.C. "Spanish for Spanish-Speaking Pupils." *Hispania* 28 (February 1945): 132-34.

2321. Milor, John H. "Junior High for Mexican-Americans." *California Journal of Secondary Education* 20, no. 3 (March 1945): 160-62.

2322. Currie, Mona Boyd. "Problems of Teaching Spanish to Spanish-Speaking Students in California." Master's thesis, Claremont Graduate School, 1950.

2323. Martin, Mary Etta Clift. "Improving the Teaching of Spanish in a Small High School of Texas." Master's thesis, University of Texas at Austin, 1950.

2324. Brewer, Sam A., Jr. "Latin-American in Texas High Schools." Master's thesis, University of Texas at Austin, 1952.

2325. Cramer, Martin J. "Causes, Symptoms, and Specialized Reading Difficulties and a Series of Biographical Stories Constructed for Use in Remedial Reading Classes." Doctoral dissertation, University of Texas at Austin, 1953.

2326. de Geer, Frank James. "A Program of Beginning English for Junior High School." Master's thesis, University of Texas at Austin, 1954.

2327. Mellenbruch, Julia Ida K. "Teaching Spanish to Spanish Speaking Students in Texas High Schools." Master's thesis, University of Texas at Austin, 1954.

2328. Mellenbruch, Julia Ida K. "Let's Teach Spanish to Spanish-Speaking Students at School." *Texas Outlook* 39, no. 7 (July 1955): 14-15.

2329. Baker, William Pitt. "A High School Program Evaluation by Means of a Cooperative Follow-Up Study." Doctoral dissertation, Stanford University, 1956.

2330. Edwards, Lester Chase. "A Program for Slow Learners in the Seventh and Eighth Grades in the Leander Public Schools." Master's thesis, University of Texas at Austin, 1956.

2331. Reuthinger, Hortense. "A Comparative Study of Two Methods of Theory Instruction for Seventh Grade Latin-American Girls." Master's thesis, University of Texas at Austin, 1956.

2332. Davis, Jack Emory. "Teaching Spanish in a Bilingual Area." *Hispania* 40, no. 2 (May 1957): 206-7.

2333. Means, Johnny Clinton. "A Proposal for a Program of Education for the Migrant Students in the Secondary Schools of Harlingen, Texas." Master's thesis, Southwest Texas State University, 1959.

2334. Guertin, Carol. "Perceived Life-Chances in the Opportunity Structure: A Study of a Tri-Ethnic High School." Master's thesis, University of Colorado at Boulder, 1962.

2335. "A Minority of One. The Story of the Franklin Junior High School Training Natural Talent Project, 1959-1963." San Bernardino, California: San Bernardino City Unified School District, 1964. ERIC ED 032 350.

2336. Perales, Alonso M. "The Audio-Lingual Approach and the Spanish-Speaking Student." *Hispania* 48 (March 1965): 99-102.

2337. Adkins, Patricia Guynes. "An Investigation of the Essentiality of Idioms and Figures of Speech in the Education of Bilingual Students in the Ninth Grade in Texas and New Mexico." Doctoral dissertation, University of Colorado at Boulder, 1966.

2338. Clark, Jack Whitman. "A Description and Evaluation of a High School Program for Culturally Disadvantaged Students." Doctoral dissertation, Arizona State University, 1968.

2339. Moses, Ruth Aline. "Teaching English to Native Spanish Speakers at the Secondary Level." Master's thesis, University of Texas at Austin, 1969.

2340. Davidson, Walter Craig. "The Mexican-American High School Graduate of Laredo Independent School District Study." Laredo, Texas: Laredo Independent School District, 1970. ERIC ED 052 508.

2341. "Mexican and Mexican-American Literature for the Junior High School. Poetry, Essay, Drama." San Jose, California: San Jose Unified School District, 1970.

2342. "Mexican and Mexican-American Literature for the Junior High School. Short Story, Novel, Biography." San Jose, California: San Jose Unified School District, 1970.

2343. "Mexican and Mexican-American Literature for the Senior High School. Poetry, Essay, Drama." San Jose, California: San Jose Unified School District, 1970.

2344. "Mexican and Mexican-American Literature for the Senior High School. Short Story, Novel, Biography." San Jose, California: San Jose Unified School District, 1970.

2345. Salazar, Tony. "A Summer Program for Hispano High School Students. A Report for the Second Year, June 15-July 10, 1970." Boulder, University of Colorado, Department of Physics and Astrophysics, 1970. ERIC ED 058 978.

2346. Blanco, George M. "Teaching Spanish as a Standard Dialect in Grades 7-12: A Rationale for a Fundamental-Skills Approach." Doctoral dissertation, University of Texas at Austin, 1971.

2347. Childers, Jean. "Some Secondary Level Curriculum Considerations for Teaching Spanish to the Mexican American in Austin, Texas." Master's thesis, University of Texas at Austin, 1971. ERIC ED 060 737.

2348. Stodola, Robert Edmund. "Improvement of Communicative Skills for Mexican-American Pupils in Secondary School." Doctoral dissertation, United States International University, 1971.

2349. Lux, Guillermo. "Ethnicization of Social Studies in the Secondary School: The 'Browning' of America." Revision of a paper presented at the Southwestern Social Science Convention, San Antonio, Texas, March 1972. ERIC ED 080 232.

2350. Moreno, Phillip Hector. "Art Experiences for the Economically Disadvantaged Spanish-Speaking High School Student in Arizona." Master's thesis, Arizona State University, 1972.

2351. Smith, Bert Kruger. *Project STAY.* Austin, Texas: Hogg Foundation for Mental Health, 1972.

2352. Calvert, John David. "An Exploratory Study to Adapt the Language Experience Approach to Remedial Seventh and Tenth Grade, Mexican-American Students." Doctoral dissertation, Arizona State University, 1973.

2353. Linton, Thomas H. "Region One Right-to-Read Project: 1972-73 Evaluation Report." Edinburg, Texas: Education Service Center Region 1, 1973. ERIC ED 086 424.

2354. Treviño, Albert Dwight. "Mexican-American Literature in the High School English Program: A Theoretical and Practical Approach." Doctoral dissertation, University of Texas at Austin, 1974.

2355. Hobson, Arthur Tilman, Jr. "Special Practices for Mexican American Students in Selected Southern California High Schools." Doctoral dissertation, University of Southern California, 1975.

2356. Cowan, Edgar Evans. "Evaluation of Elementary and Secondary Education Act, Title I, Compensatory Education Programs Involving Mexican-Americans in Selected Urban Junior High Schools." Doctoral dissertation, University of Southern California, 1976.

5.5 Vocational

2357. Clark, Madeline. "A Preliminary Survey of the Employment Possibilities of the Spanish-American Girls Receiving Commercial Training in the San Antonio Secondary Schools." Master's thesis, University of Texas at Austin, 1936.

2358. Arizona. State Employment Service. Employment Security Commission. *Careers for Youth and the Mexican-American Community of Phoenix, Arizona. Mexican-American Seminar.* Phoenix: Arizona State Employment Service, January 1963. ERIC ED 002 617.

2359. Goen, Louis. "Disadvantaged Youth Need Vocational Agriculture." *Agricultural Education Magazine* 38, no. 4 (October 1965): 92.

2360. California. State Department of Education. Bureau of Industrial Education. *The Mexican-American Curriculum Study. Report of a Coupled Basic Education—On-the-Job Training Program for Monolingual Mexican-Americans,* by John K. López. Sacramento: California State Department of Education, 1968. ERIC ED 028 853.

2361. Wright, David E., Jr., and Kuvlesky, William P. "Occupational Status Projections of Mexican American Youth Residing in the Rio Grande Valley." Dallas, Texas: Southwestern Sociological Association, April 1968. ERIC ED 023 496.

2362. Saavedra, Louis E. "Vocational-Technical Education and the Mexican-American." Albuquerque, New Mexico: Southwestern Cooperative Educational Lab., 1970. ERIC ED 051 927.

2363. Kleibrink, Michael C. "Training and Relocation of Mexican-Americans: Implications for Manpower Policy." Denver, Colorado: Rural Sociological Society, 27 August 1971. ERIC ED 054 881.

2364. Soldahl, Thomas A. "The Development of a Vocational Decision Making Environmental Construct Scale for Chicano High School Students. Final Report, Phase V." Hayward: California State College at Hayward, Department of Educational Psychology, 1971. ERIC ED 072 301.

2365. "CVAE (Coordinated Vocational-Academic Education) Academic Curriculum Project. Evaluation Report, 1971-72." Edinburg, Texas: Education Service Center Region 1, 1972. ERIC ED 066 289.

2366. McClinton, Johnnie W. "Effectiveness of a Bilingual Vocational-Technical Developmental Program." Doctoral dissertation, University of Missouri at Columbia, 1972.

2367. Smith, Jean L. "Bienvenidos! Mexican-Americans Hail Opening of Occupational Center." *American Vocational Journal* 47, no. 8 (November 1972): 44-46.

2368. Bullock, Paul. *Aspiration Vs. Opportunity: "Careers" in the Inner City. Policy Papers in Human Resources and Industrial Relations, Number 20.* Ann Arbor, Michigan: University of Michigan, Institute of Labor and Industrial Relations, 1973.

2369. Laney, John Clemens. "Vocational Needs of the Mexican-American in South Texas." Doctoral dissertation, Texas Tech University, 1973.

2370. Schulman, Sam, et al. "Mexican American Youth and Vocational Education in Texas: Summary and Recommendations." Houston, Texas: University of Houston, Center for Human Resources, February 1973. ERIC ED 075 117.

2371. U.S. Department of Health, Education, and Welfare. Office of Youth Development. *IMAGE: Involvement of Mexican-Americans in Gainful Endeavors.* Washington, D.C.: Government Printing Office, June 1973. ERIC ED 089 157.

2372. Guerra, Roberto S. "Occupational Education in Texas: Summary and Conclusions." Houston, Texas: University of Houston, Center for Human Resources, June 1974. ERIC ED 097 149.

2373. Guerra, Roberto S., and Schulman, Sam. "Occupational Education in Texas: An Ethnic Comparison." Houston, Texas: University of Houston, Center for Human Resources, June 1974. ERIC ED 097 146.

2374. Ingram, Theodore, and Robinson, Clarence L. "Making It." *Technical Education Reporter* 1, no. 2 (July/August 1974): 50-55.

2375. Mullins, Terry W., and Guerra, Roberto S. "Manpower and Vocational Education in Texas." 1974. ERIC ED 097 148.

5.6 Compensatory

2376. Boye, Bernice, et al. "Compensatory Education in the Chicago Public Schools. Study Report Number Four, 1964 Series." Chicago, Illinois: Chicago Public Schools, August 1964. ERIC ED 014 337.
2377. Coffin, Edwin C. "Compensatory Education at Chualar." *California Education* 2, no. 3 (November 1964): 11-12 + .
2378. "State Compensatory Education Program." San Francisco, California: San Francisco Unified School District, 1965.
2379. Badal, Alden W. "Evaluation Report: ESEA Program of Compensatory Education." Oakland, California: Oakland Unified School District, 1966.
2380. California. State Department of Education. Office of Compensatory Education. *Compensatory Education in California, 1966-67. Annual Evaluation Report,* by Robert A. Braund, et al. Sacramento: California State Department of Education, 1967. ERIC ED 023 502.
2381. Rapp, M.L., et al. "An Evaluation Design for San Jose Unified School District's Compensatory Education Program." San Jose, California: San Jose Unified School District, May 1969. ERIC ED 053 822.
2382. Idaho. State Department of Education. Division of Instruction. Compensatory Education Section. *Idaho State Annual Evaluation Report. Fiscal Year 1970 (School Year 1969-70).* Boise: Idaho State Department of Education, 1970. ERIC ED 046 584.

5.7 Textbooks

2383. Rojas, Arnold R. "A Critical Analysis of the Vocabulary of Three Standard Series of Pre-Primers and Primers in Terms of How the Words Are Used, with Special Reference to the Language Problems of the Spanish-Speaking Children of Puerto Rico." Doctoral dissertation, University of Michigan, 1945.
2384. Villarreal, Armando. "The Suitability of State-Adopted Basal Readers for Teaching a Reading Vocabulary to Spanish Speaking Children in the Pre-Primer, Primer, and First Grade." Master's thesis, University of Texas at Austin, 1951.
2385. Sawyers, Emanuel Cosmo Gordon Lang. "An Analysis of the Content of Later Elementary Basic Readers in Relation to Their Treatment of Selected Minority Groups." Doctoral dissertation, Wayne State University, 1962.
2386. Golden, Loretta. "The Treatment of Minority Groups in Primary Social Studies Textbooks." Doctoral dissertation, Stanford University, 1964.
2387. Gast, David Karl. "Characteristics and Concepts of Minority Americans in Contemporary Children's Fictional Literature." Doctoral dissertation, Arizona State University, 1965.
2388. Blatt, Gloria T. "The Mexican American in Children's Literature." *Elementary English* 15, no. 4 (April 1968): 446-51.

2389. "Development and Evaluation of Educational Materials on Mexican Americans. Final Report." New York: B'nai B'rith Anti-Defamation League, September 1970. ERIC ED 044 230.

2390. Gaines, John Strother. "The Treatment of Mexican-American History in Contemporary American High School Textbooks." Doctoral dissertation, University of Southern California, 1971.

2391. McKay, Ralph Yarnell. "A Comparative Study of the Character Representation of California's Dominant Minority Groups in the Officially Adopted California Reading Textbooks of the 1950's, 1960's, and 1970's." Doctoral dissertation, University of the Pacific, 1971.

2392. Gurule, Kay. "Truthful Textbooks and Mexican Americans." *Integrated Education* 11 (March 1973): 35-42.

2393. Michigan. State Department of Education. *A Study of Elementary and Secondary Social Studies Textbooks*, by Carlos E. Cortes. Lansing, Michigan: Michigan Department of Education, 1973.

2394. Moyer, Dorothy Clauser. "The Growth and Development of Children's Books about Mexico and Mexican Americans." Doctoral dissertation, Lehigh University, 1974.

2395. Ortega, Manuel Geoffrey Rivera. "A Content Analysis of the Mexican-American in Elementary Basal Readers." Doctoral dissertation, University of Oregon, 1974.

2396. Rosenoff, Wayne E., et al., comps. "Perspectives on School Print Materials: Ethnic, Non-Sexist and Others." San Francisco, California: Far West Lab. for Educational Research and Development, October 1975. ERIC ED 114 213.

5.8 Ethnic Studies

2397. "Outline of Content: Mexican American Studies. Grades 10-12." Los Angeles, California: Los Angeles City Schools, Division of Instructional Planning and Services, 1968. ERIC ED 065 384.

2398. Carranza, Eliu; Rivera, F.; and Cordova, H.Z. *Perspectives in Mexican American Studies,* New York: Holt, Rinehart, and Winston, 1971.

2399. Sánchez, Lionel. "La Raza Community and Chicano Studies." *Epoca: The National Concilio for Chicano Studies Journal* 1, no. 2 (winter 1971): 55-59.

2400. Psencik, Leroy F. "Teaching the History and Culture of the Mexican American in Social Studies." *Social Studies* 58, no. 7 (December 1972): 307-11.

2401. "1973 ATLAS Curriculum Guide for Mexican-American and Puerto Rican Studies." Brooklyn, New York: Association of Teachers of Latin American Studies, 1973. ERIC ED 106 188.

2402. Cortés, Carlos E. "Concepts and Strategies for Teaching the Mexican American Experience." Riverside, California: Systems and Evaluation in Education, 1973.

2403. Cortés, Carlos E. "Teaching the Chicano Experience." *Teaching Ethnic Studies: National Council for the Social Studies, Yearbook* 43 (1973): 180-99.

2404. Durán, Livie Isauro, and Bernard, Russell H. *Introduction to Chicano Studies: A Reader.* New York: Macmillan, 1973.

2405. "Interdisciplinary Seventh Grade Chicano Cultural Awareness Unit." Lincoln, Nebraska: Lincoln Public Schools, March 1973. ERIC ED 106 202.

2406. "Chicano Mobile Institutes, 1973-1974." Las Vegas: New Mexico Highlands University, June 1974. ERIC ED 113 117.

2407. Villarreal, Abelardo, et al. "Presentaciones escolares. Serie de programas para conmemorar acontecimientos de valor cultural para el méxico americano (School Assembly Presentations. Series of Programs to Commemorate Events of Cultural Value to the Mexican American.)" San Antonio, Texas: Curriculum Adaptation Network for Bilingual/Bicultural Education, April 1974. ERIC ED 108 489.
2408. Banks, James A. *Teaching Strategies for Ethnic Studies*. Boston: Allyn and Bacon, Inc., 1975.
2409. Tatum, Charles M. "Mexican American Culture: A Model Program." *Hispania* 58, no. 2 (May 1975): 317-22.

6. MIGRANT EDUCATION

6.1 General

2410. [Byerly, Carl, and Merberger, Carl]. "Increasing the Competence of In-Migrant Pupils by Improving Teaching and Community Services. Great Cities School Improvement Project. The Detroit Proposal." Detroit, Michigan: Detroit Public Schools, n.d. ERIC ED 020 253.

2411. Pullis, Jessica K. "Helping the Migratory Mexican Child To Belong." In *California Elementary School Principals' Association: Elementary School Faces the Problems of Migration; Fifteenth Yearbook* (1943): 97-101.

2412. Wueste, Gladys (Riskind). "A Survey of Factors Relating to the Education of the Children of Migratory Parents of Eagle Pass, Texas." Master's thesis, University of Texas at Austin, 1950.

2413. Tubbs, Lowell Lester. "A Survey of the Problems of the Migratory Mexicans." Master's thesis, University of Texas at Austin, 1952.

2414. Greene, Shirley E. *The Education of Migrant Children: A Study of Educational Opportunities and Experiences of Agricultural Migrants.* Washington, D.C.: National Council on Agricultural Life and Labor, 1954.

2415. Osborne, Marie A.S. "The Educational Status of Intrastate Migrants in Texas, 1935-40." Master's thesis, University of Texas at Austin, 1954.

2416. "Office of Education Cooperates in the National Effort for Agricultural Migrants." *School Life* 38, no. 4 (January 1956): 6-7, 11.

2417. Reynolds, Evelyn Dolores. "A Study of Migratory Factors Affecting Education in North Kern County." Master's thesis, University of Southern California, 1957.

2418. Yeager, Barbara Ann. "Meeting the Educational Needs of Migrant Children." Master's thesis, University of Texas at Austin, 1957.

2419. Potts, Alfred M. "School Bells for Children Who Follow the Crops." *Elementary School Journal* 60, no. 8 (May 1960): 437-41.

2420. Sutton, Elizabeth. *Knowing and Teaching the Migrant Child.* Washington, D.C.: National Education Association, Department of Rural Education, 1960.

2421. U.S. Congress. House. Education and Labor Committee. *Migrant Children Education. Hearings before Subcommittee on General Education, 86th Congress, 2nd Session, on H.R. 9872 and H.R. 10378, May 2-13, 1960.* Washington, D.C.: Government Printing Office, 1960.

2422. Colorado. State Department of Education. *Providing Education for Migrant Children,* by Alfred M. Potts. Denver: Colorado State Department of Education, 1961.

2423. Thomas, Donald R. "Determining an Effective Educational Program for Children of Migratory Workers in Wisconsin, Phase I: A Report of Research." Madison: University of Wisconsin, School of Education, 1961.

2424. U.S. Congress. House. Education and Labor Committee. *Migratory Labor. Hearings before Select Subcommittee on Labor, 87th Congress, 1st Session, on H.R. 5288, H.R. 5289, H.R. 5290, H.R. 5291 and Related Bills.* Washington, D.C.: Government Printing Office, 1961.

2425. Texas. Education Agency. *Report on the Educational Needs of Migrant Workers.* Austin: Texas Education Agency, 1962.

2426. U.S. Congress. House. *Health Clinics for Domestic Migratory Farm Workers. House Reports on Public Bills, 87th Congress, 2253. Report from Committee on Interstate and Foreign Commerce to Accompany H.R. 12365.* Washington, D.C.: Government Printing Office, 1962.

2427. U.S. Congress. House. *Migrant Agricultural Employees and Children Educational Assistance Act of 1961. House Reports on Public Bills, 87th Congress, 1962. Report from Committee on Education and Labor to Accompany S. 1124.* Washington, D.C.: Government Printing Office, 1962.

2428. U.S. Congress. House. Education and Labor Committee. *Education of Migrant Agricultural Employees and Their Children.* Washington, D.C.: Government Printing Office, 1962.

2429. Freedman, Marcia K. "Some Aspects of Urban Programming for Rural In-Migrant Youth." Speech delivered at the National Conference on Problems of Rural Youth in a Changing Environment, n.p., September 1963. ERIC ED 012 207.

2430. Haney, George E. "Problems and Trends in Migrant Education." *School Life* 45, no. 9 (July 1963): 5-9.

2431. Conde, Carlos. "School for the Migrant Child." *American School and University* 36, no. 10 (June 1964): 34-36.

2432. Heffernan, Helen. "Reality, Responsibility and Respect in the Education of Children from Families Who Follow the Crops." Paper presented at the Fourth Annual Statewide Conference on Families Who Follow the Crops, Sacramento, California, February 1964. ERIC ED 013 675.

2433. Coles, R. "What Migrant Farm Children Learn." *Saturday Review* 48 (15 May 1965): 73-74, 88-89.

2434. Kidd, Margaret C. "Chance to Succeed; Program for Migratory Children." *Texas Outlook* 49, no. 8 (August 1965): 16-17, 30.

2435. New Jersey. State Department of Health. *Migrant Life Education Component,* by William J. Dougherty and Leila Morgan. Trenton: New Jersey State Department of Health, 1965. ERIC ED 017 345.

2436. Fowler, William L. "The Disadvantaged Migrant and Urban Public Education." Paper presented at the annual conference of the California Association of School Psychologists and Psychometrists, San Francisco, California, 25 January 1966. ERIC ED 020 254.

2437. "So You Want To Help Migrants; Suggestions for Churches and Their Communities Wishing to Establish Helping Programs for Seasonal Farm Workers." New York: National Council of Churches of Christ, The Migrant Ministry, 1966. ERIC ED 015 045.

2438. Thonis, Eleanor. "A Program for Children Who Follow the Crops." Marysville, California: Sutter-Yuba Education Committee, 15 January 1966. ERIC ED 019 152.

2439. Blanton, Dolly, et al. "Suggestions for Teaching the Migratory Pupil." Shafter, California: Richland School District, 1967. ERIC ED 024 489.

2440. Delaware. State Department of Public Instruction. *An Approach to Migrant Bilingual Education,* by Charles C. Jacobs. Dover: Delaware State Department of Public Instruction, 1967. ERIC ED 022 619.

2441. Indiana. State Department of Public Instruction. *Some New Approaches to Migrant Education,* by Fred A. Croft. Indianapolis: Indiana State Department of Public Instruction, 1967. ERIC ED 010 747.

2442. Abeytia, H., et al. "Agencies and the Migrant: Theory and Reality of the Migrant Condition. First Papers on Migrancy and Rural Poverty: An Introduction to the Education of Mexican-Americans in Rural Areas." Los Angeles, California: University of Southern California, 1968. ERIC ED 026 173.

2443. Baine, C.F. "Migrant Education Has New Meaning?" *Wisconsin Journal of Education* 100, no. 8 (March 1968): 7-8.

2444. Blubaugh, Roland. "School Bells for Migrants." *American Education* 4, no. 3 (March 1968): 5-7.

2445. California. State Department of Education. *Guidelines for the Education of Migrant Children as Authorized under Public Law 89-750, Title I, Elementary and Secondary Education Act of 1965,* by Max Rafferty. Sacramento: California State Department of Education, 1968. ERIC ED 020 851.

2446. California. State Department of Education. Office of Compensatory Education. *Focus on Innovation,* by John F. Hughes, et al. Sacramento: California State Department of Education, January 1968. ERIC ED 021 670.

2447. Cheyney, Arnold B., and Wey, Herbert W. "National Goals for Migrant Education." Paper presented at the National Conference on Migrant Education, Denver, Colorado, May 15-17, 1968. ERIC ED 023 500.

2448. Edington, Everett D., and Tamblyn, Lewis, comps. "Research Abstracts in Rural Education: Rural, Small Schools, Indian Education, Migrant Education, Mexican American Education, Outdoor Education." Washington, D.C.: National Education Association, Department of Rural Education, 1968. ERIC ED 025 357.

2449. Graham, Richard, et al. "The Mexican-American Heritage: Developing Cultural Understanding. First Papers on Migrancy and Rural Poverty: An Introduction to the Education of Mexican-Americans in Rural Areas." Los Angeles: University of Southern California, School of Education, 1968. ERIC ED 026 174.

2450. New York. State Department of Education. *Educating Migrant Children,* by Gloria Mattera et al. Albany: New York State Department of Education, 1968. ERIC ED 024 482.

2451. Orsini, Bette. "New Road for Young Migrants." *Southern Education* Report 3, no. 7 (March 1968): 19-23.

2452. U.S. Department of Health, Education, and Welfare. Office of Education. Bureau of Elementary and Secondary Education. Office of Programs for the Disadvantaged. *The Direction of Migrant Education as Revealed by Site Visits in Selected Counties of Six States,* by Emanuel Reiser. Washington, D.C.: Government Printing Office, 1968. ERIC ED 031 354.

2453. Wey, Herbert. "Coordination of Programs for Migrants, Working Paper for National Meeting on Migrant Problems." Coral Gables, Florida: University of Miami, 1968. ERIC ED 017 356.

2454. *Alternate Strategies for Migrant Secondary Education.* Austin, Texas: Southwest Educational Development Lab., 15 April 1969.

2455. Oregon. State Board of Education. *To Teach a Migrant Child; Programs and Concepts in Migrant Education,* by Elton D. Minkler. Salem: Oregon State Board of Education, 1969. ERIC ED 047 852.

2456. Schnur, James O. "A Synthesis of Current Research in Migrant Education." University Park: New Mexico State University, May 1970. ERIC ED 039 049.

2457. U.S. Congress. *Public Law. Act To Amend Public Health Service Act To Extend Program of Assistance for Health Services for Domestic Migrant Agricultural Workers and for Other Purposes. 91st Congress, 209. H.R. 14733.* Washington, D.C.: Government Printing Office, 1970.

2458. U.S. Department of Health, Education, and Welfare. Office of Education. Office of Programs for the Disadvantaged. *Questions and Answers: Program for Migrant Children under ESEA Title I, 1970.* Washington, D.C.: Government Printing Office, 1970. ERIC ED 046 585.

2459. Kraman, Ann. "Basic Business for Migrant Workers' Children. *Business Education Forum* 25, no. 6 (March 1971): 16-17.

2460. Ohio. State Department of Education. *Educational Opportunities through Federal Assistance Programs, Fiscal Year 1970. Annual Report,* by R.A. Horn et al. Columbus: Ohio State Department of Education, 1971. ERIC ED 050 209.

2461. Price, Daniel O. "Rural-Urban Migration and Poverty: A Synthesis of Research Findings, with a Look at the Literature. Final Report, Tracor Project 073-914." Austin, Texas: Tracor, Inc., 28 July 1971. ERIC ED 114 236.

2462. Saville, Muriel R. "Providing for Mobile Populations in Bilingual and Migrant Educational Programs." Paper presented at the fifth annual TESOL Convention, New Orleans, Louisiana, 5 March 1971. ERIC ED 052 649.

2463. Stockburger, Cassandra, et al. *Migrant Children: Their Education.* Washington, D.C.: Association for Childhood Education International, 1971.

2464. Tindall, Lloyd Wilbur. "Receptivity of Mexican-American and Anglo Rural Disadvantaged to Educational Programs." Doctoral dissertation, Michigan State University, 1971.

2465. Wilson, Alfred P., et al. "Alienation Evaluation for Migrant Programs." Paper presented at the annual meeting of the Rocky Mountain Educational Research Association, Boulder, Colorado, October 1971. ERIC ED 058 280.

2466. Cheyney, Arnold B., ed. *The Ripe Harvest: Educating Migrant Children.* Coral Gables, Florida: University of Miami Press, 1972.

2467. Cohen, Monroe D., ed. *When Children Move from School to School.* Rev. ed. Washington, D.C.: Association for Education International, 1972.

2468. Fransecky, Roger B. "Visual Literacy and Teaching Migrant Youth." Geneseo: State University of New York College at Geneseo, Center for Migrant Studies, 1972. ERIC ED 066 906.

2469. Hogan, Patrick F. "Improving the Education of Migrant Children." *American Education* 9, no. 3 (April 1973): 20-24.

2470. Long, Larry H. "Does Migration Interfere with Children's Progress in School?" Paper presented at the annual meeting of the American Sociological Association, New York, August 1973. ERIC ED 091 475.

2471. Friedman, Paul G. "Awareness Groups for Migrant Children." Paper presented at the annual meeting of the Central States Speech Association, Milwaukee, Wisconsin, April 1974. ERIC ED 093 001.

2472. Hintz, Joy, and Mecartney, John. "Who Are Ohio's Migrants?" Cleveland, Ohio: Elizabeth S. Magee Education and Research Foundation, 1974. ERIC ED 086 406.

2473. Fuentes, Roy O. "Statement of the National Education Association on Migrant Education before the Subcommittee on Agricultural Labor of the House Committee on Education and Labor." Washington, D.C.: National Education Association, 5 December 1975. ERIC ED 121 540.

2474. Haney, Wava G. "The Occupational Attainment of Migrant and Nonmigrant Farm-Reared Youth: A Colombian Case." Paper presented at the annual meeting of the Rural Sociological Society, San Francisco, California, 21-24 August 1975. ERIC ED 118 346.

2475. Kalman, Marjorie. "Use of Responsive Evaluation in Statewide Program Evaluation." Paper presented at the annual meeting of the American Educational Research Association, Washington, D.C., 30 March-3 April 1975. ERIC ED 104 944.

2476. Pittman, Eric A. "How To Cope with the Transient Child." Paper presented at the annual meeting of the National School Boards Association, Miami Beach, Florida, April 1975. ERIC ED 106 916.

2477. Bragdon, Ida Brownlee. "How to Help Migrant Children." *Today's Education* 65, no. 1 (1976): 57-58.

6.2 Migrant Child

2478. Outland, George E. "Educational Background of Migrant Boys." *School Review* 43 (November 1935): 683-89.

2479. Rohrbaugh, Lewis. "More Light on Migrant Boys; Employment Histories and Training Preferences." *School Review* 44, no. 2 (February 1936): 89-92.

2480. Taylor, Paul S. "Migratory Agricultural Workers on the Pacific Coast." *American Sociological Review* 3, no. 2 (April 1938): 225-32.

2481. Law, William. "Problems for the Migratory Student." *California Journal of Secondary Education* 14, no. 3 (March 1939): 170-73.

2482. Warburton, Amber Arthun. "Children in the Fields." *Survey Midmonthly* 80, no. 1 (January 1944): 13-15.

2483. Nicola, Petra Castro. "The Educational Problem of the Mexican Migrants of Texas, with Specific Reference to San Marcos, Texas." Master's thesis, Southwest Texas State University, 1952.

2484. Valle, Emma. "The Adjustment of Migrant Pupils in a Junior High School." Master's thesis, University of Texas at Austin, 1953.

2485. Harding, Bill. "Migrant Pupils: Challenge to Texas Education." *Texas Outlook* 39, no. 7 (July 1955): 6-13.

2486. Hudson, Lois Phillips. "Children of the Harvest: A Reminiscence of Childhood Travels." *Reporter* 19, no. 6 (16 October 1958): 35-38.

2487. Sutton, Elizabeth. "When the Migrant Child Comes to School." *National Education Association Journal* 50, no. 7 (October 1961): 32-34.

2488. Metzler, William H., and Sargent, Frederic O. "Problems of Children, Youth, and Education among Mid-Continent Migrants." *Southwestern Social Science Quarterly* 43, no. 1 (June 1962): 29-38.

2489. Ulibarri, Horacio. "Social and Attitudinal Characteristics of Migrant and Ex-Migrant Workers—New Mexico, Colorado, Arizona, and Texas." 1966. ERIC ED 011 215.

2490. Soderstrom, Joan. "An Investigation of Mexican-American Migrant Children Population in Idaho and the Educational Opportunities Provided by Selected School Districts." Pocatello: Idaho State University, College of Education, April 1967. ERIC ED 014 364.

2491. Southard, J.K. "A Survey of School Age Children from Migrant Agricultural Families within Doña Ana County, New Mexico." Las Cruces, New Mexico: Las Cruces School District, 1967. ERIC ED 013 069.

2492. Segalman, Ralph. *Army of Despair: The Migrant Worker Stream.* Washington, D.C.: Educational Systems Corporation, 1968. ERIC ED 021 671.

2493. Sutton, Elizabeth. "New Focus on Migrant Children." *Instructor* 77, no. 10 (1968): 74.

2494. Ulibarri, Horacio. "Attitudinal Characteristics of Migrant Farm Workers. First Papers on Migrancy and Rural Poverty: An Introduction to the Education of Mexican Americans in Rural Areas." Los Angeles: University of Southern California, School of Education, 1968. ERIC ED 026 172.

2495. Kirby, Helen. "Children of Mexican American Migrants—Aliens in Their Own Homeland." *Today's Education* 58 (November 1969): 44-45.

2496. Kleinert, E. John, et al. "Migrant Children in Florida. The Phase II Report of the Florida Migratory Child Survey Project, 1968-1969." 2 vols. Coral Gables, Florida: University of Miami, Florida Migratory Child Survey Center, August 1969. ERIC EDS 045 255, 045 256.

2497. Postelle, Yvonne. "Migrant Youngsters. Our Forgotten Children." *Parents' Magazine and Better Family Living* 45, no. 5 (May 1970): 60-63.

2498. Rivera, Vidal A. "The Forgotten Ones: Children of Migrants." *National Elementary Principal* 50 (November 1970): 41-44.

2499. Utah. State Board of Education. Division of General Education and Planning Unit. *The Utah Migrant—An Education Survey.* Salt Lake City: Utah State Board of Education, 1 December 1971. ERIC ED 067 191.

2500. Alfaro, Manuel R., Jr., and Hawkins, Homer C. "The Chicano Migrant Child." East Lansing: Michigan State University Center for Urban Affairs, 1972. ERIC ED 072 900.

2501. Gutiérrez, Elizabeth, and Luján, Herman D. "The Kansas Migrant Survey: An Interpretive Profile of the Mexican-American Migrant Family." Lawrence: University of Kansas, Institute for Social and Environmental Studies, May 1973. ERIC ED 107 419.

2502. Horn, Patrice. "Self-Esteem among Mexican-American Migrants." *Psychology Today* 8, no. 2 (July 1974): 19-20.

2503. Park, Jeanne. "Children Who Follow the Sun." *Today's Education* 65, no. 1 (1976): 53-54, 56.

6.3 Programs

6.3.1 National

2504. Scott, Ellis Bryan. "A Survey of Educational Programs for Agricultural Migrant Children during 1967." Doctoral dissertation, New Mexico State University, 1968. ERIC ED 026 178.

2505. U.S. Department of Health, Education, and Welfare. Office of Education. Bureau of Elementary and Secondary Education. *Children at the Crossroad. A Report on State Programs for the Education of Migrant Children under Title I of the Elementary and Secondary Education Act.* Washington, D.C.: Government Printing Office, 1970. ERIC ED 045 280.

2506. U.S. Department of Health, Education, and Welfare. Office of Education. National Center for Educational Communication. *Migrant Education. PREP-19.* Washington, D.C.: Government Printing Office, December 1970. ERIC ED 042 936.

2507. U.S. Department of Health, Education, and Welfare. Office of Education. Office of Programs for the Disadvantaged. *Preguntas y respuestas, programa para niños migratorios bajo el título I de ESEA. 1971. (Questions and Answers, Program for Migrant Children under ESEA Title I. 1971.)* Washington, D.C.: Government Printing Office, 1971. ERIC ED 064 031.

2508. "Wednesday's Children; A Report on Programs Funded under the Migrant Amendment to Title I of the Elementary and Secondary Education Act." New York: National Committee on the Education of Migrant Children, 1971. ERIC ED 049 875.

2509. "Interstate Migrant Human Development Project." Laredo: Texas Migrant Council, Inc., 1972. ERIC ED 097 107.

2510. *Evaluation of the Impact of ESEA Title I Programs for Migrant Children of Migrant Agricultural Workers.* Vol. 1: *Executive Summary, Summary of Findings, and Recommendations. Final Report.* Falls Church, Virginia: Exotech Systems, Inc., 25 January 1974. ERIC ED 093 524.

2511. *Evaluation of the Impact of ESEA Title I Programs for Migrant Children of Migrant Agricultural Workers.* Vol. 2: *Impact Analysis. Final Report.* Falls Church, Virginia: Exotech Systems, Inc., 25 January 1974. ERIC ED 093 525.

2512. *Evaluation of the Impact of ESEA Title I Programs for Migrant Children of Migrant Agricultural Workers.* Vol. 3: *State Assessment. Final Report.* Falls Church, Virginia: Exotech Systems, Inc., 25 January 1974. ERIC ED 093 526.

2513. *Evaluation of the Impact of ESEA Title I Programs for Migrant Children of Migrant Agricultural Workers.* Vol. 4: *Appendices. Final Report.* Falls Church, Virginia: Exotech Systems, Inc., 25 January 1974. ERIC ED 093 527.

6.3.2 State

2514. Johnston, Edgar G. *The Education of Children of Spanish Speaking Migrants in Michigan.* New York: Macmillan Company, 1946.

2515. Johnston, Edgar G. "The Education of Children of Spanish-Speaking Migrants in Michigan." *The Papers of the Michigan Academy of Science, Arts, and Letters* 32 (1946): 509-20.

2516. Heffernan, Helen. "Migrant Children in California Schools." *California Journal of Elementary Education* 30 (May 1962): 228-36.

2517. Texas. Education Agency. *Proposed Curriculum Program for Texas Migratory Children.* Austin: Texas Education Agency, October 1963. ERIC ED 012 630.

2518. Texas. Education Agency. *The Texas Project for Migrant Children: An Evaluation of First Year Operation: A Pilot Project in Five School Districts.* Austin: Texas Education Agency, 1964.

2519. California. State Office of Economic Opportunity. *State of California Migrant Master Plan.* Sacramento: California State Office of Economic Opportunity, 1965. ERIC ED 013 681.

2520. Michigan. State Employment Security Commission. *Post Season Farm Labor Report.* Detroit: Michigan Employment Security Commission, 1965-66.

2521. California. State Department of Education. *California Plan for the Education of Migrant Children. Annual Evaluation Report, Fiscal Year Ending June 30, 1967,* by Ralph Benner and Ramiro Reyes. Sacramento: California State Department of Education, 1967. ERIC ED 020 831.

2522. California. State Department of Education. Office of Compensatory Education. *Migrant Education Handbook,* edited by Alice Michael. Sacramento: California State Department of Education, 1967. ERIC ED 031 319.

2523. Connecticut. State Department of Education. *Educational Program for Children of Migratory Agricultural Workers under the Provisions of Title I of the Elementary and Secondary Education Act of 1965,* by Dewey McGowen, Jr. Hartford: Connecticut State Department of Education, November 1967. ERIC ED 019 165.

2524. Florida. State Department of Education. *Handbook for the Florida Migratory Child Compensatory Program, Program Established under the Provisions of Title I ESEA. Preliminary Draft,* by Joseph W. Crenshaw et al. Tallahassee: Florida State Department of Education, December 1967. ERIC ED 015 032.

2525. Florida. State Department of Education. *Planning Florida's Migrant Education Program, Report of the Workshop (Chinsegut Hill, July 18-27, 1966).* Tallahassee: Florida State Department of Education, 24 January 1967. ERIC ED 011 471.

2526. Illinois. State Commission on Children. *County Profile of Agricultural Migrant Workers in Illinois. A Report of the Committee on Agricultural Migrant Workers.* Springfield: Illinois State Commission on Children, January 1967.

2527. Kansas. State Department of Education. *State Programs for Migrant Children. Kansas Annual Evaluation Report, 1967,* by Clyde J. Ahlstrom, comp. Topeka: Kansas State Department of Education, 1967. ERIC ED 066 262.

2528. New Mexico. State Department of Education. *New Mexico Title I, ESEA Migrant Program: Projects for Migratory Children of Migratory Agricultural Workers. State Annual Evaluation Report for Fiscal Year 1967,* by Bill Caperton et al. Santa Fe: New Mexico State Department of Education, 15 November 1967. ERIC ED 070 538.

2529. Texas. Education Agency. Division of Compensatory Education. *The Texas Project for Education of Migrant Children.* Austin: Texas Education Agency, September 1967. ERIC ED 017 351.

2530. Texas. Education Agency. Division of Compensatory Education. *Texas Project for the Education of Migrant Children. Annual Evaluation Report.* Austin: Texas Education Agency, December 1967. ERIC ED 023 505.

2531. California. State Department of Education. Office of Compensatory Education. *California Plan for the Education of Migrant Children. Evaluation Report July 1, 1967-June 30, 1968.* Sacramento: California State Department of Education, 1968. ERIC ED 028 009.

2532. Connecticut. State Department of Education. *Program Guidelines for Children of Migratory Agricultural Workers,* by Dewey McGowen, Jr. Hartford: Connecticut State Department of Education, 1968. ERIC ED 019 164.

2533. Idaho. State Department of Education. Division of Instruction. *State Annual Evaluation Report. Fiscal Year 1968 (School Year 1967-68),* by Ardis M. Snyder. Boise: Idaho State Department of Education, 1968. ERIC ED 046 596.

2534. Iowa. State Department of Public Instruction. Division of Pupil Personnel Services. *Migrant Programs, Fiscal Year 1968 (School Year 1967-1968). Annual Evaluation Report.* Des Moines: Iowa State Department of Public Instruction, October 1968. ERIC ED 028 007.

2535. Kansas. State Department of Education. *Title I of E.S.E.A. Projects, 1968. Kansas Annual Evaluation Report,* by Clyde J. Ahlstrom, comp. Topeka: Kansas State Department of Education, 1968. ERIC ED 066 263.

2536. Michigan. State Civil Rights Commission. *Report and Recommendations on the Status of Migratory Farm Labor in Michigan.* Lansing: Michigan Civil Rights Commission, 1968.

2537. New York. State Department of Education. *New York State Migrant Education Program,* by Francis E. Griffin et al. Albany: New York State Department of Education, 1968. ERIC ED 020 848.

2538. New York. State Department of Education. Bureau of Migrant Education. *"Migrant Education: A Comprehensive Program." Report of the Fiscal 1968 Program for the Education of Migratory Children.* Albany: New York State Department of Education, 1968. ERIC ED 037 262.

2539. New York. State Department of Education. Division of Evaluation. *The New York State Annual Evaluation Report for 1967-68 Fiscal Year: Programs for Children of Migratory Workers. ESEA, 1965—Title I.* Albany: New York State Department of Education, 1 December 1968. ERIC ED 036 584.

2540. Oregon. State Board of Education. Oregon State Migrant Education Program. *Annual Project Report and Evaluation 1967-1968,* by Dale Parnell et al. Salem: Oregon State Board of Education, 1968. ERIC ED 046 563.

2541. *Survey of Migrant Students in Texas. Final Report, March 7, 1968—August 31, 1968.* Austin, Texas: Southwest Educational Development Lab., 1968.

2542. Texas. Education Agency. Division of Assessment and Evaluation. Evaluation Section. *Texas Project for the Education of Migrant Children, 1967-68. Evaluation Report.* Austin: Texas Education Agency, October 1968. ERIC ED 028 881.

2543. Texas. Education Agency. Migrant and Preschool Programs. *A Guide for Programs for the Education of Migrant Children.* Austin: Texas Education Agency, 1968. ERIC ED 025 339.

2544. Utah. State Department of Public Instruction. *Migrants in Utah,* by Kerry D. Nelson. Salt Lake City: Utah State Department of Public Instruction, August 1968. ERIC ED 033 802.

2545. Washington. State Office of Public Instruction. *Evaluation, Washington State Migrant Programs Implemented under Title I, Public Law 89-750, 1967-68.* Olympia: Washington State Office of Public Instruction, 1968. ERIC ED 047 827.

2546. Wisconsin. State Department of Public Instruction. *State Evaluation Report for Migrant Programs, Title I, E.S.E.A.—Wisconsin, 1968,* by William C. Kahl. Madison: Wisconsin State Department of Public Instruction, 1968. ERIC ED 034 647.

2547. California. State Department of Education. Bureau of Community Services and Migrant Education. *California Plan for the Education of Migrant Children,* by Ralph Benner and Jack Beckett. Sacramento: California State Department of Education, 30 June 1969. ERIC ED 053 858.

2548. Connecticut. State Department of Education. *Evaluation of Connecticut School Programs for Migrant Children, Title I 89-750, Fiscal Year 1968,* by Dewey McGowen, Jr. Hartford: Connecticut State Department of Education, 1969. ERIC ED 028 891.

2549. "Evaluation of Migrant Education in Texas: A Summary." Austin, Texas: South-west Educational Development Lab., 1969. ERIC ED 058 973.

2550. "Evaluation Report of the Center for the Study of Migrant and Indian Educa-tion, Toppenish, Washington." Ellensburg: Central Washington State College, 12 September 1969. ERIC ED 035 702.

2551. Idaho. State Department of Education. Division of Instruction. Compensatory Edu-cation Section. *State Annual Evaluation Report. Fiscal Year 1969 (School Year 1968-69).* Boise: Idaho State Department of Education, 1969. ERIC ED 046 571.

2552. Iowa. State Department of Public Instruction. *Annual Evaluation Report for Migrant Programs, Fiscal Year 1969 (School Year 1968-69).* Des Moines: Iowa State De-partment of Public Instruction, October 1969. ERIC ED 033 809.

2553. Kansas. State Department of Education. *State Programs for Migrant Children. Kansas Annual Evaluation Report, 1969,* by Clyde J. Ahlstrom, comp. Topeka: Kansas State Department of Education, 1969. ERIC ED 066 264.

2554. Michigan. State Civil Rights Commission. *Report and Recommendations on the Status of Migratory Farm Labor in Michigan, 1968.* Lansing: Michigan Civil Rights Commission, 1969.

2555. Michigan. State Employment Security Commission. Central Office Manpower Division. *Farm Labor and Rural Manpower Post Season Report.* Detroit: Michigan Employment Security Commission, 1969.

2556. Michigan. State Governor's Office. *Final Report—Governor's Task Force on Migrant Labor.* Mimeographed. Lansing: Michigan State Governor's Office, October 1969.

2557. New York. State Department of Education. Bureau of Migrant Education. *"Caring Makes a Difference." Report of the Fiscal 1969 Program for the Education of Migratory Children,* by John O. Dunn et al. Albany: New York State Depart-ment of Education, December 1969. ERIC ED 037 261.

2558. Oregon. State Department of Education. *Evaluation: Oregon State Migrant Edu-cation Program 1968-1969,* by Elton D. Minkler. Salem: Oregon State Board of Education, 1969. ERIC ED 046 564.

2559. *Study of Modified School Programs for Migrant Children.* Austin, Texas: South-west Educational Development Lab., 15 April 1969.

2560. Washington. State Office of Public Instruction. *Evaluation, Washington State Mi-grant Programs Implemented under Title I, Public Law 89-750, 1968-69.* Olym-pia: Washington State Office of Public Instruction, 1969. ERIC ED 047 883.

2561. Wisconsin. State Department of Public Instruction. *Migrant Children in Wiscon-sin.* Madison: Wisconsin State Department of Public Instruction, 1969. ERIC ED 039 071.

2562. California. State Department of Education. Bureau of Community Services and Migrant Education. *California Plan for the Education of Migrant Children. Evalu-ation Report: July 1, 1969-June 30, 1970.* Sacramento: California State Depart-ment of Education, 1970. ERIC ED 056 796.

2563. Colorado. State Department of Education. Office of Instructional Services. *Colorado Migrant Education Program. September 1, 1968, through August 31, 1969. Sum-mary Report,* by Nick Rossi. Denver: Colorado State Department of Education, January 1970. ERIC ED 038 202.

2564. Idaho. State Department of Education. *Learning Together. A Handbook for Mi-grant Education.* Boise: Idaho State Department of Education, May 1970. ERIC ED 046 570.

2565. Iowa. State Advisory Committee to the United States Commission on Civil Rights. ¿A donde vamos ahora? (Where Are We Going Now?) A Report on the Problems of the Spanish Surnamed and Migrant Population in Iowa. Des Moines: Iowa State Advisory Committee to the U.S. Commission on Civil Rights, September 1970.

2566. Kansas. State Department of Education. State Programs for Migrant Children. Kansas Annual Evaluation Report, 1970, by Clyde J. Ahlstrom, comp. Topeka: Kansas State Department of Education, 1970. ERIC ED 066 265.

2567. Morgan, Don A., ed. "Educational Programs for By-Passed Populations." Minneapolis: University of Minnesota, College of Education. October 1970. ERIC ED 047 866.

2568. "North Carolina Migrant Education Program Evaluation Report, 1970." Durham: Learning Institute of North Carolina, October 1970. ERIC ED 044 219.

2569. Oregon. State Board of Education. Evaluation of Oregon State Migrant Education Program, 1969-70. Title I, ESEA, Migrant Amendment, by Elton D. Minkler. Salem: Oregon State Board of Education, 1970. ERIC ED 093 509.

2570. Texas. Education Agency. Migrant and Preschool Programs. Texas Child Migrant Program. Austin: Texas Education Agency, December 1970. ERIC ED 046 565.

2571. "Texas Migrant Labor. Annual Report 1970." Austin, Texas: Good Neighbor Commission of Texas, 1970. ERIC ED 057 936.

2572. Washington. State Legislature. Joint Committee on Education. Indian and Migrant Education Programs: A Report to the Washington State Legislature by the Subcommittee on Indian and Migrant Education of the Joint Committee on Education. Olympia: Washington State Legislature, 23 December 1970. ERIC ED 053 841.

2573. Washington. State Office of Public Instruction. Evaluation, Washington State Migrant Programs Implemented under Title I, Public Law 89-750, 1969-70. Olympia: Washington State Office of Public Instruction, 1970. ERIC ED 047 884.

2574. Curtis, Hazen A., and Caputo, Edward M. "Florida Agricultural Migrant Right-to-Read Program: A Suggested Set of Objectives." Tallahassee: Florida State University, College of Education, April 1971. ERIC ED 068 904.

2575. "Demonstration and Training Project for Migrant Children, McAllen, Texas. Early Childhood Learning System. Final Evaluation Report, 1970-71." Austin, Texas: Southwest Educational Development Lab., July 1971. ERIC ED 053 812.

2576. Florida. State Department of Education. Florida Compensatory Migrant "Learn and Earn" Program: An Evaluation, by Bob N. Cage et al. Tallahassee: Florida State Department of Education, August 1971. ERIC ED 056 802.

2577. Idaho. State Department of Education. Title I, ESEA Migrant Education. State Annual Evaluation Report, Fiscal Year 1971 (School Year 1970-71), by Donald Carpenter. Boise: Idaho State Department of Education, 1971. ERIC ED 059 824.

2578. Kansas. State Department of Education. A Handbook for Migrant Education Programs in Kansas, by Edith L. Dobbs, comp. Topeka: Kansas State Department of Education, 1971. ERIC ED 065 251.

2579. Kansas. State Department of Education. State Programs for Migrant Children. Kansas Annual Evaluation Report, 1971, by Clyde J. Ahlstrom, comp. Topeka: Kansas State Department of Education, 1971. ERIC ED 065 252.

2580. "1970 Evaluation Report of the North Carolina Migrant Education Program." Durham: Learning Institute of North Carolina, 1971. ERIC ED 050 846.

2581. North Carolina. State Department of Public Instruction. *1971 Migrant Education State Evaluation Report.* Raleigh: North Carolina State Department of Public Instruction, November 1971. ERIC ED 057 978.

2582. North Carolina. State Department of Public Instruction. Division of Research. *North Carolina Migrant Education Program. 1971 Project Evaluation Reports.* Vols. 1-2. Raleigh: North Carolina State Department of Public Instruction, 1971. ERIC EDS 057 979, 057 980.

2583. Oregon. State Board of Education. *Evaluation of Oregon State Migrant Education Program, 1970-71. Title I, ESEA, Migrant Amendment,* by Elton D. Minkler. Salem: Oregon State Board of Education, 1971. ERIC ED 093 510.

2584. Texas. Education Agency, Division of Evaluation. *Annual Evaluation Report for Texas Child Migrant Program, 1970-71.* Austin: Texas Education Agency, November 1971. ERIC ED 085 165.

2585. "Texas Migrant Labor. Annual Report, 1971." Austin: Good Neighbor Commission of Texas, 1971. ERIC ED 070 555.

2586. Texas. State Department of Health. *Migrant Health Program. Annual Report, 1970.* Austin: Texas State Department of Health, April 1971. ERIC ED 057 935.

2587. Washington. Office of the State Superintendent of Public Instruction. *Washington State Migrant Programs. Annual Report and Evaluation, 1970-71.* Olympia: Washington Office of the State Superintendent of Public Instruction, 1971. ERIC ED 067 200.

2588. Wisconsin. State Department of Public Instruction. *Wisconsin Migrant Education Program. 1971 Evaluation.* Madison: Wisconsin State Department of Public Instruction, 1971. ERIC ED 067 204.

2589. "Evaluation of Michigan Migrant Education, Summer 1971 Programs." Mount Pleasant, Michigan: Central Michigan University, Michigan Migrant Education Center, March 1972. ERIC ED 064 012.

2590. Idaho. State Department of Education. *Title I, ESEA Migrant Education. State Annual Evaluation Report, Fiscal Year 1972 (School Year 1971-1972).* Boise: Idaho State Department of Education, 1972. ERIC ED 071 817.

2591. North Carolina. State Department of Public Instruction. Division of Research. *1972 Migrant Education State Evaluation Report.* Raleigh: North Carolina State Department of Public Instruction, October 1972. ERIC ED 068 241.

2592. Oregon. State System of Higher Education. Teaching Research Division. *Evaluation of Migrant Education, Número Uno. Title 1-M Programs in the State of Oregon, September, 1971-August, 1972,* by William G. Moore, comp. Monmouth: Oregon State System of Higher Education, 1972. ERIC ED 077 628.

2593. Texas. Education Agency. Division of Evaluation. *Annual Report of the Texas Child Migrant Program, 1971-72.* Austin: Texas Education Agency, December 1972. ERIC ED 103 187.

2594. Texas. Education Agency. Migrant and Preschool Programs. *Texas Child Migrant Program.* Austin: Texas Education Agency, 1972. ERIC ED 070 554.

2595. Texas. State Department of Health. *Texas State Department of Health Migrant Project. Annual Report 1971.* Austin: Texas State Department of Health, 1972. ERIC ED 082 863.

2596. Washington. Office of the State Superintendent of Public Instruction. *Annual Report and Evaluation, ESEA Title I (P.L. 89-10), Fiscal Year 1972*, by Marion E. Cupp and Dale Farris. Olympia: Washington Office of the State Superintendent of Public Instruction, 1972. ERIC ED 086 776.

2597. Washington. Office of the State Superintendent of Public Instruction. *Washington State Migrant Programs. Annual Report and Evaluation, 1971-1972*, by Leonard Winchell. Olympia: Washington Office of the State Superintendent of Public Instruction, 1972. ERIC ED 080 285.

2598. Arizona. State Department of Public Instruction. Division of Migrant Child Education. *The Arizona Migrant Story*, by J.O. Maynes. Phoenix: Arizona State Department of Public Instruction, 1973. ERIC ED 116 848.

2599. Baird, Janet Rae. "An Analysis of Mexican-American Culture Taught in Kansas Migrant Programs." Doctoral dissertation, University of Kansas, 1973.

2600. Colorado. State Department of Education. Compensatory Education Services Unit. *Colorado Migrant Education Program, 1971-1972. Summary and Evaluation Report*. Denver: Colorado State Department of Education, April 1973. ERIC ED 116 851.

2601. Idaho. State Department of Education. *Title I, ESEA Migrant Education. State Annual Evaluation Report, Fiscal Year 1973 (School Year 1972-73)*. Boise: Idaho State Department of Education, 1973. ERIC ED 097 156.

2602. North Carolina. State Department of Public Instruction. Division of Compensatory Education. *1973 Migrant Education State Evaluation Report*. Raleigh: North Carolina State Department of Public Instruction, October 1973. ERIC ED 084 072.

2603. Oregon. State System of Higher Education. Teaching Research Division. *Evaluation of Migrant Education, Número Dos, Title I-M Programs in the State of Oregon. September 1972-August 1973*, by William G. Moore et al. Monmouth: Oregon State System of Higher Education, 1973. ERIC ED 088 624.

2604. Texas. Education Agency. Division of Evaluation. *Annual Report of the Texas Child Migrant Program, ESEA, Title I, 1972-73*. Austin: Texas Education Agency, November 1973. ERIC ED 085 155.

2605. "Texas Migrant Labor. Annual Report, 1972." Austin: Good Neighbor Commission of Texas, 1973. ERIC ED 079 009.

2606. "Texas Migrant Labor. 1973 Annual Report." Austin, Texas: Good Neighbor Commission of Texas, 1973. ERIC ED 091 134.

2607. Colorado. State Department of Education. Compensatory Education Services Unit. *Colorado Migrant Education Program, 1972-1973. Summary and Evaluation Report*, by James D. Hennes. Denver: Colorado State Department of Education, March 1974. ERIC ED 116 852.

2608. Illinois. State Office of Education. *State of Illinois Report on Title I, Public Law 89-750, Migrant. 1974 Annual Report*, by Marjorie Kalman, comp. Springfield: Illinois State Office of Education, 1974. ERIC ED 116 832.

2609. New York. State Department of Education. Bureau of Migrant Education. *Providing Opportunities: Report of the Fiscal 1974 Program for the Education of Children of Migratory Agricultural Workers in New York State*, by Tad Thompson. Albany: New York State Department of Education, 1974. ERIC ED 115 413.

2610. North Carolina. State Department of Public Instruction. Division of Compensatory Education. *1974 Migrant Education. State Evaluation Report,* by Barbara Oliver, ed. Raleigh: North Carolina State Department of Public Instruction, October 1974. ERIC ED 097 166.

2611. Texas. Education Agency. Division of Evaluation. *Annual Report of the Texas Child Migrant Program, ESEA, Title I, 1974.* Austin: Texas Education Agency, November 1974. ERIC ED 100 576 .

2612. Texas. Education Agency. Migrant and Preschool Programs. *Texas Child Migrant Program, Migrant and Preschool Programs, February 1974.* Austin: Texas Education Agency, February 1974. ERIC ED 089 922.

2613. Vega, Jaime I., et al., eds. "Migrant Programs in Alabama, Arkansas, Illinois, Indiana, Mississippi, and Oklahoma." Austin, Texas: National Migrant Information Clearinghouse, August 1974. ERIC ED 155 417.

2614. Vega, Jaime I., et al., eds. "Migrant Programs in Wisconsin and Ohio." Austin, Texas: National Migrant Information Clearinghouse, May 1974. ERIC ED 118 298.

2615. Colorado. State Department of Education. Compensatory Education Services Unit. *Colorado Migrant Education Program, 1973-1974. Summary and Evaluation Report,* by Jerry L. Dunn. Denver: Colorado State Department of Education, 1975. ERIC ED 116 853.

2616. Florida. State Department of Education. Migratory Child Division. *Florida Migratory Child Compensatory Program. State Annual Evaluation Report, Fiscal Year 1975.* Tallahassee: Florida State Department of Education, 1975. ERIC ED 121 507.

2617. Idaho. State Department of Education. *Title I ESEA, Migrant Education. State Annual Evaluation Report, Fiscal Year 1975 (School Year 1974-1975),* by Antonio Ochoa. Boise: Idaho State Department of Education, 1975. ERIC ED 121 506.

2618. Illinois. State Office of Education. *Illinois Migrant Program Guidelines, Public Law 89-750 (Amendment to Public Law 89-10, Elementary and Secondary Education Act of 1965).* Springfield: Illinois State Office of Education, November 1975. ERIC ED 116 833.

2619. Iowa. State Department of Public Instruction. Division of Pupil Personnel Services. *Annual Evaluation Report for Migrant Programs Fiscal Year 1975 (School Year 1974-1975),* by Drexel D. Lange et al., comps. Des Moines: Iowa State Department of Public Instruction, December 1975. ERIC ED 116 865.

2620. Kansas. State Department of Education. ESEA Title I Office. *Kansas State Migrant Education Program. 1972, 1973, 1974 Evaluation Report.* Topeka: Kansas State Department of Education, 1975. ERIC ED 115 441.

2621. Kryza, Frank, T., II. "Migrant Education in Connecticut: An Introduction to the Connecticut Migratory Children's Program." New Haven, Connecticut: Area Cooperative Educational Services, Educational Resources Center, October 1975. ERIC ED 113 121.

2622. North Carolina. State Department of Public Instruction. Division of Compensatory Education. *1975 Migrant Education. State Evaluation Report,* by Barbara Oliver, ed. Raleigh: North Carolina State Department of Public Instruction, October 1975. ERIC ED 116 836.

2623. Nutt, Andrew T., et al. "Annual Report of the Texas Child Migrant Program, ESEA Title I, 1974-75." Albany: State University of New York at Albany, November 1975. ERIC ED 121 505.

2624. Oklahoma. State Department of Education. *Migrant Education Handbook, 1975.* Oklahoma City: Oklahoma State Department of Education, 1975. ERIC ED 115 434.

2625. Oregon. State Department of Education. *Migrant Education Programs under ESEA Title I Migrant Amendment. (Programas de educación migrante bajo el título I de ESEA),* by Elton D. Minkler. Salem: Oregon State Department of Education, March 1975. ERIC ED 114 238.

2626. Pennsylvania. State Department of Education. Bureau of Special and Compensatory Education. *State Annual Evaluation Report for Migrant Programs in Pennsylvania, ESEA Title I, Fiscal Year 1974,* by George B. Inskip. Harrisburg: Pennsylvania State Department of Education, 1975. ERIC ED 113 107.

2627. Schnur, James O. "A Handbook for Migrant Education in Iowa." Cedar Falls: University of Northern Iowa, 18 June 1975. ERIC ED 115 643.

2628. South Carolina. State Department of Education. Division of Instruction. *ESEA Title I Migrant Annual Evaluation Report, FY 1975 (South Carolina).* Columbia: South Carolina State Department of Education, November 1975. ERIC ED 119 922.

2629. Texas. Education Agency. Migrant and Preschool Programs. *Texas Child Migrant Program, Migrant and Preschool Programs, Educational Programs for Special Populations.* Austin: Texas Education Agency, March 1975. ERIC ED 106 014.

2630. Washington. Office of the State Superintendent of Public Instruction. Migrant Education Program. *The Washington State Migrant Education Program, 1974-75.* Olympia: Washington Office of the State Superintendent of Public Instruction, 1975. ERIC ED 115 443.

2631. Oregon. State Department of Education. Compensatory Education Section. *Evaluation of Migrant Education. Title I-M Programs in the State of Oregon, September 1974-August 1975,* by J.J. Garza. Salem: Oregon State Department of Education, February 1976. ERIC ED 121 528.

6.3.3 Regional-Local

2632. "Great Cities School Improvement Project. A Milwaukee Project Proposal. A Special Program for In-Migrant and Transient Children in Depressed Areas." Milwaukee, Wisconsin: Milwaukee Public Schools, n.d. ERIC ED 020 251.

2633. Davis, Edward Everett, and Gray, C.T. "A Study of Rural Schools in Karnes County." Austin: University of Texas at Austin, Bulletin No. 2246, December 1922.

2634. Hanson, Rita M . "Educating the Children of Seasonally Migrant Agricultural Workers in the San Joaquin Valley." *California Journal of Elementary Education* 18 (May 1950): 244-51.

2635. Miller, Bonnie Belle Moore. "Meeting the Needs of the Spanish Speaking Migrant in the Coahoma Elementary School, Howard County, Texas, 1950-53, Inclusive." Master's thesis, University of Texas at Austin, 1953.

2636. Wood, Helen Cowan. "Teaching Children Who Move with the Crops. Report and Recommendations of the Fresno County Project, the Educational Program for Migrant Children." Fresno, California: Fresno County Schools, September 1955. ERIC ED 012 625.

2637. How, Beatrice. "Committee on Coordination of Services to Migrant Workers." St. Joseph County, Indiana: Council of Community Services of St. Joseph County, Inc., 16 February 1956.

2638. Burnett, Calvin W. "Evaluation of Title III-B Migrant Project Office of Economic Opportunity in Collier County, Florida." Washington, D.C.: Catholic University of America, 1966. ERIC ED 010 961.

2639. "An Evaluation of the Special Educational Project for Migrant Children in Dade County Public Schools, Miami, Florida." Naranja, Florida: Naranja Elementary School, Special Educational Project for Migrant Children, July 1966. ERIC ED 023 761.

2640. Pittman, Kenneth C., et al. "Migrant Non-Curricular Supportive Education Program. Pilot Project Number CG 8561 A/1. Evaluation Report." Naples, Florida: Collier County Board of Public Instruction, 1 July 1966. ERIC ED 013 130.

2641. Sandage, Richard (Mrs.). "Migrant Action 'Program. Annual Report 1966." Mason City, Iowa: Migrant Action Program, 1966. ERIC ED 019 159.

2642. Schelby, Floyd A. "Education Program for Migrant Farm Workers and Their Families. Final Report, 1965." Merced, California: Merced County Schools, January 1966. ERIC ED 014 354.

2643. Canning, William M. "What Chicago Does for the Mobile Family." Paper presented at the American Psychological Association Convention, Washington, D.C., 4 September 1967. ERIC ED 014 783.

2644. Southard, J.K., et al. "Project Move Ahead, Development of a Program for Students from Migrant Agricultural Families in the Public Schools of the Mesilla Valley, New Mexico." Las Cruces, New Mexico: Las Cruces School District No. 2, Office of Research and Development, 1967. ERIC ED 018 317.

2645. "Migrant Education Regional Demonstration Project, Component of the California Plan for Migrant Education. Procedural Handbook." Merced, California: Regional Migrant Demonstration Project, 1968. ERIC ED 025 340.

2646. Skinner, Jann, and Brunstein, James J. "The Somerton Story, Part I. A Progress Report on the Somerton Demonstration School for Migrant Child Education." Tempe, Arizona: Arizona State University, November 1968. ERIC ED 044 187.

2647. Guernsey, John. "Rise and Shine; Eastern Oregon Program for Migrant Children." *American Education* 5, no. 9 (November 1969): 20-21.

2648. López, Frances. "Regional Program for Migrant Education." *Education Digest* 34, no. 5 (January 1969): 10-12.

2649. McDonald, Thomas F., and Moody, Earl. "The ABC Project. A Report on the Program for Migrant Child Education at Tolleson Elementary School." Tolleson, Arizona: Tolleson Elementary School, 1969. ERIC ED 032 990.

2650. Porter, Pearl. "Children of the Harvesters; A Study in Migrant Education." Lehigh Acres, Florida 33936: By the Author, 707 Buchanan Avenue, 1969.

2651. U.S. Department of Health, Education, and Welfare. Office of Education. *The Center for the Study of Migrant and Indian Education; An Overview of the History and Purpose of an Educational Service Center for Teachers of Migrant and Indian Children in the State of Washington.* Washington, D.C.: Government Printing Office, 1969. ERIC ED 046 594.

2652. Utah. State Department of Public Instruction. Research Coordinating Unit for Vocational and Technical Education. *Evaluation of Mobile Office Education Unit Utilization with Migrant Workers in Box Elder School District. Final Report,* by Maurine B. Lee and John F. Stephens. Salt Lake City: Utah State Department of Public Instruction, 1969. ERIC ED 043 446.

2653. Arizona. State Department of Education. *The Arlington-Harquaha Story; A Step Forward Program for the Education of Migrant Children,* by James L. Hickman. Phoenix: Arizona State Department of Education, 1970. ERIC ED 048 974.

2654. Arizona. State Department of Education. *The Somerton Story: Part II. A Progress Report on the Somerton Demonstration School for Migrant Child Education*, by James J. Burnstein. Phoenix: Arizona State Department of Education, 1970. ERIC ED 044 226.

2655. Biller, Julian, and Meredith, William. "Markham: Report of the Evaluation of an Educational Program, 1968-70." Fort Lauderdale, Florida: Broward County Schools, 1970. ERIC ED 047 053.

2656. "NRO Migrant Child Development Centers, Pasco, Washington: Childhood Education. Model Programs. A Report to the White House Conference on Children, Washington, D.C., December, 1970." Palo Alto, California: American Institutes for Research, 1970. ERIC ED 045 253.

2657. Skinner, Jann. "The Somerton Story: Teaching Spanish Surname Children." Paper presented at the International Reading Association Conference, Anaheim, California, 6-9 May 1970. ERIC ED 040 032.

2658. Utah. State Department of Public Instruction. Research Coordinating Unit for Vocational and Technical Education. *Evaluation of Mobile Office Education Unit Utilization with Migrant Workers in Box Elder School District. Final Report, March 1971*, by Richard Keene and John F. Stephens. Salt Lake City: Utah State Department of Public Instruction, March 1971. ERIC ED 050 866.

2659. Arizona. State Department of Education. *The Somerton Story: Part III. A Progress Report on the Somerton Demonstration School for Migrant Child Education*, by James J. Burnstein, comp. Phoenix: Arizona State Department of Education, August 1972. ERIC ED 067 216.

2660. Arizona. State Department of Public Instruction. Division of Migrant Child Education. *The Somerton Story: Part 4. A Progress Report on the Somerton Demonstration School for Migrant Child Education*. Phoenix: Arizona State Department of Public Instruction, August 1972. ERIC ED 116 829.

2661. Blancett, Bob L. "Implementation of a Migrant Education Program in the Richgrove School District." Doctoral dissertation, Walden University, 1972. ERIC ED 063 990.

2662. "Visions of Sugarplums." Greenwood, Mississippi: Laflore County Schools, 1972. ERIC ED 067 427.

2663. Thomson, Peggy. "Visit to Pasco; Child Development Center for Children of Migrant Workers in Pasco, Washington." *American Education* 9, no. 8 (October 1973): 13-19.

2664. California. State Department of Education. Bureau of Community Services and Migrant Education. *A Study of Two Methods of Delivering Supplementary Educational Services to Mobile Migrant Children in California*, by Jack Beckett, comp. Sacramento: California State Department of Education, 4 February 1974. ERIC ED 087 602.

2665. Hartman, David W., ed. *Immigrants and Migrants: The Detroit Ethnic Experience. Ethnic Studies Reader*. Detroit, Michigan: New University Thought Publishing Co., 1974.

2666. Mattera, Gloria, and Steel, Eric M. "Exemplary Programs for Migrant Children." University Park: New Mexico State University, ERIC/CRESS, June 1974. ERIC ED 092 278.

2667. Arizona. State Department of Public Instruction. Division of Migrant Child Education. *The Somerton Story: Part 5. Bilingual Education in Conjunction with a Migrant-Child Demonstration Project*. Phoenix: Arizona State Department of Public Instruction, June 1975. ERIC ED 116 846.

6.3.4 Summer

2668. Wisconsin. Governor's Commission on Human Rights. *Education on the Move. Part II, Report of a 1961 Demonstration Summer School for Migrant Children in Manitowoc County, Wisconsin.* Madison: Wisconsin Governor's Commission on Human Rights, 1962. ERIC ED 033 814.

2669. Wood, Nancy. "Summer-School Help for Migrant Workers' Children." *National Educational Association Journal* 51, no. 5 (May 1962): 18-19.

2670. Howsden, Arley L., et al. "Report of Chico State College Gridley Farm Labor Camp, Summer Project (1964)." Chico, California: Chico State College, September 1964. ERIC ED 012 636.

2671. Harris, Alton E. "Summer Migrant Project, Unified School District Number 467, Wichita County, Leoti, Kansas. Evaluation Report." Leoti, Kansas: Leoti Unified School District No. 467, 1967. ERIC ED 019 162.

2672. New York. State Department of Education. Migrant Education Office. Bureau of Elementary School Supervision. *"These Too Are Our Children," Report of the 1967 Summer School Program for Children of Migratory Farm Workers.* Albany: New York State Department of Education, December 1967. ERIC ED 032 142.

2673. Garofalo, V. James. "Evaluation of Migrant Summer School Programs Supported by the New York State Department of Education during 1968. Final Report." Syracuse, New York: Syracuse University, 1968. ERIC ED 026 162.

2674. Washington. Office of the State Superintendent of Public Instruction. *Summer Programs for Migrant Children. Special Issue, Your Public Schools, Volume 6, Number 8,* by Dorothee Brown and Zita Lichtenberg, eds. Olympia: Washington Office of the State Superintendent of Public Instruction, July 1968. ERIC ED 028 850.

2675. Wrezesinski, Conrad. "Summer School for Migrant Children." *Catholic School Journal* 68, no. 4 (April 1968): 54-55.

2676. Arizona. State Department of Education. *The Willcox Story. A Report from the Willcox Elementary School's Summer Migrant Project,* by James C. Henderson and Alfred P. Wilson. Phoenix: Arizona State Department of Education, 1970. ERIC ED 049 863.

2677. "Report of Experimental Demonstration Project; School Lunch—Emergency Food for Families—Migrant Summer School—Minnesota." Washington, D.C.: Manpower Evaluation and Development Institute. Migrant Research Project, August 1970. ERIC ED 046 614.

2678. Virginia. State Department of Education. *"Eight Weeks at Accomack": A Report on the Migrant Education Program—Accomack County Public Schools—Accomack, Virginia—Summer 1970.* Richmond: Virginia State Department of Education, December 1970. ERIC ED 048 973.

2679. Arizona. State Department of Education. *The Eloy Story. A Report from the Eloy Elementary School Summer Migrant Program for Kindergarten through Second Grade Level Children,* by Dan M. Baxley and Max Hinton, comps. Phoenix: Arizona State Department of Education, November 1971. ERIC ED 067 217.

2680. DeLing, Elli. "In-Depth Evaluation of Oral Language Instruction in the 1971 Migrant Education Summer Program." Mount Pleasant: Central Michigan University, Michigan Migrant Education Center, March 1972. ERIC ED 064 014.

2681. Eiszler, Charles F. "Self-Concept, Attitude toward School, and Reading Achievement: A Study of Michigan Migrant Education Summer School Programs." Mount Pleasant: Central Michigan University, Michigan Migrant Education Center, March 1972. ERIC ED 064 013.

2682. Gadjo, Henry W., and Hayden, Laurie. "1972 Sodus Migrant Summer Program." Sodus, New York: Sodus Central School, 1972. ERIC ED 071 833.

2683. Eiszler, Charles F., and Kirk, Barbara V. "Achievement and Attitude Change in Michigan Migrant Education, Summer Classrooms, 1972." Mount Pleasant: Central Michigan University, Michigan Migrant Education Center, January 1973. ERIC ED 072 876.

2684. Gadjo, Henry W. "You and Your Community. 1973 Sodus Migrant Summer Laboratory School Program. Sodus Central School, New York." Sodus, New York: Sodus Central School, 1973. ERIC ED 086 387.

2685. Arizona. State Department of Public Instruction. Division of Migrant Child Education. *Parker Migrant Summer Story. A Report from Parker Summer School Migrant Program: Kindergarten through Grade Six,* by Merel E. Pollard, comp. Phoenix: Arizona State Department of Public Instruction, 1974. ERIC ED 116 847.

2686. Gadjo, Henry, and Knapp, William. "Reaching Out—1974 Sodus Migrant Summer Programs." Sodus, New York: Sodus Central School, 1974. ERIC ED 100 575.

2687. "Altus Migrant Summer Programs, Title I ESEA (Altus Independent School District 18, June 2, 1975-July 11, 1975)." Altus, Oklahoma: Altus Independent School District 18, 1975. ERIC ED 115 432.

2688. Seriale, J.K., et al. "We're Off To See the Wizard. A Report from Mohawk Valley School, Summer School Migrant Program, Kindergarten through Grade 7. A Pictorial Account." Mohawk Valley, Arizona: Mohawk Valley Elementary School District 17, February 1976. ERIC ED 121 523.

6.3.5 Preschool

2689. Hagen, John W., and Hallahan, Daniel P. "A Language Training Program for Preschool Migrant Children." Ann Arbor, Michigan: University of Michigan, Center for Research on Language and Language Behavior, 1968. ERIC ED 028 878.

2690. Texas. Education Agency. *A Program for Five-Year-Old Migrant Children.* Austin: Texas Education Agency, 1968. ERIC ED 028 879.

2691. "Early Childhood Education Learning System for Three- and Four-Year-Old Migrant Children, McAllen, Texas. Evaluation Report. 1968-1969." Austin, Texas: Southwest Educational Development Lab., 31 July 1969. ERIC ED 043 370.

2692. "Mobile Head Start Program for Migrant Children and Parents. Final Report and Strategies for Continuation Activities." Austin, Texas: Southwest Educational Development Lab., 1 November 1970. ERIC ED 052 864.

2693. Chandler, Bessie E. "A Comprehensive Study of the Educational Program and Related Components of Preschool and Day Care Centers Serving Children of Migrant Families." Geneseo: State University of New York College at Geneseo, Center for Migrant Studies, 1971. ERIC ED 081 545.

2694. Combs, Eloyce F. "Florida's Early Childhood Learning Program for Migrant Children." *Young Children* 26, no. 6 (August 1971): 359-63.

2695. Newell, John, et al. "Migrant Early Childhood Education Program in Hardee County, Florida: An Evaluation." Gainesville: University of Florida, College of Education and Institute for Development of Human Resources, August 1971. ERIC ED 060 960.

2696. "Early Childhood Programs for Migrants: Alternatives for the States. The Second
Report of the Education Commission of the States, Task Force on Early Child-
hood Education, May 1972." Denver, Colorado: Education Commission of the
States, May 1972. ERIC ED 063 996.

2697. Spinks, Nellie J., comp. "Early Childhood Education for Migrants: An Evaluation
of Behavioral and Physical Change. Research Monograph No. 3." Lowndes,
Georgia: Lowndes County Schools, 1972. ERIC ED 067 190.

2698. Florida. State Department of Education. Migratory Child Division. *Early Childhood
Objectives for Five-Year-Old Migrant Children. Florida Migratory Child Compensatory Program.* Tallahassee: Florida State Department of Education, August
1973. ERIC ED 092 285.

6.3.6 Special

2699. *Computer-Assisted Instruction in the Education of the Migrant Mexican American.*
Austin, Texas: Southwest Educational Development Lab., 1968.

2700. Dik, David. "A Study of Informal Out-of-School Programs with Migrant Children."
Geneseo: State University of New York College at Geneseo, Center for Migrant
Studies, 1970. ERIC ED 081 546.

2701. Heffernan-Cabrera, Patricia. "The Camera as the 'Eye of the Mind.' A Pilot Project
for Visual Literacy and the Teaching of English as a Second Language to Disadvantaged Spanish Speaking Migrant Children." 1970. ERIC ED 041 254.

2702. Hick, Thomas L. "Response of Migrant Children to Outdoor Education." Geneseo:
State University of New York College at Geneseo, 1970. ERIC ED 048 988.

2703. Lewis, David A. "Computer Aids Educationally Deprived Migrant Students."
Journal Systems Management 21, no. 10 (October 1970): 30-33.

2704. McDonald, Thomas F., and Moody, Earl. "Basic Communication Project for Migrant Children." *Reading Teacher* 24, no. 1 (October 1970): 29-32.

2705. Olson, George H. "The Effectiveness of a Programmed Method of Instruction for
Teaching Handwriting Skills to Migrant Children." Paper presented at the na-
tional meeting of the American Educational Research Association, Minneapolis,
Minnesota, March 1970. ERIC ED 039 062.

2706. Mackin, Eva, et al. "ITV and Education of Children of Migrant Farm Workers,
Indians, and Inner-City Poor: Cross-Cultural Comparisons of International Uses
of Media. Volume I." Washington, D.C.: American University, Development
Education and Training Research Institute, January 1971. ERIC ED 050 570.

2707. Early, L.F. "FM Radio; An Oral Communication Project for Migrants in Palm
Beach County." West Palm Beach, Florida: Palm Beach County Board of Public
Instruction, April 1972. ERIC ED 061 739.

2708. Jasper, Gary, and Sloan, Jerry. "School Projects for Migrant Children." *Today's
Education* 62, no. 6 (1973): 26-27.

2709. Miles, Guy H., and Henry, William F. "An Experimental Program for Ethnic Minority Youth from the Rural Southwest. Volume 4 of a Four Volume Final Report."
Minneapolis, Minnesota: North Star Research and Development Institute, September 1974. ERIC ED 100 541.

2710. Washington. Office of the State Superintendent of Public Instruction. *Night
School for Secondary Migrant Students.* Olympia: Washington Office of the State
Superintendent of Public Instruction, 1974. ERIC ED 115 442.

2711. Perrine, Jay R. "Telecommunications Technology and Rural Education in the
United States." St. Louis, Missouri: Washington University, Center for Development Technology, March 1975. ERIC ED 106 009.

2712. Guerra, Roberto S. "Work Experience and Career Education Programs for Migrant Children." University Park: New Mexico State University, ERIC/CRESS, January 1976. ERIC ED 118 289.

6.4 Conferences

2713. McCuistion, F. "Education of Minority and Special Groups in Rural Areas." *White House Conference on Rural Education, Proceedings* (1944): 172-80.
2714. U.S. Department of Health, Education, and Welfare. Office of Education. *Report of Regional Conferences on the Education of Migrant Children, 1952.* Washington, D.C.: Government Printing Office, 1952.
2715. Kern, Rev. Clement H. "The Migrants in the North." In *Proceedings of the Ninth Regional Conference*, pp. 47-52. San Antonio, Texas: Catholic Council for the Spanish-Speaking, 15-17 April 1958.
2716. *Southwest Conference on Educational and Social Problems of Rural and Urban Mexican-American Youth. Summary of Proceedings. Saturday, April 6, 1963.* Southwest Intercollegiate Conference. 12th. Los Angeles, California: Occidental College, 1963.
2717. U.S. Department of Health, Education, and Welfare. Office of Education. Division of Compensatory Education. *Report on Conferences on Special Educational Programs for Migratory Children of Migratory Agricultural Workers.* Washington, D.C.: Government Printing Office, September 1966. ERIC ED 020 808.
2718. Cake, Ralph H., Jr., et al. "First Western Region Conference of OEO Migrant Projects (Woodburn, Oregon, June 7-9, 1967)." Woodburn, Oregon: Valley Migrant League, June 1967. ERIC ED 068 208.
2719. California. Governor's Advisory Committee on Children and Youth. *Report and Recommendations of the Conference on Families Who Follow the Crops (5th, Davis, California, March 20-21, 1967),* by Mrs. Wilson W. Wood. Sacramento: California Governor's Advisory Committee on Children and Youth, 20 March 1967. ERIC ED 018 316.
2720. California. State Department of Education. Title V Interstate Migrant Education Project. *Basis for a Plan of Action for Improving the Education of Migrant Children. A Summary of Recommendations Made at the Conference on the Education of Migrant Children and Youth (January 1967),* by Max Rafferty and Eugene Gonzales. Sacramento: California State Department of Education, January 1967. ERIC ED 011 805.
2721. Goodwin, William L., ed. "Bucknell Conference on Learning Problems of the Migrant Child, Report of Proceedings (Bucknell University, August 13-18, 1967)." Lewisburg, Pennsylvania, Bucknell University, 1967. ERIC ED 023 498.
2722. Goodwin, William L., and Cieslak, Paul J., eds. "Bucknell Conference on Facilitating the Learning of the Migrant Child. Report of Proceedings (August 19-30, 1968)." Lewisburg, Pennsylvania: Bucknell University, Department of Education, 1968. ERIC ED 028 880.
2723. Robinson, Raymond D., comp. "Presentations, Educational Training Conference for IMC, Illinios Migrant Council (December 7-8, 1968)." Washington, D.C.: Educational Systems Corporation, December 1968. ERIC ED 030 053.

2724. U.S. Department of Health, Education, and Welfare. Office of Education. Bureau of Elementary and Secondary Education. *Report of Title I, ESEA, Migrant Coordinators Meeting.* Washington, D.C.: Government Printing Office, 4 December 1968. ERIC ED 039 056.

2725. Walker, Jess, et al. "Ohio Conference on Migrant Education." Papers presented at the Ohio Conference on Migrant Education, Columbus, Ohio, [1968]. ERIC ED 028 875.

2726. "Exceptional Children Conference Papers: Environmental Influences in the Early Education of Migrant and Disadvantaged Students." Papers presented at the Special Conference on Early Childhood Education, New Orleans, Louisiana, 10-13 December 1969. ERIC ED 034 908.

2727. Hinz, Marian C., ed. "Resume of Materials, Suggestions, and References Gathered during the Shippensburg Conference on the Education of the Migrant Child (June 10-21, 1968)." Shippensburg, Pennsylvania: Shippensburg State College, 1969. ERIC ED 029 722.

2728. Ohio. State Department of Education. *Ohio Conference on Migrant Education; 1969,* by Carlos Rivera et al. Columbus: Ohio State Department of Education, 1969. ERIC ED 037 284.

2729. Ohio. State Department of Education. *Partners in Learning. . .Teachers & Migrant Children. Proceedings of Glen Helen Workshop (Yellow Springs, Ohio, April 30-May 2, 1970).* Columbus: Ohio State Department of Education, 2 May 1970. ERIC ED 044 204.

2730. New York. State Department of Education. Bureau of Migrant Education. *Statewide Conference on Migrant Education (State University College in Geneseo, New York, July 8, 1971).* Albany: New York State Department of Education, 8 July 1971. ERIC ED 069 460.

2731. Virginia. State Department of Education. Office of Federal Programs. *Migrant Education. Third Annual Regional Workshop (Virginia Beach, Va., March 5-9, 1972),* by Cynthia P. Machman, comp. Richmond: Virginia State Department of Education, 6 April 1972. ERIC ED 078 974.

2732. Georgia. State Department of Education. *Educational Continuity of the Migrant Child. Annual Eastern Stream Conference (5th, Atlanta, Georgia, March 5-8, 1974).* Atlanta: Georgia State Department of Education, 8 March 1974. ERIC ED 093 531.

6.5 Administration

2733. Dougherty, Sarah E., and Uhde, Madeline. "School Health Program for Children of Seasonal Agricultural Workers." *Journal of School Health* 35, no. 2 (February 1965): 85-90.

2734. Moore, Harold E., and Schufletowski, Charles. "Southwestern States Developmental Project Relating to Educational Needs of Adult Agricultural Migrants. The Arizona Report." Tempe: Arizona State University, January 1965. ERIC ED 015 031.

2735. U.S. Department of Health, Education, and Welfare. Office of Education. *A School Transfer Record System for Farm Migrant Children,* by George E. Haney. Washington, D.C.: Government Printing Office, 1965. ERIC ED 020 032.

2736. "Bulletins for Teachers of the Migratory Pupil." Shafter, California: Richland School District, 1967. ERIC ED 032 144.

2737. California. State Department of Education. *A School and Health Record Transfer System for Migratory Children of Migratory Agricultural Workers (California).* Sacramento: California State Department of Education, 1967. ERIC ED 014 367.

2738. Arizona. State Department of Public Instruction. *Arizona Teacher Exchange 1969; A Component of Migrant Child Education.* Phoenix: Arizona State Department of Public Instruction, 1969.

2739. *Handbook for Auxiliary Services for Migrant Education.* Austin, Texas: Southwest Educational Development Lab., 1969. ERIC ED 086 392.

2740. "Migrant Children in Alabama. A Survey to Identify Children of Migrant Workers and Certain Former Migrant Workers in Alabama." Tuscaloosa: University of Alabama, August 1969. ERIC ED 042 545.

2741. Swanson, Patricia. "Health Care and Education. A Guide for the Migrant School Nurse; A Resource in Health Education for the Migrant School Teacher." St. Paul, Minnesota: Migrants, Inc., 1969. ERIC ED 038 191.

2742. U.S. Department of Health, Education, and Welfare. Office of Education. Bureau of Elementary and Secondary Education. *Directory of Consultants on Migrant Education, National and State Lists for Migrant Education Programs under Title I, Elementary and Secondary Education Act, Public Law 89-10, as Amended.* Washington, D.C.: Government Printing Office, August 1969. ERIC ED 032 159.

2743. Pfeil, Mary P. "Computer Harvests Migrant Records." *American Education* 6, no. 9 (November 1970): 6-9.

2744. Scott, Norval C., Jr. "Zip Test: A Quick Locator Test for Migrant Children." *Journal of Educational Measurement* 7, no. 1 (spring 1970): 49-50.

2745. U.S. Department of Health, Education, and Welfare. Office of Education. Bureau of Elementary and Secondary Education. *Directory of Consultants on Migrant Education. National and State Lists for Migrant Education Programs under Title I, Elementary and Secondary Education Act, Public Law 89-10, as Amended.* Washington, D.C.: Government Printing Office, 1970. ERIC ED 045 277.

2746. Cappelluzzo, Emma M. *Guidance and the Migrant Child.* New York: Houghton Mifflin Company, 1971.

2747. Krebs, Robert E., and Stevens, Gail A. "An Assessment of Needs Related to the Education of Migrant Children in the State of Washington." Topenish, Washington: Center for the Study of Migrant and Indian Education, February 1971. ERIC ED 050 851.

2748. Patterson, Mary G.; Gabel, Ann; Holmes, Lillian, et al. "Extending the Role of the School Nurse to Migrant Families: Fresno County." *Journal of School Health* 41, no. 8 (October 1971): 421-24.

2749. "Migrant Health—Legislation and Programs." Austin, Texas: National Migrant Information Clearinghouse, Juarez-Lincoln Center, 1972. ERIC ED 081 531.

2750. New Jersey. State Department of Education. Division of Curriculum and Instruction. *Pilot V Needs Assessment: A Study Conducted during the Year 1972 to Ascertain Data as the Basis of Curriculum Development for Migrant Children,* by Georgianna Badaracca et al., comps. Trenton: New Jersey State Department of Education, 1972. ERIC ED 091 129.

2751. U.S. Congress. Senate. *Migrant Children's Nutrition, 1972: Migrant Children's Food Program Failures. Joint Hearing before the Subcommittee on Migratory Labor of the Committee on Labor and Public Welfare and the Select Committee on Nutrition and Human Needs, U.S. Senate, 92nd Congress, 2nd Session*. 1 May 1972. ERIC ED 118 333.

2752. Barba, Alma Maria Acevedo. "New Mexico Migrant Project Aides: Perceptions of Their Functions." Doctoral dissertation, New Mexico State University, 1973. ERIC ED 081 542.

2753. Dyer, Maxwell. "Children of the Four Winds: The Migrant Student Record Transfer System." Paper presented at the Association for the Educational Data Systems Annual Convention, New Orleans, Louisiana, 16-19 April 1973. ERIC ED 087 456.

2754. Hagwood, Richard Andrew. "Decision-Making in Migrant Mexican-American Education in an Illinois Community." Doctoral dissertation, University of Illinois at Urbana-Champaign, 1973.

2755. Roberts, James A. "A Study of the Feasibility of Using the Existing Migrant Student Record Transfer System to Promote Continuity of Learning for Adult Migratory Farmworkers." Geneseo: State University of New York College at Geneseo, Migrant Center, 1973. ERIC ED 111 568.

2756. Scott, Norval C. "Locator Tests: Useful or Ornamental?" Paper presented at the American Educational Research Association annual meeting, Chicago, Illinois, 15-19 April 1974. ERIC ED 090 281.

2757. Archuleta, George L., and Archuleta, Sherrie L. "Colorado Migrant Child Identification and Recruitment Project: Field Guide." Weld Board of Cooperative Educational Services. La Salle, Colorado, August 1975. ERIC ED 116 854.

2758. Illinois. State Office of Education. *Directory of Services for Migrant Families*. Springfield: Illinois State Office of Education, 1975. ERIC ED 116 834.

2759. New York. State Department of Education. Bureau of Migrant Education. *Migrant Student Record Transfer System in New York State*. Albany: New York State Department of Education, 1975. ERIC ED 121 541.

2760. U.S. Comptroller General. *Evaluation of the Migrant Student Record Transfer System (Office of Education, DHEW). Report of the Comptroller General of the United States*. Washington, D.C.: Government Printing Office, 16 September 1975. ERIC ED 114 235.

2761. Washington. Office of the State Superintendent of Public Instruction. Migrant Education Program. *MSRTS—A Handbook to the Migrant Student Record Transfer System (State of Washington)*. Olympia: Washington Office of the State Superintendent, 1975. ERIC ED 115 444.

6.6 Teacher Training

2762. Colorado. State Department of Education. *Learning on the Move; A Guide for Migrant Education*, by Neil W. Sherman and Alfred M. Potts. Denver: Colorado State Department of Education, 1960. ERIC ED 032 139.

2763. "The Use of Teaching Teams to Improve the Education of In-Migrant Transient Pupils in Depressed Areas. Project Proposal." Pittsburgh, Pennsylvania: Pittsburgh Public Schools, 1960. ERIC ED 020 252.

2764. "A Policy Statement on the Education of Children of Migrant Farm Workers." Washington, D.C.: National Committee on the Education of Migrant Children, 6 June 1968. ERIC ED 077 636.

2765. Wyoming. State Department of Education. *A Handbook for Teachers of Migrant Children in Wyoming.* Cheyenne: Wyoming State Department of Education, 1968. ERIC ED 028 000.

2766. "Florida Migratory Child Compensatory Program Announcement of Staff Development Activities." Boca Raton: Florida Atlanta University, January 1969. ERIC ED 030 524.

2767. Michigan. State Department of Education. *Handbook for Teachers of Migrant Children.* Lansing: Michigan State Department of Education, 1970. ERIC ED 038 203.

2768. *1970 Institute for Individualizing Mathematics for Migrant Students. Summary and Evaluation Analysis.* Austin, Texas: Southwest Educational Development Lab., September 1970.

2769. North Carolina. State Department of Public Instruction. Learning Institute of North Carolina. *Migrant Education Institute.* Raleigh: North Carolina State Department of Public Instruction, May 1970. ERIC ED 040 799.

2770. U.S. Comptroller General. *Assessment of the Teacher Corps Program at the University of Southern California and Participating Schools in Tulare County Serving Rural-Migrant Children.* Washington, D.C.: Government Printing Office, 25 August 1971. ERIC ED 054 079.

2771. McConnell, Beverly. "Training Migrant Paraprofessionals in the Bilingual Mini Head Start, April 1972." Ephrata: Washington State Intermediate School District 104, April 1972. ERIC ED 116 866.

2772. McConnell, Beverly. "Training Migrant Paraprofessionals in the Bilingual Mini Head Start, February 1973." Ephrata: Washington State Intermediate School District 104, February 1973. ERIC ED 116 867.

2773. "A Policy Statement on Staff Development for Migrant Education." New York: National Committee on the Education of Migrant Children, 1973. ERIC ED 088 634.

2774. Bermea, María Teresa Cruz. "Training Migrant Paraprofessionals in Bilingual Mini Head Start. Mexican Cultural Heritage Materials for Preschool Children." Ephrata, Washington: Washington State Intermediate School District 104, 1974. ERIC ED 114 223.

2775. "Bilingual-Bicultural Teacher Education Program." Austin, Texas: Saint Edward's University, 1974. ERIC ED 102 152.

2776. Arizona. State Department of Public Instruction. Division of Migrant Child Education. *Arizona's Annual Migrant Child Teacher Institute (6th, June 9-June 27, 1975).* Phoenix: Arizona State Department of Public Instruction, 9 June 1975. ERIC ED 121 524.

2777. Arizona. State Department of Public Instruction. Division of Migrant Child Education. *Arizona's Migrant Child Education Teacher Exchange with Florida.* Phoenix: Arizona State Department of Public Instruction, August 1975. ERIC ED 116 849.

2778. McConnell, Beverly. "Bilingual MiniSchool Tutoring Project. A State of Washington URRD (Urban, Rural, Racial, Disadvantaged) Program. Mid-Year Evaluation, 1975-76 Program Year." Ephrata: Washington State Intermediate School District 104, December 1975. ERIC ED 121 497.

2779. McConnell, Beverly. "Training Migrant Paraprofessionals in Bilingual Mini Head Start. Evaluation of Progress, Mid-Year Evaluation, 1974-75 Program Year." Ephrata: Washington State Intermediate School District 104, 1975. ERIC ED 116 868.

2780. McConnell, Beverly. "Training Migrant Paraprofessionals in Bilingual Mini Head Start. Final Evaluation, 1974-75 Program Year. Progress Report No. 7." Ephrata: Washington State Intermediate School District 104, September 1975. ERIC ED 114 222.

7. BILINGUAL EDUCATION

7.1 General

2781. Fallis, Guadalupe Valdes. "Teaching Spanish to the Spanish-Speaking: Classroom Strategies." n.d. ERIC ED 097 806.

2782. Goodman, Frank M. "Bilingual Bicultural Education in the Compton Unified School District and Its Relevance to a Multi-Ethnic Community." Compton, California: Compton City Schools, n.d. ERIC ED 060 705.

2783. Mireles, E.E. "Corpus Christi Kids Are Bilingual." *Texas Outlook* 35, no. 5 (May 1951): 10-12.

2784. Baca, Fidel García. "Bilingual Education in Certain Southwest School Districts." Doctoral dissertation, University of Utah, 1956.

2785. Chávez, Simón J. "Preserve Their Language Heritage." *Childhood Education* 33, no. 4 (December 1956): 165-85.

2786. Ulibarri, Horacio, and Cooper, James G., directors. "Bilingual Research Project: Final Report." Albuquerque: University of New Mexico, College of Education, 1959.

2787. California. State Department of Education. *Spanish for Spanish-Speaking Pupils*, by A.D. Nance. Mimeographed. Sacramento: California State Department of Education, 1963.

2788. Leighton, E. Roby, ed. "Bicultural Linguistic Concepts in Education. A Handbook of Suggestions, Primary to Adult, for the Classroom Teacher, the Guidance Counselor, the Administrator." September 1964. ERIC ED 001 493.

2789. Andersson, Theodore. "New Focus on the Bilingual Child." *Modern Language Journal* 49 (March 1965): 156-60.

2790. Ching, D.C. "Methods for the Bilingual Child." *Elementary English* 42, no. 1 (January 1965): 22-27.

2791. Christian, Chester C. "Suggested Objectives for a Bilingual Program." In *Reports on Bilingualism to the Annual Conference of the Southwest Council of Foreign Language Teachers, El Paso, Texas, November 4-5, 1966*, pp. 31-32. El Paso, Texas: Southwest Council of Foreign Language Teachers, 1966.

2792. Cooper, Lloyd G. "Awakening at Socorro." *Texas Outlook* 50, no. 11 (November 1966): 34-35.

2793. Hoben, Nancy, and Hood, John T. "Help for the Language Handicapped." *Texas Outlook* 50, no. 3 (March 1966): 28-29.

2794. Michel, Joseph. "Tentative Guidelines for a Bilingual Curriculum." In *Reports on Bilingualism to the Annual Conference of the Southwest Council of Foreign Language Teachers, El Paso, Texas, November 4-5, 1966*, pp. 38-43. El Paso, Texas: Southwest Council of Foreign Language Teachers, 1966.

2795. Noreen, Sister D.C. "A Bilingual Curriculum for Spanish-Americans: A Regional Problem with Nation-Wide Implications." *Catholic School Journal* 66, no. 1 (January 1966): 25-26.

2796. Anderson, Merlin D. "Bilingual Education in Nevada." In *Bilingual Education, Research and Teaching. Reports to the Annual Conference of the Southwest Council of Foreign Language Teachers, El Paso, November 10-11, 1967*, pp. 68-69. El Paso: Southwest Council of Foreign Language Teachers, 1967. ERIC ED 017 387.

2797. California. State Department of Education. *Bilingual Education for Mexican-American Children*, by Eleanor Wall Thonis. Sacramento: California State Department of Education, 1967.

2798. California. State Department of Education. *Bilingual Education for Mexican American Children: A Report of an Experiment Conducted in the Mayville Joint Unified School District*, by Eugene González and John Plakos. Sacramento: California State Department of Education, 1967.

2799. Christian, Chester C., ed. *Bilingual Education, Research and Teaching. Annual Conference of the Southwest Council of Foreign Language Teachers (4th, El Paso, November 10-11, 1967). Reports*. El Paso, Texas: Southwest Council of Foreign Language Teachers, 1967. ERIC ED 016 434.

2800. Consalves, Julia. "Bilingual Education in California." Paper presented at the annual conference of the Southwest Council of Foreign Language Teachers, El Paso, Texas, 10 November 1967. ERIC ED 017 386.

2801. Maynes, J.O., Jr. "Bilingual Education in Arizona. Report 3, Bilingual Programs in the Southwest." Paper presented at the annual conference of the Southwest Council of Foreign Language Teachers, El Paso, Texas, 10-11 November 1967. ERIC ED 017 385.

2802. Skrabanck, R.L., and Mahoney, Mary K. "The Use of English and Spanish by Spanish-Americans in Two South Texas Counties." In *Proceedings of the Southwestern Sociological Association, 1967*, pp. 189-94. Arlington, Texas: University of Texas at Arlington, 1967.

2803. U.S. Congress. House. *Bilingual Education Act. House Reports on Public Bills, 90th Congress, 915. Report together with Minority Views from Committee on Education and Labor to Accompany H.R. 13103*. Washington, D.C.: Government Printing Office, 1967.

2804. U.S. Congress. House. Education and Labor Committee. *Bilingual Education Programs. Hearings before General Subcommittee on Education, 90th Congress, 1st Session*. Washington, D.C.: Government Printing Office, 1967.

2805. U.S. Congress. Senate. *Hearings before the Special Subcommittee on Bilingual Education of the Committee on Labor and Public Welfare*. Washington, D.C.: Government Printing Office, 1967. (Testimony of officials, school personnel, and representatives of Mexican-American organizations.)

2806. U.S. Department of Health, Education, and Welfare. Office of Education. *Science Instruction in Spanish for Pupils of Spanish Background: An Experiment in Bilingualism*, by Arnold Raisner; Philip Bolger; and Carmen Sanguinetti. Final Report Project No. 407-9. Vol. 181. Washington, D.C.: Government Printing Office, 1967.

2807. Wapple, R.J., and Foder, A.A. "Bilingual Education for Mexican-American Children: An Experiment." Marysville, California: Marysville Joint Unified School District, 1967.

2808. California. State Department of Education. *Administrative Procedures for the Bilingual Education Act, Elementary and Secondary Education Act, Title VII as Amended.* Sacramento: California State Department of Education, 1968.

2809. California. State Department of Education. *Development of a Bilingual Task Force to Improve Education of Mexican American Students.* Sacramento: California State Department of Education, 1968. ERIC ED 024 493.

2810. Ott, Elizabeth H. "Basic Education for Spanish Speaking Disadvantaged Pupils." Austin, Texas: Southwest Educational Development Lab., 1968. ERIC ED 020 497.

2811. Ott, Elizabeth H. "English in Bilingual Education." Paper presented at the "Bilingual Education in Three Cultures" Annual Conference of the Southwest Council for Bilingual Education, El Paso, November 8-9, 1968. Las Cruces, New Mexico: New Mexico State University, Department of Modern Languages, 1968.

2812. Spencer, Maria Gutierrez. "B.O.L.D.: Bicultural Orientation and Language Development." Paper presented at the American Association of Teachers of Spanish and Portuguese, San Antonio, Texas, August 1968. ERIC ED 030 342.

2813. Ury, Claude M. "Bilingual Education Act: Bridge to Understanding." *Catholic School Journal* 68, no. 7 (September 1968): 33-34.

2814. Benjamin, Richard C. "A Bilingual Oral Language and Conceptual Development Program for Spanish-Speaking Pre-School Children." *TESOL Quarterly* 3, no . 4 (December 1969): 315-19.

2815. Bernal, Ernest M., Jr., ed. "The San Antonio Conference. Bilingual-Bicultural Education—Where Do We Go from Here? (San Antonio, Texas, March 28-29, 1969)." San Antonio, Texas: Saint Mary's University, 28 March 1969. ERIC ED 033 777.

2816. "Escuela con dos lenguas; J.T. Brackenridge School, San Antonio, Texas." *Instructor* 78, no. 6 (February 1969): 56-58.

2817. Lance, D.M. "Conclusions and Implications." In *A Brief Study of Spanish-English Bilinguals: Final Report,* pp. 91-95. Unpublished Document. College Station: Texas A&M University, Research Project ORR-Liberal Arts 15504, 1969.

2818. *National Conference on Bilingual Education: Language Skills.* Washington, D.C.: Educational Systems Corporation, 1969.

2819. Ott, Elizabeth H. "The Bilingual Education Program of the Southwest Educational Development Laboratory." *Florida FL Reporter: A Language Education Journal. (Special Anthology Issue: Linguistic-Cultural Differences and American Education.)* 7, no. 1 (spring/summer 1969): 147-48, 159.

2820. "Projects under the New Bilingual Program." *American Education* 5, no. 8 (October 1969): 26-27.

2821. Pucinski, Roman C. "The Federal Investment in Bilingual Education." Paper presented at the 3rd Annual TESOL Convention, Chicago, Illinois, 5-8 March 1969. ERIC ED 030 099.

2822. Ulibarri, Horacio. "Administration of Bilingual Education." Albuquerque, New Mexico: University of New Mexico, College of Education, 1969.

2823. Vásquez, Librado Keno. "An Experimental Pilot Bilingual Model School for Transient Mexican-American Students." Doctoral dissertation, University of Oregon, 1969.

2824. Andersson, Theodore, et al. "An Experimental Study of Bilingual-Affective Education for Mexican American Children in Grades K and 1." Austin, Texas: Southwest Educational Development Lab., 27 April 1970. ERIC ED 056 536.

2825. "A Bilingual Approach: Education for Understanding. Leadership Report." Austin, Texas: Southwest Intergroup Relations Council, Inc., January 1970. ERIC ED 075 106.

2826. Fedder, Ruth, and Gabaldon, Jacqueline. *No Longer Deprived. The Use of Minority Cultures and Languages in the Education of Disadvantaged Children and Their Teachers*. New York: Teachers College Press, 1970.

2827. Jourdaine, John R. "A Bilingual Math-Science Learning Center." In *In Reaching: Creative Approaches to Bilingual/Bicultural Education*. Los Angeles, California: University of Southern California, September 1970. ERIC ED 051 716.

2828. Lindt, John, and Nosse, Marilyn. "The Cutler-Orosi Intercultural Center." In *In Reaching: Creative Approaches to Bilingual/Bicultural Education*. Los Angeles: University of Southern California, School of Education, September 1970. ERIC ED 051 715.

2829. Logan, J. Lee. "One Will Do But We Like Two: Coral Way Bilingual Pilot Project." *National Elementary Principal* 50, no. 2 (November 1970): 85-87.

2830. López, Thomas F. "Staff Development of Bilingual Programs." Master's thesis, Sacramento State College, 1970. ERIC ED 044 233.

2831. Malkoc, Anna Maria, and Roberts, A. Hood. "Bilingual Education: A Special Report from CAL/ERIC." *Elementary English* 47, no. 5 (May 1970): 713-25.

2832. Micotti, Antonia R. "Dance School Project (Bi-Lingual Preschool Project), Santa Clara County Office of Education. Final Report, August 1, 1970." San Jose, California: Santa Clara County Office of Education, August 1970. ERIC ED 046 514.

2833. "Peso Bilingual Language Development Project. Project Evaluation, June 30, 1970." Amarillo, Texas: Peso Education Service Center Region 16, 30 June 1970. ERIC ED 064 010.

2834. Stubing, C.H., et al. "Reports: 'Bilingual Education: The Status of the Art, 1970.' (7th Annual Conference of the Southwest Council for Bilingual Education, El Paso, Texas, November 20-21, 1970)." Las Cruces, New Mexico: Southwest Council for Bilingual Education, 1970. ERIC ED 059 818.

2835. Texas. Education Agency. *A Resource Manual for Implementing Bilingual Education Programs*. Austin: Texas Education Agency, 1970.

2836. Treviño, Bertha G. "Bilingual Instruction in the Primary Grades." *Modern Language Journal* 54, no. 4 (April 1970): 255-56.

2837. Black, Eric D. "Bilingual Education for Nation's Spanish Speaking." *International American Scene* 3, nos. 1-2 (1971): 20-28.

2838. Cannon, Garland. "Bilingual Problems and Developments in the United States." *Publications of the Modern Language Association* 86, no. 3 (May 1971): 452-58.

2839. Cottrell, Milford C. "Bilingual Education in San Juan County, Utah: A Cross Cultural Emphasis." Paper presented at the American Educational Research Association annual convention, New York, February 4-7, 1971. ERIC ED 047 855.

2840. Gingras, Rosario C. "An Analysis of Two Sets of Mexican-American Bilingual Data." Los Alamitos, California: Southwest Regional Laboratory for Educational Research and Development, 25 June 1971. ERIC ED 110 205.

2841. Herbert, Charles H., Jr. "Initial Reading in Spanish for Bilinguals." Paper presented at the Conference on Child Language, Chicago, Illinois, 22-24 November 1971. ERIC ED 061 813.

2842. Lesley, Tay. "Bilingual Education in California." Master's thesis, University of California at Los Angeles, 1971. ERIC ED 057 661.

2843. Levenson, Stanley. "Planning Curriculum for Bilingual Education Programs: Kindergarten through Grade 12." Paper presented at the Fifth Annual TESOL Convention, New Orleans, Louisiana, 5 March 1971. ERIC ED 053 587.

2844. Nedler, S. "Language, the Vehicle; Culture, the Content; Southwest Educational Development Laboratory: Early Childhood Learning System." *Journal of Research and Development in Education* 4 (summer 1971): 3-10.

2845. Ramírez, Karen G. "Bilingualism and Bilingual Programs in El Paso: Kindergarten and First Grade." Master's thesis, University of Texas at El Paso, 1971.

2846. Stern, H.H. "Bilingual Education Conference." Mimeographed. Toronto: Ontario Institute for Studies in Education, 1971.

2847. Zirkel, Perry A. "Two Languages Spoken Here." *Grade Teacher* 88, no. 8 (April 1971): 36-40, 59.

2848. Ainsworth, Len, and Alford, Gay. "Responsive Environment Program for Spanish American Children. Evaluation Report, 1971-72." June 1972. ERIC ED 068 219.

2849. Herbert, Charles H., Jr., and Sancho, Anthony R. "Puedo leer: I Can Read. Initial Reading in Spanish for Bilingual Children." 1972. ERIC ED 071 525.

2850. Kobrick, Jeffrey W. "Compelling Case for Bilingual Education." *Saturday Review* 55 (29 April 1972): 54-58.

2851. "A Resource Manual for Implementing Bilingual Education Programs." 1972. ERIC ED 070 552.

2852. Bernal, Elias R., comp. "A Report of the Final Session of the National Bilingual/Bicultural Institute (Albuquerque, New Mexico, November 28-December 1, 1973)." Albuquerque, New Mexico: National Education Task Force de la Raza, 1973. ERIC ED 100 601.

2853. Brisk, Maria. *Directory of Bilingual Programs in the United States 1972-1973.* Washington, D.C.: Center for Applied Linguistics, 1973.

2854. Cross, William C., and Bridgewater, Mike. "Toward Bicultural Education for the Southwestern Mexican-American." *Education* 94, no. 1 (September/October 1973): 18-22.

2855. Flores Macías, Reynaldo. "Developing a Bilingual Culturally-Relevant Educational Program for Chicanos." *Aztlán* 4, no. 1 (spring 1973): 61-84.

2856. García, Robert, and Truan, Carlos. "State Legislation in Bilingual Education." Report presented at the International Multilingual-Multicultural Conference, San Diego, California, April 1973.

2857. López, Ronald W., et al. *The Role and Functions of Spanish-Language-Only Television in Los Angeles.* Claremont, California: Claremont Graduate School, Center for Urban and Regional Studies, Claremont University Center, Chicano Studies Center, 1973.

2858. Martínez, Frank, et al. *Bilingual/Bicultural Education Models. Final Report.* Portland, Oregon: Northwest Regional Educational Lab.; Salem, Oregon: Valley Migrant League, 7 February 1973.

2859. "Opportunities for Youth in Education. Final Report, 1971-1973." Crystal City, Texas: Crystal City Independent School District, July 1973. ERIC ED 089 913.

2860. "Report of a National Bilingual Bicultural Institute: A Relook at Tucson '66 and Beyond (Albuquerque, New Mexico, November 28-December 1, 1973)." Albuquerque, New Mexico: National Education Task Force de la Raza, December 1973. ERIC ED 101 923.

2861. Rodríguez, Rodolfo, comp. "A Preliminary Study of 5th Year ESEA Title VII Bilingual Bicultural Programs with High Concentrations of Mexican American Students." Albuquerque, New Mexico: National Education Task Force de la Raza, 1973. ERIC ED 100 600.

2862. U.S. Congress. Senate. *Bilingual Education, Health, and Manpower Programs, 1973. Joint Hearing before the Subcommittee on Education and the Special Subcommittee on Labor and Public Welfare, U.S. Senate, 93rd Congress, 1st Session on Examination of the Problems of Bilingual Education, Health, and Manpower Programs (Los Angeles, California, February 26, 1973).* Washington, D.C.: Government Printing Office, 1973. ERIC ED 089 890.

2863. Bernal, Ernest M., Jr. "Models of Bilingual Education, Grades K-3, for a Planned Variation Study." Paper presented at the annual meeting of the American Educational Research Association, 59th, Chicago, Illinois, April 1974. ERIC ED 097 157.

2864. Casso, Henry J., comp. "Observations from a National Bilingual Bicultural Institute Recommendations for a State Wide Design. Annual Illinois Bilingual Bicultural Conference (1st, Chicago, Illinois, March 28-29, 1974)." Albuquerque, New Mexico: National Education Task Force de la Raza, 1974. ERIC ED 103 143.

2865. "The Daily Curriculum Guide, Year 1: A Preschool Program for the Spanish-Speaking Child." San Jose, California: Spanish Dame Bilingual Bicultural Project, 1974. ERIC ED 108 507.

2866. Elwell, Richard. "This Way to 'Villa Alegre': Bilingual TV Program." *American Education* 10, no. 9 (November 1974): 12-15.

2867. Fisher, R.I. "Study of Non-Intellectual Attributes of Children in First Grade Bilingual-Bicultural Program." *Journal of Educational Research* 67 (March 1974): 323-28.

2868. Gaillard, Frye. "Chicanos Push Bilingual Education." *Race Relations Reporter* 5, no. 17 (September 1974): 4-6.

2869. "Happiness Is Bilingual Education for the Children in the San Luis Valley Schools, School Year 1973-74." Alamosa, Colorado: San Luis Valley Board of Cooperative Services, 1974. ERIC ED 113 115.

2870. "Language Development Resources for Bilingual Bicultural Education: An Aid to Primary Teachers of Mexican American Children." Tucson: University of Arizona, Experienced Teacher Fellowship Program, February 1974. ERIC ED 108 490.

2871. Linton, Thomas H. "Region One Right to Read Project. Right to Read Annual Performance Report." Edinburg, Texas: Education Service Center Region 1, 1974. ERIC ED 096 070.

2872. Montgomery, Linda. "Carnival of Bilingual Learning: Carrascolendas TV Program." *American Education* 10, no. 7 (August/September 1974): 34-37.

2873. Teschner, Richard V. "Bilingual Education and the Materials Explosion, or, a Guide for the Bibliographer-by-Necessity." *Bilingual Review/La revista bilingue* 1, no. 3 (September-December 1974): 259-69.

2874. Villarreal, Abelardo, et al. "¡Que bonito es leer! (How Nice It Is To Read!)." San Antonio, Texas: Curriculum Adaptation Network for Bilingual/Bicultural Education, February 1974. ERIC ED 108 503.

2875. Williams, Frederick, and Van Wart, Geraldine. *Carrascolendas: Bilingual Education through Television.* Praeger Special Studies in U.S. Economic, Social, and Political Issues. New York: Praeger, 1974.

2876. de los Santos, Gilberto. "An Operational Model for Bilingual Education." Paper presented at the Symposium on Bilingual/Bicultural Education: Effects on the Language, Individual and Society, El Paso, Texas, June 12-14, 1975. ERIC ED 108 819.

2877. Engle, Patricia Lee. *The Use of Vernacular Languages in Education: Language Medium in Early School Years for Minority Language Groups.* Papers in Applied Linguistics/Bilingual Education Series, No. 3, Arlington, Virginia: Center for Applied Linguistics, 1975.

2878. Gonzales, Tobias. "An Economic and Political Analysis of Bilingual Bicultural Education Legislation at the Federal Level." In *Perspectives on Chicano Education.* Stanford, California: Stanford University, Office of Chicano Affairs, 1975.

2879. Hardgrave, Robert L., Jr., and Hinojosa, Santiago. *The Politics of Bilingual Education: A Study of Four Southwest Texas Communities.* Manchaca, Texas: Sterling Swift Publishing Co., 1975.

2880. Metzger, Gerhard Rudolf. "Spanish Bilingual Programs in Industrial Arts." Master's thesis, California State University at Long Beach, 1975.

2881. Troike, Rudolf C., and Modiano, Nancy, eds. *Proceedings of the First Inter-American Conference on Bilingual Education.* Arlington, Virginia: Center for Applied Linguistics, 1975.

2882. Chambers, Joanna F., comp. *Directory of Title VII ESEA Bilingual Education Programs: 1975-76.* Austin, Texas: Dissemination and Assessment Center for Bilingual Education, 1976.

7.2 Theory

2883. Coronel, Paul. "Underlying Philosophy of a Bi-Lingual Program." *Claremont College Reading Conference Yearbook* 10 (1945): 51-57.

2884. de León, Marcos. "Wanted: A New Educational Philosophy for the Mexican-American." *California Journal of Secondary Education* 34, no. 7 (November 1959): 398-402.

2885. Gaarder, A. Bruce, et al. "Teaching the Bilingual Child: Research, Development, and Policy." *Modern Language Journal* 49 (March 1965): 165-75.

2886. Crow, Lester D.; Murray, Walter I.; and Smythe, Hugh H. *Educating the Culturally Disadvantaged Child: Principles and Programs.* New York: David McKay Company, Inc., 1966.

2887. Nostrand, Howard Lee. "Toward a Bi-Cultural Curriculum. Report 1, Areas Where Research Is Needed in Bilingual Education." Paper presented at the annual conference of the Southwest Council of Foreign Language Teachers, El Paso, Texas, November 10-11, 1967. ERIC ED 018 285.

2888. Pascual, Henry. "Teaching Spanish to Native Speakers of Spanish in New Mexico." 10 November 1967. ERIC ED 018 303.

2889. Forbes, Jack D. *Education of the Culturally Different: A Multi-Cultural Approach.* Berkeley, California: Far West Laboratory for Educational Research and Development, 1968.

2890. Olstad, Charles, ed. *Bilingual Education in Three Cultures. Reports to the Annual Conference of the Southwest Council for Bilingual Education, El Paso, November 8-9, 1968.* Las Cruces: New Mexico State University, Department of Modern Languages, 1968.

2891. Rodríguez, Armando M. "Bilingual Education Now." In *Proceedings of the National Conference on Educational Opportunities for the Mexican American, May 1968.* Austin, Texas: Southwest Educational Development Lab., 1968.

2892. Andersson, Theodore. "Bilingual Elementary Schooling: A Report to Texas Educators." *Florida Foreign Language Reporter* 7, no. 1 (spring/summer 1969): 37-40.

2893. Andersson, Theodore. "Bilingual Schooling: Oasis or Mirage?" *Hispania* 52, no. 1 (March 1969): 69-74.

2894. Olstad, Charles, ed. *Bilingual Education Commitment and Involvement. Reports to the Sixth Annual Conference of the Southwest Council for Bilingual Education, Tucson, Arizona, November 14-15, 1969.* Las Cruces: New Mexico State University, November 1969. ERIC ED 033 791.

2895. Rodríguez, Armando M . "Bilingual Education—A Look Ahead." 1969. ERIC ED 030 505.

2896. Rodríguez, Armando M. "The Realities of Bilingual Education." In *National Conference on Bilingual Education: Language Skills*, pp. 14-21. Washington, D.C.: Educational Systems Corporation, 1969.

2897. Treviño, Bertha G. "Bilingual Education—A Psychological Helping Hand." *Texas Outlook* 53, no. 5 (May 1969): 24-25.

2898. Ulibarri, Horacio, and Cooper, James G. "Interpretive Studies on Bilingual Education. Final Report." Albuquerque: University of New Mexico, College of Education, 1969.

2899. Ulibarri, Horacio, et al. "Bilingual Education, PREP-6." Albuquerque: University of New Mexico, 1969. ERIC ED 034 082.

2900. Zintz, Miles V. "Chapter 8. Foundations for Education of Spanish American Children." In *Education across Cultures*, pp. 220-49. 2nd ed. Dubuque, Iowa: Kendall/Hunt Publishing Company, 1969.

2901. Andersson, Theodore, and Boyer, Mildred. *Bilingual Schooling in the United States.* 2 vols. Austin, Texas: Southwest Educational Development Laboratory [for sale by the Superintendent of Documents, U.S. Government Printing Office, Washington, D.C.], 1970.

2902. Ballesteros, David. "Toward an Advantaged Society: Bilingual Education in the 70's." *National Elementary Principal* 50, no. 2 (November 1970): 25-28.

2903. Carter, Thomas P. "The Way beyond Bilingual Education." *Civil Rights Digest* 3, no. 4 (fall 1970): 14-21.

2904. Cordasco, Francesco M. "Educational Enlightenment out of Texas: Toward Bilingualism." *Teachers College Record* 71, no. 4 (May 1970): 608-12.

2905. Felder, Dell. "The Education of Mexican Americans: Fallacies of the Monoculture Approach." *Social Education* 34, no. 6 (October 1970): 639-42.

2906. Fishman, Joshua A., and Lovas, John. "Bilingual Education in Sociolinguistic Perspective." *TESOL Quarterly* 4, no. 3 (September 1970): 215-22.

2907. Lara-Braud, Jorge. *Bilingualism for Texas; Education for Fraternity.* Austin: Hispanic-American Institute, 1970.

2908. Mondale, Walter F.; González, Henry B.; and Roybal, Edward R. "Education for the Spanish Speaking: The Role of the Federal Government." *National Elementary Principal* 50, no. 2 (November 1970): 116-22.

2909. Ramírez, Manuel. "Cultural Democracy: A New Philosophy for Educating the Mexican-American Child." *National Elementary Principal* 50, no. 2 (November 1970): 45-46.

2910. Rodríguez, Armando M. "The Necessity for Bilingual Education." *Wilson Library Bulletin* 44, no. 7 (March 1970): 724-30.

2911. Rodríguez, Emilia Margarita. "La educación bilingüe: sus implicaciones." Master's thesis, University of Texas at Austin, 1970.

2912. Ulibarri, Horacio. "The Effects and Implications of Culturally Pluralistic Education on the Mexican-American." Albuquerque, New Mexico: Southwestern Cooperative Educational Lab., 1970. ERIC ED 058 971.

2913. Andersson, Theodore. "Bilingual Education: The American Experience." *Modern Language Journal* 55, no. 7 (November 1971): 427-40.

2914. Ayala, Armando A. "Rationale for Early Childhood Bilingual-Bicultural Education." Paper presented at the American Educational Research Association Annual Convention, New York, 4-7 February 1971. ERIC ED 047 869.

2915. Benitez, Mario. "Bilingual Education: The What, the How, and the How Far." *Hispania* 54, no. 3 (September 1971): 499-503.

2916. Gómez, Severo. "Innovations in Education, Bilingual Education in Texas." *Educational Leader* 28, no. 7 (April 1971): 757-62.

2917. Ivie, Stanley D. *Mexican Education in Cultural Perspective. Monograph Series, No. 5 (1971).* Tucson: University of Arizona, College of Education, 1971.

2918. John, Vera P., and Horner, Vivian M., co-directors. *Early Bilingual Education Project.* New York: The Modern Language Association of America, 1971.

2919. Rendon, Armando B. *Chicano Manifesto.* "Chapter XI." New York: The Macmillan Company, 1971.

2920. Tucker, G. Richard, and D'Anglejan, Alison. "Some Thoughts Concerning Bilingual Education." *Modern Language Journal* 55, no. 8 (December 1971): 491-93.

2921. Badillo, Herman. "The Politics and Realities of Bilingual Education." *Foreign Language Annals* 5, no. 3 (March 1972): 297-301.

2922. Christian, Chester C., Jr., and Sharp, John M. "Bilingualism in a Pluralistic Society." In *ACTFL Review of Foreign Language Education.* Vol. 4: *Foreign Language Education: A Reappraisal,* pp. 341-75. Edited by Dale L. Lange and Charles J. James. Skokie, Illinois: National Textbook Company, 1972.

2923. Ramírez, Manuel. "Current Educational Research: The Basis for a New Philosophy for Educating Mexican-Americans." In *Adelante: An Emerging Design for Mexican-American Education.* Edited by Manuel Reyes Mazon. Austin: University of Texas at Austin, Center for Communication Research, 1972.

2924. Reyes Mazon, Manuel. *Adelante: An Emerging Design for Mexican American Education.* Austin: The University of Texas at Austin, Center for Communication Research, 1972.

2925. Valencia, Atilano A. *Bilingual-Bicultural Education for the Spanish-English Bilingual.* Las Vegas, New Mexico: New Mexico Highlands University Press, 1972.

2926. Benitez, Mario. "A Blueprint for the Education of the Mexican American." Paper presented at the annual convention of the Comparative and International Education Society, San Antonio, Texas, 25-27 March 1973. ERIC ED 076 294.

2927. Poblano, Ralph, ed. *Ghosts in the Barrio. Issues in Bilingual-Bicultural Education.* San Rafael, California: Leswing Press, 1973.

2928. Treviño, Robert E. "Is Bilingual Education Shortchanging the Chicano?" Paper read at the Symposium on the Education of Mexican-Americans, Meeting of the Society for Applied Anthropology, Tucson, Arizona, 12-14 April 1973. ERIC ED 077 617.

2929. *Casa de la Raza: Separatism or Segregation—Chicanos in Public Education.* Hayward, California: Southwest Network, January 1974.

2930. Castañeda, Alfredo, et al. "New Approaches to Bilingual Bicultural Education, No. 1: A New Philosophy of Education." Santa Cruz, California: Systems and Evaluation in Education, August 1974. ERIC ED 111 181.

2931. Cortés, Carlos E. "Concepts and Strategies for Teaching the Mexican American Experience. New Approaches to Bilingual Bicultural Education, No. 7." Austin, Texas: Dissemination Center for Bilingual Bicultural Education, August 1974. ERIC ED 108 494.

2932. Illinois. State Advisory Committee. *Bilingual/Bicultural Education—A Privilege or a Right? ¿Educación bilingue/bicultural—un privilegio o un derecho?,* by Frank Steiner et al., comps. Springfield: Illinois State Advisory Committee, May 1974. ERIC ED 097 167.

2933. Pialorsi, Frank, ed. *Teaching the Bilingual: New Methods and Old Traditions.* Tucson: University of Arizona Press, 1974.

2934. "Position Papers on Bilingual Bicultural Educational Manpower Development." Papers from Symposium for Bilingual Bicultural Educational Manpower Development, Washington, D.C., 14-16 March 1974. ERIC ED 096 039.

2935. Ramírez, Manuel, and Castañeda, Alfredo. *Cultural Democracy, Bicognitive Development, and Education.* New York: Academic Press, 1974.

2936. Ramírez, Manuel, et al. "Mexican American Values and Culturally Democratic Educational Environments. New Approaches to Bilingual Bicultural Education, No. 2." Austin, Texas: Dissemination Center for Bilingual Bicultural Education, August 1974. ERIC ED 108 496.

2937. Rhode, Robert D. "Bilingual Education for Teachers: English-Spanish." *Educational Forum* 38, no. 2 (January 1974): 203-9.

2938. Santana, Ray, et al. *Parameters of Institutional Change: Chicano Experience in Education.* Hayward, California: Southwest Network, May 1974.

2939. Swanson, Maria Medina. "Bilingual Education: The National Perspective." In *ACTFL Review of Foreign Language Education.* Vol. 5: *Responding to New Realities,* pp. 75-127. Edited by Gilbert A. Jarvis. Skokie, Illinois: National Textbook Company, 1974.

2940. Trueba, Henry T. "Bilingual Bicultural Education for Chicanos in the Southwest." *Council on Anthropology and Education Quarterly* 5, no. 3 (1974): 8-15.

2941. Flores Macías, Reynaldo, et al. *Educación alternativa: On the Development of Chicano Bilingual Schools.* Hayward, California: Southwest Network, 1975.

2942. Peña, Albar A., ed. "Special Feature on Bilingual Education: An Overview." *Today's Education* 64, no. 1 (1975): 70-73.

2943. "A Position Paper on Bilingual Education." Tucson: Arizona Association of Mexican American Educators, Tucson Chapter, 1975. ERIC ED 121 117.

2944. U.S. Commission on Civil Rights. *A Better Chance to Learn: Bilingual-Bicultural Education. Publication No. 51.* Washington, D.C.: Government Printing Office, May 1975.

2945. von Maltitz, Frances Willard. *Living and Learning in Two Languages: Bilingual-Bicultural Education in the United States.* New York: McGraw-Hill Book Co., 1975.

7.3 Evaluation

2946. Loretan, J.O. "Evaluation of Science Instruction in Spanish for Students of Spanish Speaking Background—Steps in Implementing Experimental Project. Report." Brooklyn, New York: New York City Board of Education, 1964.

2947. Pryor, Guy C. "Evaluation of the Bilingual Project of Harlandale Independent School District, San Antonio, Texas, in the First and Second Grades of Four Elementary Schools during 1967-68 School Year." San Antonio, Texas: Harlandale Independent School District, July 1968. ERIC ED 026 158.

2948. Pryor, Guy C. "Evaluation of the Bilingual Project of Harlandale Independent School District, San Antonio, Texas, in the First, Second, and Third Grades of Four Elementary Schools during 1968-69 School Year." San Antonio, Texas: Harlandale Independent School District, July 1969.

2949. "ABE Phase III: Progress and Problems. September 1, 1969-April 1, 1970." Albuquerque, New Mexico: Southwestern Cooperative Educational Lab., 1 April 1970. ERIC ED 060 406.

2950. Ainsworth, C.L., and Christian, Chester C., Jr. "Lubbock Bilingual Elementary Education Program, Title VII, Elementary and Secondary Education Act of 1965. Evaluation Report, 1970." Lubbock, Texas: Lubbock Independent School District, 1970. ERIC ED 065 213.

2951. "Clark County School District ESEA Title I Final Evaluation, 1969-70." 1970. ERIC ED 053 629.

2952. Cordova, Ignacio R., et al. "Evaluation of the Second Year (1968-1969) of the Sustained Primary Program for Bilingual Students in the Las Cruces, New Mexico Public School System." Las Cruces, New Mexico: Las Cruces School District No. 2, Elementary School Bilingual Program, June 1970. ERIC ED 052 855.

2953. Hughes, B.E. "Evaluation Report of the Bilingual Education Program. Harlandale Independent School District, San Marcos Independent School District, Southwest Texas State University, 1969-70." 1970. ERIC ED 078 973.

2954. Ayala, Armando, and Vatsula, John. "Area III Valley Intercultural Report: 1970-71 Final Evaluation Report." 1971. ERIC ED 069 708.

2955. Baker, Jean M. "Bicultural Socialization Project: A Group Process Approach to Bilingual Instruction—Title VII. Final Report, 1970-71." Tucson: University of Arizona, Arizona Center for Early Childhood Education, August 1971. ERIC ED 057 973.

2956. Cline, Marvin G., and Joyce, John F. "An Evaluation of the EDC Role in the Bilingual Transitional Clusters of the Boston Public Schools." Newton, Massachusetts: Educational Development Center, Inc., January 1971. ERIC ED 050 652.

2957. Dillon, Paul L., Jr., comp. "San Francisco Bilingual-Bicultural Education Project for Spanish-English Speaking Children. Final Evaluation Report: 1970-71." San Francisco, California: San Francisco Unified School District, December 1971. ERIC ED 068 222.

2958. Ehrlich, Roselin S., and Shore, Marietta Saravia. "Content Analysis Schedule for Bilingual Education Programs: Catch-Up." New York: City University of New York, 30 June 1971. ERIC ED 072 701.

2959. Glick, Toby. "Content Analysis Schedule for Bilingual Education Programs: Pomona Bilingual Leadership Program." New York: City University of New York, 2 July 1971. ERIC ED 074 877.

2960. Glick, Toby, and González, Castor. "Content Analysis Schedule for Bilingual Education Programs: Bilingual Instruction for Spanish Speaking Pupils." New York: City University of New York, 28 June 1971. ERIC ED 072 698.

2961. Goodman, Frank M., and Stern, Carolyn. "Bilingual Program Evaluation Report, ESEA Title VII, 1970-1971." Compton, California: Compton City Schools, 1971. ERIC ED 054 672.

2962. "Hacer vida. First Year Evaluation Report, 1970-71." Riverside, California: Riverside County Superintendent of Schools, 3 August 1971. ERIC ED 064 018.

2963. "Helping Advance Bilingual Learning in Abernathy (HABLA). Evaluation Report, 1970-71." 1971. ERIC ED 065 209.

2964. Hess, Richard T. "Content Analysis Schedule for Bilingual Education Programs: Bilingual Elementary Education Program. Project BEST." Lubbock, Texas: 30 June 1971. ERIC ED 074 872.

2965. Hess, Richard T., and Shore, Marietta Saravia. "Content Analysis Schedule for Bilingual Education Programs: Habla—Helping Advance Bilingual Learning in Abernathy. Project BEST." Abernathy, Texas: Abernathy Independent School District, 29 June 1971. ERIC ED 072 714.

2966. Hess, Richard T., et al. "Content Analysis Schedule for Bilingual Education Programs: Albuquerque Public School Bicultural-Bilingual Program." New York: City University of New York, November 1971. ERIC ED 074 863.

2967. Hess, Richard T., et al. "Content Analysis Schedule for Bilingual Education Programs: Tucson Bilingual Bicultural Project." 30 June 1971. ERIC ED 080 018.

2968. Hughes, B.E., and Harrison, Helene W. "Evaluation Report of the Bilingual Education Program: Harlandale Independent School District; San Marcos Independent School District; Southwest Texas State University, 1970-1971." 1971. ERIC ED 055 686.

2969. La Noue, Joan. "Content Analysis Schedule for Bilingual Education Programs: Las Cruces Elementary School Bilingual Project. Project BEST." Las Cruces, New Mexico: 30 June 1971. ERIC ED 074 875.

2970. López-Ferrer, Edgardo, et al. "Content Analysis Schedule for Bilingual Education Programs: Bilingual Education Center. Project BEST." New York: City University of New York, 1971. ERIC ED 078 705.

2971. "Lubbock Bilingual (Elementary) Education Program. Evaluation Report, 1971." Lubbock, Texas: Lubbock Independent School District, 1971. ERIC ED 065 216.

2972. Ludanyi, R.P., and Shore, Marietta Saravia. "Content Analysis for Bilingual Education Programs: Programa en dos lenguas. Project BEST." Fort Worth, Texas: 15 November 1971. ERIC ED 072 710.

2973. Mackelduff, Eleanor, and Glick, Toby. "Content Analysis Schedule for Bilingual Education Programs: Pilot Bilingual Program Grades 1, 2, 3. Project BEST." Redwood, California: Redwood City School District, 26 April 1971. ERIC ED 072 703.

2974. Natalicio, Diana S., and Williams, Frederick. "Carrascolendas: Evaluation of a Bilingual Television Series. Final Report." Austin: University of Texas at Austin, June 1971. ERIC ED 054 612.

2975. Owens, Thomas R., et al. "Final Evaluation Report for ABRAZO—Title VII Bilingual Project, 1970-71." San Jose, California: Santa Clara County Office of Education and San Jose Unified School District, September 1971. ERIC ED 065 212.

2976. "Rowland Bilingual/Bicultural Education Project. Evaluation Report." Rowland Heights, California: Rowland School District, 1971. ERIC ED 064 015.

2977. Simons, Raymond S. "Final Evaluation Report for Colorado [City] Bilingual Education Program, Colorado [City] Independent School District, Colorado City, Texas." Colorado City, Texas: Colorado City Independent School District, 1971. ERIC ED 064 022.

2978. Texas. Education Agency. *Region One Bilingual Education Project. 1970-1971 Final Evaluation Report.* Austin: Texas Education Agency, 31 July 1971. ERIC ED 051 955.

2979. Texas. Education Agency. *Region XIII Bilingual Education Program Evaluation Report.* Austin: Texas Education Agency, 1971. ERIC ED 065 221.

2980. "Bilingual Education Project, Santa Clara County, California. Final Report, 1972." San Jose, California: Santa Clara County Office of Education, 1 July 1972. ERIC ED 067 182.

2981. Ehrlich, Alan. "Content Analysis Schedule for Bilingual Education Programs: Ukiah Indian, Mexican-American Bilingual-Bicultural Program." New York: City University of New York, 14 January 1972. ERIC ED 074 856.

2982. Ehrlich, Alan, and Shore, Marietta Saravia. "Content Analysis Schedule for Bilingual Education Programs: Bilingualism for Conceptualization of Learning." New York: City University of New York, February 1972. ERIC ED 072 709.

2983. Ehrlich, Roselin S., and Shore, Marietta Saravia. "Content Analysis Schedule for Bilingual Education Programs: Collier County Bilingual Project." New York: City University of New York, 15 May 1972. ERIC ED 072 715.

2984. Ehrlich, Roselin S., and Shore, Marietta Saravia. "Content Analysis Schedule for Bilingual Education Programs: Del Valle Bilingual Education Program." New York: City University of New York, June 1972. ERIC ED 074 880.

2985. González, Castor. "Content Analysis Schedule for Bilingual Education Programs: Proyecto PAL." New York: City University of New York, 4 January 1972. ERIC ED 078 704.

2986. Goodman, Frank M. "Compton Bilingual Plan Review Report 1971-72." 1972. ERIC ED 072 676.

2987. Harrison, Helene W. "Evaluation Report of the Bilingual Education Program. Harlandale Independent School District, San Marcos Independent School District, Southwest Texas State University. 1971-72." 1972. ERIC ED 071 795.

2988. Hess, Richard T. "Content Analysis Schedule for Bilingual Education Programs: Adaptations of Bilingual Education. Project BEST." Orange, California: March 1972. ERIC ED 074 882.

2989. Hess, Richard T. "Content Analysis Schedule for Bilingual Education Programs: Compton Elementary Bilingual Education Plan. Project BEST." Compton, California: June 1972. ERIC ED 074 874.

2990. Hess, Richard T. "Content Analysis Schedule for Bilingual Education Programs: Santa Barbara County Bilingual Project. Project BEST." Santa Barbara, California: June 1972. ERIC ED 072 716.

2991. Hess, Richard T., and Shore, Marietta Saravia. "Content Analysis for Bilingual Education Programs: Española Bilingual Education Program. Project BEST." Española, New Mexico: Española Municipal Schools, 20 May 1972. ERIC ED 072 711.

2992. Hess, Richard T., and Shore, Marietta Saravia. "Content Analysis Schedule for Bilingual Education Programs: Heraldsburg Bilingual Education." 10 June 1972. ERIC ED 080 016.

2993. Mackelduff, Eleanor, et al. "Content Analysis Schedule for Bilingual Education Programs: Brentwood Bilingual Education Project. Project BEST." Brentwood, California: Brentwood Union School District, 24 June 1972. ERIC ED 072 712.

2994. Nafus, Charles. "Content Analysis Schedule for Bilingual Education Programs: Region XIII Bilingual Education." New York: City University of New York, 31 March 1972. ERIC ED 074 870.

2995. Shore, Marietta Saravia, and Nafus, Charles. "Content Analysis Schedule for Bilingual Education Programs: BICEP Intercambio de la cultura. Project BEST." San Bernardino, California: 11 February 1972. ERIC ED 072 708.

2996. Skoczylas, Rudolph V. "An Evaluation of Some Cognitive and Affective Aspects of a Spanish-English Bilingual Education Program." Doctoral dissertation, University of New Mexico, 1972.

2997. Texas. Education Agency. *Region One Bilingual Education Project. 1971-1972. Final Evaluation Report.* Austin: Texas Education Agency, 1972. ERIC ED 068 243.

2998. Williams, Frederick, and Natalicio, Diana S. "Evaluating Carrascolendas: A Television Series for Mexican-American Children." Austin, Texas: University of Texas at Austin, Center for Communication Research, April 1972. ERIC ED 062 367.

2999. Williams, Frederick, et al. "Carroscolendas: Effects of a Spanish/English Television Series for Primary School Children. Final Report. Evaluation Component." Austin, Texas: University of Texas at Austin, Center for Communication Research, June 1972. ERIC ED 066 048.

3000. Zajic, Vlad, and Shore, Marietta Saravia. "Content Analysis Schedule for Bilingual Education Programs: Colorado City Center to Aid Bilingual Education. Project BEST." Colorado City, Texas: Colorado City Independent School District, July 1972. ERIC ED 074 879.

3001. Cohen, Andrew David. "Innovative Education for La Raza: A Sociolinguistic Assessment of a Bilingual Education Program in California." Doctoral dissertation, Stanford University, 1973.

3002. Díaz, Agapito, and Smidt, Robert K. "Final Evaluation, Title VII, Community School District No. 10. Bilingual Mini School." New York, 15 June 1973. ERIC ED 092 657.

3003. Ehrlich, Roselin S., and Shore, Marietta Saravia. "Content Analysis Schedule for Bilingual Education Programs: Bilingual Education Program, Adelante." New York: City University of New York, February 1973. ERIC ED 080 019.

3004. García, Joseph O., and Peralta, Alex. "An Evaluation of the National Bilingual Bicultural Institute (Albuquerque, New Mexico, November 28-December 1, 1973.)" Albuquerque, New Mexico: National Education Task Force de la Raza, 28 November 1973. ERIC ED 111 573.

3005. Harrison, Helene W. "Evaluation Report of the Harlandale Independent School District's Bilingual Education Program." San Antonio, Texas: Harlandale Independent School District, 1973. ERIC ED 081 555.

3006. Harrison, Helene W. "Evaluation Report of the San Marcos Independent School District's Bilingual Education Program." San Marcos, Texas: San Marcos Independent School District, 1973. ERIC ED 081 553.

3007. Molina, Huberto, and Shoemaker, David M. "A Preliminary Evaluation of a Bilingual Spanish/English Program Using Multiple Matrix Sampling." Paper presented at the International Seminar on Language Testing, San Juan, Puerto Rico, May 1973. ERIC ED 093 911.

3008. Prochnow, Harold G. "Final Evaluation Accomplishment Audit of the Harlandale Independent School District's Bilingual Education Program." San Antonio, Texas: Harlandale Independent School District, 12 June 1973. ERIC ED 081 556.

3009. Ramírez, A.R., et al. "An Evaluative Study of the ROCK English as a Second Language Program in Spanish-English Bilingual Projects." Edinburg, Texas: Region One Educational Service Center, 1973. ERIC ED 078 071.

3010. Williams, Frederick, et al. "Carrascolendas: National Evaluation of a Spanish/English Educational Television Series. Final Report." June 1973. ERIC ED 078 679.

3011. Casso, Henry J., and García, Joseph O. "An Analysis of the Evaluation of the Arizona First Annual Bilingual Institute (Nogales, Arizona, March 21-23, 1974)" Albuquerque, New Mexico: National Education Task Force de la Raza, 23 March 1974. ERIC ED 100 598.

3012. Casso, Henry J., and García, Joseph O. "An Analysis of the Evaluation of the Wisconsin First Bilingual Institute (Milwaukee, Wisconsin, March 29-30, 1974)." Albuquerque, New Mexico: National Education Task Force de la Raza, 30 March 1974. ERIC ED 100 599.

3013. Harrison, Helene W. "Final Evaluation Report of the Harlandale Independent School District's Bilingual Education Program." San Antonio, Texas: Harlandale Independent School District, 1974. ERIC ED 091 108.

3014. Harrison, Helene W. "Final Evaluation Report of the San Marcos Independent School District's Bilingual Education Program." San Marcos, Texas: San Marcos Independent School District, 1974. ERIC ED 091 107.

3015. Laosa, Luis M. "Carrascolendas: A Formative Evaluation." Formative Research Project, March 1974. ERIC ED 090 968.

3016. Van Wart, Geraldine. "Carrascolendas: Evaluation of a Spanish/English Educational Television Series within Region XIII. Final Report. Evaluation Component." Austin, Texas: Education Service Center Region 13, June 1974. ERIC ED 092 089.

3017. Washington. Office of the State Superintendent of Public Instruction. *Bilingual Mini-School Tutoring Project. Evaluation Progress Report Number 1, March 1974,* by Beverly McConnell. Olympia: Washington Office of the State Superintendent of Public Instruction, March 1974. ERIC ED 116 872.

3018. Washington. Office of the State Superintendent of Public Instruction. *Bilingual Mini-School Tutoring Project. Evaluation Progress Report Number 2, Final Evaluation, Program Year 1, July 1974,* by Beverly McConnell. Olympia: Washington Office of the State Superintendent of Public Instruction, July 1974. ERIC ED 116 873.

3019. Washington. Office of the State Superintendent of Public Instruction. *Bilingual Mini-School Tutoring Project. Evaluation Progress Report, Number 3, Mid-Year Evaluation, Program Year 2, December 1974,* by Beverly McConnell. Olympia: Washington Office of the State Superintendent of Public Instruction, December 1974. ERIC ED 116 874.

3020. "Bi-Lingual Bi-Cultural Program, Title VII, ESEA. Final Evaluation." Alamosa, Colorado: San Luis Valley Board of Cooperative Services, 1975. ERIC ED 118 338.

3021. Harrison, Helene W. "Final Evaluation Report of the Harlandale Independent School District's Bilingual Education Program, 1974-75." San Antonio, Texas: Harlandale Independent School District, 1975. ERIC ED 111 557.

3022. Harrison, Helene W. "Final Evaluation Report of the San Marcos Consolidated Independent School District's Bilingual Education Program, 1974-1975." San Marcos, Texas: San Marcos Independent School District, 1975. ERIC ED 111 556.

3023. Washington. Office of the State Superintendent of Public Instruction. *Bilingual Mini-School Tutoring Project. Evaluation Progress Report Number 4, Final Evaluation, Program Year 2, July 1975*, by Beverly McConnell. Olympia: Washington Office of the State Superintendent of Public Instruction, July 1975. ERIC ED 116 875.

7.4 Effects

3024. Irish, Dorothy C. "An Experiment to Determine the Value of Use of the Mother-Tongue in Teaching a Beginning Class of Spanish-Speaking Children." Master's thesis, University of New Mexico, 1945.

3025. Patterson, Charles J. "A Comparison of Performances of Mexican and American Children in a Bicultural Setting on Measures of Ability, Achievement and Adjustment." Doctoral dissertation, Michigan State University, 1960.

3026. Bolger, Philip Albert. "The Effect of Teacher Spanish Language Fluency upon Student Achievement in a Bilingual Science Program." Jamaica, New York: Saint Johns University, 1967. ERIC ED 027 198.

3027. Treviño, Bertha Alicia Gamez. "An Analysis of the Effectiveness of a Bilingual Program in the Teaching of Mathematics in the Primary Grades." Doctoral dissertation, University of Texas at Austin, 1968.

3028. Valencia, Atilano A. "Identification and Assessment of Ongoing Educational and Community Programs for Spanish Speaking People. A Report Submitted to the Southwest Council of La Raza, Phoenix, Arizona." Albuquerque, New Mexico: Southwestern Cooperative Educational Lab., March 1969. ERIC ED 028 013.

3029. Valencia, Atilano A. "An Analysis and Assessment of Oral Spanish and Oral English Development among Children with Limited Proficiency in English and/or Spanish: An Evaluation Report for the Wilson School District Bilingual Education Program, Phoenix, Arizona." Albuquerque, New Mexico: Southwestern Cooperative Educational Lab., June 1970. ERIC ED 041 647.

3030. Valencia, Atilano A. "The Effects of Bilingual/Bicultural Instruction among Spanish-Speaking, English-Speaking, and Sioux-Speaking Kindergarten Children. A Report of Statistical Findings and Recommendations for Educational Unit No. 18, Scottsbluff, Nebraska." Albuquerque, New Mexico: Southwestern Cooperative Educational Lab., August 1970. ERIC ED 043 415.

3031. Valencia, Atilano A. "The Relative Effects of Early Spanish Language Instruction on Spanish and English Linguistic Development; An Evaluation Report on the Pecos Language Arts Program for the Western States Small Schools Project." Albuquerque, New Mexico: Southwestern Cooperative Educational Lab., 1970. ERIC ED 036 382.

3032. Solini, J. "The Effects of Bilingual Instruction on the Achievement of Elementary Pupils." Doctoral dissertation, East Texas State University, May 1971.

3033. Valencia, Atilano A. "Bilingual/Bicultural Education—An Effective Learning Scheme for First Grade and Second Grade Spanish Speaking, English Speaking, and American Indian Children in New Mexico." Albuquerque; New Mexico: Southwestern Cooperative Educational Lab., August 1971. ERIC ED 054 883.

3034. de Weffer, R. del C.E. "Effects of First Language Instruction in Academic and Psychological Development of Bilingual Children." Doctoral dissertation, Illinois Institute of Technology, 1972.

3035. Valencia, Atilano A. "Bilingual-Bicultural Development for Spanish, English and Indian Speaking Children in a Southwestern Multicultural Environment. A Report of Statistical Findings and Recommendations for the Grants Bilingual Educational Project, Grants, New Mexico." Albuquerque, New Mexico: Southwestern Cooperative Educational Lab., 31 July 1972.

3036. Valencia, Atilano A. "Bilingual/Bicultural Education—An Effective Learning Scheme for First Grade Spanish Speaking, English Speaking and American Indian Children in New Mexico. A Report of Statistical Findings and Recommendations for the Grants Bilingual Education Project. Grants, New Mexico, September 1972." Albuquerque, New Mexico: Southwestern Cooperative Educational Lab., 1972. ERIC ED 043 418.

3037. Covey, Donald David. "An Analytical Study of Secondary Freshmen Bilingual Education and Its Effect on Academic Achievement and Attitude of Mexican American Students." Doctoral dissertation, Arizona State University, 1973.

3038. Cornejo, Ricardo J. "A Synthesis of Theories and Research on the Effects of Teaching in First and Second Languages: Implications for Bilingual Education." University Park: New Mexico State University, June 1974. ERIC ED 092 265.

3039. Kingsbury, Ramona Lee Bent. "The Effects of the Las Cruces, New Mexico, Bilingual Program on Selected Aspects of English." Master's thesis, New Mexico State University, 1974. ERIC ED 093 528.

3040. Valencia, Atilano A. "The Cognitive and Affective Development of Elementary School Children in a Bilingual-Bicultural Learning Environment. A Study of the Grants Bilingual-Bicultural Education Program, Grants, New Mexico." Grants, New Mexico: Grants Municipal Schools, 1974.

3041. Alvarez, Juan M. "Comparison of Academic Aspirations and Achievement in Bilingual Versus Monolingual Classrooms." Doctoral dissertation, University of Texas at Austin, 1975.

3042. Ortiz, Berta E. "The Effects of Bilingual Oral Language Development on Initial Tested Ability in English and Spanish Reading." Master's thesis, Texas A&I University at Kingsville, 1976.

8. HIGHER EDUCATION

3043. Elerick, Charles. "An Instructional Model for Teaching 'University' English to Mexican-American Bilinguals." El Paso: University of Texas at El Paso, n.d. ERIC ED 078 714.

3044. MacDougall, Allan. "Completion and Performance of Ethnic Groups in the English Department at Southwestern College as Compared with All Other Departments, Fall 1973 and Spring 1974." Chula Vista, California: Southwestern College, n.d. ERIC ED 097 940.

3045. Ward, Robert, and Hedley, Carolyn. "Interaction Analysis of Mexican-American and Negro High School Students to College Orientation." Santa Barbara: University of California at Santa Barbara, n.d. ERIC ED 020 537.

3046. Hall, Faye Benson. "A Study of the Educational Progress of Graduates of Chaffey Union High School." Master's thesis, University of Southern California, 1931.

3047. Cantwell, George C. "Differential Prediction of College Grades for Spanish American and Anglo American Students." Master's thesis, University of New Mexico, 1946.

3048. Fogartie, Ruth Ann. "Spanish-Name People in Texas with Special Emphasis on Those Who Are Students in Texas Colleges and Universities." Master's thesis, University of Texas at Austin, 1948.

3049. Fogartie, Ruth Ann. *Texas-Born Spanish-Name Students in Texas Colleges and Universities. A Survey Conducted for Winter Semester 1945-1946.* Austin: University of Texas Press, 1948.

3050. Sincoff, Martin. "A Study of the Racial Prejudices of Students at Arizona State University." Master's thesis, Arizona State University, 1952.

3051. Putnam, Howard L. "The Relation of College Programs of Community Services to the Needs of the Spanish Speaking People." Doctoral dissertation, University of Texas at Austin, 1956.

3052. Bailey, Helen M. "A Junior College Helps Students of Mexican Ancestry Serve Their Community." *Journal of Secondary Education* 32, no. 2 (February 1957): 86-89.

3053. Hamilton, Emma Frances. "A Comparison of Scores Made on College Entrance Examinations by 'Latin' and 'Anglo' Students." Master's thesis, Texas A&I University at Kingsville, 1957.

3054. Renner, Richard R. "Some Characteristics of Spanish-Name Texans and Foreign Latin Americans in Texas Higher Education." Doctoral dissertation, University of Texas at Austin, 1957.

3055. Soffer, Virginia M. "Socio-Cultural Changes in the Lives of Five Mexican-American College Graduates." Master's thesis, University of Southern California, 1958.

3056. Richards, Eugene S. "Attitudes of College Students on the Southwest toward Ethnic Groups in the U.S." *Sociology and Social Research* 35, no. 1 (September-October 1959): 22-30.

3057. Meyer, Samuel L., and Cullen, Arthur J. "A Spanish-Speaking College in North America: A 'Prospectus' of a Unique Adventure in Inter-American Education." *Liberal Education* 49 (May 1963): 218-25.

3058. Cabrera, Y. Arturo. "A Survey of Spanish-Surname Enrolled Students, San Jose State College 1963-1964." San Jose, California. San Jose State College, 1964. ERIC ED 020 031.

3059. Martyn, Kenneth A. *Increasing Opportunities in Higher Education for Disadvantaged Students.* Sacramento, California: Coordinating Council for Higher Education, 1966.

3060. Olsen, James. "Drop Out Patterns in the New Hope Project. Stanislaus County Multi-Occupational Adult Training Project, Report No. 22." Modesto, California: Modesto Junior College, 1966.

3061. Katz, Jerry M. "The Educational Shibboleth: Equality of Opportunity in a Democratic Institution, the Public Junior College." Doctoral dissertation, University of California at Los Angeles, 1967.

3062. "Law School Preparatory Program for College Graduates of Spanish American Descent. Progress Report to the Ford Foundation." Denver, Colorado: University of Denver, 1 September 1967. ERIC ED 021 682.

3063. Van Ditmar, E. "Latin American Students in the United States Universities. An Exploratory Study." Doctoral dissertation, University of California at Los Angeles, 1967.

3064. California. State Legislature. Joint Committee on Higher Education. *Equal Opportunity in Higher Education.* Sacramento: California State Legislature, 25 May 1968.

3065. Greene, Roger L., and Clark, John R. "Birth Order and College Attendance in a Cross-Cultural Setting." *Journal of Social Psychology* 75 (August 1968): 289-90.

3066. Rodríguez, Armando. "The Mexican-American and Higher Education." 1968. ERIC ED 030 507.

3067. "Annual Report of the United Scholarship Service, Inc., 1969." Denver, Colorado: United Scholarship Service, Inc., 1969. ERIC ED 043 422.

3068. Cheeves, Lyndell. "Mexican-American Studies: Guidelines for a Junior College Program." August 1969. ERIC ED 036 286.

3069. Edington, Everett D., and Angel, Frank. "Recruitment of Spanish-Speaking Students into Higher Education." Long Beach: California State College, May 1969. ERIC ED 031 320.

3070. Franklin, Mayer J., et al. "Proceedings of the Conference of Increasing Opportunities for Mexican-American Students in Higher Education (Los Angeles Harbor College, California, May 15-17, 1969)." Los Angeles, California: Los Angeles Harbor College, 1969. ERIC ED 031 350.

3071. Gómez, Anna Nieto, and Vasquez, J. Anthony. "The Needs of the Chicano on the College Campus." Long Beach: California State College, School of Education, May 1969. ERIC ED 031 323.

3072. Guerra, Manuel H. "The Retention of Mexican-American Students in Higher Education with Special Reference to Bicultural and Bilingual Problems." Long Beach: California State College, May 1969. ERIC ED 031 324.

3073. Lopate, Carol. "The College Readiness Program: A Program for Third World Students at the College of San Mateo, California. The Study of Collegiate Compensatory Programs for Minority Group Youth." New York: Columbia University, November 1969. ERIC ED 035 686.

3074. Núñez, René, comp. "A Proposal of Guidelines for Reordering Educational Processes of Recruitment and Admissions." Long Beach: California State College, May 1969. ERIC ED 031 321.

3075. "Proceedings of the Conference of Increasing Opportunities for Mexican American Students in Higher Education (Los Angeles Harbor College, California, May 15-17, 1969)." Los Angeles: California State College, 1969. ERIC ED 031 350.

3076. Rodríguez, Armando. "Financial Assistance of Mexican-American Students in Higher Education." Long Beach: California State College, May 1969. ERIC ED 031 322.

3077. Scott, Helen B. "Educational Attainment and Aspirations of Rural and Urban Spanish-Americans in Two South Texas Counties." College Station: Texas A&M College, January 1969. ERIC ED 037 293.

3078. Boucher, Stanley W., et al., eds. "Mexican-American Mental Health Issues: Present Realities and Future Strategies." Boulder, Colorado: Western Interstate Commission for Higher Education, Mental Health Manpower Office, 10 June 1970. ERIC ED 121 553.

3079. California. State Department of Education. *Variables Differentiating Mexican American College and High School Graduates.* Sacramento: California State Department of Education, 1970.

3080. Fernández, Jose R., comp. "Chicano Studies and the California Community Colleges. Chicano Course Descriptions." Ventura, California: Ventura College, 1970. ERIC ED 094 803.

3081. Gámez, George López. "T-Groups as a Tool for Developing Trust and Cooperation between Mexican-American and Anglo-American College Students." Doctoral dissertation, University of Texas at Austin, 1970.

3082. Godoy, Charles Edward. "Variables Differentiating Mexican-American College and High School Graduates." Doctoral dissertation, University of Southern California, 1970. ERIC ED 049 877.

3083. *Graduate Education and Ethnic Minorities.* Boulder: Western Interstate Commission for Higher Education, 1970.

3084. Immenhausen, Richard L. "Academic Performance of Mexican-American Educational Opportunity Grant Recipients." Specialist in Education thesis, University of the Pacific, 1970. ERIC ED 099 702.

3085. McGuire, John Bennett. "The Reisman Typology and Mexican-American Junior College Students." Doctoral dissertation, University of Texas at Austin, 1970.

3086. McNamara, Patrick H. "Some Factors Associated with Differential Grade Performance of Mexican American and Non-Mexican American College Students." Paper presented at the annual meeting of the Southwestern Social Science Association, Dallas, Texas, March 1970. ERIC ED 042 541. Also: Doctoral dissertation, University of Texas at El Paso, 1970.

3087. Meléndez-Craig, Mario. "A Study of the Academic Achievement and Related Problems among Latin American Students Enrolled in the Major Utah Universities." Doctoral dissertation, Brigham Young University, 1970.

3088. "Narrative Evaluation Report on the Institute for: A Multi-Media Approach to Library Services for the Spanish Surnamed at: Colorado State College, Greeley." Greeley: Colorado State College, 1970. ERIC ED 089 752.

3089. Parsons, Paul J. "A Study of Values of Spanish-Surname Undergraduate College Students at Five State Colleges in Colorado." Doctoral dissertation, University of Northern Colorado, 1970.

3090. Reilley, Robert R., and Knight, Glenn E. "MMPI Scores of Mexican-American College Students." *Journal of College Student Personnel* 11, no. 6 (1970): 419-22.

3091. U.S. Cabinet. Committee on Opportunity for Spanish Speaking People. *Spanish Surnamed American College Graduates.* Washington, D.C.: Government Printing Office, 1970.

3092. Valencia, Atilano A. "The Effects of a College Teacher Training Project with Emphasis on Mexican American Cultural Characteristics. An Evaluation Report." Sacramento, California: Sacramento State College, 18 September 1970. ERIC ED 045 267.

3093. Aguirre, Rueben E. "Toward Higher Education for Chicanos." *Educational Resources and Techniques* 12, no. 2 (summer 1971): 25-26.

3094. Altman, Robert A., and Snyder, Patricia O., eds. *The Minority Student on the Campus: Expectations and Possibilities.* Boulder, Colorado: Western Interstate Commission for Higher Education, 1971.

3095. Barron, Jose. "Chicanos in the Community College." *Junior College Journal* 42, no. 9 (June-July 1971): 23-26.

3096. Chappell, Willard R., and Baur, James F. "A Physics-Oriented College Motivation Program for Minority Students." Boulder: University of Colorado, Department of Physics and Astrophysics, 1971. ERIC ED 058 977.

3097. Collymore, Raymond Quintin. "A Survey of the Educational Aspirations and Cultural Needs of the Negro and Mexican-American Students in Two Community Colleges in the State of Colorado." Doctoral dissertation, University of Colorado, 1971.

3098. Despain, Loy K., and Orrantia, Gilbert D. "Fiesta de oportunidades for [sic] mesa." *Junior College Journal* 42, no. 2 (October 1971): 20, 22, 24.

3099. Howell, James Oliver. "A Comparison of Academic Characteristics and Predictability of Academic Success of Mexican American Students with That of Non-Mexican American Students at New Mexico State University." Doctoral dissertation, New Mexico State University, 1971.

3100. Lezmama, Juan A. "Bilingualism, the Mexican American College Student and His Community." Paper presented at the Fifth Annual TESOL Convention, New Orleans, Louisiana, 4 March 1971. ERIC ED 066 935.

3101. Macmurdo, Lee M. "The Effect of Selected Retail Operating Characteristics on the Patronage Decisions of Mexican-American University Students." Master's thesis, Southwest Texas State University, 1971.

3102. *El plan de Santa Barbara; A Chicano Plan for Higher Education.* Santa Barbara, California: La Causa Publications, 1971.

3103. "A Report of the University of New Mexico's College Enrichment Program." Albuquerque: New Mexico University, Institute for Social Research and Development, 15 October 1971. ERIC ED 058 997.

3104. U.S. Cabinet. Committee on Opportunity for Spanish Speaking People. *Spanish Surnamed American College Graduates, 1971-72.* Washington, D.C.: Government Printing Office, 1971.

3105. Willard, Caroline Corser. "A Linguistic Analysis of Written Compositions by Mexican-American Students on College English Placement Examinations." Master's thesis, University of Texas at Austin, 1971.

3106. "Access to College for Mexican Americans in the Southwest. Report of Action Conferences, July 31-August 4, 1972." Palo Alto, California: Southwestern Committee for Higher Education, Survey No. 6, 1972. ERIC ED 068 218.

3107. "Aims College Operation Bridge Project. Phase 1, Preliminary Evaluation Report." Washington, D.C.: National Spanish Speaking Management Association, 21 September 1972. ERIC ED 074 269.

3108. Bess, Robert Oliver. "Academic Performance and Persistence Characteristics of Special Admission Minority-Poor Freshmen and Regular Freshmen at Six California State Colleges." Doctoral dissertation, University of Southern California, 1972.

3109. California. State Legislature. Joint Committee on the Master Plan for Higher Education. *Chicanos and Public Higher Education in California.* Sacramento: California State Legislature, December 1972. ERIC ED 071 627.

3110. Carlson, Nils Sigfred. "An Investigation of the Self-Concept and Values of Selected Spanish-American Male College Students Enrolled in the University of New Mexico." Doctoral dissertation, University of New Mexico, 1972.

3111. Castro, Felix; Gómez, Raul; and Castro, Robert. *A Proposal: College Opportunity Program for California Spanish-Surnamed Students.* Los Angeles: Youth Opportunities Foundation, 1972.

3112. "Chicano Enrollment Not Proportional. CEEB Survey Shows." *College and University Business* 53, no. 4 (October 1972): 29.

3113. Cottle, Thomas J. "Run to Freedom: Chicanos and Higher Education." *Change* 4, no. 1 (February 1972): 34-41.

3114. de los Santos, Gilbert. "An Analysis of Strategies Used by Community Junior Colleges to Serve the Educational and Cultural Needs of Their Mexican-American Students." Doctoral dissertation, University of Texas at Austin, 1972.

3115. Duling, John A. "The Use of the Miller Analogies Test as a Screening Device for Mexican-American Graduate Students." Paper presented at the Rocky Mountain Educational Research Association meeting, Las Cruces, New Mexico, 16-17 November 1972. ERIC ED 071 789.

3116. Ferrin, Richard I., et al. "Access to College for Mexican Americans in the Southwest." Palo Alto, California: College Entrance Examination Board, July 1972. ERIC ED 067 015.

3117. Goldman, Roy D., and Richards, Regina. "The SAT Prediction of Grades for Mexican-American Versus Anglo-American Students at the University of California, Riverside." Riverside: University of California at Riverside, 1972. ERIC ED 088 904.

3118. Hall, Lincoln H. "Personality Variables of Achieving and Non-Achieving Mexican-American and Other Community College Freshmen." *Journal of Educational Research* 65, no. 5 (1972): 224-28.

3119. Murray, Wayne R., and Pettibone, Timothy J. "Mexican American and Anglo Perceptions of a University Environment." Paper presented at the Rocky Mountain Educational Research Association meetings, Las Cruces, New Mexico, 16-17 November 1972. ERIC ED 072 905.

3120. Murray, Wayne Robert. "Ethnic and Sex Differences as Related to Student Perceptions of a University Environment." Doctoral dissertation, New Mexico State University, 1972. ERIC ED 065 208.

3121. Rudolph, James Edward. "Self Perceived and Ascribed Characteristics of Mexican-American, Anglo, and Bicultural College Students." Doctoral dissertation, St. John's University, 1972.

3122. Russo, John V. "The Administrative Aspects of the Development of a Bilingual Secretarial/Clerical Program at Santa Ana College." Seminar paper, June 1972. ERIC ED 062 985.

3123. Suter, Jon Michael. "The Response of Academic Librarians in the Southwest to Mexican-American Undergraduates." Doctoral dissertation, Indiana University, 1972.

3124. Young, Gary Eugene. "Differential Predictive Validity of the American College Test (ACT) for Minority and Non-Minority Students." Doctoral dissertation, Ohio State University, 1972.

3125. Barron, Pepe. "Miguel Mendez-M.: Chicano Teacher in a Community College." *Community and Junior College Journal* 43, no. 6 (March 1973): 56.

3126. Burns, Ruth Aline Ketchum. "Model for a Career/Life-Planning Program for Mexican-American College Students." Doctoral dissertation, University of Oregon, 1973.

3127. Cruz, Rodolfo, and Segura, Roberto. "The Potential Application of the Model Learning Concept to a Chicano Studies Curricula in the Community Colleges. Final Report." Pullman: Washington State University, June 1973. ERIC ED 082 720.

3128. Curren, D.J., and Fimbres, Manuel, eds. *The Chicano Faculty Development Program: A Report.* New York: Council on Social Work Education, 1973.

3129. "Enrollment of Minority Doctoral Students by Institution and Program." St. Louis, Missouri: American Assembly of Collegiate Schools of Business, October 1973. ERIC ED 092 030.

3130. Goho, Tom, and Smith, David. "A College Degree: Does It Substantially Enhance the Economic Achievement of Chicanos? Center for Business Services Occasional Paper No. 503." Paper presented at the Southwestern and Rocky Mountain Division, American Association for Advancement of Science, Lubbock, Texas, 19 April 1973. ERIC ED 079 011.

3131. Gómez, Angel I. "Mexican Americans in Higher Education." Paper presented before the Symposium on Mexican American Education, Society for Applied Anthropology meeting, Tucson, Arizona, 12-14 April 1973. ERIC ED 077 618.

3132. Goodman, Paul Wershub. "Grade Point Average of Mexican American and Anglo College Students Attending the Same University." Paper presented at the Symposium on the Education of Mexican Americans, Society for Applied Anthropology meeting, Tucson, Arizona, 12-14 April 1973. ERIC ED 077 616.

3133. Hernández, John Lawrence. "The Perception of Students and Parents toward College Advicement with Implications for Mexican-Americans." Doctoral dissertation, University of Southern California, 1973.

3134. "Higher Education for Indians and Spanish-Speaking Americans: South Dakota and New Mexico." *Intellect* 101, no. 3 (January 1973): 208-9.

3135. Knoell, Dorothy M. "The New Student in 1973." *Community and Junior College Journal* 43, no. 5 (February 1973): 39-41.

3136. "Materiales en marcha para el esfuerzo bilingüe-bicultural (Materials on the March for the Promotion of Bilingualism/Biculturalism), July 1973." San Diego, California: San Diego City Schools, July 1973. ERIC ED 082 581.

3137. Mornell, Eugene S. "The Program of Special Directed Studies: A Five Year Summary. A Report of the Special Admission Program and Compensatory Education at Claremont University." Claremont, California: Claremont University, June 1973. ERIC ED 088 638.

3138. Negrete, Louis R. "Chicano Studies and Rio Hondo College." Whittier, California: Rio Hondo Junior College, May 1973. ERIC ED 077 483.

3139. Ornstein, Jacob. "Some Findings of Sociolinguistic Research on Mexican-American College Age Bilinguals." Paper presented at the Society for Applied Anthropology, Tucson, Arizona, 12-14 April 1973. ERIC ED 080 253.

3140. Pesqueira, Richard E. "Mexican American Student (Staying) Power in College." College Board Review 90 (winter 1973-74): 6-9, 26, 28.

3141. Sánchez, Corinne. "Higher Education y la Chicana." Encuentro Femenil 1, no. 1 (spring 1973): 27-33.

3142. Tindol, William Allen. "The Administration of an Admission Program at Sul Ross State University, Based on the American College Testing Program." Doctoral dissertation, East Texas State University, 1973.

3143. Brooks, Glenwood C., Jr., and Sedlacek, William E. "Fall 1973 University Racial Census. Report." College Park: University of Maryland, 1974. ERIC ED 089 643.

3144. Cardenas, Isaac. "Equality of Educational Opportunity: A Descriptive Study on Mexican-American Access to Higher Education." Doctoral dissertation, University of Massachusetts, 1974.

3145. El-Khawas, Elaine H., and Kinzer, Joan L. "Enrollment of Minority Graduate Students at Ph.D. Granting Institutions. Higher Education Panel Report No. 19." Washington, D.C.: American Council on Education, Higher Education Panel, 1974. ERIC ED 094 620.

3146. Felger, R.V. "H.E.A.P. of Personalization; Higher Education Achievement Program." Community and Junior College Journal 44, no. 7 (April 1974): 10-11.

3147. Flores Macías, Reynaldo, and Gómez-Quiñones, Juan, eds. The National Directory of Chicano Faculty and Research. Los Angeles, California: Aztlán Publications, 1974.

3148. García, Ernest Lucero. "A Comparative Study of Community College Mexican-American and Anglo Graduates and Dropouts." Doctoral dissertation, University of California at Los Angeles, 1974.

3149. Gonzales, Arnold. "Analysis of a Challenge Program in Relation to Entry and Success of Mexican-American Students in Higher Education and the Effect on Their Self-Image, Attitude toward Education and Degree of Community Participation." Doctoral dissertation, University of Michigan, 1974.

3150. Hernández, Armand Patrick. "An Exploratory Field Study of the Relationship between Pre-Service Mexican-American Law Enforcement Students and the Educational Community at San Jose City College." Doctoral dissertation, University of Southern California, 1974.

3151. Hernández, Edward, Jr. "An Examination of the Chicano Advisory Committee's Effect on the Establishment of College Policy. An Examination of the Committee's Implementation of a Chicano Recruitment Project." Doctoral dissertation, Nova University, August 1974. ERIC ED 111 452.

3152. Herrera, Frank. "In Reach in Delano: California." Community and Junior College Journal 44, no. 9 (June 1974): 8-9.

3153. Leman, Kevin Anderson. "Parental Attitudes toward Higher Education and Academic Success among Mexican-American, Black and Anglo Economically Disadvantaged College Students." Doctoral dissertation, University of Arizona, 1974.

3154. Light, Jere Cook. "A Critical Analysis of Anglo and Mexican American Cultural Patterns in Two Texas Border City Junior Colleges." Doctoral dissertation, University of Texas at Austin, 1974.

3155. Rangel, Diego Raul. "A Longitudinal Study of Special Services Experienced by Twenty-Three Post-Secondary Students for Mexican-American and Puerto Rican Communities in Chicago." Doctoral dissertation, Northwestern University, 1974.

3156. Silliman, Janet Caroline. "Academic Achievement of Mexican-American Females in a College of Nursing." Doctoral dissertation, University of Arizona, 1974.

3157. Simmons, Stephen. "A Comparison of the Perceived Body-Images of Mexican-American and Anglo-American College Students." Master's thesis, Texas A&I University at Kingsville, 1974.

3158. Casso, Henry Joseph. "Higher Education and the Mexican-American." In *Mexican-Americans Tomorrow: Educational and Economic Perspectives*, pp. 137-63. Edited by Gus Tyler. Albuquerque: University of New Mexico Press, 1975 .

3159. Crawford, Carole Ann. "A Comparative Study of Two Experimental Humanities Programs for Mexican-American University Students." Doctoral dissertation, University of Michigan, 1975.

3160. Crisco, James Jeffrey. "The Prediction of Academic Performance for Minority Engineering Students from Selected Achievement-Proficiency, Personality, Cognitive Style, and Demographic Variables." Doctoral dissertation, Marquette University, 1975.

3161. Gallegos, Samuel, Jr. "Academic Survival and Performance of United Mexican American Students in the Equal Opportunity Program at the University of Colorado in Boulder." Doctoral dissertation, University of Northern Colorado, 1975.

3162. González, Jess. "Chicano Studies and Self-Concept: Implications for the Community Colleges." Doctoral dissertation, Nova University, 1975. ERIC ED 118 160.

3163. Hinrichsen, Keith A. "Administrative Reorganizational Needs in Chicano Studies at Cerritos College." Doctoral dissertation, Nova University, 1975. ERIC ED 114 133.

3164. "Interning in Chicano Studies." *American Libraries* 6, no. 2 (February 1975): 78-79.

3165. Lowman, Robert P., and Spuck, Dennis W. "Predicators of College Success for the Disadvantaged Mexican-American." *Journal of College Student Personnel* 16, no. 1 (January 1975): 40-48.

3166. New York. State Department of Education. Bureau of Migrant Education. *College Level Financial Aid Opportunities for Migrant Students within The State University of New York,* by Barbara Stratton et al. Albany: New York State Department of Education, August 1975. ERIC ED 121 542.

3167. Ovando, Carlos Julio. "Factors Influencing Midwestern High School Latino Students' Aspirations to Go to College." Doctoral dissertation, Indiana University, 1975.

3168. Rainwater, Jerry A. "Comprehension Characteristics of Chicano and Non-Chicano Students at Eastern New Mexico University." Paper presented at the Farwest Regional Conference of the International Reading Association, 3rd, Reno, Nevada, 6-8 February 1975. ERIC ED 108 183.

3169. Ramírez, Ernesto, Jr. "The Identification of Special Problems as Perceived by Mexican American Chief Executive Officers in Selected Community Colleges in the Southwest and Public School Districts in Texas." Doctoral dissertation, University of Texas at Austin, 1975.

3170. Tabor, Barry A. "Stereotypic Attitudes and Attitude Shift in Anglo- and Mexican-American College Students." Master's thesis, Texas A&I University at Kingsville, 1975.

3171. Weaver, Marleen E. "Mexican-American Women: Diversity in Depth." Paper read at the annual meeting of the Conference on College Composition and Communication, 26th, St. Louis, Missouri, 13-15 March 1975. ERIC ED 103 900.

3172. Zúñiga, Alfredo H., and Rigby-Acosta, Barbara. "A Study of the Nature of Chicano Studies Derived from the Twelve Proposals for Chicano Studies Written between 1968 and 1974: A Tentative Description." In *Perspectives on Chicano Education*. Edited by Tobias Gonzales and Sandra Gonzales. Palo Alto, California: Stanford University, Office of Chicano Affairs, 1975.

3173. Binder, Fremont Eugene. "A Study of Migrant Farmworker Students Enrolled at Saint Edward's University." Doctoral dissertation, Washington State University, 1976.

3174. Hook, Ora MacDonald. "The Relationship of Cognitive, Affective, Demographic, and School-Related Variables to Membership of Community College Students in Four Ethnic Groups and to Their Academic Achievement." Doctoral dissertation, University of Southern California, 1976.

3175. Slotkin, Jacquelyn Hersh. "Role Conflict among Selected Anglo and Mexican-American Female College Graduates." Doctoral dissertation, University of Arizona, 1976.

9. ADULT EDUCATION

3176. Reeves, Grace Elizabeth. "Adult Mexican Education in the United States." Master's thesis, Claremont College, 1929.

3177. Ackerman, R.E. "Trends in Illiteracy in New Mexico." Master's thesis, University of New Mexico, 1933.

3178. Texas. Education Agency. *Texas Adult Migrant Education. Progress Report.* Austin: Texas Education Agency, January 1966. ERIC ED 015 361.

3179. Ulibarri, Horacio. "Education of the Adult Spanish-Speaking Migrant and Ex-Migrant Worker." *Adult Leadership* 15, no. 3 (September 1966): 80-82.

3180. Burrichter, Arthur, and Jensen, Glenn. "Research Studies with Implications for Adult Education, Mountain-Plains Region, 1945-1966." Laramie: University of Wyoming, Department of Adult Education and Instructional Services, 1967.

3181. California. State Department of Education. *Recommendations Relative to the Organization of Advisory Committees When Working with Adults with Spanish Surnames,* by Patricia Cabrera et al, comps. Sacramento: California State Department of Education, 1967. ERIC ED 017 844.

3182. Jackson, Vera Madeleine. "A Program for Teaching English to Spanish Speaking Adults of Miami, Arizona." Master's thesis, Arizona State University, 1967.

3183. Maurer, Wayne F. "Adult Education for Migrant and Seasonal Farm Workers. Project Report, June 12-September 1, 1967." Naples, Florida: Collier County Board of Public Instruction, September 1967. ERIC ED 016 539.

3184. Pinnock, Theodore James. "Testing in Adult Basic Education Programs Catering to Seasonal and Migrant Farmers." Tuskegee, Illinois: Tuskegee Institute, 29 April 1967. ERIC ED 013 692.

3185. "A Regional Educational Television Project for Non-English Speaking Spanish-Surname Adults. Final Report." Albuquerque, New Mexico: Southwestern Cooperative Educational Lab., 1967. ERIC ED 061 477.

3186. "Adult Basic Education, Milwaukee. Annual Report, July 1, 1967-June 30, 1968." Milwaukee, Wisconsin: Council for Spanish Speaking, 1968.

3187. Etienne, Jerald Francis. "The Relationship between Language and Employment of Caucasian, Negroid, and Spanish-American Male Educable Mentally Retarded Adults." Doctoral dissertation, Colorado State College, 1968.

3188. Gromatzky, Irene. "Consumer Education for Mexican-Americans." University Park: New Mexico State University, March 1968. ERIC ED 016 563.

3189. Olivero, James L., et al. "The Chicano Is Coming Out of Tortilla Flats. . . One Way or the Other. Proceedings of the Conference on Adult Basic Education Sponsored by the Southwestern Cooperative Educational Laboratory, Inc. (Albuquerque, July 29-30, 1968)." Albuquerque, New Mexico: Southwestern Cooperative Educational Laboratory, Inc., 1968. ERIC ED 025 351.

3190. Pfannstiel, Daniel C., and Hunter, Starley M. "Extending Cooperative Extension Education to Mexican-American Families: Program, Methods and Evaluation. A Report of a Research Study, El Paso, Texas, 1962-1967." College Station: Texas A&M University, October 1968. ERIC ED 028 005.

3191. Smoker, David E. "Southwestern Cooperative Educational Laboratory: Adult Basic Education Project." *Adult Leadership* 17, no. 2 (June 1968): 73-74.

3192. Ulibarri, Horacio. "Acculturation Problems of the Mexican-American. Report of Conference on Adult Basic Education." Albuquerque, New Mexico: Southwestern Cooperative Educational Laboratory, Inc., 1968.

3193. Balbuena, Wesley; Morton, Edward W.; and Robinson, Byrl. "Adult Bilingual Experimental School." *Journal of Secondary Education* 44, no. 5 (May 1969): 225-30.

3194. California. State Department of Education. Bureau of Industrial Education. *Attitudes of Administrators toward Instructional Programs for Adults with Spanish Surnames,* by Roy W. Steeves. Sacramento: California State Department of Education, 1969.

3195. "Changes in Attitudinal Characteristics of Migrant and Ex-Migrant Workers Involved in Adult Education. Final Report." Albuquerque: University of New Mexico, College of Education, October 1969. ERIC ED 034 621.

3196. Bradtmueller, Weldon, and Ulmer, Curtis. "Basic Education and the Adult Migrant." Paper presented at the Conference of the Association for Children with Learning Disabilities. Philadelphia, Pennsylvania, 12-14 February 1970. ERIC ED 040 818.

3197. Chávez, Gilbert. "Adult Education." *National Elementary Principal* 50, no. 2 (November 1970): 114-15.

3198. Amador, Richard S., and McCune, Jalayne. *Project HEART (Hospital Employment and Related Training). Final Report.* Los Angeles, California: Community and Human Resources Agency, November 1971.

3199. Bartley, Diana E., and James, Carl. "Institute in Adult Basic Education: 1971. Final Report. TESOL." 1971. ERIC ED 090 415.

3200. Bartley, Diana E. "Institute in Adult Basic Education: A Model Program 1972. Final Report. TESOL." 1972. ERIC ED 090 416.

3201. Jensen, Gerald M. "Investigation of Occupational Training Needs of Migrant Workers Which May Point toward Employment in Other Than Migrant Employment. Final Report." El Centro, California: Imperial County Schools, 28 April 1972. ERIC ED 065 262.

3202. Larson, Lora B., and Massoth, Donna M. "Nutrition Education Program for Texas Migrant Families." *Journal of Home Economics* 65, no. 8 (November 1973): 36-40.

3203. Martínez, Linda K. "Adult Education: A Key to Aiding the Mexican-American." *Education* 94, no. 2 (November-December 1973): 120-21.

3204. Cotera, Martha. *Profile on the Mexican American Woman.* Austin, Texas: National Educational Laboratory Publishers, Inc., 1976.

10. COMMUNITY

3205. Schroff, Ruth. "A Study of Social Distance between Mexican Parents and American Teachers in San Bernardino, California." Master's thesis, University of Southern California, 1936.

3206. Newell, Elizabeth Virginia. "The Social Significance of Padua Hills as a Cultural and Educational Center." Master's thesis, University of Southern California, 1938.

3207. Tireman, Lloyd S. "Discovery and Use of Community Resources in the Education of Spanish-Speaking Pupils." *National Education Association, Department of Rural Education, Yearbook* (1939): 72-85.

3208. Carlson, Glen E. "Community Organization Turns a Corner." *Sociology and Social Research* 32, no. 4 (March-April 1948): 782-86.

3209. Tinsley, Willa Vaughn. "Building Better School Community Relations in Latin-American Communities." Master's thesis, Southwest Texas State Teachers College, 1949.

3210. Mills, Helen Risinger. "Home-School Cooperation for Child Development in the Latin-American Primary School." Master's thesis, Southwest Texas State University, 1951.

3211. Peña-Flores, Estela. "Parent-Teacher Relations in an Elementary School System." Master's thesis, University of Texas at Austin, 1955.

3212. "Mama Goes to Nursery School; Malabar Street School in East L.A." *American Education* 3, no. 8 (September 1967): 10-11.

3213. Rodríguez, Armando. "Understanding and Working with the Power Structure in the Mexican-American Community." Kansas City, Missouri: National Academy for School Executives, 31 October 1968. ERIC ED 030 506.

3214. Friedland, William H. "The Community, the Teacher and the Migrant Child." Geneseo: State University of New York College at Geneseo, Geneseo Migrant Center, 1969. ERIC ED 111 567.

3215. Picchiotti, N. "Community Involvement in the Bilingual Center." Paper presented at the 3rd Annual TESOL Convention, Chicago, Illinois, 5-8 March 1969. ERIC ED 031 690.

3216. "The Community Speaks." *National Elementary Principal* 50, no. 2 (November 1970): 29-33.

3217. Fierro, Leonard. "Chicano Community Action Efforts at the Local Level and Their Effects on Promoting Educational Change for Mexican-Americans. A Research Paper." Albuquerque, New Mexico: Southwestern Cooperative Educational Lab., 1970. ERIC ED 057 972.

3218. Harmon, Genevieve Coon. "Participation of Mexican-American Parents in School Activities at Kindergarten Level in Poverty Areas of Los Angeles." Doctoral dissertation, University of Southern California, 1971.

3219. Holladay, Howard Preston. "Communication of Mexican-Americans with Public School Personnel: A Study of Channel, Code, Receiver, and Source Preference." Doctoral dissertation, University of Southern California, 1971.

3220. Hughes, Marie M. "Community Components in Teacher Education." Storrs: University of Connecticut, November 1971. ERIC ED 084 248.

3221. *Program Handbook for Parent-School-Community Involvement and Parent Education.* Austin, Texas: Southwest Educational Development Lab., 1971.

3222. "Building Communication Skills: Home-School-Community, July 1, 1970 to June 30, 1972. Florence-Firestone Project. Final Report." Los Angeles, California: Los Angeles Unified School District, 1972 ERIC ED 075 689.

3223. García, Angela B., et al. "Description of a Program to Train Parents to Influence the Development of Question-Asking Skills in Their Young Children." Tucson, Arizona: University of Arizona, Arizona Center for Early Childhood Education, 1972. ERIC ED 089 853.

3224. Gutiérrez, Lorraine Padilla. "Attitudes toward Bilingual Education: A Study of Parents with Children in Selected Bilingual Programs." Doctoral dissertation, University of New Mexico, 1972. ERIC ED 070 550.

3225. Henderson, Ronald W., and García, Angela B. "The Effects of a Parent Training Program on the Question-Asking Behavior of Mexican-American Children." Tucson: University of Arizona, Arizona Center for Early Childhood Education, 1972. ERIC ED 094 861.

3226. Larson, James R. "Community Involvement and Educational Decision Making; The Development of a Mexican American Curriculum Office in the Toledo Public Schools." Doctoral dissertation, University of Toledo, December 1972. ERIC ED 082 902.

3227. Martínez, Irma Herrera. "A Study of Parental Views toward Spanish Instruction in Kindergarten Conducted at Ollie P. Storm Elementary School in San Antonio, Texas." Master's thesis, University of Texas at Austin, 1972.

3228. Adorno, William. "The Attitudes of Selected Mexican and Mexican-American Parents in Regards to Bilingual/Bicultural Education." Doctoral dissertation, United States International University, 1973.

3229. Carrillo, Rafael Abeyta. "An In-Depth Survey of Attitudes and Desires of Parents in a School Community to Determine the Nature of a Bilingual-Bicultural Program." Doctoral dissertation, University of New Mexico, 1973.

3230. Steward, Margaret, and Steward, David. "The Observation of Anglo-, Mexican-, and Chinese-American Mothers Teaching Their Young Sons." *Child Development* 44, no. 2 (June 1973): 329-37.

3231. Anchor, Kenneth N., and Anchor, Felicia N. "School Failure and Parental School Involvement in an Ethnically Mixed School: A Survey." *Journal of Community Psychology* 2, no. 3 (July 1974): 265-67.

3232. "Handbook for a Parent-School-Community Involvement Program." Austin, Texas: Southwest Educational Development Lab., January 1974. ERIC ED 118 709.

3233. Johnson, Dale L.; Leler, Hazel; Rios, Laurel, et al. "Houston Parent-Child Development Center: A Parent Education Program for Mexican-American Families." *American Journal of Orthopsychiatry* 44 (January 1974): 121-28.

3234. Leler, Hazel, et al. "A Parent Involvement Program for Low-Income Mexican-American Families." Paper presented at the annual meeting of the American Psychological Association, New Orleans, Louisiana, 1 September 1974. ERIC ED 104 544.

3235. Montes, Mary. "School Community Relations: A View from the Barrio." Doctoral dissertation, Claremont Graduate School, 1974.

3236. Moreno, Peggy Roanne. "Vertical Diffusion Effects within Black and Mexican-American Families Participating in the Florida Parent Education Model." Doctoral dissertation, University of Florida, 1974.

3237. Soto, John Anthony. "Mexican-American Community Leadership for Education." Doctoral dissertation, University of Michigan, 1974.

3238. Texas. Education Agency. *Handbook for a Parent-School-Community Involvement Program; Migrant and Preschool Programs*. Austin: Texas Education Agency, 1974.

3239. Valadez, Senon Monreal. "An Exploratory Study of Chicano Parent Perceptions of School and the Education of Their Children in Two Oregon Community Settings." Doctoral dissertation, University of Oregon, 1974.

3240. Colvin, Willis Dwayne. "A Comparison of Attitudes toward Education of Persons in the Anglo-American and the Mexican-American Power Structures within Four Selected Oklahoma Communities." Doctoral dissertation, Oklahoma State University, 1975.

3241. Melody, Sister Laura. "Mexican American Mothers' Teaching Style and Their Children's Need for Structure." Doctoral dissertation, University of Illinois at Urbana-Champaign, 1975.

3242. Oregon. State Department of Education. *Parent Councils for Migrant Education under ESEA Title I Migrant Amendment. (Concilios de padres para educación migratoria bajo el título I de ESEA)*, by Elton D. Minkler. Salem: Oregon State Department of Education, July 1975. ERIC ED 114 239.

3243. Sonquist, Hanne, et al. "A Model for Low-Income and Chicano Parent Education. Final Report." Santa Barbara, California: Santa Barbara Family Care Center, June 1975. ERIC ED 113 063.

3244. Riley, Mary Tom. *Project LATON: The Parent Book*. Lubbock: Texas Tech Press, 1976.

AUTHOR INDEX

AUTHOR INDEX

CHRONOLOGICAL INDEX

CHRONOLOGICAL INDEX

Note: For the convenience of the user, the references under each year are listed in numerical order rather than in an order which would conform to the alphabetical arrangement of authors.

1896
1129

1911
1130

1917
1131

1920
247

1921
1088
1089
1409
1410

1922
1411
1412
2633

1923
248
1322
1997

1925
249
613
1413

1926
676
1414
1544

1927

997	1416	1545
1415	1491	2091

1928

415	1417	1419
998	1418	1546

1929

250	1132	2092
677	1420	3176
875	1421	
1113	1998	

1930

251	614	1422
252	649	2196
442	678	2267
557	679	

1931

416	1323	1756
680	1423	1779
681	1424	3046
1114	1492	
1133	1493	

1932

199	683	1495
229	1134	1547
254	1425	2093
417	1426	2094
418	1427	2197
632	1428	
682	1494	

1967

27	328	969	1524	2056	2521	2801
28	329	970	1525	2057	2522	2802
29	471	1011	1526	2141	2523	2803
30	472	1012	1572	2142	2524	2804
31	473	1013	1573	2143	2525	2805
32	474	1014	1574	2144	2526	2806
33	597	1040	1575	2145	2527	2807
34	598	1041	1576	2146	2528	2887
35	660	1064	1577	2147	2529	2888
36	746	1098	1578	2229	2530	3026
176	747	1166	1673	2230	2643	3061
215	748	1167	1674	2231	2644	3062
216	749	1220	1739	2232	2671	3063
316	750	1221	1765	2233	2672	3180
317	751	1264	1823	2234	2718	3181
318	752	1265	1847	2286	2719	3182
319	753	1266	1872	2287	2720	3183
320	754	1308	1873	2288	2721	3184
321	755	1309	1948	2289	2736	3185
322	756	1351	1949	2380	2737	3212
323	757	1352	2004	2439	2796	
324	758	1353	2052	2440	2797	
325	888	1396	2053	2441	2798	
326	889	1397	2054	2490	2799	
327	923	1467	2055	2491	2800	

1968

37	483	989	1579	2238	2531	2808
38	484	1015	1580	2239	2532	2809
39	485	1016	1581	2240	2533	2810
40	599	1017	1582	2241	2534	2811
41	600	1042	1583	2242	2535	2812
42	601	1043	1675	2243	2536	2813
43	602	1044	1721	2244	2537	2889
217	661	1099	1740	2290	2538	2890
240	759	1100	1766	2291	2539	2891
330	760	1101	1767	2338	2540	2947
331	761	1168	1874	2360	2541	3027
332	762	1169	1875	2361	2542	3064
333	763	1170	1914	2388	2543	3065
334	764	1222	1915	2397	2544	3066
335	765	1223	1916	2442	2545	3186
336	766	1310	1950	2443	2546	3187
337	767	1354	2005	2444	2645	3188
338	768	1355	2006	2445	2646	3189
339	769	1356	2007	2446	2673	3190
340	770	1357	2008	2447	2674	3191
341	771	1398	2058	2448	2675	3192
433	772	1399	2059	2449	2689	3213
475	773	1400	2060	2450	2690	
476	774	1401	2148	2451	2699	
477	775	1468	2149	2452	2722	
478	776	1469	2150	2453	2723	
479	777	1527	2151	2492	2724	
480	890	1528	2235	2493	2725	
481	924	1529	2236	2494	2764	
482	971	1530	2237	2504	2765	

1969

44	346	788	1360	1918	2551	2819
45	347	789	1361	1919	2552	2820
46	348	891	1470	1920	2553	2821
47	349	892	1531	1921	2554	2822
48	350	925	1584	1922	2555	2823
49	434	926	1585	1951	2556	2892
50	486	927	1586	1952	2557	2893
51	487	928	1587	1953	2558	2894
52	488	972	1588	1954	2559	2895
53	489	973	1589	2009	2560	2896
54	490	1018	1590	2061	2561	2897
55	491	1045	1591	2152	2647	2898
56	558	1065	1592	2153	2648	2899
57	559	1066	1593	2154	2649	2900
58	603	1125	1676	2155	2650	2948
59	604	1126	1677	2245	2651	3028
60	605	1171	1678	2246	2652	3067
61	606	1172	1722	2247	2691	3068
62	607	1173	1723	2292	2726	3069
63	637	1174	1741	2293	2727	3070
64	662	1175	1742	2294	2728	3071
65	663	1176	1768	2295	2738	3072
66	778	1177	1769	2339	2739	3073
67	779	1178	1770	2381	2740	3074
68	780	1224	1797	2454	2741	3075
69	781	1225	1798	2455	2742	3076
177	782	1267	1824	2495	2766	3077
241	783	1268	1825	2496	2814	3193
342	784	1269	1848	2547	2815	3194
343	785	1311	1876	2548	2816	3195
344	786	1358	1877	2549	2817	3214
345	787	1359	1917	2550	2818	3215

1970

70	436	975	1402	1993	2505	2834
71	437	976	1471	2010	2506	2835
72	438	977	1472	2011	2562	2836
73	492	978	1473	2012	2563	2901
74	493	990	1532	2013	2564	2902
75	494	1019	1533	2014	2565	2903
76	495	1020	1594	2062	2566	2904
77	496	1021	1595	2063	2567	2905
78	497	1022	1596	2064	2568	2906
79	498	1046	1597	2065	2569	2907
80	499	1047	1598	2066	2570	2908
81	560	1067	1599	2156	2571	2909
82	561	1068	1600	2157	2572	2910
83	574	1069	1601	2158	2573	2911
84	576	1070	1602	2159	2653	2912
85	608	1102	1603	2160	2654	2949
86	629	1103	1604	2161	2655	2950
87	630	1104	1605	2248	2656	2951
178	638	1179	1606	2249	2657	2952
179	639	1180	1607	2250	2676	2953
180	640	1181	1679	2251	2677	3029
181	664	1182	1743	2296	2678	3030
182	665	1183	1744	2297	2692	3031
183	790	1184	1799	2298	2700	3078
184	791	1185	1800	2299	2701	3079
185	792	1186	1826	2300	2702	3080
351	793	1187	1849	2301	2703	3081
352	794	1188	1850	2302	2704	3082
353	795	1226	1878	2303	2705	3083
354	796	1227	1879	2304	2729	3084
355	797	1228	1880	2305	2743	3085
356	798	1229	1923	2306	2744	3086
357	799	1230	1924	2340	2745	3087
358	800	1270	1925	2341	2767	3088
359	893	1271	1926	2342	2768	3089
360	894	1272	1955	2343	2769	3090
361	895	1273	1983	2344	2824	3091
362	929	1274	1984	2345	2825	3092
363	930	1312	1985	2362	2826	3196
364	931	1313	1986	2382	2827	3197
365	932	1314	1987	2389	2828	3216
366	933	1362	1988	2456	2829	3217
367	934	1363	1989	2457	2830	
368	935	1364	1990	2458	2831	
369	936	1365	1991	2497	2832	
435	974	1366	1992	2498	2833	

1971

88	577	941	1616	2255	2839	3098
89	583	979	1680	2256	2840	3099
90	584	991	1681	2307	2841	3100
91	609	992	1682	2346	2842	3101
92	641	1023	1683	2347	2843	3102
93	642	1048	1724	2348	2844	3103
94	643	1049	1745	2363	2845	3104
95	666	1050	1746	2364	2846	3105
96	667	1051	1747	2390	2847	3198
97	668	1052	1748	2391	2913	3199
98	801	1053	1827	2398	2914	3218
99	802	1105	1828	2399	2915	3219
100	803	1106	1829	2459	2916	3220
101	804	1107	1851	2460	2917	3221
102	805	1189	1881	2461	2918	
103	806	1190	1882	2462	2919	
104	807	1191	1883	2463	2920	
105	808	1192	1927	2464	2954	
106	809	1193	1928	2465	2955	
186	810	1231	1956	2499	2956	
187	811	1232	1957	2507	2957	
188	812	1233	1958	2508	2958	
189	813	1234	1959	2574	2959	
218	814	1235	1960	2575	2960	
219	815	1275	2015	2576	2961	
220	816	1276	2016	2577	2962	
221	817	1277	2017	2578	2963	
370	818	1315	2018	2579	2964	
371	819	1316	2019	2580	2965	
372	820	1367	2020	2581	2966	
373	821	1368	2021	2582	2967	
374	822	1369	2067	2583	2968	
375	823	1370	2068	2584	2969	
376	824	1371	2069	2585	2970	
377	825	1474	2070	2586	2971	
378	826	1475	2071	2587	2972	
379	827	1476	2072	2588	2973	
380	828	1534	2162	2658	2974	
439	829	1535	2163	2679	2975	
500	896	1536	2164	2693	2976	
501	897	1537	2165	2694	2977	
502	898	1538	2166	2695	2978	
503	899	1608	2167	2706	2979	
504	900	1609	2168	2730	3032	
505	901	1610	2169	2746	3033	
506	902	1611	2170	2747	3093	
507	937	1612	2171	2748	3094	
508	938	1613	2252	2770	3095	
549	939	1614	2253	2837	3096	
562	940	1615	2254	2838	3097	

1972

107	550	1075	1624	2025	2662	2999
108	581	1108	1625	2026	2680	3000
109	585	1127	1626	2073	2681	3034
110	610	1194	1684	2074	2682	3035
111	611	1195	1685	2075	2696	3036
112	631	1196	1686	2076	2697	3106
113	644	1197	1687	2077	2707	3107
114	669	1198	1725	2172	2731	3108
190	670	1199	1726	2173	2749	3109
191	671	1200	1749	2174	2750	3110
192	830	1236	1750	2175	2751	3111
222	831	1237	1751	2176	2771	3112
223	832	1238	1801	2257	2848	3113
381	833	1239	1802	2258	2849	3114
382	834	1240	1852	2308	2850	3115
383	835	1278	1853	2309	2851	3116
384	836	1279	1884	2349	2921	3117
385	837	1280	1885	2350	2922	3118
386	838	1281	1886	2351	2923	3119
387	839	1282	1887	2365	2924	3120
388	840	1317	1888	2366	2925	3121
389	841	1372	1889	2367	2980	3122
390	842	1373	1890	2400	2981	3123
391	903	1374	1891	2466	2982	3124
392	942	1375	1929	2467	2983	3200
393	943	1376	1930	2468	2984	3201
394	944	1377	1931	2500	2985	3222
509	945	1403	1932	2509	2986	3223
510	946	1404	1933	2589	2987	3224
511	993	1477	1934	2590	2988	3225
512	994	1478	1935	2591	2989	3226
513	1024	1479	1961	2592	2990	3227
514	1025	1480	1962	2593	2991	
515	1054	1617	1963	2594	2992	
516	1055	1618	1964	2595	2993	
517	1056	1619	1965	2596	2994	
518	1071	1620	1994	2597	2995	
519	1072	1621	2022	2659	2996	
520	1073	1622	2023	2660	2997	
521	1074	1623	2024	2661	2998	

1973

115	524	980	1483	2031	2602	3007
116	525	995	1539	2032	2603	3008
117	526	1026	1627	2033	2604	3009
118	527	1027	1628	2078	2605	3010
119	528	1057	1629	2079	2606	3037
120	529	1058	1630	2080	2663	3125
121	530	1059	1631	2177	2683	3126
122	531	1076	1632	2178	2684	3127
123	543	1077	1633	2179	2698	3128
124	551	1078	1634	2180	2708	3129
125	563	1079	1635	2181	2752	3130
126	564	1080	1636	2259	2753	3131
127	567	1081	1688	2260	2754	3132
128	578	1082	1689	2261	2755	3133
129	579	1201	1690	2310	2772	3134
130	582	1202	1691	2311	2773	3135
193	645	1203	1692	2352	2852	3136
194	843	1204	1752	2353	2853	3137
195	844	1205	1757	2368	2854	3138
224	845	1206	1771	2369	2855	3139
225	846	1207	1803	2370	2856	3140
242	847	1241	1804	2371	2857	3141
243	848	1242	1830	2392	2858	3142
244	849	1283	1831	2393	2859	3202
395	904	1284	1854	2401	2860	3203
396	905	1285	1892	2402	2861	3228
397	906	1286	1893	2403	2862	3229
398	907	1318	1894	2404	2926	3230
399	908	1319	1936	2405	2927	
400	947	1378	1937	2469	2928	
401	948	1379	1966	2470	3001	
402	949	1380	1967	2501	3002	
403	950	1381	2027	2598	3003	
440	951	1382	2028	2599	3004	
522	952	1481	2029	2600	3005	
523	953	1482	2030	2601	3006	

1974

131	539	1031	1641	1996	2611	3012
132	540	1060	1642	2034	2612	3013
133	544	1061	1643	2035	2613	3014
134	565	1083	1644	2036	2614	3015
135	568	1084	1693	2081	2664	3016
136	570	1085	1694	2082	2665	3017
137	580	1086	1695	2083	2666	3018
138	612	1109	1727	2084	2685	3019
139	646	1128	1753	2182	2686	3038
140	647	1208	1754	2183	2709	3039
141	672	1209	1755	2184	2710	3040
142	673	1210	1758	2185	2732	3143
143	674	1211	1759	2186	2756	3144
144	850	1243	1772	2187	2774	3145
145	851	1244	1773	2188	2775	3146
146	852	1245	1805	2189	2863	3147
147	853	1246	1806	2262	2864	3148
148	854	1287	1855	2263	2865	3149
149	855	1288	1856	2264	2866	3150
150	856	1289	1857	2265	2867	3151
151	857	1290	1858	2312	2868	3152
196	858	1291	1895	2354	2869	3153
197	859	1320	1896	2372	2870	3154
226	860	1383	1897	2373	2871	3155
227	861	1384	1898	2374	2872	3156
228	862	1385	1899	2375	2873	3157
245	863	1386	1900	2394	2874	3231
246	909	1387	1901	2395	2875	3232
253	910	1405	1902	2406	2929	3233
404	911	1484	1903	2407	2930	3234
405	912	1485	1904	2471	2931	3235
406	954	1486	1938	2472	2932	3236
407	955	1487	1939	2502	2933	3237
441	956	1488	1940	2510	2934	3238
532	957	1540	1968	2511	2935	3239
533	958	1541	1969	2512	2936	
534	981	1542	1970	2513	2937	
535	982	1637	1971	2607	2938	
536	1028	1638	1972	2608	2939	
537	1029	1639	1973	2609	2940	
538	1030	1640	1995	2610	3011	

1975

152	648	1292	1731	2089	2627	3020
153	675	1293	1732	2190	2628	3021
154	864	1321	1733	2191	2629	3022
155	865	1406	1734	2192	2630	3023
156	866	1489	1774	2193	2667	3041
157	867	1490	1775	2266	2687	3158
158	868	1645	1776	2313	2711	3159
159	869	1646	1777	2314	2757	3160
160	870	1647	1832	2355	2758	3161
161	913	1648	1833	2396	2759	3162
162	914	1649	1834	2408	2760	3163
198	915	1650	1859	2409	2761	3164
408	916	1651	1860	2473	2776	3165
409	959	1652	1861	2474	2777	3166
410	960	1653	1905	2475	2778	3167
411	983	1654	1941	2476	2779	3168
412	984	1655	1942	2615	2780	3169
413	1062	1656	1974	2616	2876	3170
414	1063	1696	1975	2617	2877	3171
541	1087	1697	1976	2618	2878	3172
545	1110	1698	1977	2619	2879	3240
546	1111	1699	1978	2620	2880	3241
547	1112	1700	2037	2621	2881	3242
553	1212	1701	2038	2622	2941	3243
566	1213	1702	2085	2623	2942	
571	1214	1728	2086	2624	2943	
572	1247	1729	2087	2625	2944	
573	1248	1730	2088	2626	2945	

1976

163	542	985	1408	1980	2631	3174
164	871	996	1543	2090	2688	3175
165	872	1249	1657	2194	2712	3204
166	873	1250	1703	2356	2882	3244
167	874	1388	1943	2477	3042	
168	917	1407	1979	2503	3173	